WITTGENSTEIN IN AMERICA

Wittgenstein in America

edited by
TIMOTHY McCARTHY
and
SEAN C. STIDD

CLARENDON PRESS · OXFORD
2001

OXFORD

UNIVERSITY PRESS

Great Clarendon Street, Oxford OX2 6DP

Oxford University Press is a department of the University of Oxford
It furthers the University's objective of excellence in research, scholarship,
and education by publishing worldwide in

Oxford New York

Athens Auckland Bangkok Bogotá Buenos Aires
Cape Town Chennai Dar es Salaam Delhi Florence Hong Kong Istanbul
Karachi Kolkata Kuala Lumpur Madrid Melbourne Mexico City Mumbai
Nairobi Paris São Paulo Shanghai Singapore Taipei Tokyo Toronto Warsaw

with associated companies in Berlin Ibadan

Oxford is a registered trade mark of Oxford University Press
in the UK and in certain other countries

Published in the United States
by Oxford University Press Inc., New York

British Library Cataloguing in Publication Data

Data available

Library of Congress Cataloging in Publication Data
Wittgenstein in America / edited by Timothy McCarthy and Sean C. Stidd.
p. cm.
Based on a conference held in Sept. 1995 at the University of Illinois
at Urbana-Champaign.
Includes bibliographical references (p.) and indexes.
1. Wittgenstein, Ludwig, 1889–1951—Congresses. I. McCarthy, Timothy
(Timothy G.) II. Stidd, Sean C.
B3376.W564 W568 2001 192—dc21 00–053736
ISBN 0–19–924159–7

1 3 5 7 9 10 8 6 4 2

Typeset by Invisible Ink
Printed in Great Britain
on acid-free paper by
T. J. International Ltd.,
Padstow, Cornwall

To Peter Winch
in memoriam

CONTENTS

ACKNOWLEDGMENTS

Our main debt is to Peter Winch, who played a central role in organizing the conference from which these papers descended, and who was originally a co-editor of this book. We would also like to express our gratitude to the following persons and organizations: the College of Liberal Arts and Sciences at the University of Illinois at Urbana-Champaign for its generous sponsorship of the original conference, "Wittgenstein in America"; the UIUC Research Board for a grant that materially aided the editorial process for this volume; the administrative staff of the Philosophy Department at UIUC for all its support during both the conference and the editorial process; the literary estate of Peter Winch, and in particular Helen Geyer, for permission to use the essay by Winch here reprinted; the American Philosophical Association for the same reason; Blackwell Publishers, for permission to use the essay by Stanley Cavell, which was read at the original conference, but which first reached print in *The Cavell Reader*; Josh Finkler, Don Moulds, and the late Randy Cooper for assistance and support during the conference; Kira Berman for her unfailing intellectual and spiritual support of, and patience with, the long editorial process which has led to the present volume; and finally to Noreen Sugrue, whose help was essential both in organizing the conference and in making it run, and whose tiramisu was and continues to be an inspiration for much philosophical discussion.

CONTRIBUTORS

STANLEY CAVELL is Walter M. Cabot Professor of Aesthetics and the General Theory of Value emeritus at Harvard University. Long one of the foremost American interpreters of Wittgenstein, he is the author and subject of numerous books and essays. His many writings include *Must We Mean What We Say?*, *The Claim of Reason*, *The Senses of Walden*, and *This New yet Unapproachable America*.

JAMES CONANT is professor of philosophy at the University of Chicago and one of the most prominent interpreters of Wittgenstein working in the USA today. He has written extensively on Wittgenstein and the history of early analytic philosophy. He has also worked closely with Hilary Putnam as editor for several of his works.

CORA DIAMOND is professor of philosophy at the University of Virginia. Her widely influential book *The Realistic Spirit: Wittgenstein, Philosophy, and the Mind* was published in 1991, and could fairly be said to have re-shaped the landscape of contemporary Wittgenstein studies. She has written articles contributing to many areas of philosophy in the Wittgensteinian tradition, and edited Wittgenstein's *Lectures on the Foundations of Mathematics*.

DAVID H. FINKELSTEIN is assistant professor of philosophy at the University of Indiana in Bloomington. He has published articles on Wittgenstein, philosophy of psychology, and philosophy of language.

LARS HERTZBERG is professor of philosophy at the Åbo Academy in Finland. A student of Norman Malcolm's, he has written extensively on Wittgenstein, philosophy of social science, philosophy of language, and philosophy of religion. He is author of *The Limits of Experience*.

TIMOTHY MCCARTHY is associate professor of philosophy at the University of Illinois at Urbana-Champaign. His research interests center on philosophy of language, philosophy of logic, and philosophy of mathematics. With Peter Winch, he organized the conference on which this volume is based. His book *Radical Interpretation and Indeterminacy* will be published by Oxford University Press in 2001.

HILARY PUTNAM is Cogan University Professor emeritus at Harvard University, and has been one of the most influential figures in analytic philosophy over the last half-century. Three volumes of his collected papers have been published. His other books include *Reason, Truth, and History*, *Realism with a Human Face*, and his John Dewey Lectures, recently published as *The Threefold Cord*.

SEAN STIDD is a graduate student in philosophy at the University of Illinois at Urbana-Champaign who worked with Peter Winch. He has presented work on Plato, Wittgenstein, Heidegger, and Simon Weil, and is currently completing a doctoral dissertation in the philosophy of mathematics.

BEN TILGHMAN is professor emeritus of philosophy at Kansas State University. He has written several books on Wittgenstein and aesthetics, most recently *Wittgenstein, Ethics, and Aesthetics: The View from Eternity*. He has also written an introductory text in the philosophy of religion, which has been translated into Portuguese.

MEREDITH WILLIAMS is professor of philosophy at the Johns Hopkins University. Her research interests include the philosophies of mind, psychology, and language, and she has written extensively on Wittgenstein. She is the author of *Wittgenstein, Mind, and Meaning: Towards a Social Conception of Mind*.

PETER WINCH was professor of philosophy at the University of Illinois at Urbana-Champaign until his death in 1997. He was the author, editor, and subject of many books and essays, his own books including *The Idea of a Social Science, Ethics and Action, Trying to Make Sense*, and *Simone Weil: The Just Balance*. A student of Rush Rhees's, he was among the foremost interpreters of Wittgenstein of his generation.

ABBREVIATIONS

Standard abbreviations for Wittgenstein's works in the text are as follows:

CV	*Culture and Value*
LaWrPP1	*Last Writings on the Philosophy of Psychology*, vol. 1
LaWrPP2	*Last Writings on the Philosophy of Psychology*, vol. 2
LFM	*Wittgenstein's Lectures on the Foundations of Mathematics, Cambridge, 1939*
LO	*Letters to C. K. Ogden with Comments on the English Translation of the Tractatus Logico-Philosophicus*
OC	*On Certainty*
PG	*Philosophical Grammar*
PI	*Philosophical Investigations*
PR	*Philosophical Remarks*
RFM	*Remarks on the Foundations of Mathematics*. Unless otherwise specified, references to this book are to the revised edition.
RPP1	*Remarks on the Philosophy of Psychology*, vol. 1
RPP2	*Remarks on the Philosophy of Psychology*, vol. 2
WNL	Wittgenstein's "Notes for Lectures on 'Private Experience' and 'Sense Data'"
Z	*Zettel*

INTRODUCTION

Timothy McCarthy and Sean C. Stidd

The nine essays collected here represent some of the most important recent work on Wittgenstein. The papers have descended from talks given by the authors at a conference under the heading "Wittgenstein in America" at the University of Illinois at Urbana-Champaign in September of 1995, which brought together a number of philosophers from different generations concerned with Wittgenstein from a number of different points of view. However, the collection does not attempt to present a systematic picture of the reception of Wittgenstein's thought in the USA. Rather, the authors have found in Wittgenstein a voice that speaks to some of the most salient issues in recent American philosophy: the topics of meaning, truth, reference, understanding, realism, indeterminacy, intentionality, and the nature of philosophy are treated, in each case by more than one writer. The unity of the collection arises from the connections that bind these themes together, on the one hand, and from certain commonalities of approach among the authors, on the other. In what follows, we have provided short introductions to the essays, grouped thematically, with special attention to their interrelations and to their connection to salient themes in recent philosophy.

SENSE, NONSENSE, AND UNDERSTANDING

The first triad of papers, by James Conant, Meredith Williams, and Lars Hertzberg, deal with a fundamental (if possibly—according to Wittgenstein's thinking—intrinsically confused) question in the philosophy of logic. In order for us to understand a sentence, it has to make sense; what are the logical grounds on which sentences become able to make sense? A common view, which James Conant's contribution to this volume is dedicated to criticizing in detail, is that such sentences must be constructed with the proper logical syntax—very roughly, in terms of a set of rules that determinately circumscribe the class of significant sentences. After this view is refuted, however, the question concerning the origins of sense and nonsense may still remain; and Conant, Williams, and Hertzberg all have their own observations on this matter.

Conant's paper deals, by way of a sustained and perceptive interrogation of Carnap and Wittgenstein, with a question of central importance to both: what is nonsense? Conant argues that in Carnap, as in Frege, there is a tension between two views of nonsense, the 'substantial' and the 'austere' view, and that it is one of the central goals of the *Tractatus* to resolve this tension in favor of the austere view. Along these lines, Conant brings out important features of Carnap's and the early Wittgenstein's conceptions of logic and nonsense by considering their strategies for elucidating these concepts.

The central distinction of Conant's article, between substantial and austere conceptions of nonsense, owes much to Cora Diamond's seminal "What Nonsense Might Be,"[1] a paper which is also crucially important for Lars Hertzberg's contribution to this collection. In that paper, Diamond criticized a set of very commonly held views of nonsense, on which certain sentences (e.g. "Caesar is a prime number") are nonsense *because* the meanings of the words in them ("Caesar" and "prime number"), in some not-too-clearly understood sense, clash with one another. These are paradigmatically substantial views of nonsense, views in which the 'pieces' of sentences have their own meanings, which are compatible or incompatible with one another in ways which will determine whether the sentence which combines a given set of words makes sense or not. In contrast to such views, Conant and Diamond would suggest, stands the idea (embodied in Frege's context principle) that sentences succeed or fail in making sense as wholes, and so in the absence of some given understanding of what is meant by a properly contextualized assertion of some sentence, we have no ground for saying what the words in the sentence mean, or what logical category they belong to. This is an 'austere' conception because it treats sense and nonsense as given with the whole sentence, rather than as 'constructed' out of the 'substantial' meanings of the sentential constituents. For Conant and Diamond, as for Frege, a sentence's making sense to us is, as it were, a primary datum of cognition, which any conception of word meaning, grammar, or logical categories must presume; and it is also the case that it is only on the basis of a sentence's making sense to us in context that we are entitled to draw any conclusions about the contributions of its parts to the sense of the whole. Conant's essay develops this

---

[1] In Cora Diamond, *The Realistic Spirit* (Cambridge, Mass.: MIT Press, 1991).

distinction in important ways while deploying it to illustrate substantial problems with Carnap's conception of nonsense and with many standard interpretations of Wittgenstein, between which he finds a surprising affinity.

Conant manages to shed considerable light on questions of meaning without providing an explanation of where, if not from the meanings of sentential constituents, the sense or nonsense of a sentence comes from. Williams and Hertzberg attempt to fill this gap in their essays, Williams by offering a recognizably Wittgensteinian strategy for providing such explanations, Hertzberg by arguing that it is mistaken to ask for such explanations in the first place.

Meredith Williams's paper starts out from what she calls the 'problem of normative similarity'. Putting Wittgenstein into an illuminating dialogue with Quine, Williams inquires into the relations of our judgments of sameness to our shared training in techniques which involve the use or application of particular concepts. Arguing that Quine's account of language cannot account for the normativity of language, she attempts to find a ground for this normativity in terms of a "shared, unquestioned, and certain sense of the obvious,"[2] which is imparted by our training in various linguistic techniques and language-games. That is, the 'grounds of sense' of our language are to be found in our training in a multiplicity of language-games and in particular in the basic judgments of sameness or similarity that are to be found within them. Taking certain distinctions and similarities as basic, we learn that different objects can play similar logical roles; it is our shared training in these games which grounds our reliance on these distinctions. On this basis, she argues that an investigation of our training in linguistic techniques and language-games can show us important aspects of the nature and necessity of our conceptual judgments. Whether or not Wittgenstein would have approved of the turn of phrase by which such an investigation can provide a sort of *justification* for, or even an explanation of, the way we do in fact judge—as Williams sometimes suggests—is unclear; but that he thought such investigations were fundamentally important for understanding what was going on with our ways of judging and reasoning is not, and Williams provides a comprehensive and interesting account of the issues which arise in relation to Wittgenstein's conception of the 'foundations' of our judgments.

Lars Hertzberg's "The Sense Is Where You Find It" returns to the problem of nonsense, considering the logical 'place' of sense and

---

[2] Williams, p. 69.

nonsense in our language (are they a matter of clashes between words? Sentences which suggest no obvious meaning? Utterances which are out of place in the present context?) and calling into question the status of invocations of nonsense in philosophical writing. Hertzberg argues that (for example) the word 'Caesar' does not have any more determinate a meaning in 'Caesar crossed the Rubicon' than it does in 'Caesar is a prime number,' where both sentences are being considered without a context of significant use. He then tries to show that there is something misguided in the philosophical desire to lay down the general conditions under which a sentence might or might not make sense in the first place. Because "questions about the sense of a sentence are only to be asked about sentences as used by particular speakers on particular occasions,"[3] and because in real-life situations we do not resort to the ideas of a violation of logical syntax or of "the rules of language"[4] to explain a mysterious utterance in a philosophically innocent context, the philosophical accusation of nonsensicality is for Hertzberg a mark of philosophical impatience. The task of the philosopher, for Hertzberg as for Wittgenstein, is to understand how people are using words rather than to legislate about what they can say. Therefore, if someone puts things in an odd or misleading way, says something which sounds strikingly incoherent, one might quite reasonably ask them to explain themselves—ask them what they mean. If they cannot explain it, or continue to be incoherent, there is perhaps a serious question about whether they meant anything at all; but it is the philosopher's task to get them to see that, not to put a rubber stamp marked "sense" or "nonsense" on their prior utterance. If they can explain themselves, then that might be all; or the philosopher may feel that they are putting things misleadingly, and try to persuade them to change the way they express themselves by pointing out problematic connections that others might make with their words, or by offering them a different metaphor or picture.[5]

In common with Conant and Williams, and following Wittgenstein, Hertzberg wants to argue that there is something misguided about the very idea of a general, context-independent theory of sentential meaning. He is particularly concerned to cast doubt upon attempts in the style of Paul Grice to salvage such a theory of meaning by grounding pragmatics on a conception of language as a formal system supple-

---

[3] Hertzberg, p. 97.

[4] Ibid. p. 102.

[5] Wittgenstein's discussion of a physicist who "discovers how to see what people look like in the dark" (*LFM*, p. 17) makes precisely Hertzberg's point. This lecture of Wittgenstein's is in general an excellent discussion of many of the same issues that Hertzberg is dealing with.

mented with 'conversational maxims'. For Hertzberg, the ways in which our languages can succeed or fail in making sense cannot ultimately be rendered any less complex than those languages themselves. How precisely the seeming and real differences between Conant, Williams, and Hertzberg will be resolved is not clear at the present time; but what is clear is that the seeds of an interesting and potentially rewarding debate have been sown in these three essays.

REALISMS, METAPHYSICAL AND ORDINARY

The next two essays, by Cora Diamond and Hilary Putnam, attempt to sketch out Wittgensteinian lines on issues where the temptation to slide into metaphysical realism (or the anti-realism that corresponds to it) is especially great. Each tries to do justice to the subject by carefully articulating the ways in which a 'realist' grammar emerges out of a background of practice and experience, while showing how the urge to hypostatize that realist grammar in the manner of traditional metaphysics is both unnecessary and born from philosophical illusion. Both also discuss Wittgenstein's views in relation to those of his most prominent realist interpreter, Saul Kripke.

Cora Diamond's contribution to this collection takes up what has become a canonical problem of modern metaphysics: what was the length, if any, of the standard meter bar in Paris?[6] Her discussion of this problem revolves around an incisive criticism of Kripke's view, together with a careful diagnosis of the points of disagreement between Kripke and Wittgenstein on these issues. Diamond tries to show clearly the proper place of "the whole business of actually putting objects alongside each other, reading properly off instruments, and so on"[7] in constituting the meanings of 'length' and 'meter' without sliding either into the verificationism which identifies the meanings with the practices or into a realism which postulates an abstract object as a denotation for every measure term.

In Diamond's estimation, the issue which lies at the heart of this problem is identity. The (metaphysical) realist à la Kripke attempts to

---

[6] That is, prior to 1960, when the logical problems pertaining to our standards of measurement became even more difficult, because the basis of our systems of length and time was transferred to the properties of Cesium atoms, which are of course invisible to the naked eye.

[7] Diamond, p. 122.

treat intransitive uses of a sentence as special reflexive cases of transitive ones. Relative to our actual practices of measuring, Diamond argues, this is like treating "Susan is Susan's height" (and, consequently, "The meter bar is a meter long") as a proposition of exactly the same type as "Susan is a meter tall." The former has no practical content; but by treating it as exactly the same kind of proposition as arises out of our actual practices of measuring, and so on, the realist creates a need for it to have a meaning, and offers as a vehicle for such a meaning a class of abstract objects, 'lengths', which are supposed to fix or be the denotations of our measure terms. Like Wittgenstein, Diamond thinks that this move is representative of a certain kind of philosophical confusion, but she goes further than a number of Wittgenstein's interpreters by showing how the division between Wittgenstein and the realist arises not simply over the existence of abstract objects, but over the concept of identity itself. In the course of her argument, she connects Kripke's discussion of Wittgenstein on the standard meter with his discussion of Wittgenstein on rules, and considers important discussions of both of these matters by Malcolm, Putnam, and Winch. The result is a discussion which brings the Wittgensteinean tradition squarely and forcefully into dialogue with mainline analytic philosophy, something both needed and welcome at the present time.

Hilary Putnam's extended essay "Was Wittgenstein *Really* an Antirealist about Mathematics?" sketches out a Wittgensteinian program in the philosophy of mathematics. Contrary to a long interpretive tradition, however, Putnam wants to read Wittgenstein as espousing a kind of *realism* about mathematics. He calls this position more generally "commonsense realism," no doubt partly influenced by Cora Diamond's new gloss on the idea of realism in "Realism and the Realistic Spirit,"[8] and identifies the following two ideas as its tenets:

(1) Taking perfectly seriously our ordinary claims to know about the existence of birds and automobiles and what Austin referred to as "middle-sized dry goods," and our ordinary explanations of how we know these things, and

(2) Meeting the objection that these ordinary claims simply ignore a philosophical problem by challenging the very intelligibility of the supposed problem.[9]

This is a familiar strategy, but Putnam's applications of it to Kripke's 'skeptical paradoxes' about rule-following in the context of the philo-

---

[8] Diamond, *The Realistic Spirit*.
[9] Putnam, p. 165.

sophy of mathematics is an important new development.[10] One promising idea that comes out of the later sections of the paper, for example, is that appeals in the course of mathematical argument to the law of excluded middle get their sense from the practice of (for instance) number theory itself. Far from relying on a metaphysical realist understanding of the reference of mathematical terms, therefore, the law of excluded middle could be seen as arising out of purely ordinary canons of mathematical reasoning—at least, at the points where mathematicians themselves would naturally and unproblematically apply it. Along the way, Quine's doctrine of ontological commitment, the Benacerraf problem, and a number of Dummett's views also come up for serious scrutiny, making the present paper a characteristic example of the breadth of synthetic vision to be found in Putnam's later writings.

THE LOGIC OF PSYCHOLOGICAL CONCEPTS

In the final section of *Philosophical Investigations*, Wittgenstein wrote: "In psychology there are experimental methods and *conceptual confusion* . . . The existence of experimental methods makes us think we have the means of solving the problems which trouble us; though problem and methods pass one another by" (*PI* II. xiv). This conceptual confusion in psychology was of great concern to Wittgenstein: he believed that simplified philosophical pictures of the mind and misleading analogies between our various mental terms fundamentally distort our thinking about many psychological concepts, from belief and hope to fear and pain.

Much of *Philosophical Investigations* and several volumes of the notebooks are dedicated to the 'grammar', in Wittgenstein's special sense, of words like these, and the contributions of Peter Winch and David Finkelstein to the present collection focus on some of the problems which arise in this connection. Peter Winch's "The Expression of Belief," given as a presidential address to the American Philosophical Association in 1996, offers a canny interpretation of Wittgenstein's analyses of belief in the *Tractatus* and the *Investigations*. Noting that in both texts the discussion of belief is immediately followed by a discussion of seeing aspects and the Necker cube, Winch argues that this is

---

[10] With respect to the latter, it is worth comparing Arthur Fine's discussion of the 'natural ontological attitude' in *The Shaky Game* (Chicago: University of Chicago Press, 1992).

not accidental. Wittgenstein means to illustrate the logic of the belief proposition by analogy in both cases: the belief proposition is essentially connected to at least two different language-games, which is to say that there are at least two entirely different things that we can do with expressions of belief. Winch writes:

Suppose you hear the words "This lecture is going to last too long." It is only if this incident takes place in a certain very familiar kind of context that you will hear them as the expression of a belief: not, for instance if the sound emanates from a tape-recorder on which an English lesson is being played. If, on the other hand, the sound has been produced by a worried-looking human being who you know to be called Winch and who you know plans to give a lecture directly . . . your interest in this may be of two sorts. You may thereupon resolve not to go to the lecture, since it will probably keep you from a more attractive engagement later in the evening. In that case you are simply interested in p [the proposition believed—eds.]. On the other hand you may be interested in reassuring me, fearing that my nervousness over the coming lecture's length will prevent me from delivering it intelligibly. Now you are interested, not so much in the proposition that the utterance "p" expresses, as in the fact that what it expresses is my belief. You will now give emphasis to quite different elements in the circumstances of the utterance than in the first case.[11]

The analogy between the belief proposition and the Necker cube is that the same proposition can play two distinct logical roles which remain interlocked in the same proposition. Winch extends this discussion of the logic of expressions of belief a great deal, trying to shed light on the wide variety of functions such expressions can play in different areas of human life. Of special interest are discussions of Moore's paradox, and of the logical status of seeming contradictions between belief and action.

David Finkelstein's contribution to the present volume gives an excellent and thorough treatment of one of the later Wittgenstein's most striking pieces of conceptual analysis—the idea that the first-person use of many of our psychological words (in sentences such as "I am in pain") is in many cases best understood as an expression of our state, in roughly the way that, unaccompanied by words, crying can express sadness or pain. Consequently, for Wittgenstein, in many respects such sentences do not function as statements or descriptions at all in terms of their grammar or, indeed, in terms of the kind of contribution they make to our understanding and lives. If Wittgenstein was right, then, that "the verbal expression of pain replaces crying" (*PI* §144), it follows that a whole host of positions taken by philosophers and psychologists

---

[11] Winch, p. 201.

on the epistemic relation of a person to the 'inner objects' (or even 'outer' behavior) which putatively ground such statements are off the mark.

Finkelstein gives an insightful and entertaining critique of the various positions which devolve from the understanding of expressions of fear, pain, hope, desire, expectation, and intention as grammatically similar to statements such as "I see a red apple." These include various 'detectivist' views, held by Russell nearly a hundred years ago and found down to the present day in certain behaviorist and materialist theories, as well as the radical 'constitutivism' of Crispin Wright, who holds that our stating that we have such-and-such a feeling or mental state actually makes it the case that we do have it. Perhaps most significantly, however, Finkelstein also cautions against the *purely* expressivist interpretation of Wittgenstein's remarks on this subject, which would *identify* the meaning of (rather than merely note a kinship between), say, a statement of sadness in the first person with the shedding of tears. The statement does, after all, have an assertoric dimension that the tears do not.[12] Winch's suggestive interpretation of Wittgenstein's use of the Necker cube to illustrate the dual aspect of expressions of belief seems applicable in a slightly different way to Finkelstein's subtle treatment of this topic as well. Along the way Finkelstein also shows what it was that Wittgenstein disagreed with in these various positions, and how Wittgenstein's treatment of our psychological concepts addresses many of the philosophical problems which can arise in our thinking about them.

MORALITY, AESTHETICS, AND THE UNITIES OF WITTGENSTEIN'S PHILOSOPHY

The final two essays in this collection, by Ben Tilghman and Stanley Cavell, explore the ways in which Wittgenstein's conception of the ingredients of understanding is connected to issues in ethics and aesthetics. Tilghman's "Morality, Human Understanding, and the Limits of Language" takes up some of the same issues discussed in Hertzberg's, Winch's, and Finkelstein's papers, but with a few twists. Tilghman's central concerns are with the moral dimensions of our understanding of human beings, both ourselves and others, and with the conceptual difficulties involved in trying to reduce or eliminate our standards for

---

[12] Finkelstein, p. 232.

judgment of human feelings in favor of a simplified set of criteria, as advocated by some modern materialists and others.

Tilghman starts out with a discussion of what makes for an expert judge of character or human emotion, noting both the epistemic and the moral ramifications of the possibility of such judgment. He specifically analyzes Wittgenstein's notion of "imponderable evidence" in such judgment, and notes some of the more striking features of such evidence:

- that one person (the 'expert', for lack of a better term) may sometimes be able to see it when another is not;

- that persons may sometimes disagree about whether a particular observation even counts as evidence;

- that such evidence may be fundamentally indeterminate in its indication.

Arguing that the logical features of such evidence are too fine-grained and subtle always to be reducible to those of insufficient evidence in the more traditional sense, Tilghman then illustrates various ways in which the importance of imponderable evidence to human understanding influences the moral aspects of that understanding. The paper concludes with a vigorous critique of reductive and eliminative materialist programs in the philosophy of mind, arguing that such programs rely on distortingly simple conceptions of evidence, self-knowledge, and human relations. For Tilghman this makes reductive materialism impossible, and turns eliminative materialism into the construction of "an altogether new practice of talking about feelings and relating to people," which would be "a new way of living."[13] Quite naturally, he regards this possibility without much relish, since what would be 'eliminated' in such a program are parts of our conceptual scheme for dealing with people which fundamentally enrich (if sometimes obscure) our intercourse with others, and form an essential part of our moral existence as well.

Stanley Cavell's essay in this collection deals with the fundamental literary question of Wittgenstein's writing, a question which could be asked of the *Tractatus* as well as (as Cavell does) of the *Investigations*. What is the connection between Wittgenstein's style of writing, the structure and motifs of his works, and his conception of his reader, with the philosophical arguments, examples, and discussions one finds in those works? Cavell's ingenious answer to this question emerges from

---

[13] Tilghman, p. 247.

an analysis of Wittgenstein's "fundamentally significant" idea of a "perspicuous representation" (*PI* §122; Cavell translates this with 'perspicuous *presentation*') as a literary trope in his writing, as well as from a philosophical point of view. Cavell writes:

Wittgenstein is claiming for the ordinary or everyday its own possibility of perspicuousness, as different from that of the mathematical as the experience of an interesting sentence is from the experience of an interesting theorem. But how can this be? Doesn't Wittgenstein's idea of the perspicuous just mean, as it were, the look of a formal proof? My proposal is rather to conceive that Wittgenstein once hit off an experience of the convincingness, perhaps of the unity, of a proof, with the concept of perspicuousnes and for some reason, later (or earlier), he hits off an experience of a unity, or a reordering, of ordinary words with the same concept, as if discovering a new manifestation of the concept in discovering something new about the ordinary.[14]

At least one other major thinker, Socrates, had an idea like this one before; but while Socrates' conception of a perspicuous ordering of the ordinary is essentially acontextual, for Wittgenstein the idea of such an ordering, while perhaps always a possibility, will take a different form in every case. Cavell analyzes the writing of the *Investigations* in terms of this notion, attempting to exhibit a unity of aim and style between the more demonstrative passages of the work, which employ language-games, counterexamples, and even traditional arguments, with the more aphoristic ones, which seem to go, poetically, straight to the heart of the matter.

Cavell also provides an interesting analysis of the thematics of the *Philosophical Investigations*—temptation, disappointment, and perversity, "suffocation, illness, strangeness,"[15] "human self-destructiveness at war with itself"[16]—and of the essentially modern subject to which the book addresses itself. He also explores some fascinating resonances of Wittgenstein's thought with the Schlegel brothers and with Emerson.

With Cavell's essay we come to the end of this introduction; and we have also, in a way, come full circle. For in his discussion of a 'perspicuity' or 'clarity' which links the ideas of a formal proof or argument and of finding precisely the right thing to say in our ordinary languages, Cavell calls us back to a possibility which seemed to be implicit in Conant's and Hertzberg's ruminations on the 'location' and grounds of sense and nonsense in our languages. This is the possibility of a conception of understanding which does not presuppose the modern

---

[14] Cavell, p. 252.
[15] Ibid. p. 257.
[16] Ibid. p. 256.

dichotomy between science and interpretation, which allows each way of speaking to realize the possibilities of clarity and perspicuity appropriate to it, and which allows each conceptual problem to be solved with the tools that it calls for, in the language-game which is its proper home. Long ago, Peter Winch also pointed in the direction of such a possibility:

The scientist, for instance, tries to make the world more intelligible; but so do the historian, the religious prophet, and the artist; so too does the philosopher . . . It is clear that in very many important ways, the objectives of each of them differ from the objectives of any of the others . . . [But] it does not follow from this that we are just punning when we speak of the activities of all these enquirers in terms of the notion of making things intelligible. That no more follows than does a similar conclusion with regard to the word 'game' when Wittgenstein shows us that there is no set of properties common and peculiar to all the activities correctly so called . . . On my view, then, the philosophy of science will be concerned with the kind of understanding sought and conveyed by the scientist; the philosophy of religion will be concerned with the way in which religion attempts to present an intelligible picture of the world; and so on . . . The purpose of such philosophical enquiries will be to contribute to our understanding of what is involved in the concept of intelligibility, so that we may better understand what it means to call reality intelligible.[17]

It is just such a conception of understanding, one which takes into account the unities and differences between its manifold forms, that Winch was centrally concerned to explicate, in various ways, throughout much of his writing. With affection and respect, we dedicate this volume to his memory.

---

[17] Winch, *The Idea of a Social Science and Its Relation to Philosophy* (London: Routledge & Kegan Paul, 1958), pp. 18–20.

Two Conceptions of *Die Überwindung der Metaphysik*

Carnap and Early Wittgenstein

James Conant

For me personally, Wittgenstein was perhaps the philosopher who, besides Russell and Frege, had the greatest influence on my thinking.

Rudolf Carnap, "Intellectual Autobiography"

I cannot imagine that Carnap should have so completely and utterly misunderstood the last sentences of my book—and therefore the fundamental conception of the whole book.

Ludwig Wittgenstein, letter to Moritz Schlick, 8 August 1932

This paper has two aims: first, to show that if most commentators on Wittgenstein are correct in the views that they attribute to Wittgenstein, then Carnap is a far more important philosopher (and one whose thought is far closer to that of Wittgenstein) than is generally acknowledged in such commentaries, and second, to suggest that the views that are thus attributed to Wittgenstein in such commentaries, although they are to be found in some of the writings of Carnap, are not to be found in the writings of Wittgenstein—not even those of early Wittgenstein.

In broadest outline, the sort of reading of Wittgenstein I have in mind might be put as follows: Wittgenstein seeks to show that the utterances of metaphysicians are nonsense by exposing them to be logically (or conceptually) *flawed*, where these flaws are to be traced to *specifiable infringements* upon the conditions of meaningful discourse. Put this broadly, the preceding summary can serve equally well as an outline of currently standard readings of Wittgenstein's early work or of his later work. If Wittgenstein's early work is under discussion, it will be said that these infringements arise through violations of "the principles of logical syntax"; if Wittgenstein's later work is under discussion, it will be said that they arise through violations of "the rules of grammar." What such readings have in common is the idea that Wittgenstein seeks a method which would enable him (a) to expose the sentences of metaphysicians as *intrinsically* nonsensical, and (b) through the application of such a method to *demarcate* meaningful from meaningless discourse.

Such readings attribute to Wittgenstein a particular conception of nonsense—which I will call the *substantial conception of nonsense*. This conception of nonsense distinguishes between two different kinds of nonsense: mere nonsense and substantial nonsense. Mere nonsense is simply unintelligible—it expresses no thought. Substantial nonsense is composed of intelligible ingredients combined in an illegitimate way— it expresses a logically incoherent thought. According to the substantial conception, these two kinds of nonsense are logically distinct: the former is mere gibberish, whereas the latter involves (what commentators on the *Tractatus* are fond of calling) a "violation of logical syntax" or (what commentators on Wittgenstein's later work are fond of calling) a "violation of grammar." The substantial conception of nonsense can be contrasted with another conception of nonsense which I will call the *austere conception of nonsense*. According to the latter, mere nonsense is, from a logical point of view, the only kind of nonsense there is.

The two aims of this paper stated above can now be rearticulated as three: first, to show that Carnap's method of philosophical analysis presupposes the substantial conception of nonsense;[1] second, to argue that the method of Wittgenstein's *Tractatus* can be understood only in the light of his commitment to an austere conception of nonsense;[2] third, to suggest that the *Tractatus* seeks to expose as a misunderstanding the very "understanding of the logic of our language" most commonly attributed to it.

CARNAP ON THE OVERCOMING OF METAPHYSICS
THROUGH THE LOGICAL ANALYSIS OF LANGUAGE

Carnap repeatedly explicitly acknowledges that his understanding of the nature of metaphysics is enormously indebted to the *Tractatus* and

---

[1] I think that this is true of Carnap's work from *Der Logische Aufbau der Welt* on, but considerations of space dictate that I restrict my argument in this paper to a particular phase of Carnap's career.

[2] I think the same claim can be made with regard to the method of philosophical clarification practiced in Wittgenstein's later work, but considerations of space also preclude me from defending that claim here.

that he takes himself to be borrowing from (what he takes to be) ideas of the *Tractatus* in elaborating his own successive attempts to mount a critique of metaphysics.[3] Due to the considerable influence of Carnap's own ideas on several generations of analytic philosophers, subsequent commentators on the *Tractatus* have, often unknowingly, read Wittgenstein's work through Carnap's spectacles, construing the *Tractatus*'s often quite distinctive notions along more familiar Carnapian lines and importing additional Carnapian terminology to fill in the gaps in Wittgenstein's original exposition.

Before I attempt to illustrate this, it should be noted that, for the purposes of this essay, I am going to focus narrowly on one particular phase of Carnap's thought. Carnap's thought about metaphysics—about what metaphysics is, what gives rise to it, and what means should be employed to eliminate it—passes through at least[4] the following four broad phases: (1) the *Der Logische Aufbau der Welt* phase, (2) the (comparatively brief) verificationist phase, (3) the logical syntax phase, and (4) the semantic frameworks phase. As Carnap's own philosophical views evolve so does his understanding of what is most significant and enduring in Wittgenstein's contribution to philosophy. With the transition to each of these phases of his thought, Carnap's understanding both of the sources and of the proper mode of treatment of metaphysics undergoes, each time, a considerable evolution. Nonetheless, Carnap continues, throughout all four of these phases of his thought, to express considerable indebtedness to Wittgenstein—and, in particular, to Wittgenstein's *Tractatus*—not only for having shown that metaphysical problems are *Scheinprobleme*, but for having shown what kind of problems such problems are and how they are to be diagnosed and dissolved. Thus a comparison of the sort that this paper seeks to furnish—between Carnap's critique of metaphysics and that of the *Tractatus*—must not pretend to be able to treat Carnap's thought on these matters as a single homogeneous whole. One must distinguish between the various distinct *Tractatus*-inspired projects that Carnap pursues in the course of his career, and examine the relation between the *Tractatus* and each of these phases of Carnap's thought separately.

---

[3] That Carnap took his views on what metaphysics is and how it is to be overcome to be influenced by Wittgenstein is evident from his generous references and acknowledgments to the *Tractatus*. See e.g. *The Logical Structure of the World* (Berkeley: University of California Press, 1967), esp. pp. 290-2, 297-8); *The Logical Syntax of Language* (New York: Harcourt, Brace & Co., 1937), esp. pp. 282-4); and "Intellectual Autobiography," in P. A. Schilpp, ed., *The Philosophy of Rudof Carnap* (Carbondale, Ill.: Open Court, 1963), esp. pp. 24-9, 45).

[4] This overview could be considerably refined: within each of these phases (especially the last), Carnap's philosophy undergoes further shifts in doctrine.

It would be an interesting project to trace the successive shifts in Carnap's view of what the *Tractatus* should be credited with having anticipated in each of his own successive understandings of the proper method of exposing and eliminating metaphysics. But that is not the project of the present paper. The aim of this paper is to exploit certain features of Carnap's misunderstanding of Wittgenstein as a foil to furthering our understanding of Wittgenstein. It will therefore suffice, for the comparatively limited purposes of this paper, if we confine ourselves to an examination of the third of the above phases of Carnap's thought—the logical syntax phase—and, primarily, to the earliest expression of that phase of his thought.[5] The three most important publications in this phase of Carnap's thought are "The Elimination of Metaphysics through the Logical Analysis of Language,"[6] *Philosophy and Logical Syntax,*[7] and *The Logical Syntax of Language*. All three of these works purport to be developing and applying the method of philosophical elucidation that Wittgenstein advanced in the *Tractatus*. There are, however, substantial differences of doctrine and method across these three closely allied works. In what follows, my references to Carnap will pertain only to his views in "The Elimination of Metaphysics through the Logical Analysis of Language," unless otherwise noted.

The word "elimination" in the title of Carnap's essay is Arthur Pap's translation of the German word *Überwindung*, which might be better translated "overcoming" or even "subjugation." In the final sentence of §6.54, it is said of the reader of the *Tractatus* that *er muß diese Sätze überwinden*: he must overcome [or defeat] these sentences[8]—the sen-

---

[5] As already indicated, Carnap, throughout this phase, took himself to be following Wittgenstein's lead: "It was Wittgenstein who first exhibited the close connection between the logic of science (or 'philosophy', as he calls it) and syntax . . . He has shown that all the so-called sentences of metaphysics are nonsense" (*The Logical Syntax of Language*, p. 282n).

[6] "The Elimination of Metaphysics through the Logical Analysis of Language" (henceforth EMLAL), trans. Arthur Pap; collected in A. J. Ayer, ed., *Logical Positivism* (New York: Macmillan, 1959), pp. 59–81. I have occasionally amended Pap's translations. References to the original German are to "Überwindung der Metaphysik durch logische Analyse der Sprache" [henceforth ÜMLAS], *Erkenntnis*, 2 (1932): 219–41.

[7] First published in 1935; repr. Bristol: Thoemmes, 1997.

[8] Carnap thus, interestingly, seizes upon and takes up into the title of his essay the very word (from the closing lines of the *Tractatus*) which—once translated into English or French—has often been seized upon by commentators to advocate a reading of the *Tractatus* diametrically opposed to Carnap's own. Pears and McGuinness translate *überwinden* as "transcend," thus inviting (what I call in "The Method of the *Tractatus*") *the ineffability interpretation* of the work—an invitation which is reinforced through their translation of *schweigen* in the next sentence (which calls merely for silence) as an injunction to the reader to "to *pass over* [something] in silence" (see "The Method of

tences which serve as elucidations in that book are, eventually, to be recognized by the reader as nonsense. How faithful an inheritance of Wittgenstein's project (to teach his reader to "overcome" the sentences of the *Tractatus*) is Carnap's project of "overcoming" metaphysics? In a footnote to the essay, Carnap writes: "For the logical and epistemological conception which underlies our exposition, but can only be briefly intimated here, cf. Wittgenstein, *Tractatus Logico-Philosophicus*."[9] In order to begin to get a sense both of how Carnap takes his own views in this essay to derive from Wittgenstein and how standard readings of the *Tractatus* owe more than they think to Carnap's reading of that work, consider §4.003 of the *Tractatus*:

> Most propositions and questions, that have been written about philosophical matters, are not false, but nonsensical . . . Most questions and propositions of the philosophers result from the fact that we do not understand the logic of our language.[10]

On what has become the standard interpretation of the *Tractatus*, this passage is interpreted to mean (1) that "the nonsensical pseudo-propositions of the philosophers" are nonsensical because they "violate the

the *Tractatus*," in Eric H. Reck, ed., *From Frege to Wittgenstein: Perspectives on Early Analytic Philosophy* (Oxford: Oxford University Press, 2000). These mistranslations are mirrored in Gilles-Gaston Granger's French translation of the *Tractatus* (Paris: Gallimard, 1993) in which *überwinden* is rendered *dépasser* ("to go beyond") and *schweigen* is rendered *garder le silence* ("to keep silent" [in the sense of *observing* a rule of silence]). These translations are philosophically consequential: talk of "transcending" or "going beyond" only makes sense where there is a *beyond*, and talk of "passing [something] over in silence" or "guarding one's silence [with respect to something]" only makes sense where *breaking* one's silence is a possibility. My aim in noting these consequential features of certain standard translations of the *Tractatus* is not to give aid and comfort to Carnap's reading of the work, but merely to prepare the way for the claim that these translations foreclose the reading of the text for which this essay as a whole is concerned to make room—a reading according to which the work as a whole aims to show that such "transcendence" of "the limits of language" (of the sort which these translations invite us to imagine is possible) is revealed to be a putative description of a possible state of affairs upon which we have failed to confer a *Sinn*, thus revealing that (as Wittgenstein's Preface puts it) "what lies on the other side of the [supposed] limit will be *einfach Unsinn*."

[9] EMLAL, p. 69n.

[10] The whole passage runs as follows:

> Most propositions and questions, that have been written about philosophical matters, are not false, but nonsensical. We cannot, therefore, answers questions of this kind at all, but only determine their nonsensicality. Most questions and propositions of the philosophers result from the fact that we do not understand the logic of our language.
>
> (They are of the same kind as the question whether the Good is more or less identical than the Beautiful.)
>
> And so it is not to be wondered at that the deepest problems are no problems. (§4.003)

rules of logical syntax," (2) that this is what philosophers need to be brought to see about their pseudo-propositions, (3) that this requires that they be instructed in logical syntax (so as to be able to identify such violations), and hence (4) that "the misunderstanding of the logic of our language" which is the source of the confusions of philosophers is to be traced to their present inability to identify such violations. This (standard) interpretation of the *Tractatus* is broadly Carnapian: it takes the Tractarian project of uncovering *nonsense* (*Unsinn*) to be a project of uncovering instances of substantial nonsense, it takes Tractarian *logical syntax* to be a combinatorial theory governing the legitimate employment of signs or symbols, and it takes Tractarian *elucidation* to consist in the specification of ill-formed sequences of signs or symbols. In the following pages we will be concerned to recover the original sense of each of these three pieces of Tractarian terminology—'nonsense', 'logical syntax', 'elucidation'—each of which has, due to the Carnapian inflection it has acquired, become all but inaudible to the ears of contemporary commentary. We will proceed by examining the senses of each of the terms as they respectively figure in the Carnapian and Tractarian projects of *Überwindung der Metaphysik*.[11]

Let us begin with Carnap on *nonsense*. Carnap distinguishes two kinds of *unsinnige* pseudo-propositions:

(i) those which contain a meaningless word or words;
(ii) those which contain only meaningful words, but put together in such a way that no meaning results.[12]

I will refer to these as *type (i) nonsense* and *type (ii) nonsense* respectively. Metaphysical nonsense, Carnap thinks, can occasionally be traced to an unwitting attraction to type (i) nonsense. He speculates that some stretches of metaphysical discourse about "God" are of this sort. They involve a simple failure to settle on any specific meaning for

---

[11] I have no wish to deny that EMLAL contains a number of ideas that represent a self-conscious effort on Carnap's part to depart from (what he takes to be) Wittgenstein's teaching. My discussion of Carnap's essay will be intentionally and unscrupulously partial, focusing only on those aspects of its doctrine which rhyme with aspects of accepted interpretations of the *Tractatus*.

[12] Here is Carnap on the two kinds of pseudo-statements:

There are . . . those pseudo-statements which contain a meaningless word. But there is also a second kind of pseudo-statement. They consist of meaningful words, but the words are put together in such a way that nevertheless no meaning results. The syntax of a language specifies which combinations of words are admissible and which inadmissible. The grammatical syntax of natural languages, however, does not fulfill the task of elimination of senseless combinations of words in all cases. (EMLAL, p. 67)

the term 'God'. In such cases, the metaphysician, in point of fact, simply does not know what he means by 'God' but nonetheless continues to employ the term under the impression that it does have a definite and familiar meaning.[13] The tools of logical syntax only play an indirect role in the exposure of type (i) nonsense. Such an employment of the term 'God' can be seen to be nonsense from the fact that it fails to satisfy "the first requirement of logic": the requirement that one be able to specify how it occurs meaningfully in elementary statements of the form "x is a God." The diagnosis and cure of type (i) nonsense does not require any detailed attention to the *logical structure* of the speaker's propositions; and, indeed, strictly speaking, type (i) nonsense has no (fully) determinate logical syntax. All that is required to "overcome metaphysics" in such a case is to bring the speaker to realize that she is unable to provide a specification of the meaning of the word in question.

Carnap is of the view that an unwitting attraction to type (i) nonsense accounts for a certain portion of the pseudo-statements of metaphysicians. But, more often, a metaphysician does know what she means by each of her words. When a speaker is able to specify what each of her words mean (i.e. how it occurs in elementary propositions), and yet sense fails to result from the combination of her words, then the source of the failure is to be traced (not to an absence of meaning on the part of one of the constituents of her propositions, but rather) to the illicit character of the combination—to its being a case of type (ii) nonsense. Type (i) nonsense is mere nonsense; it is literally unintelligible: it contains (at a point where something with meaning should be) a void. Type (ii) nonsense is substantial nonsense; it is not literally unintelligible: we know what each of the parts of the proposition mean—the trouble lies with the composite which they form. Carnap thinks it is often not evident to speakers of a natural language that type (ii) sequences are meaningless because the sequences in question do not violate the excessively permissive combinatorial rules of ordinary grammar. Their accord with the rules of ordinary grammar *masks from view* their true underlying character. The point of translating a type (ii)

---

[13] Carnap is not of the view that *all* discourse involving the term 'God' is of this sort. He distinguishes (EMLAL, pp. 66–7) between four sorts of usage: (1) type (i) nonsense; (2) the *mythological* usage—in which 'God' has a determinate meaning, occurs in empirically verifiable statements, and refers to a kind of physical being with specifiable properties whose possibility and existence is a possible topic of scientific inquiry; (3) the *theological* usage which involves an oscillation between uses (1) and (2); and (4) cases in which a definition of 'God' is furnished but involves type (ii) nonsense.

sequence of words into logical notation is to bring to the surface what natural-language syntax obscures from view.

In the case of type (i) nonsense, what is classified as nonsense is, strictly speaking, not a grammatical or logical unit of a language, but a mere mark on paper (or noise) or sequence of marks (or noises). What about the case of type (ii) nonsense? *What* is here classified as non-sense—a string of marks (or noises) or what the string of words says (something with semantic content)? In the third paragraph of his essay, Carnap writes:

In saying that the so-called statements [*Sätze*] of metaphysics are *meaningless*, we intend this word in its strictest sense . . . In the strict sense . . . a sequence of words [*Wortreihe*] is *meaningless* if it does not, within a specified language, constitute a statement [*gar keinen Satz bildet*]. It may happen that such a sequence of words looks like a statement [*Satz*] at first glance; in that case we call it a *pseudo-statement* [*Scheinsatz*]. Our thesis, now, is that logical analysis reveals the alleged statements [*Sätze*] of metaphysics to be pseudo-statements [*Scheinsätze*].[14]

There are two possible readings of this passage. I will call them the *weaker reading* and the *stronger reading* respectively. In the quotation above, I have presented the text of Arthur Pap's translation of this passage. Pap's translation, on the whole, encourages the weaker reading. Thus translated, the passage might appear to claim that the problem with metaphysical propositions is that, given what they mean, they fail to *assert* anything—they fall short of being *statements*. This would suggest that the class of ("sequences of words" properly classified as) "propositions" is wider than that of "statements." We see what the parts of the metaphysician's statement mean, but they do not add up to a coherent whole and *therefore* fail to state anything. Some propositions have what it takes to be a statement, some do not; metaphysical propositions are of this latter sort. Carnap's original German seems, however, to invite a stronger reading. Carnap (in the original German) appears to wish to claim that the so-called "propositions" (*Sätze*) of metaphysics are not even propositions; they are only apparent propositions (*Scheinsätze*)—mere strings of words masquerading as propositions. When Carnap says that they are meaningless, he "intend[s] this word in its strictest sense"; and the import of this would appear to be that, in the strict sense, only "a sequence of words" (*Wortreihe*) can be meaningless—not a proposition. A sequence of words is meaningless, if, within some specified language, it fails so much as to form a proposition (*gar keinen Satz bildet*). Metaphysics appears to consist of propositions, but they are only apparent propositions; and an apparent proposition is not a kind of proposition at all.

This is one of a number of passages in (the original German version of) Carnap's essay that invite the stronger reading more readily than the weaker reading. If Carnap, in the course of his essay, resolutely adhered to what the stronger reading of this passage takes him to be saying, then he would be espousing the austere conception of nonsense. It is central to the teaching of the *Tractatus* that it is extraordinarily difficult to succeed in being resolute in this matter. Carnap does not succeed. His irresoluteness is, however, both philosophically instructive (about the shortcomings of any program of philosophical critique which resembles Carnap's) and exegetically illuminating (as to why Wittgenstein's own method of philosophical elucidation in the *Tractatus* differs so radically from that of Carnap).

This brings us to Carnap on *logical syntax*. The syntax of a language, for Carnap, specifies which combinations of words are admissible and which are not. The syntax of a natural language allows for the formation of type (ii) nonsense—sequences of words which are meaningless because of the incompatible meanings of the words involved. In the case of type (ii) nonsense, the meaninglessness of the combination is to be traced to what Carnap calls "a violation of *logical* syntax" or, alternatively, "*logically* counter-syntactic formation." Such formations can be demonstrated to be irremediably flawed as vehicles for the expression of thought. Now how is this to be understood? This, too, admits of a weaker and a stronger reading. On the weaker reading, there are certain kinds of thought—logically incoherent thoughts—which cannot be expressed in a proper logical syntax. These thoughts have a logical structure, but the sort of structure that they have renders them incapable of being either true or false. They therefore belong to a logically defective species of thought. On the stronger reading, there are no logically incoherent thoughts—a logically incoherent "thought" is not a kind of thought at all. Only that which can be represented in a proper logical syntax can be thought. What we (are tempted to) refer to as "a logically incoherent thought" is really a form of words that gives merely apparent expression to a thought.

Neither the weaker nor the stronger reading taken by itself can suffice as a reading of Carnap's essay. Carnap wants to be able—needs to be able—to have it both ways.

Carnap, in order further to clarify what kind of a thing "a violation of logical syntax" is, introduces (what is alleged to be) a concrete example of one. Here is Carnap's discussion of his example:

Let us take as examples the following sequences of words:

1. "Caesar us and"
2. "Caesar is a prime number"

The word sequence (1) is formed countersyntactically; the rules of syntax require that the third position be occupied, not by a conjunction, but by a predicate, hence by a noun (with article) or by an adjective. The word sequence "Caesar is a general", e.g., is formed in accordance with the rules of syntax. It is a meaningful word sequence, a genuine sentence. But, now, word sequence (2) is likewise syntactically correct, for it has the same grammatical form as the sentence just mentioned. Nevertheless (2) is meaningless. "Prime number" is a predicate of numbers; it can be neither affirmed nor denied of a person. Since (2) looks like a statement yet is not a statement, does not assert anything, expresses neither a true nor a false proposition, we call this word sequence a "pseudo-statement". The fact that the rules of grammatical syntax are not violated easily seduces one at first glance into the erroneous opinion that one still has to do with a statement, albeit a false one. But "a is a prime number" is false if and only if a is divisible by a natural number different from a and from 1; evidently it is illicit to put here "Caesar" for "a". This example has been so chosen that the nonsense is easily detectable. Many so-called statements of metaphysics are not so easily recognized to be pseudo-statements. The fact that natural languages allow the formation of meaningless sequences of words without violating the rules of grammar, indicates that grammatical syntax is, from a logical point of view, inadequate.[15]

We are offered two "sentences" here: (1) "Caesar us and" and (2) "Caesar is a prime number." The first is an example of something that is not even well formed by the lights of the syntax of natural language; the latter is well formed by those lights but nonetheless involves a violation of (the more stringent principles of a proper) logical syntax. In considering the example which Carnap himself here offers of a violation of logical syntax—"Caesar is a prime number"[16]—what kind of a thing are we meant to be considering? Are we meant to be considering a mere sequence of words or what this sequence of words says? Carnap's interest here is evidently not confined to the words considered as mere marks on paper. He wants us to consider this as a sequence each of whose constituents has a determinate meaning. He wants to say that in ordinary language it is possible to form the nonsensical sentence (c) by combining the underlined portions of the (meaningful) propositions (a) and (b) below:

---

[15] EMLAL, pp. 67–8.
[16] This is by no means an uncontroversial example of nonsense: Frege would have regarded it not as nonsensical, but as simply false.

(a) *Caesar* crossed the Rubicon   (b) 53 *is a prime number*

(c) *Caesar is a prime number*

About this example Carnap wants to say that it is nonsense, but not that it is type (i) nonsense. The resulting nonsense is not due to the absence of meaning on the part of some word or words, but rather to precisely the meanings that the words already have: meanings which clash with one another when imported into this context. It is supposed to be an example of a kind of nonsense which is due to the way in which the meanings of the parts of the sentence fail to fit together so as to make sense.

What we have here is alleged by Carnap to be a case of *fully determinate* nonsense: (1) it is *logically distinct* from other fully determinate cases of substantial nonsense; (2) each of the "parts" of this proposition has a *fully determinate sense*; and (3) though the sense of the resulting whole is flawed, it is a flawed in a *determinately specifiable respect*—it involves a determinate kind of failure of significance (whereas other cases of substantial nonsense each involve some other equally determinate "violation" of the principles of logical syntax). That we have here to do with a logically determinate example of nonsense can be seen from the fact that the grammatical/syntactical formation-rules of other natural languages, unlike a properly logical syntax, are thought by Carnap equally to permit the construction of *this* substantially nonsensical sentence—that is, they permit the formation of a string which can be said to correspond in the sort of flawed sense it possesses to this one. Thus Carnap's German example of type (ii) nonsense can be translated into English in such a way that the English counterpart can be said to have the same (flawed) "sense" as Carnap's original German example. The determinately specifiable respect in which Carnap's case of substantial nonsense possesses a (flawed) "sense" is the following: it represents "an attempt" to put *that* proper name for a person into *that* argument place where only a numerical expression will fit. But it won't fit—thus we get nonsense; not mere nonsense, but a special variety of nonsense which arises from attempting to do something logically impossible. Carnap, in taking himself to be building upon the ideas of the *Tractatus*, here implicitly attributes to the *Tractatus* an idea which many others have explicitly attributed to it. Moreover, it is the very idea that, as we shall see, that work is most concerned to criticize: the idea that we can so much as try to put a logical item into an argument place in which it doesn't fit—the idea that we can have a proposition that has a fully determinate kind of sense but the kind of sense that it has is nonsense.

EARLY WITTGENSTEIN'S DISTINCTION
BETWEEN SIGN AND SYMBOL

Here are the first two of Frege's three principles (which he presents at the beginning of his *Grundlagen der Arithmetik*):

[1] always to separate sharply the psychological from the logical, the subjective from the objective;

[2] never to ask for the meaning of a word in isolation, but only in the context of a proposition.

The methodological import of these principles is developed in the *Tractatus* through the claim that in ordinary language it is often the case that the same sign symbolizes in different ways. The distinction between sign and symbol as it is drawn in the *Tractatus* is introduced as part of the commentary on §3.3, which is the *Tractatus*'s reformulation of Frege's second principle.[17] Section 3.3 runs as follows: "Only the proposition has sense; only in the context of a proposition has a name meaning." Then, beginning immediately thereafter (with §3.31), comes the following commentary:

Every part of a proposition which characterizes its sense I call an expression (a symbol).

(The proposition itself is an expression.)

Everything essential to their sense that propositions can have in common with one another is an expression.

An expression is the mark of a form and a content.

An expression presupposes the forms of all propositions in which it can occur. It is the common characteristic mark of a class of propositions. (§§3.31–3.311)

An expression has meaning only in a proposition. (§3.314)

I conceive the proposition—like Frege and Russell—as a function of the expressions contained in it. (§3.318)

The sign is that in the symbol which is perceptible by the senses. (§3.32)

Two different symbols can therefore have the sign (the written sign or the sound sign) in common—they then signify in different ways. (§3.321)

---

[17] I say "reformulation of Frege's second principle" (rather than restatement of it) because the *Tractatus* is concerned to refashion Frege's distinction between *Sinn* and *Bedeutung*. Section 3.3 is worded as it is precisely in order to mark a departure from Frege in this regard. In the following discussion, I will ignore this difference in Frege's and Wittgenstein's understandings of the context principle.

It can never indicate the common characteristic of two objects that we symbolize them with the same signs but by different *methods of symbolizing*. For the sign is arbitrary.

We could therefore equally well choose two different signs [to symbolize the two different objects] and where then would remain that which the signs shared in common? (§3.322)

The point of the commentary is in part to clarify the notion of 'proposition' which figures in the context principle (only the *proposition* has sense; only in the context of a *proposition* has a name meaning).[18] The relevant notion is one of a certain kind of a symbol—not a certain kind of a sign—something which only has life in language.[19] The sign,

---

[18] A number of commentators have attributed to the *Tractatus* the view that a special mental act (of intending to mean a particular object by a particular word) is what endows a name with meaning (see e.g. P. M. S. Hacker, *Insight and Illusion* (Oxford: Oxford University Press, 1986), pp. 73–80; Max Black, *A Companion to Wittgenstein's Tractatus* (Ithaca, N.Y.: Cornell University Press, 1982), pp. 114–22; Norman Malcolm, *Nothing is Hidden: Wittgenstein's Criticisms of His Early Thought* (Oxford: Blackwell, 1986), pp. 63–82. There is, however, no reference anywhere in the *Tractatus* to a distinct act of meaning (through which a *Bedeutung* is conferred on a sign). The passage from the *Tractatus* most commonly adduced to provide a semblance of textual support for this psychologistic attribution is §3.11, which Pears and McGuinness translate as follows: "The method of projection is to think of the sense of the proposition." So translated, this remark can be taken to refer to an act of thinking and to ascribe an explanatory role to such an act. The Ogden translation is more faithful: "The method of projection is the thinking of the sense of the proposition." Rush Rhees glosses this (quite properly, I think) as: "The method of projection is what we mean by 'thinking' or 'understanding' the sense of the proposition." Rhees comments: "Pears and McGuinness read it [i.e. §3.11] . . . as though the remark were to explain the expression 'method of projection' . . . [On the contrary], 'projection', which is a logical operation, is . . . to explain '*das Denken des Satz-Sinnes*'. The '*ist*' after '*Projektionsmethode*' might have been italicized" (*Discussions of Wittgenstein* (London: Routledge & Kegan Paul, 1970), p. 39). Rhees's point here is that the last sentence of §3.11 has the same structure as e.g. the last sentence of §3.316: the explanans is on the left and the explanandum on the right—not the other way around. (Acknowledging the justice of Rhees's criticism, and finding it more natural in English to place the explanandum on the left, McGuinness later recanted his and Pears's original translation of §3.11 and proposed the following translation instead: "Thinking the sense of the proposition is the method of projection." McGuinness then goes on to offer the following lucid summary of the actual point of the passage: "Thinking the sense into the proposition is nothing other than so using the words of the sentence that their logical behaviour is that of the desired proposition": "On the So-Called Realism of the *Tractatus*," in Irving Block, ed., *Perspectives on the Philosophy of Wittgenstein* (Cambridge, Mass.: MIT Press, 1981), pp. 69–70.) The point being made here in the work about "thinking" is an illustration of a general feature of Wittgenstein's method. What the *Tractatus* does throughout is explicate putatively psychological explananda in terms of logical explanantes. The Malcolm/Black/Hacker reading of §3.11 takes Wittgenstein to be explaining one of the central logical notions of the book in terms of a psychological notion, thus utterly missing the way Wittgenstein here takes himself to be elaborating and building upon Frege's first two principles.

[19] Although the notion of *Satz* which figures in the context principle (only the *Satz* has sense; only in the context of a *Satz* has a name meaning) is of a certain kind of a

Wittgenstein says, "is that in the symbol which is perceptible by the senses" (what is now sometimes called the sign design). The symbol is a logical unit, it expresses something which propositions—as opposed to propositional signs—have in common.[20] Once transposed into a proper logical notation, it would be manifest which of the following three propositions have a propositional symbol in common:

(a) Socrates was bald.
(b) Socrates, who taught Plato, was bald.
(c) A philosopher whose teacher was Socrates was bald.

It would become clear, from the manner in which these three propositional symbols were expressed in the notation, that (a) and (b) have a propositional symbol in common (though they have no three-word sequence in common), and that (a) and (c) have no propositional symbol in common (despite their having the sequence of words 'Socrates was bald' in common). Taken together, (a) and (b) furnish an example of how in ordinary language different sequences of signs can have the symbol in common; and, taken together, (a) and (c) furnish an example of how in ordinary language the same sequence of signs can have no symbol in common, and thus how the same signs can belong to different symbols. Wittgenstein comments on these features of ordinary language:

---

symbol, the term 'Satz' in the *Tractatus* floats between meaning (1) a propositional symbol (as e.g. in §§3.3ff and §§4ff) and (2) a propositional sign (as e.g. in §§5.473 and §6.54). It is important to the method of the *Tractatus* that the recognition that certain apparent cases of (1) are merely cases of (2) be a recognition that the reader achieve on his own. Consequently, at certain junctures, the method of the *Tractatus* requires that the reference of *Satz* remain provisionally neutral as between (1) and (2).

[20] Wittgenstein's notion of an expression or symbol (that which is common to a set of propositions)—as opposed to a sign (that which is common to what Frege calls forms of words)—builds on Frege's idea that what determines the logical segmentation of a sentence are the inferential relations which obtain between the judgment that the sentence expresses and other judgments. *Language* (*Sprache*) is Wittgenstein's term for the totality of such propositional symbols; and *logical space* is his term for the resulting overall network of inferential relations within which each of these propositional symbols has its life. Sections 4–4.001 build on the notion of *Satz* qua *propositional symbol* developed in §§3.31ff. ("The thought is the *sinnvolle Satz*. The totality of *Sätze* is the language.") *Language* (*Sprache*) in the *Tractatus* refers to the totality of *possible* propositional symbols. One might think of this as Wittgenstein's attempting to follow Frege's example (in his exchange with Kerry about concepts) by "keeping to the strictly logical use" of a word, here the word 'language'. It is trivially true, if one employs this idiom, that *there is only one language*—though there are, of course, countless alternative systems of signs which may differ widely from one another in their respective expressive powers (and thus in how much and which aspects of *die Sprache* they are each able to express).

In the language of everyday life it very often happens that the same word signifies in two different ways—and therefore belongs to two different symbols—or that two words, which signify in different ways, are apparently applied in the same way in the proposition.

Thus the word "is" appears as the copula, as the sign of equality, and as the expression of existence; "to exist" as an intransitive verb like "to go"; "identical" as an adjective; we speak of *something* but also of the fact of *something* happening.

(In the proposition "Green is green"—where the first word is a proper name and the last an adjective—these words have not merely different meanings but they are *different symbols*.) (§3.323)

It is worth elaborating how Wittgenstein's example in the last paragraph illustrates the point of the first paragraph of §3.323. The propositional sign "Green is green" can be naturally taken as symbolizing in any of three different ways[21]—and hence can be understood as an expression for any one of three different thoughts:

(a) Mr. Green is green   Gg
(b) Mr. Green is Mr. Green   g = g
(c) The color green is the color green $(\forall x)(Gx \Leftrightarrow Gx)$

One way of noticing how the same sign symbolizes differently in each of these three cases is to focus on the word 'is'. In each of the propositions expressing each of these three different thoughts, the sign 'is' symbolizes a different logical relation. In (a), the sign 'is' symbolizes the copula (a relation between a concept and an object); in (b) we have the 'is' of identity (a relation between objects); in (c), we have the 'is' of coextensionality (a relation between concepts).[22] In the ordinary language

---

[21] The ensuing exposition of this example only really works if we assume all the letters of the sentence to be capitalized so that we have no orthographic clues as to when the expression 'GREEN' is being used as the proper name of a person and when as a concept expression.

[22] The sequence of (a), (b), and (c) nicely brings out a further asymmetry between sign and symbol. In the rendition of (b) into logical notation, we might think of the sign '=' as corresponding to the sign 'is' in the ordinary language version of (b); that is, we might think of these two signs ('=', 'is') as symbolizing the same relation (the relation of identity). But in the rendition of (a) into logical notation, there is no candidate for a sign that corresponds to 'is'—there is here nothing which is *the* sign which symbolizes the copula. The *Tractatus* draws five morals from this: (M1) a method of symbolizing is not simply a matter of a sign *naming* an item of a particular logical category; (M2) a symbol is expressed not simply through a sign but through *a mode of arrangement* of signs; (M3) not every logically significant aspect of a mode of arrangement of signs corresponds to an argument place (into which a different sign can be substituted); (M4) it is not the case that each method of symbolizing requires the employment of a distinct sign to express the method of symbolizing (a method of symbolizing can be expressed through a mode of arrangement of signs, such as the method of symbolizing the copula

version of (a)—"where the first word is a proper name and the last an adjective"—'green' can be seen to be not merely ambiguous with respect to its meaning (the way 'bank' is in "The bank is on the left bank"), but ambiguous with respect to its logical type: "these words have not merely different meanings but they are *different symbols.*" The point of the example is to show us that we cannot gather from the nota-tion of ordinary language how a given sign (e.g. 'green', or 'is') sym-bolizes in a given instance. Wittgenstein suddenly follows this example with the observation: "Thus there easily arise the most fundamental confusions (of which the whole of philosophy is full)" (§3.324). In a proper *Begriffsschrift*, a different sign would express each of these "dif-ferent methods of symbolizing," thus enabling us to identify the sources of certain confusions. In §3.325, Wittgenstein immediately goes on to say that in order "to avoid such errors" we require a symbolism which obeys the rules of *logical* grammar.

In the *Tractatus*, Wittgenstein argues that there will always be room for a question as to whether a given sign, when it occurs in two differ-ent sentences of ordinary language, is symbolizing the same way in each of those occurrences. And this question cannot be settled simply by appealing to the fact that the same word (sign) ordinarily occurs (sym-bolizes) as a name;[23] nor by appealing to the fact that if I were asked what I meant when I uttered one of those sentences I would reply that I meant the word in the same sense as I have on other occasions; nor by appealing to the fact that I, on this occasion of utterance, exert a spe-cial effort to mean the word in the same way as before. How can this question be settled? Wittgenstein says: "In order to recognize the sym-bol in the sign we must consider the context of significant use" (§3.326). We must ask ourselves on what occasion we would utter this sentence and what, in that context of use, we would then mean by it.[24]

in modern logical notation); (M5) for certain methods of symbolizing, the employment of a distinct sign is required.

[23] This is not to claim that it is possible to understand a sentence, if none of its con-stituent signs symbolize in the same manner in which they symbolize in other sentences. (Hence *Tractatus*, §4.03: "A proposition must use old expressions to communicate new senses.") It is only to claim that not *all* of the constituent signs must symbolize in a prece-dented fashion. But an unprecedented usage of a sign will only be intelligible if the con-stituent signs which symbolize in the "old" manner determine a possible segmentation of the propositional sign—where such a segmentation specifies both (1) the logical role of the sign which symbolizes in an unprecedented manner and (2) the position of the resulting propositional symbol in logical space.

[24] One standard way of contrasting early and later Wittgenstein is to say that later Wittgenstein rejected his earlier (allegedly truth-conditional) account of meaning—on which considerations of use have no role to play in fixing the meaning of an expres-sion—in favor of (what gets called) "a use theory of meaning." Our brief examination

CARNAP ON HEIDEGGER

We are now ready to look at Carnap's conception of *elucidation*. Carnap furnishes a detailed example of how the elucidation and elimination of metaphysical nonsense is supposed to proceed. Carnap takes a passage from Heidegger as his illustration. Heidegger's text allegedly furnishes a particularly vivid case of type (ii) nonsense. Indeed, it is adduced as a *typical* case of type (ii) metaphysical nonsense—one ripe for the application of Carnap's method. Hence Carnap remarks: "We could just as well have selected passages from any other of the numerous metaphysicians of the present or the past; yet the selected passages seem to us to illustrate our thesis especially well."[25] Could Carnap just as well have selected passages from any other of the numerous metaphysicians of the present or the past? And does the passage selected from Heidegger illustrate Carnap's thesis regarding the syntactically ill-formed character of metaphysical utterances?

Here is the text of the Heidegger passage as Carnap presents it:

What is to be investigated is Being only and—*nothing* else; Being alone and further—*nothing*; solely Being, and beyond Being *nothing . . . Does the Nothing exist only because the Not, i.e. Negation, exists?* Or is it the other way around? *Does Negation and the Not exist only because the Nothing exists?. . .* We assert: *the Nothing is prior to the Not and the Negation . . .* Where do we seek the Nothing? How do we find the Nothing . . . We know the Nothing . . . *Anxiety reveals the Nothing . . .* That for which and because of which we were anxious, was 'really'—nothing. Indeed, the Nothing itself—as such—was present . . . *What about this Nothing?—The Nothing itself nothings.*[26]

of §3.326 should already make one wary of such a story. The popularity of this story rests largely on an additional piece of potted history, according to which the *Tractatus* advances the doctrine that it is possible (and indeed, according to most readings, semantically necessary) to fix the meanings of names prior to and independently of their use in propositions (either through ostensive definition or through some special mental act which endows a name with meaning; see n. 18). This putative teaching of the *Tractatus* is standardly taken to be the primary target of the opening sections of *Philosophical Investigations*. But the whole point of §3.3–3.344 of the *Tractatus* is that the identity of the object referred to by a name is only fixed by the use of the name in a set of significant (*sinnvolle*) propositions. An appeal to use thus already plays a critical role in Wittgenstein's early account of what determines both the meaning of a proposition as a whole and the meanings of each of its "parts." With respect to this topic, the opening sections of *Philosophical Investigations* are properly seen as recasting and extending a critique of Russellian doctrines already begun in the *Tractatus*.

[25] EMLAL, p. 69n.

[26] I have (except for capitalizing the word "Being") reproduced Pap's translation of this passage as it occurs in EMLAL, p. 69 (Carnap's emphases). For reasons which will become clear, it should be noted that Heidegger's last sentence contains a neologism and thus would be more faithfully rendered into English by something that contained an

What basis does Carnap have for suspecting these statements of Heidegger's of being nonsense? One suspects that what initially brought them under a cloud of suspicion is that they are not obviously even *grammatically* well formed. The same word ('nothing') which ordinarily signifies a particle (used to form negative existential statements) appears in this text sometimes in the grammatical role of a substantive, sometimes in that of a verb. Carnap introduces the example by saying: "Let us now take a look at some examples of metaphysical pseudo-statements of a kind where the violation of logical syntax is especially obvious, though they accord with historical-grammatical syntax."[27] This nicely summarizes the two features that Carnap wants his example simultaneously to possess: first, it is well formed by the lights of ordinary grammatical syntax; second, it is comparatively obvious nonetheless that it is ill formed by the lights of a proper logical syntax. But the worry that immediately comes to mind is that the example manages to possess the second feature to the conveniently glaring degree that it does precisely because it does not possess the first. Carnap therefore goes to some lengths to attempt to demonstrate that the word 'nothing' sometimes occurs in sentences of ordinary language in a manner which might lead one to mistake it for a noun. Carnap even furnishes the reader with an elaborate chart which purports to demonstrate how someone might be misled by features of surface grammar into thinking that he was employing the word 'nothing' in a grammatically unobjectionable manner when, in reality, employing it in the logically illicit manner of a Heidegger. To mention only one of the countless problems with this "demonstration," it overlooks the fact that the syntax of ordinary German marks the distinction Carnap claims it fails to track: in order to employ a term as a substantive in German one has to capitalize it (and thus employ a term which is orthographically distinct from a term which denotes a logical particle); and Heidegger, in the proper fashion, in accordance with ordinary grammatical syntax, clearly distinguishes between his substantival and non-

expression which is not itself an English word but which nonetheless manages to offer the appearance of being a verbal form of 'nothing' conjugated in the third person singular—e.g. "The nothing itself noths." Though Pap's translation of the Heidegger passage is also in other respects atrocious (failing, for example, even to distinguish between *Sein* and *Seiende*), I have left the passage in this form, as it is in this form that it has achieved its considerable notoriety among anglophone philosophers, and to make clear that my concern here is solely with Carnap's analysis of Heidegger's passage and not with the interpretation of Heidegger per se. Indeed, nothing I say in this essay should be taken to endorse a particular reading of any one of the passages from Heidegger quoted by Carnap.

[27] EMLAL, p. 69.

substantival uses of the terms 'nichts' and 'das Nichts' in his text. But even if one takes Carnap's analysis to be sound as far as it goes, it still remains hard to see how Heidegger's text is supposed to furnish an illustration of Carnap's theory. Reading through this remarkably peculiar passage from Heidegger, one ought to be moved to expostulate: *this* is supposed to be an example of how metaphysical nonsense remains *undetected* until brought to the surface through the application of the principles of logical syntax? Whatever one thinks of its independent merits, Carnap's elaborate analysis of the different contexts in which the term 'nothing' can occur in ordinary language is scarcely credible as an account of how Heidegger is led to employ the word 'nothing' as he does here. It won't do to say of Heidegger's sentences that "the fact that the rules of the grammatical syntax of ordinary language are not violated [is what] seduces one into the erroneous opinion that one still has to do with a statement."[28] Such a diagnosis would be blind to the stunningly virtuosic character of Heidegger's employment of the word, even when judged by the allegedly comparatively permissive lights of ordinary grammatical syntax. This virtuosity renders Heidegger's text utterly unsuitable as an example of that of which it was allegedly introduced as an example: the surreptitious misuse of language. It is hard to credit the hypothesis that the author of this text has been led astray by the surface grammar of ordinary language; for precisely what puzzles and challenges us in Heidegger's assertions is their peculiar surface grammar. The disclosure that language is under some extraordinary pressure in this text does not wait on the application of the principles of logical syntax. Heidegger is evidently speaking here in an unusual way: openly forcing his reader to reflect on how his words are meant.

Carnap's analysis clings nonetheless to the supposition that Heidegger's words are employed by him in nothing other than their usual senses. The problem then becomes one of seeing how it is that this author *could* imagine that he was employing the words in their usual senses. Carnap sees this problem. Here is his first line of response:

In view of the gross logical errors which we find [in Heidegger's text] . . ., we might be led to conjecture that perhaps the word "nothing" has in Heidegger's treatise a meaning entirely different from the customary one. And this presumption is further strengthened as we go on to read there that anxiety reveals the Nothing, that the Nothing itself is present as such in anxiety. For here the word "nothing" seems to refer to a certain emotional constitution, possibly of a religious sort, or something or other that underlies such emotions. If such were the case, then the mentioned logical errors . . . would not pertain. But the

---

[28] EMLAL, p. 67.

first sentence of the quotation at the beginning of this section proves that this interpretation is not possible. The combination of "only" and "nothing else" shows unmistakably that the word "nothing" here has the usual meaning of a logical particle that serves for the formulation of a negative existential statement.[29]

If we were to adopt the assumption that "the word 'nothing' has in Heidegger's treatise a meaning entirely different from the customary one," then we would have to know what Heidegger means by the word 'nothing' before we could conclude that its occurrence here violated the principles of logical syntax. Carnap therefore needs to rule out the possibility that the meaning of 'nothing' here might be different from the customary one. How does Carnap know that Heidegger means the word 'nothing' throughout the course of his enigmatic assertions always in the same way and always only in its usual sense (and thus, in most of its occurrences, incoherently)? His evidence for this claim is that in the *first* sentence (of the sequence of sentences that Carnap has strategically chosen to excerpt from Heidegger's essay)[30] we find the author using the word 'nothing' in the usual way: "What is to be investigated is Being only and—*nothing* else; Being alone and further—*nothing*; solely Being, and beyond Being *nothing*." The employment of the word 'nothing' in this sentence is, by Carnap's lights, grammatically and logically unobjectionable. The sentence is nonetheless included as part of Carnap's extract from Heidegger because of the light it ostensibly sheds on the rest of the text. Its role is to show that the overall context of Heidegger's remarks supports Carnap's reading of them.[31] The occurrence of the word 'nothing' in this first sentence "shows unmistakably," says Carnap, that the word 'nothing' is used univocally in none other than its usual meaning throughout Heidegger's text. Both Frege and Wittgenstein would object: to imagine that an examination of Heidegger's first sentence suffices to establish that the word 'nothing' retains its usual meaning in its occurrences throughout the subsequent sentences just is to violate Frege's context principle (and with it, *Tractatus* §3.3). Moreover, Carnap's basis for his conclusion (i.e. the claim that Heidegger *intends* to continue to use the word the same way in the subsequent sentences) runs afoul of Frege's first principle: it

---

[29] EMLAL, p. 71.

[30] And which, moreover, do not occur consecutively in Heidegger's essay.

[31] If it were possible to tell what Carnap says it is possible to tell from a consideration of the context of use, then any speaker of the language (regardless of their knowledge of the finer points of Carnapian logical syntax) has cause to charge Heidegger with a misuse of language. There would be no need for appeal to a higher court—for deferral of judgment until it was established that these sentences additionally drew the verdict: "inadequate from a strictly logical point of view."

depends upon an appeal to Heidegger's psychological intentions in employing the sign. Carnap proceeds towards his conclusion in just the manner that Frege and Wittgenstein seek to expose as confused: first, Carnap notices how the sign is used in a previous context of use; then, secondly, he attempts to establish what is meant in a subsequent context of use by appealing to an intention to employ the same sign in the same way as in the original context; and finally, he imagines that the existence of the postulated intention can fix the meaning of the sign in the subsequent context, enabling it to continue to symbolize in the same way (regardless of its logical role within the subsequent context). Carnap here succumbs to (what Frege calls) *psychologism*. Psychologism? Carnap?

The putative achievement of the identification of cases of Carnapian type (ii) nonsense can be said to involve a lapse into psychologism in this sense: it takes the meaning of a word to be fixed by something independently of its logical role in a construction to which it makes a contribution. Admittedly, no part is played in Carnap's *theory* by a claim to the effect that the correct way to determine what someone means is to determine something about their psychological state of mind while writing or uttering a sequence of words. Nonetheless, when Carnap claims that he knows what Heidegger must want to mean—that is, when he claims that he knows that in Heidegger's case "the combination of 'only' and 'nothing else' shows unmistakably that the word 'nothing' here has the usual meaning of a logical particle that serves for the formulation of a negative existential statement"—his ability to know this rests on a tacit appeal to Heidegger *intending* the word 'nothing' here to have the meaning of a logical particle in each of its several occurrences throughout this sequence of sentences. Carnap's ability to know this about Heidegger's sentences cannot rest on anything that Carnap's theory officially sanctions as a method of determining the meaning of an expression: namely, the logico-syntactic behavior of the expression in the context of a proposition. Thus, to say that Carnap succumbs to psychologism, in this extended sense of the term, is not a matter of attributing to him a commitment to a certain kind of theory— say, a theory which accounts for what it is to mean a particular expression in a particular way by appealing to a psychological act performed by the speaker of that expression, or to the presence of certain psychological associations in the mind of the speaker, and so on. Carnap, who in this respect—as in so many others—is a faithful student of Frege's, would immediately repudiate any theory which rested on such an appeal. The formulation of the charge here as one of psychologism must seem perverse, if one fails to appreciate that this formulation invokes a particular philosophical understanding of the realm of the psychological, and with it a peculiar (Fregean and early Wittgensteinian) employment of term 'psychological'—one which Carnap himself, following Frege, claims to adopt—in which the category of the *psychological* gets its content from its contrast with that of the *logical*.[32] All extra-logical determinants of (what the metaphysician mistakes for a kind of) "meaning" are, Carnap himself declares, merely psychological. (Thus Carnap concludes that, though metaphysical pseudo-propositions lack "theoretical content," they possess "psychological content" qua expressions of psychological feelings or attitudes.)[33] Precisely because he has deprived himself of any logical basis for a segmentation of Heidegger's sentences into their logical components, and yet persists in believing that he knows what Heidegger must mean (when he says things like "We know the nothing"), Carnap can be charged—in accordance with his own extended, Fregean use of the term 'psychological'—with lapsing into psychologism. In this extended sense of the term 'psychologism', one lapses into psychologism whenever one takes oneself to be able to settle the meaning a word imports into a construction independently of the word's *logical* contribution to that construction.

Even if an appeal to Heidegger's intentions could suffice to settle what Heidegger's sentences mean, how can Carnap be so sure that in Heidegger's passage the sign 'nothing' is "intended" by Heidegger to

[32] I do not mean to suggest that such an invocation of the category of the psychological is itself philosophically inconsequential. The extraordinarily inclusive, garbage-can conception of the nature and scope of the psychological that such an invocation presupposes in turn rests upon a correlatively narrow conception of the nature and scope of (what Frege and Wittgenstein call) the logical (which later Wittgenstein, in reconceiving the nature and scope of its provenance, will call the grammatical). The important break here between the philosophy of later Wittgenstein and that of Frege and early Wittgenstein is nicely captured in the following aphorism due to Stanley Cavell: as Kant sought to undo Hume's psychologizing of knowledge, and Frege and Husserl sought to undo the psychologizing of logic, so later Wittgenstein seeks to undo the psychologizing of psychology ("Aesthetic Problems of Modern Philosophy," in *Must We Mean What We Say?* (Cambridge: Cambridge University Press, 1969), p. 91).

[33] It is, for Carnap, constitutive of *metaphysics* that it confuses these two kinds of content. (If the metaphysician merely gave expression to his psychological feelings or attitudes without mistaking his performance for one that had theoretical content, then he would not be open to the charge of "metaphysics.") It is, for Carnap, correlatively constitutive of art that it provides the forum in which the elaborate expression of psychological content may occur without pretense of traffic in theoretical content. (Thus, from among those philosophers commonly referred to as metaphysicians, Carnap singles out Nietzsche for praise on the ground that, when moved to give expression to his general attitude toward life, he abandons a theoretical mode of discourse and has recourse to art; EMLAL, p. 80.) The irony here is that—since the confusion of that which has logical with that which has psychological content defines metaphysics for Carnap—Carnap, in his method of identifying instances of substantial nonsense, opens himself up to the charge of metaphysics.

symbolize the same way throughout its successive occurrences? How can he be sure that Heidegger's later uses of the word do not represent the expression of an intention to employ the word 'nothing' in a linguistically innovative yet (potentially) intelligible manner?[34] Carnap recognizes that he needs to say more here; and his way of dispensing with this worry ought to come as a surprise. We can be sure, Carnap tells us, that Heidegger means to employ the word 'nothing' in the aforementioned self-defeating fashion because Heidegger is someone who *self-consciously* aspires to speak nonsense. It is actually Heidegger's *aim*, in these sentences, to (try to) jam the negative existential quantifier first into an argument place that can only accommodate an object expression, then into an argument place that can only accommodate an expression for a first-level function, and so on.[35] The attribution of such an intention would be uncharitable in the absence of any evidence suggesting that Heidegger does possess such an extraordinary aim. Carnap (imagines he) possesses a way of ruling out any alternative comparatively charitable construal.[36] He has *evidence* which shows that

[34] Indeed, Carnap himself concedes that Heidegger is no longer using the sign to symbolize in the same way as in the earlier sentences in the remarkable final sentence: "The Nothing itself nothings." In German, this sentence reads: "das Nichts selbst nichtet" (ÜMLAS, p. 229). There simply is no established usage, of *any* sort, for the sign 'nichtet'. Carnap remarks: "[H]ere we confront one of those rare cases where a new word is introduced which never had a meaning to begin with" (EMLAL, p. 71). Why not draw the same conclusion about 'das Nichts? Carnap never explains why the presence of the last sentence in Heidegger's text doesn't threaten his classification of the previous sentences as type (ii) nonsense. Presumably, he would want to try to claim that two distinct sorts of cases are to be distinguished here: the last sentence is type (i), whereas the others are all type (ii). But this raises the question: how does he know the other sentences aren't type (i)? In the absence of some criterion for distinguishing these cases, Carnap's chosen example threatens to fail to illustrate what it is supposed to illustrate: namely, how to identify real live cases of type (ii) metaphysical nonsense as simultaneously distinct from both cases of type (i) nonsense and *sinnvolle* sentences.

[35] Carnap's argument here still rests on the claim that Heidegger's intentions fix the meaning of the word 'nothing' in his sentences—only now the appeal is to a very different sort of intention on Heidegger's part: an intention to violate the logical structure of language on purpose.

[36] Someone might object that the claim that Heidegger intends to speak nonsense does not play a weight-bearing role in the argument of Carnap's essay, and that I am attaching too much significance to Carnap's observation (EMLAL, pp. 71–2) that Heidegger does so intend. It is true that the claim is not represented by Carnap as playing an important role in his argument. But his argument nonetheless requires it. Faced with the choice of (1) attributing to someone the intention to fail to make sense, and (2) attributing to him the intention to use words in an unprecedented but potentially intelligible manner, any sound theory of interpretation will prescribe that we settle for (1) only if we have excellent grounds for preferring it over (2). If Carnap is unable to rule out the possibility of a more charitable construal of Heidegger's sentences, then his entire analysis stands under threat of failing to make contact with Heidegger's text. He therefore needs an argument for why we should go with (1).

Heidegger intends to speak nonsense. Heidegger elsewhere in his work, Carnap tells us, explicitly avows the intention to speak nonsense that Carnap here attributes to him.

The evidence that Heidegger means to speak nonsense is drawn from the same essay of Heidegger's from which Carnap's original exhibit is drawn. Carnap quotes the following passage from Heidegger:

> Question and answer in regard to the Nothing are equally absurd in themselves . . . The fundamental rule of thinking commonly appealed to, the law of prohibited contradiction, general 'logic', destroys this question . . . If thus the power of the understanding in the field of questions concerning Nothing and Being is broken, then the fate of the sovereignty of 'logic' within philosophy is thereby decided as well. The very idea of 'logic' dissolves into the whirl of a more basic questioning.[37]

This evidence, Carnap claims, shows that "the author of the treatise is clearly aware of the conflict between his questions and statements and logic."[38] Carnap concludes: "Thus we find here a good confirmation of our thesis; a metaphysician himself states that his questions and answers are irreconcilable with logic and the scientific way of thinking."[39] Carnap here "confirms" his claim that Heidegger speaks nonsense by relying on statements of Heidegger's—statements which Carnap evidently takes himself to be able to understand (and hence which he presumably takes to make some sort of sense). Carnap needs this additional evidence to show that he is not reading Heidegger uncharitably. Unless he assumes that his additional evidence is reliable, Carnap is unable to evade the objection that Heidegger's use of the word 'nothing' might represent a linguistically innovative use of the word. But, once he has his additional evidence in hand and assumes it to be reliable (which he is obliged to assume if it is to serve its intended purpose), then, in response to the question "How do you know Heidegger speaks nonsense?" Carnap does not need to look beyond this one piece of evidence to settle the matter.

The presumption behind Carnap's procedures initially appeared to be that no one would intentionally speak nonsense. The original idea was supposed to be that if the nonsensical character of the metaphysician's utterances were made evident to him, he would no longer be attracted to them. It is hard to see how Carnap can attribute to the author of a purportedly typical case of metaphysical nonsense an intention to speak nonsense without abandoning his original claims concerning how to diagnose and cure metaphysical nonsense (or at least

---

[37] Quoted in EMLAL, pp. 71–2.   [38] EMLAL, p. 71.
[39] EMLAL, p. 72.

abandoning his claim that Heidegger is a representative example of the phenomenon that Carnap's essay seeks to bring to his reader's attention).[40] The advent of the cure was originally advertised as coinciding with the metaphysician's epiphany that his employment of words involved an illegitimate combination of meanings. It is difficult to see how, by Carnap's own lights, the application of the principles of logical syntax could ever lead to a cure of the philosopher who self-consciously aspires to produce nonsensical combinations of words.

It is no accident that Carnap has fixed upon an example which has the features exhibited by this passage from Heidegger. Though it fails to accord with his own description of metaphysical nonsense, Carnap needs to avail himself of an example with these features to be able so much as to appear to provide any sort of illustration of the practical application of his theory. Heidegger's text offers the appearance of simultaneously satisfying three conditions all of which an example must satisfy if Carnap is to seem to stand a chance of unmasking it as a case of metaphysical nonsense: first, it must consist of sequences of words that a human being might actually be moved to write with the intention of communicating a thought; second, it must be possible to identify it as a case of nonsense simply by attending to the words as they stand on the page; third, it must be possible to forestall the objection that the words have been construed in an uncharitable manner. If Carnap fixed upon an example in which the speaker did not exhibit the slightest paradoxical animus and uttered only statements which were by the lights of ordinary grammar apparently unimpeachable, the questions would always arise: is the speaker really speaking nonsense? How does the speaker mean her words? Is there a way to make sense of her words? (Is there a way to see the symbol in the sign?) Carnap does not want the application of his method to be forestalled by such preliminary inquiries. The only contexts in which such inquiries have a legitimate place, for Carnap, are ordinary non-metaphysical cases of obstructed comprehension—cases in which we encounter hermeneutic difficulties concerning the semantics of syntactically well-formed sentences. Carnap wants, in his application of the method of logical analysis, to be able to bypass such inquiries altogether—to eschew any consideration of the semantics of a metaphysician's utterances—by identifying metaphysical statements as cases of nonsense solely through

---

[40] The attribution also renders Carnap's chart on EMLAL, p. 70 (of misleading because grammatically superficially similar sentences) otiose, insofar as the chart aims to show how misleading features of the surface grammar of the word 'nothing' are what occasion someone like Heidegger *unwittingly* to stray into nonsense.

an attention to (what he calls) their syntax. He wants to apply his analytical tools directly to the metaphysician's words considered in isolation from possible contexts of use.

NONSENSE IN THE *TRACTATUS*

The following passage from Baker and Hacker offers a fairly standard story of how an appeal to the rules of syntax in the *Tractatus* gives way in the work of later Wittgenstein to an appeal to the rules of grammar:

> Wittgenstein had, in the *Tractatus,* seen that philosophical or conceptual investigation moves in the domain of rules. An important point of continuity was the insight that philosophy is not concerned with what is true and what is false, but rather with what makes sense and what traverses the bounds of sense . . . [W]hat he called 'rules of grammar' . . . are the direct descendants of the 'rules of logical syntax' of the *Tractatus*. Like rules of logical syntax, rules of grammar determine the bounds of sense. They distinguish sense from nonsense . . . Grammar, as Wittgenstein understood the term, is the account book of language. Its rules determine the limits of sense, and by carefully scrutinizing them the philosopher may determine at what point he has drawn an overdraft on Reason, *violated the rules for the use of an expression*, and so, in subtle and not readily identifiable ways, traversed the bounds of sense.[41]

I agree with Baker and Hacker that Wittgenstein's later conception of grammar is the heir to his earlier conception of logical syntax. But I disagree with their characterizations of these conceptions. Indeed, their characterizations fit Carnap's views far more comfortably than Wittgenstein's.[42] The idioms which Baker and Hacker employ in the above passage—"determining the limits or bounds of sense," "determining the point at which these bounds are traversed," "violating the rules for the use of an expression"—have, as we have seen, a natural

---

[41] Gordon Baker and Peter Hacker, *Wittgenstein: Rules, Grammar and Necessity,* vol. i (Oxford: Blackwell, 1985), pp. 39–40, 55 (their emphasis).

[42] It would be a mistake to think that the crucial difference between my interpretation of Wittgenstein and that of Baker and Hacker is that whereas they, on the one hand, think that when Wittgenstein wrote his early work he thought that there were ineffable truths that cannot be stated in language and later came to see that this is misconceived, I, on the other hand, think that already in his early work he thought this misconceived. The more important difference between their reading and mine is that I think that Wittgenstein (early and late) thinks that the view that they attribute to later Wittgenstein is a disguised version of the view that they attribute to early Wittgenstein. I take the continuity in Wittgenstein's thought to lie in his espousal of the austere conception of nonsense; they take it to lie in his espousal of the substantial conception.

place in the exegesis of Carnap's doctrines. Consider the following pair of passages from Baker and Hacker:

Wittgenstein's 'rules of grammar' serve only *to distinguish sense from nonsense* . . . They *settle what makes sense*, experience settles what is the case . . . Grammar is a free-floating array of rules for the use of language. It *determines what is a correct use of language*, but is not itself correct or incorrect.

What philosophers have called 'necessary truths' are, in Wittgenstein's view, typically rules of grammar, norms of representation, i.e., they fix concepts. They are expressions of internal relations between concepts . . . Hence they *license (or prohibit) transitions between concepts*, i.e. transitions from one expression of an empirical proposition to another.[43]

Each of the phrases italicized in the above passages marks a moment in which Baker and Hacker attribute to later Wittgenstein an instance of the sort of understanding of "the logic of our language" that he was already seeking to exorcise in his early work—one which conceives of the possibilities of meaningful expression as limited by "general rules of the language" (be they called "rules of logical syntax" or "rules of grammar") and which imagines that by specifying these rules one can identify in advance which combinations of words are licensed and which prohibited. And, indeed, not only much of Baker and Hacker's rhetoric but many of their attempts to apply (what they take to be) Wittgenstein's methods to particular examples of philosophical confusion are strikingly reminiscent of moments in Carnap's writings. Consider the following example:

If someone (whether philosopher or scientist) claims that colours are sensations in the mind or in the brain, the philosopher must point out that this person is misusing the words 'sensation' and 'colour'. Sensations in the brain, he should remind his interlocutor, are called 'headaches', and colours are not headaches; one can have (i.e., it makes sense to speak of) sensations in the knee or in the back, but not in the mind. It is, he must stress, extended things that are coloured. But this is not a factual claim about the world (an opinion which the scientist might intelligibly gainsay). It is a grammatical observation . . . Such utterances are not false (for then they could be true) but senseless.[44]

Baker and Hacker's analysis of "Colors are sensations in the mind" here closely parallels Carnap's analysis of "Caesar is a prime number." Just as the expression 'prime number' cannot be predicated of an expression denoting a person, so 'color' cannot be predicated of an

---

[43] *Wittgenstein: Rules, Grammar and Necessity*, pp. 40, 269. I am indebted to Martin Gustafsson for drawing these two passages to my attention.

[44] Ibid. p. 53.

expression denoting a sensation. The nonsensicality of the statement is to be traced to an attempt to combine terms in an illegitimate manner and the nonsense is to be exposed by invoking a principle (now called a principle of "grammar") that forbids such a combination.

Baker and Hacker's understanding of such cases of *violating the rules for the use of an expression*—like Carnap's understanding of type (ii) nonsense—rests on affirming something that the *Tractatus* is centrally concerned to repudiate: the possibility of identifying the logical (or grammatical) category of a term outside the context of legitimate combination—of identifying the manner in which a sign symbolizes in a context in which the reference of the parts of a sentence does not determine the reference of the whole. This repudiation is explicit in the following series of remarks:

Logic must take care itself.

A *possible* sign must also be able to signify. Everything which is possible in logic is also permitted. ("Socrates is identical" means nothing because there is no property which is called "identical". The proposition is nonsensical because we have not made some arbitrary determination, not because the symbol itself is impermissible.)

In a certain sense we cannot make mistakes in logic. (§5.473)

We cannot give a sign the wrong sense. (§5.4732)

Frege says: Every legitimately constructed proposition must have a sense; and I say: Every possible proposition is legitimately constructed, and if it has no sense this can only be because we have given no *meaning* to some of its constituent parts.

(Even if we believe that we have done so.)

Thus "Socrates is identical" says nothing, because we have given *no* meaning to the word "identical" as *adjective*. For when it occurs as the sign of equality it symbolizes in an entirely different way—the symbolizing relation is another—therefore the symbol is in the two cases entirely different; the two symbols have the sign in common with one another only by accident. (§5.4733)

These remarks express in an extremely compressed fashion some of the central ideas of the *Tractatus*. Let us begin by looking at the example ("Socrates is identical") and the commentary on it which Wittgenstein offers here. It is the sort of combination of words that Carnap would be tempted to analyze as an instance of type (ii) nonsense—as an attempt to employ the identity sign (i.e. an expression which symbolizes the relation of identity between objects) as if it were a concept expression. Wittgenstein says in this passage that the nonsensicality of the string is due not to an impermissible employment of a symbol, but rather to our failing to make a determination of meaning. Wittgenstein's refusal to accept a Carnapian analysis of the matter here is not due to some peculiarity of the example.[45] Wittgenstein says: "If it has no sense this can *only* be because we have given no meaning to some of its constituent parts." The "only" here signals that for Wittgenstein all apparent cases of type (ii) nonsense are (in the words of §6.54) "eventually to be recognized as" cases of type (i) nonsense. Carnap's own example could be substituted for Wittgenstein's without affecting the point of the passage. On the Tractarian view, if "Caesar is a prime number" has no sense, "this can only be because we have given no *meaning* to some of its constituent parts" (§5.4733)—regardless of how strong our inclination may be "to believe that we have done so."

LOGICAL SYNTAX IN THE *TRACTATUS*

Logical syntax, in the *Tractatus*, is concerned neither with what Carnap calls "logical syntax" nor with what Russell calls "a theory of types." To express the same point in the idiom of the *Tractatus*: logical syntax

---

[45] The following two excerpts from §§5.473–5.4733 are potentially misleading and might appear to conflict with what I say about the point of the passage:

(1) "'Socrates is identical' means nothing because there is no property which is called 'identical'" (§5.473).
(2) "'Socrates is identical' says nothing, because we have given *no* meaning to the word 'identical' as *adjective*" (§5.4733).

The point of remark (1)—about "identical" naming an unspecified property—is to offer a suggestion intended to enable us, based on the surface grammar of this peculiar string, to find a way to see a symbol in the sign. There is an invitation present in the pattern of ordinary language for us to try to read the sign in this way (on the model of "Socrates is happy"). But we can only go so far in this direction. We can assimilate "Socrates is identical" to an established pattern (and thereby recognize the symbol in the sign); but we still do not yet know *what* the sentence says, because there is no established use of "identical" as a concept expression. When Wittgenstein talks in remark (1) about a property, he is talking about a method of *symbolizing*. When he talks in remark (2) about "identical" as adjective, he is referring to a feature of the "external form" (§4.002) of certain sentences—a grammatical surface pattern—of ordinary language (a certain sort of configuration of signs). The term "adjective" in §3.323 and in §5.473 refers to a feature of the surface grammar (the sign-structure) of ordinary language—not a proper *logical* category. The point here is about the sign "identical," not the symbol. Consider sentences (a) and (b):

(a) Socrates and the teacher of Plato are identical.
(b) Socrates and the teacher of Aristotle are happy.

As it occurs in sentence (b), "identical" has the same surface grammar as an adjective such as "happy." This is what Wittgenstein means when he says in §3.323 that "'identical' sometimes appears as an adjective."

is concerned neither with the proscription of combinations of signs nor with the proscription of combinations of symbols. It is not concerned with the proscription of combinations of signs, because Tractarian logical syntax does not treat of (mere) *signs*; it treats of symbols—and a symbol only has life in the context of a significant proposition. It is not concerned with the *proscription* of combinations of symbols, because there is nothing to proscribe[46]—"Every possible proposition is legitimately constructed" (§5.4733). Tractarian logical syntax treats of the categorically distinct kinds of logically significant components into which *sinnvolle Sätze* can be segmented—such components being the sorts of components they are only in virtue of their participation in a *possible* proposition.

Two years after his "Elimination of Metaphysics" essay, in his book *The Logical Syntax of Language,* Carnap writes that logical syntax "should have no reference to the meaning of signs."[47] This means: logical syntax is concerned with strings of *uninterpreted* signs—that is, strings of (mere) marks on paper. In Carnap's work, from *The Logical Syntax of Language* on, "logical syntax" treats of a class of *formal* structures—combinatorial structures generated by sequences of signs— where "formal" means formal in the Hilbertian sense: void of semantic content or structure.[48] "Formal" for Wittgenstein means pertaining to

---

[46] There is therefore an asymmetry in the attitude of the *Tractatus* toward these two sorts of proscription. The latter sort (i.e. the proscription of combinations of symbols) rests on philosophical confusion; the former does not. The *Tractatus* clearly thinks it is desirable for certain purposes (and for systems of notation which facilitate those purposes) to introduce principles which proscribe combinations of signs (as e.g. a *Begriffsschrift* does). But there is reason to think the *Tractatus* would not look favorably upon a general reform of natural language based on principles that sought to proscribe sequences of natural language icons. (§§4.002 and 5.5563 taken in conjunction yield: "Our everyday language is part of the human organism and no less complicated than it . . . and in perfect logical order, just as it is.") It is important that natural languages be able to tolerate the sorts of innovative use of signs exemplified in a mild way by Frege's example about 'Vienna' (see "On Concept and Object," *Collected Papers* (Oxford: Blackwell, 1984), p. 189), with a vengeance by Heidegger's employment of 'nothing', and by Wittgenstein's own remarks (in §§5.473, 5.4733) about the possibility of giving 'identical' an adjectival use.

[47] *The Logical Syntax of Language*, p. 282n. Carnap goes on to cite *Tractatus*, §3.33 as evidence that he and Wittgenstein are in agreement on this point. For an excellent discussion of what Wittgenstein does not and Carnap does think logic is, see Michael Friedman, "Carnap and Wittgenstein's *Tractatus*," in W. W. Tait, ed., *Early Analytic Philosophy* (New York: Open Court, 1996).

[48] This is not obviously what "logical syntax" means in EMLAL (most of what Carnap says about Heidegger's employment of *nothing*—see e.g. the passage from Carnap the reference for which is given in n. 29—makes no sense if he is only concerned with the sign 'nothing'); but it is not altogether clear what "logical syntax" means in this essay. The closest he comes in EMLAL to a definition of logical syntax is to say: "The syntax of a language specifies which combinations of words are admissible and which

that structure common to language and world (within which all semantic content has its life) considered in abstraction from any particular
(true or false) content. Every state of affairs has a Tractarian logical
form. The only parts of the *world* which can be said to have "formal"
properties, for the Carnap of *The Logical Syntax of Language*, are mere
marks on paper. The author of *The Logical Syntax of Language*, if he
mistook Wittgenstein's notion of "formal" for his own, would be
obliged to regard the *Tractatus*'s employment of the notion of "formal"
or "logical" properties which are equally "properties of language" and
"of the world" (§6.12) as an example of type (ii) nonsense. Wittgenstein's remark in the *Tractatus* that "in logical syntax the *Bedeutung* of
a sign ought never to play a role" (§3.33) sounds just like Carnap's
remark that logical syntax "should have no reference to the *Bedeutung*
of signs." But Wittgenstein is not saying what Carnap is saying. Mere
marks on paper have no Tractarian logical syntax. Only symbols—"the
parts of a proposition which characterize its *Sinn*"—have logical syntax. In Tractarian logical syntax, the particular *Bedeutungen* of signs
"never play a role" (not because logical syntax is concerned with *mere*
signs, but) because logical syntax is concerned only with *how* signs
symbolize—with what the *Tractatus* calls their *methods of symbolizing*
(3.322)—while abstracting from *what* (i.e. which particular object,
property, or relation) they denote. Logical syntax thus prescinds from
all content and considers only the bare form of significant thought.

   Though Wittgenstein never speaks in the *Tractatus* of "violations of
logical syntax," he does remark on the ways in which a proper logical

---

inadmissible" (EMLAL, p. 67). This reference throughout Carnap's discussion to admissible and inadmissible combinations of *words* allows Carnap, from the point of view of
the *Tractatus*, systematically to conflate questions concerning admissible combinations
of signs with questions concerning admissible combinations of symbols. Carnap wavers,
in this essay, between characterizing the principles of "logical syntax" as principles
which govern combinations of symbols (as he needs to, if they are to isolate a flawed
Sinn in the utterances of the metaphysician) and characterizing them as principles which
govern the combinations of signs (as he would need to, if he wanted to maintain—as he
does in his later work—that logical syntax is only concerned with "language" qua purely formal combinatorial syntactic object). EMLAL represents a transitional phase in
Carnap's work in which he is moving towards his 1934 Hilbertian understanding of syntax (which eschews semantics), and away from a Tractarian understanding of logical
syntax (the application of which presupposes semantic aspects of the structure of significant thought). The "logical analysis of language" practiced on many of the examples in
EMLAL only makes sense if "logical syntax" refers to something akin to a
Fregean/Tractarian *Begriffsschrift* which perspicuously exhibits the logical structure of
thoughts (and not merely the sequence-structure of uninterpreted *signs*). (Some of the
discussions of examples in the later portions of *The Logical Syntax of Language*
(§§72–81), which seek to refine the EMLAL project of unmasking metaphysics through
the logical analysis of language, continue—albeit in a subtler way—to equivocate
between symbol and sign.)

grammar would enable us to see more clearly the logical structure of ordinary language—and thus the ways in which ordinary language itself fails to reflect its own logical structure in a perspicuous manner. These remarks occur in the context of his discussion of how ordinary language allows the same sign to symbolize in different ways and the same symbol to be expressed by different signs. He goes on to say:

> Thus there easily arise the most fundamental confusions (of which the whole of philosophy is full).
>   In order to avoid these errors, we must employ a symbolism which excludes them, by not applying the same sign in different symbols and by not applying signs in the same way which signify in different ways. A symbolism, that is to say, which obeys the rules of *logical* grammar—of logical syntax. (§§3.324–3.325)

In order to understand this passage, we need to distinguish clearly between two different things one can mean by the expression "violation of logical syntax":

(1) *substantial nonsense*—the result of putting an item of one logical category in the place where an item of another category belongs;

(2) *cross-category equivocation*—the result of allowing different occurrences of the same sign to symbolize items of a different logical category.[49]

Carnap's appropriation of Tractarian logical syntax, in its talk of "violations of logical syntax," conflates these two kinds of "violation," as have many commentators after him. This allows §§3.324–3.325 to appear to offer textual evidence for the claim that the *Tractatus* holds that "the most fundamental confusions (of which the whole of philosophy is full)" (§3.324) are due to "violations" of the first kind, when all that is at issue are "violations" of the second kind. The point of a

---

[49] The following newspaper headlines offer examples of cross-category equivocation—cases in which there is an ambiguity (not just in the *Bedeutungen* of the words, but in the logical syntax of the string and thus) in the logical category of the symbol we should see in the sign:

(a) British Left Waffles on Falkland Islands
(b) British Push Bottles Up German Rear
(c) Potential Witness to Murder Drunk
(d) Legal Aid Advocates Worry
(e) Crowds Rushing To See Pope Trample 6 to Death
(f) Beating Witness Provides Names
(g) Nixon Stands Pat on Watergate Tapes
(h) University Studies Mushroom
(i) Carter Plans Swell Deficit.

proper logical symbolism for the *Tractatus* is only to exclude the latter kind of "violation," but not the former kind (because, according to the teaching of the *Tractatus*, there is no such kind). Theories of logic which seek to proscribe certain combinations of symbols seek to take care of that which *"must fall into place as a matter of course"* (§3.334). It is, Wittgenstein comes to think by the time he writes the *Tractatus*, the task of "a proper theory of symbolism" to show that all such theories are "superfluous."[50] ("Logic must take care itself," §5.473.) In rejecting such theories, the *Tractatus* rejects the project standardly attributed to it: one of demarcating the bounds of sense.[51] When, in the *Tractatus*, Wittgenstein says you cannot give a sign a wrong sense, he is claiming that there is no such thing as infringing on the bounds of sense and thus no bounds of the sort that Carnap (or Wittgenstein, early or late, according to most readings of him) seeks to demarcate.[52]

The difference between an ideal logical symbolism and ordinary language, for the *Tractatus*, is that in the former—unlike the latter—one is able to read the symbol directly off the sign. Logical syntax for the *Tractatus* is not a combinatorial theory (which demarcates legitimate from illegitimate sequences of signs or symbols) but a *tool* of elucidation (which allows us to recognize the logical contributions of the constituent parts of a *Satz*, and the absence of such a contribution on the part of the constituents of a *Scheinsatz*). The kind of cross-category

---

[50] Some version of this thought—and, with it, the insight that this might be the way out of the problems that plagued Russell's philosophy—came to Wittgenstein remarkably early. Already in January 1913, he was writing Russell as follows: "[E]very theory of types must be rendered superfluous by a proper theory of the symbolism . . . What I am *most* certain of is not however the correctness of my present way of analysis, but of the fact that all theory of types must be done away with by a theory of symbolism showing that what seem to be *different kinds of things* are symbolized by different kinds of symbols which cannot possibly be substituted in one another's places." (Wittgenstein, *Notebooks, 1914–1916*, ed. G. H. von Wright and G. E. M. Anscombe, trans. G. E. M. Anscombe (New York: Harper & Row, 1969), p. 121.)

[51] David Pears gives succinct expression to the standard reading of the *Tractatus* when he writes: "In the *Tractatus* a general theory of language is used to fix the bounds of sense" ("Wittgenstein," in Jonathan Dancy and Ernest Sosa, eds., *A Companion to Epistemology* (Oxford: Blackwell, 1992), p. 524).

[52] When Wittgenstein argues in his later writings that we cannot give a word a "senseless sense" (e.g. *Philosophical Investigations*, §500), he is refashioning the Tractarian point that we cannot give a sign "the wrong sense." Not only does Wittgenstein never speak in the *Tractatus* of "violations of logical syntax," but later Wittgenstein only occasionally mentions the idea of "violations of grammar," and always in the service of encouraging the reader to be puzzled by what such a thing could be; e.g. "How can one put together *logically* ill-assorted concepts (in violation of grammar [*gegen die Grammatik*], and therefore nonsensically) and significantly ask about the possibility of the combination?" (*Philosophical Grammar* (Oxford: Blackwell, 1974), p. 392).

equivocation exhibited by an uncontextualized sentence of ordinary language such as "Green is green" is not possible in a *Begriffsschrift*. One can, of course, if one wants, call this sort of cross-category equivocation a "violation of logical syntax" (though Wittgenstein himself never speaks in this way) but, if one chooses to speak in this way, one should be clear that what is at issue in those passages where Wittgenstein alludes to the differences between ordinary language and "a logical grammar" (§3.325) are differences in notational perspicuity between various kinds of symbolism.[53]

The preceding conclusion (that the only "logical" defects of ordinary language to be corrected by "a proper logical syntax" are defects in its notational perspicuity) runs counter to the widespread assumption that the early Wittgenstein—like Frege, Russell and Carnap—is an ideal language philosopher. This assumption is encouraged by the Pears and McGuinness translation of §4.112:

A philosophical work consists essentially of elucidations.

Philosophy does not result in 'philosophical propositions', but rather in the clarification of propositions.

Without philosophy thoughts are, as it were, cloudy and indistinct: its task is to make them clear and give them sharp boundaries.

It certainly sounds here as if the role of an elucidation is to introduce clarity into propositions which prior to elucidation lack clarity: elucidation renders what is logically cloudy and indistinct precise and sharp. The interpretative assumption underlying the standard reading of this passage is that this transformation of thoughts (that are initially cloudy and indistinct) is effected through their transposition into a medium which, unlike ordinary language, permits the expression of precise and sharp thoughts. But Wittgenstein repudiates just such an understanding of §4.112 in his correspondence with Ogden. Wittgenstein rejects "the clarification of propositions" as a translation of *das Klarwerden von Sätzen*,[54] and, after several exchanges, suggests instead: "the proposi-

[53] Wittgenstein's point in devising alternative logical notations in which certain signs (e.g. logical connectives (*logische Operationszeichen*)) are made to disappear is to devise a language which suits his elucidatory purposes in philosophy. Wittgenstein's aim is to free us from the philosophical confusions (which the outward form of our language leads us into) by showing us that we *can* dispense with such signs. It is not to encourage us, outside the context of philosophical elucidation, to prefer a language which dispenses with such signs. On the contrary, according to the *Tractatus*, the outward form of our language is already carefully designed to suit our everyday purposes in communication (see §4.002).

[54] Wittgenstein, *Letters to C. K. Ogden with Comments on the English Translation of the Tractatus-Logico-Philosophicus* (hereafter *LO*), ed. G. H. von Wright (Oxford and London: Blackwell and Routledge, 1973), p. 28.

tions *now have become clear* that they ARE clear."[55] This is such terrible English that Ogden decides simply to ignore the suggestion. But the point that is obscured by the existing translations (and which the young Wittgenstein's horrendous English seeks to bring out) is that the transition from unclarity to clarity (i.e. the kind of *Klarwerden*) that is at issue here is not one that is effected through a transformation in the logical character of the *propositions* of ordinary language, but rather through a transformation in the view that *we* command of their logical character. What is cloudy and indistinct—and is rendered transparent with the assistance of a logical syntax—is our view of the logical structure that is present in the proposition all along. The aim of elucidation is not "to clarify" in the sense of making that which is said or thought intrinsically clearer (in the sense of cleaning up and, to that extent, changing the logical character of what is said); but rather, "to clarify" in the sense of making that which is said or thought clear to us (in the sense of disencumbering our view of the logical character of that which we have been saying all along). It is a matter of making explicit the logical structure which had been implicit in our *Sätze* all along[56] (and, if our *Sätze* are *Unsinn*, it is a matter of making explicit that there has, all along, been no implicit logical structure but only the appearance of such structure).

In *Tractatus* §5.5563, we find:

All propositions of our everyday language are actually, just as they stand, logically completely in order.

Commentators have found it difficult to reconcile Wittgenstein's comment in §3.325 that "we must employ a symbolism which excludes" certain possibilities which ordinary language permits with his respectful comment here in §5.5563 concerning the logical orderliness of the

---

[55] Ibid. p. 49. Ogden's translation, as published, has: "The result of philosophy is not a number of 'philosophical propositions', but to make propositions clear." This came about as a response to Wittgenstein's initial suggestion that *das Klarwerden von Sätzen* be rendered (instead of "the clarification of propositions") as "the getting clear of propositions" (ibid. p. 28). Ogden, having convinced Wittgenstein that this isn't much help, tries "to make propositions clear." Wittgenstein (in his annotations of Ogden's revisions) changes this to "that propositions become clear." But Ogden still finds this unclear and awkward English to boot, thus prompting Wittgenstein's more illuminating (though even more awkward) suggestion on *LO*, p. 49.

[56] The *Tractatus* articulates an *expressivist* conception of logic, in so far as it conceives of logical syntax as an instrument for (1) explicating the logical structure of thought and thus enabling (what the *Tractatus* calls) *das Klarwerden von Sätzen*, (2) revealing specifically logical vocabulary (such as the logical constants) to be linguistically optional and thus subject to "disappearance," and (3) perspicuously representing the inferential relations between thoughts.

propositions of ordinary language.[57] But there is no conflict. For, according to the *Tractatus*, it is the logical imperspicuity of ordinary language which leads us to believe that it is able to accommodate a kind of thought which is not, just as it is, logically completely in order. Section 3.325 recommends a notation which eliminates the sort of notational imperspicuity ordinary language tolerates in order to help us perceive how the logically imperspicuous character of ordinary language seduces us into thinking that ordinary language tolerates the expression of logically flawed thoughts. The *Tractatus* wants to show how Frege's theory of *Begriffsschrift*—his theory of a logically perfect language which excludes the possibility of the formation of illogical thought—is in fact the correct theory of symbolism *überhaupt*. Language itself, the *Tractatus* says, prevents the possibility of every logical mistake (§§5.4731).[58] Ordinary language is in this respect already a kind of *Begriffsschrift*. What for Frege is the structure of an ideal language is for early Wittgenstein the structure of all language. In his remarks clarifying his emendations of Ogden's initial attempt to translate §5.5563, Wittgenstein explains:

> By this [i.e. §5.5563] I meant to say that the propositions of our ordinary language are not in any way logically *less correct* or less exact or *more confused* than propositions written down, say, in Russell's symbolism or any other *Begriffsschrift*. (Only it is easier for us to gather their logical form when they are expressed in an appropriate symbolism.)[59]

Already in the *Tractatus*, Wittgenstein's interest in a logical symbolism is not that of someone who seeks to overcome an imprecision in ordinary thought through recourse to a more precise medium for the expression of thought.[60] The *Tractatus* is interested in successors to

---

[57] John Koethe, for example, writes: "[To] try to read . . . the *Tractatus* as urging to adopt an ideal language analogous to Frege's *Begriffsschrift* . . . seems at odds with Wittgenstein's insistence that 'all the propositions of our everyday language, just as they stand, are in perfect logical order'" (*The Continuity of Wittgenstein's Thought* (Ithaca, N.Y.: Cornell University Press, 1996), p. 39).

[58] This, of course, does not mean that language itself prevents us from ever making "logical mistakes" in the ordinary (non-philosophical) sense of the expression "logical mistake"—i.e. that it keeps us from ever contradicting ourselves! Indeed, the possibility of forming contradictions is, according to the *Tractatus*, a constitutive feature of any symbolism (which, for the *Tractatus*, means any system capable of expressing thought). What this passage refers to rather is the prevention of the possibility of the (peculiarly philosophical) sort of "logical mistake" that Russell's theory of types or Carnap's theory of logical syntax sought to exclude. This latter notion of "a violation of logic" depends upon a philosophical *theory* (which seeks to draw a limit to the sorts of thoughts that are so much as possible).

[59] *LO*, p. 50. Emphases in the original.

[60] We see here yet another instance of how what is standardly put forward by com-

Frege's *Begriffsschrift* (in what the *Tractatus* calls "logical grammars") because such systems of notation exclude a multiplicity of kinds of use for individual signs, allowing one to see in a more perspicuous manner what kind of logical work (if any) a given term in a given sentence is doing.[61] It allows us to see *how*—and, most importantly, *whether*—the signs we call upon (in giving voice to the thoughts we seek to express) symbolize. The advantage of a logical symbolism, for the *Tractatus*, lies not in *what* it permits (or forbids) one to say, but in the perspicuity of its mode of representation: in how it allows someone who is drawn to call upon certain words to see what it is (if anything) he is saying.[62] The reason ordinary language can lead us philosophically astray is not to be traced to its (alleged) capacity to permit us to formulate illogical thoughts (i.e. to give a sign the wrong sense).[63] Rather, it is to be traced to the symbolic imperspicuity of ordinary language—our inability to read off from it what contribution, if any, the parts of a sentence make to the sense of the whole. It is this lack of perspicuity in our relation to our own words which allows us to imagine that we perceive a meaning where there is no meaning, and which brings about the need for a mode

mentators as a criticism later Wittgenstein directs against his earlier work is in fact already developed in the *Tractatus* as a criticism of Frege and Russell.

[61] It is perhaps worth mentioning that this employment of *Begriffsschrift* (as a tool for the perspicuous representation of the logical structure of sentences of ordinary language) for the purposes of philosophical clarification—though by no means Frege's primary reason for developing his ideography—was nonetheless envisioned by him from the start as one of its possible applications: "If it is one of the tasks of philosophy to break the domination of the word over the human spirit by laying bare those misconceptions which through the use of language all but unavoidably arise, then my ideography, if it is further developed with an eye to this purpose, can become a useful tool for the philosopher." (*Begriffsschrift*, Preface, eighth paragraph; my translation.) And, when advertising the virtues of his *Begriffsschrift*, Frege not infrequently remarks upon the value it could have in this regard for philosophy: "We can see from all this how easily we can be led by language to see things in the wrong perspective, and what value it must therefore have for philosophy to free ourselves from the domination of language. If one makes the attempt to construct a system of signs on quite other foundations and with quite other means, as I have tried to do in creating my concept-script, we shall have, so to speak, our very noses rubbed into the false analogies in language." (*Collected Papers on Mathematics, Logic, and Philosophy*, ed. Brian McGuinness (Oxford: Blackwell, 1984), p. 67.)

[62] The *Tractatus* sacrifices all the other ends to which Frege and Russell sought to put a *Begriffsschrift* to the sole end of notational perspicuity. Early Wittgenstein champions a logical syntax which avoids a plurality of logical constants because such a plurality frustrates the sole application which the *Tractatus* seeks to make of a logical syntax: to allow the logical form of propositions to appear with "complete clarity." A plurality of logical constants frustrates this end in two ways: first, it permits the same thought to be rendered in diverse ways, and second, it obscures the logical relations between propositions.

[63] See also §3.03 and §5.4731.

of perspicuous representation of the possibilities of meaning available to us.[64]

"CAESAR IS A PRIME NUMBER" REVISITED

In the passage that Carnap quotes from Heidegger, Heidegger begins one of his questions by asking "Does the Nothing exist because . . .?" Carnap seizes on this talk about the Nothing existing as a particularly flagrant case of type (ii) nonsense. Carnap remarks:

Even if it were admissible to introduce 'nothing' as a name or description of an entity, still the existence of this entity *would* be denied in its very definition . . . This sentence therefore *would* be contradictory, hence nonsensical [*unsinnig*] were it not already senseless [*sinnlos*].[65]

Carnap here implicitly distinguishes between two levels of nonsense: a sequence of words which is merely lacking in sense ("senseless") and one whose sense requires something which is logically prohibited ("nonsense"). Thus he seems to take himself here to be able to identify the kind of sense that the sequence of expressions "The Nothing exists"

---

[64] I have summarized the method of the *Tractatus* here in such a way as to highlight a further important continuity between early and later Wittgenstein. Both early and later Wittgenstein trace our philosophical failures of meaning to our tendency to transfer an expression without transferring its use (in the language of the *Tractatus*: to employ the same sign without transferring the method of symbolizing). Thus both have an interest in finding a mode of perspicuous representation—a mode of representation which makes perspicuous to a philosophical interlocutor (1) the contexts of use within which a word has a particular meaning (in the language of the *Tractatus*: the contexts within which a sign symbolizes in a particular way), (2) how the meaning shifts as the context shifts, (3) how "it very often happens" in philosophy that we are led into "confusions" by "the same word belonging to two different symbols" without our realizing it (§§3.323–3.234), and (4) how nothing at all is meant by a word—how one "has given no meaning to certain signs" (§6.53)—as long as one hovers indeterminately between contexts of use. The underlying thought common to early and later Wittgenstein is that we are prone to see a meaning where there is no meaning because of our inclination to imagine that a sign carries its meaning with it, enabling us to import a particular meaning into a new context merely by importing the sign.

Though the conception of philosophical elucidation remains in many respects the same (one of taking the reader from latent to patent nonsense), there are also important differences here between early and later Wittgenstein. To mention only one: on the later conception, once one has completed the work of perspicuously displaying the possible contexts of significant use, there is no elucidatory role left for a *Begriffsschrift* to come along and play. What the *Tractatus* sees as a preliminary task in the process of elucidation (namely, the consideration of contexts of significant use) becomes for later Wittgenstein a comparatively central exercise—one which usurps the role previously played by the rendition of sentences into a perspicuous logical symbolism.

[65] EMLAL, p. 65 (my emphases), ÜMLAS, p. 231; I have amended Pap's translation.

would have if it were the kind of thing which could have a sense. In his attempts, in moments like this, to make vivid the logically flawed character of the examples of type (ii) nonsense which (allegedly) occur in Heidegger's text, Carnap comes close to saying something patently incoherent: namely, that we know what each of the parts of one of Heidegger's sentences mean (including what the word 'nothing' here means), so we know what the resulting combination *would* mean, if such a combination were an admissible combination of meanings! (More briefly: we grasp what "it" *would* mean, if what "it" meant could be meant.) In §5.4733, Wittgenstein says: "if . . . [a proposition] has no sense this can only be because we have given no *meaning* to some of its constituent parts. (Even if we believe that we have done so.)" This last parenthetical remark of Wittgenstein's gently touches on the elucidatory aim of the work as a whole: to show us that we are prone to *believe* that we have given meaning to some of the constituent parts of a proposition when we have not done so. This remark highlights an important analogy between type (ii) nonsense such as "Caesar is a prime number" (as Carnap describes it) and an innocuously meaningful sentence such as "Caesar crossed the Rubicon": in each of these cases, we *believe* that we have already given a meaning to all of the constituent parts. In the former of these two cases, we undergo the phenomenology of meaning something determinate while failing to mean anything determinate by our words. Part of what causes us to hallucinate a meaning in sequences such as "Caesar is a prime number," according to Wittgenstein, is that there is more than one natural remedy for what ails the nonsensical linguistic string. (The greater the number of natural remedies which lie ready to hand for redeeming the sense of a string, the more powerful the illusion of meaning which that string is able to engender.) We could assign a meaning to 'Caesar' which would allow us to treat 'Caesar' as the kind of logical element which symbolizes a number; or, alternatively, we could assign a meaning to 'prime number' which would allow us to treat it as the kind of element which symbolizes a predicate which applies to persons. So there are two natural ways of making sense of this string: it can be taken as saying something it makes sense to say of a person—in which case it contains the proper name of a person but not a numerical predicate; or it can be taken as saying of a number something which it makes sense to say of a number—in which case it contains a numerical predicate but not a proper name for a person. But, according to the *Tractatus*, there isn't anything which is an instance of a proposition's containing two logical elements which are incompatible. What there can be is a case in which there are two natural directions in which to seek a sense for a sentence whose sense is as yet undetermined (as is the case with Carnap's example). But each of the available readings of this sentence eclipses the other—as each reading of a duck-rabbit figure eclipses the other. There isn't anything which is having a part of the sentence as it is segmented on one reading illegitimately combined with a part of the sentence as segmented on the other reading—anymore than one can have only the eye of the rabbit taken from one reading of a duck-rabbit figure occur in combination with the face of the duck. To see the drawing as a picture of the face of a duck *is* to see the, as it were, argument place for an eye in the picture filled by the eye of a duck—that is what it is to see the dot (that sign) *as* an eye of a duck (*as* that kind of a symbol).

If we have not made the necessary assignments of meaning to cure Carnap's example of its emptiness then, according to the *Tractatus*, what we have before us is simply a string of signs—a string which has a surface resemblance to propositions of two distinct logical patterns: it has a sign but no symbol in common with propositions about the great Roman general Caesar, and it also has a sign but no symbol in common with sentences such as "53 is a prime number." Its nonsensicality is to be traced not to the logical structure of the sentence, but to *our* failure to mean something by it: to what the *Tractatus* calls our failure to make certain determinations of meaning. For Wittgenstein, the source of the clash is to be located in *our relation* to the linguistic string—not in the linguistic string itself. The problem, according to the *Tractatus*, is that we often believe that we have given a meaning to all of a sentence's constituent parts when we have failed to do so. We think nonsense results in such cases not because of a failure on our part, but because of a failure on the sentence's part. We think the problem lies not in an absence of meaning (in our failing to mean anything by these words) but rather in a presence of meaning (in the incompatible senses the words already have—senses which the words import with them into the context of combination). We think the thought is flawed because the component senses of its parts logically repel one another. They fail to add up to a thought. So we feel our words are attempting to think a logically impossible thought—and that this involves a kind of impossibility of a higher order than ordinary impossibility. Wittgenstein's teaching is that the problem lies not in the words, but in our confused relation to the words: in our experiencing ourselves as meaning something definite by them, yet also feeling that what we take ourselves to be meaning with the words makes no sense. "We . . . hover between regarding it as sense and regarding it as nonsense, and hence the trouble arises."[66] We are

---

[66] The quotation is from Wittgenstein's "Lectures on Personal Experience"

confused about what it is we want to say and we project our confusion onto the linguistic string. Then we look at the linguistic string and imagine we discover what *it* is trying to say. We want to say to the string: "We know what you mean, but 'it' cannot be said." The incoherence of our desires with respect to the sentence—wishing to both mean and not mean something with it—is seen by us as an incoherence in what the words want to be saying. We displace our desire onto the words and see them as *aspiring* to say something they never quite succeed in saying (because, we tell ourselves, "it" cannot be said). We account for the confusion these words engender in us by discovering in the words a hopelessly flawed sense.

The heart of the Tractarian conception of logic is to be found in the remark that "we cannot make mistakes in logic" (§5.473). It is one of the burdens of the elucidatory strategy of the *Tractatus* to try to show us that the idea that we can violate the logical syntax of language rests upon a conception of "the logical structure of thought" according to which the nature of logic itself debars us from being able to frame certain sorts of "thoughts." Wittgenstein says: "Everything which is possible in logic is also permitted" (§5.473). If a sentence is nonsense, this is not because *it* is trying but failing to make sense (by breaking a rule of logic), but because *we* have failed to make sense with it: "the sentence is nonsensical because *we* have failed to make an arbitrary determination of sense, not because *the symbol in itself* is impermissible" (§5.473; my emphases). The idea that there can be such a thing as a kind of proposition which has an internal logical form of a sort which is debarred by the logical structure of our thought rests upon what Wittgenstein calls (in the Preface) "a misunderstanding of the logic of our language."

(Michaelmas Term, 1935, recorded by Margaret MacDonald, ed. Cora Diamond; unpublished manuscript). Its context is as follows:

> *Different kinds of nonsense.* Though it is nonsense to say "I feel his pain", this is different from inserting into an English sentence a meaningless word, say "abracadabra" (compare Moore last year on "Scott kept a runcible at Abbotsford") and from saying a string of nonsense words. Every word in this sentence is English, and we shall be inclined to say that the sentence has a meaning. The sentence with the nonsense word or the string of nonsense words can be discarded from our language, but if we discard from our language "I feel Smith's toothache" that is quite different. The second seems nonsense, we are tempted to say, because of some truth about the nature of things or the nature of the world. We have discovered in some way that pains and personality do not fit together in such a way that I can feel his pain.—The task will be to show that there is in fact no difference between these two cases of nonsense, though there is a psychological distinction, in that we are inclined to say the one and be puzzled by it and not the other. We constantly hover between regarding it as sense and regarding it as nonsense, and hence the trouble arises.

Carnap mistakes this misunderstanding of the logic of our language for Wittgenstein's own understanding of the logic of language. Carnap, however, was well aware that Wittgenstein viewed most of what was said about the *Tractatus* in Carnap's published writings as shot through with misunderstanding, so he was careful merely to express a sense of indebtedness to Wittgenstein's work while directly attributing as little as possible of his own conception of logical syntax to the *Tractatus* itself.[67] Subsequent commentators on Wittgenstein's work have been less careful, thus bringing about the following historical irony: at the present time, when much is written about Wittgenstein's and relatively little about Carnap's philosophy by authors who allege that Carnap's doctrines have been surpassed through Wittgenstein's later criticisms of the views expressed in his *Tractatus*, the philosophical teaching they disseminate under the name of Wittgenstein resembles the very one that Carnap sought to champion in some of his writings and which Wittgenstein sought to criticize already in the *Tractatus*.

ELUCIDATION IN THE *TRACTATUS*

Carnap, in what he takes to be a departure from the teaching of the *Tractatus*, soon after writing "The Elimation of Metaphysics through the Logical Analysis of Language" gives up on the idea that the key to exposing metaphysical propositions as nonsense lies in unmasking the underlying violations of logical syntax they harbor. Rather he returns to a strategy of elucidation that he had already defended in a different form earlier in his career: one of specifying principles for the construction of alternative "linguistic frameworks" (i.e. frameworks within which it is possible to make cognitively significant statements) and insisting that all dispute be conducted with reference to such principles.[68] The speaker of metaphysical utterances is invited either to

---

[67] That Wittgenstein thought Carnap repeatedly and grossly misunderstood the *Tractatus* is evident from his irate correspondence with Schlick about Carnap's efforts to build on his ideas and from his brief correspondence with Carnap himself on the subject in 1932. (See, for example, the letters reprinted in M. Nedo and M. Ranchetti, eds., *Ludwig Wittgenstein: Sein Leben in Bildern und Texten* (Frankfurt am Main: Suhrkamp, 1983), pp. 254–5, 381–2.) Passing remarks sprinkled throughout Carnap's letters and papers at the University of Pittsburgh Archives for Scientific Philosophy bear witness to Carnap's continued (and eminently justified) frustration concerning both the obscurity and the harshness of Wittgenstein's complaints about Carnap's (mis)appropriation of his work.

[68] *Philosophy and Logical Syntax*, pp. 80–1.

translate his propositions into a properly specified linguistic framework or to furnish principles which would allow a listener to translate between her own framework and that of the speaker. Carnap's picture here is the following: any dispute which can be adjudicated must turn on one of two factors—empirical factors (which can be adjudicated through observation) or linguistic factors (which can be adjudicated through appeal to the fundamental principles of the linguistic framework within which the dispute is conducted). Carnap anticipates that most metaphysical disputes will be unmasked (through a proper formalization of "the language" in which the dispute is conducted) as ones in which the parties to the "dispute" do not share a common language: the seemingly substantive matter over which the disputants appear to differ, though disguised so as to appear to be of a super-empirical nature, will be revealed to be of a merely verbal nature. However, considered as a strategy of philosophical elucidation, such a procedure is likely, as Carnap fully realizes, to fall short of its goal of assisting one's interlocutors to win their way through to clarity. Often the philosophical conversation will simply break off:

If one partner in a philosophical discussion cannot or will not give a translation of his thesis into the formal mode, or if he will not state to which language-system his thesis refers, then the other will be well-advised to refuse the debate, because the thesis of his opponent is incomplete, and discussion would lead to nothing but empty wrangling.[69]

Faced with a Heidegger, once the conversation reaches the juncture described here, presumably a Carnap will politely take his leave. Carnap's method here runs out of steam, once again, just at the point at which Wittgenstein's seeks to enter the philosophical conversation.

The Wittgenstein of the *Tractatus*, faced with Heidegger's assertions, would neither have us conclude that a sign has been given a wrong use (e.g. that a logical particle that serves for the formulation of a negative existential statement has been illegitimately employed), nor that the conversation should be abandoned if the speaker refuses to specify the ground rules of the linguistic framework within which he is conducting his inquiry. Wittgenstein would instead have us first attempt to identify alternative ways of perceiving the symbol in the sign by reflecting upon its possible contexts of significant use.[70] Each alternative way of

---

[69] Ibid.

[70] In conversation with Carnap and other members of the Vienna Circle, Wittgenstein remarked: "To be sure, I can imagine what Heidegger means by Being [*Sein*] and Anxiety [*Angst*]" (*Ludwig Wittgenstein and the Vienna Circle: Conversations*

perceiving the symbol in the sign yields a distinct segmentation of the propositional sign into symbolic constituents. In a symbolic notation of the sort which the *Tractatus* recommends (one "founded on the principles of logical grammar," designed expressly to serve the purposes of philosophical elucidation), there will correspond to each possible segmentation of the string a *unique* rendering of it in the notation. In Tractarian philosophical elucidation, the role of logical symbolism is to furnish a perspicuous means of representing alternative segmentations, thus perspicuously displaying to the speaker the range of available possibilities for meaning his words. Let us consider four possible outcomes such an elucidatory employment of logical notation might have. Let us begin with the two most straightforward possible outcomes. Faced with a perspicuous representation in logical symbolism of the possibilities for meaning his words, a speaker might:

(1) accept a particular rendition of his sentence into the symbolism; or

(2) not accept any proposed rendition of his sentence.

If the outcome is (1), then we have learned what the logical form of the speaker's statement is—we are furnished with a means for seeing the symbol in the sign. If (2), then it remains open what (if anything) he means—it remains open whether we are faced with a case of nonsense or have simply failed to discern his meaning. In both cases (1) and (2), a *Begriffsschrift* (i.e. a symbolic notation founded on the principles of logical grammar) serves a hermeneutic role. It helps us to see better what someone means by her words or what we mean by our own words. Let us now consider a third possible outcome. Faced with a perspicuous representation in logical symbolism of the possibilities for meaning his words, a speaker might:

(3) discover that he means nothing at all by his words, but rather has been unwittingly hovering between alternative possibilities of meaning his words, without determinately settling on any one.

Prior to a perspicuous overview of the available possibilities for meaning his words, the speaker in case (3) is under the impression of having conferred a method of symbolizing on each of his signs. But, confronted with the perspicuous overview which the symbolism furnishes, the

Recorded by Friedrich Waismann, ed. Brian McGuinness (Oxford: Blackwell, 1979), p. 68). Wittgenstein's response to Heidegger's remarks—in contrast with Carnap's—is to attempt to imagine what Heidegger might mean by his words. The task of philosophical elucidation, for Wittgenstein, always begins with such an attempt.

speaker discovers that he has been wavering between alternative possible methods of symbolizing.[71] The task of working through the options for how he *can* mean his words undermines his impression that there was something determinate that he did mean by them. His original conviction that there was such a "something" dissolves on him. (We will return to case (3).) We need to consider yet a fourth kind of case before we can see how a *Begriffsschrift* discharges the whole of its appointed task as an instrument of Tractarian elucidation. In this case, the speaker:

> (4) refuses to countenance the possibility that the full meaning of his words could correspond to anything expressible in the symbolism.

Such a response signals that an interlocutor has placed his foot on the penultimate rung of the Tractarian ladder. Outcome (4) resembles each of the first two outcomes in a certain respect. It resembles (1) in that the speaker accepts *parts* of thoughts which can be expressed in the symbolism as corresponding to parts of his own thought—but only parts: alternative rendition(s) of his words into the symbolism are, in each case, at most partially expressive of that which he wants to mean by his words. Case (4) resembles (2) in that the speaker refuses to accept any single rendition as definitively capturing his meaning. "Alternative renditions can express a constituent aspect of the whole which I want to mean," the speaker in case (4) responds, "but no single rendition can express the whole of what I want to mean; because what I want to mean requires the conjunction of logical features that the symbolism does not permit me to conjoin."

The speaker in case (4) feels that that which he wants to mean by his words could never be expressed in a *Begriffsschrift*, for the very features of a *Begriffsschrift* which render it capable of perspicuously reflecting the logical structure of language simultaneously render it incapable of expressing that which he wants to mean by his words. It is here that Tractarian elucidation encounters its final hurdle—the case of a speaker who not only, as in case (2), rejects all of the alternative possible ways of meaning of his words expressible in a *Begriffsschrift*, but one who rejects any *possible* rendition of what he wants to mean by his words into a *Begriffsschrift* on a priori grounds—on the grounds that what he

---

[71] The *Tractatus* works through in (its characteristically compressed) detail a wide variety of such cases (of hovering between determinate possibilities of use) as they arise in connection with the philosophical employment of *Scheinbegriffe* such as "world," "fact," "essence," "logical form," "representation," "language," "thought," "concept," "object," "generality," etc.

wants to mean cannot be accommodated by the logical structure of language. (It is against just such a speaker, as we have seen, that Carnap's methods are powerless.) Such a speaker is perfectly willing to concede (as Heidegger is) that that which he wants to mean by his words runs up against the limits of what logic will permit us to say. Only he will insist that his nonsense is unlike the nonsense which figures in outcome (3): for his nonsense is substantial nonsense, and it is his aim to produce just this sort of nonsense. The task, when faced with such an interlocutor, for the *Tractatus*, is *not* one of demonstrating to the speaker that "the proposition is nonsensical because the symbol itself is impermissible" (§5.473). (This would hardly come as news; for this is just what the sort of interlocutor that is here in question will himself maintain about his own nonsense—"logically impermissible" nonsense is just what he aims to produce, and nothing other than such a sort of nonsense would serve his purpose.) The task for the Tractarian elucidator is rather "to demonstrate to [the interlocutor] that he has given no meaning to certain signs in his propositions" (§6.53), that the "proposition" is only apparently substantially nonsensical. The elucidation is only at an end when the interlocutor arrives at the point at which he is able of his own accord to acknowledge this. Thus it is only at an end when the interlocutor "recognizes" his propositions as *Unsinn*—in the sense of *Unsinn* specified in §5.4733—that is, in the only way, according to the *Tractatus*, anything can be *Unsinn*. The activity of elucidation which the *Tractatus* seeks to practice on its reader is only at an end when the reader of the work is able to "recognize" the propositions which figure in the work as *Unsinn*, not for the reason that the interlocutor in case (4) imagines (because of incompatible determinations of meaning he has already made), but rather because the reader now sees that *no* determination of meaning has yet been made.[72] The aim is to bring the reader to the point at which he himself is able to acknowledge that, in wanting to mean these forms of words in the apparently determinate way in which he originally imagined he was able to "mean" them, he failed to mean anything (determinate) at all by those forms of words.

The "problems of philosophy" that the *Tractatus* sets itself the task

---

[72] Thus Wittgenstein says in §6.53 that the aim is to demonstrate to the metaphysically inclined speaker that he has given "no meaning to certain *signs* in his *Sätze*." If the standard reading of the *Tractatus* were correct, this is not what Wittgenstein should be saying here. The complaint should be directed not at the (mere) *signs* in the metaphysician's *Sätze* (on the grounds that no meaning—i.e. no method of symbolizing—has been conferred upon them), but at the impermissible character of the propositional *symbols* which the metaphysician employs. (Hence also the danger of translating 'Satz' as 'proposition'.)

of "solving" are all of a single sort: they are all occasioned by reflection on possibilities (of running up against the limits of thought, language, or reality) which appear to come into view when we imagine ourselves able to frame in thought violations of the logical structure of language. The "solution" to these problems (as §6.52 says) lies in their disappearance—in the dissolution of the appearance that we are so much as able to frame such thoughts. The mode of philosophy which this work practices (as §4.112 says) does not result in "philosophical propositions": the "philosophical propositions" we come out with when we attempt to frame such thoughts are to be recognized as *Unsinn*. This process of recognition is an inherently piecemeal one: our inclination to believe that we can perceive the symbol in the sign, when no method of symbolizing has yet been conferred on it, is not one that is to be extirpated, at a single stroke, by persuading the reader of some "theory" of meaning. As is made clear in §6.53, the aim is to demonstrate to the metaphysically inclined speaker that he has given "no meaning to certain signs in his sentences" on a case by case basis.[73] The sign that one of the sentences of the *Tractatus* has achieved its elucidatory purpose comes when the reader's phenomenology of having understood something determinate by the form of words in question is suddenly shattered. The reader undergoes an abrupt transition: one moment, imagining he has discovered something, the next, discovering he has not yet discovered anything, to mean by the words. The transition is from a psychological experience of entertaining what appears to be a fully determinate thought—*the* thought apparently expressed by *that* sentence—to the experience of having that appearance (the appearance of there being any such thought) disintegrate. No "theory of meaning"

---

[73] "The only strictly correct method" of philosophy described in §6.53 is quite different from the one actually practiced in the *Tractatus*. The practitioner of the strictly correct method eschews nonsense, confining himself to displaying what can be said and to pointing out where the other has failed to give a meaning to one of his signs; whereas the elucidatory method of the *Tractatus* involves the production of vast quantities of nonsense. The former method depends on the elucidator always being able to speak second; the latter attempts to achieve the aims of the former but in a situation in which the interlocutor is not present. The actual method of the *Tractatus* is thus a literary surrogate for the strictly correct method—one in which the text invites the reader alternately to adopt the roles played by each of the parties to the dialogue in the strictly correct method. As the addressees of this surrogate form of elucidation, we are furnished with a series of "propositions" whose attractiveness we are asked both to feel and to round on. This raises the question: which of the *Sätze* of which the work is composed are *really* nonsense and which not?—which belong to the voice of temptation and which to the voice of correctness? The question is based on a confusion—on the idea that *Sinn* is the sort of property a *Satz* can possess on its own steam, apart from any relation that we, as users of it, enter into with it.

could ever bring about the passage from the first of these experiences
(the hallucinatory one) to the second (the experience of discovering
oneself to be a victim of a hallucination). As long as we retain the relevant phenomenology of meaning (as long as it appears to us that, by
golly, we *do* mean something determinate by our words), our conviction in such an experience of meaning will always lie deeper than our
conviction in anything we are told by a theory of meaning concerning
what sorts of things we are and are not able to mean by our words.
Hence the ineffectuality of Carnap's earlier methods. Carnap eventually gives up on the project of furnishing "a theory of meaning" of this
sort, but in the process he gives up on the idea of an effective method
of philosophical elucidation. The *Tractatus* aims to practice a method
of elucidation which does not presuppose a theory of this sort. It does
not aim to show us that certain sequences of words possess an intrinsically flawed sense by persuading us of the truth of some theoretical
account of where to locate "the limits of sense." Any theory which
seeks to draw such "a limit to thinking" commits itself, as the Preface
says, to being "able to think both sides of the limit" and hence to being
"able to think what cannot be thought." The Tractarian attack on substantial nonsense—on the idea that we can discern the determinately
unthinkable thoughts certain pieces of nonsense are trying to say—is an
attack on the coherence of any project which thus seeks to mark the
bounds of sense.

The *Tractatus* seeks to bring its reader to the point where he can
recognize sentences within the body of the work as nonsensical, not by
means of a theory which legislates certain sentences out of the realm of
sense, but rather by bringing more clearly into view for the reader the
life with language he already leads—by harnessing the capacities for
distinguishing sense from nonsense (for recognizing the symbol in the
sign and for recognizing when no method of symbolizing has yet been
conferred upon a sign) implicit in the everyday practical mastery of language which the reader already possesses. As the Preface says: "The
limit . . . can only be drawn *in language* and what lies on the other side
of the limit will be simply nonsense." Just as, according to the
Tractatus, each propositional symbol—that is, each *sinnvoller Satz*—
shows its sense (§4.022), so the *Tractatus* shows what it shows (i.e. what
it is to make sense) by *letting language show itself*—not through "the
clarification of sentences" but through allowing "sentences themselves
to become clear" (through *das Klarwerden von Sätzen*, §4.112). The
work seeks to do this, not by instructing us in how to identify determinate cases of nonsense, but by enabling us to see more clearly what it is
we do with language when we succeed in achieving determinate forms

of sense (when we succeed in projecting a symbol into the sign) and what it is we fall short of doing when we fail to achieve such forms of sense (when we fail to confer a determinate method of symbolizing on a propositional sign). If and when we have failed to achieve sense, the acknowledgment that this is how things stand lies with us.

In the transition to Wittgenstein's later work the task of eliciting such acknowledgment plays an increasingly important role:

> The philosopher strives to find the liberating word . . . The philosopher delivers the word to us which can render the matter harmless . . . The choice of our words is so important, because the point is to hit upon the physiognomy of the matter exactly . . . Indeed, we can only convict someone else of a mistake if he . . . acknowledges the expression [we have chosen] as the correct expression . . . For only if he acknowledges it as such, is it the correct expression. (Psychoanalysis)[74]

The fundamental difference between Carnap's and Wittgenstein's approaches to philosophical elucidation might be summarized as follows: Carnap seeks a method that will furnish criteria that permit one to establish that someone else is speaking nonsense, whereas Wittgenstein (both early and late) seeks a method that ultimately can only be practiced by someone on himself. Wittgenstein's method only permits the verdict that sense has not been spoken to be passed by the one who speaks. The role of a philosophical elucidator is not to pass verdicts on the statements of others, but to help them achieve clarity about what it is that they want to say. Thus the conversation does not break off if the other cannot meet the demand to make himself intelligible to the practitioner of philosophical elucidation; rather the burden lies with the one who professes to elucidate—not to specify a priori conditions of intelligibility, but rather to find the liberating word: enabling the other to attain intelligibility, where this may require helping him first to discover that he is unintelligible to himself.[75]

---

[74] "The Big Typescript," sect. 87, in Ludwig Wittgenstein, *Philosophical Occasions, 1912–1951*, ed. James Klagge and Alfred Nordmann (Indianapolis: Hackett, 1993), p. 165.
[75] This essay borrows heavily from my "The Method of the *Tractatus*," in Reck, ed., *From Frege to Wittgenstein: Perspectives on Early Analytic Philosophy*.

2

The Etiology of the Obvious

Wittgenstein and the Elimination of Indeterminacy

Meredith Williams

Much of the discussion of Wittgenstein's later philosophy focuses on one or another of three arguments drawn from the *Philosophical Investigations*: the critique of denotational theories of meaning, the "paradox of interpretation" with respect to rule-following, and the private language argument. My aim in this paper is to identify a deep underlying issue that is common to all three (though I will consider only the first two). That is what I will call "the problem of normative similarity." This concerns the normative role played by our basic judgments of sameness or identity with respect to categorization and rule-following. The arguments Wittgenstein develops against ostensive definition and rules, as the primitive or basic devices for fixing the normative standards of language use, show that both are indeterminate in their application and so cannot account for the normativity of language. Successful ostension and rule-following presuppose a background of what is obviously the same to the participants. And, according to Wittgenstein, that background consists in the mastery of techniques of application that are acquired in the process of learning. The process of learning techniques is in this way *constitutive* of what is learned, namely, of what is the same as what or what it is to go on in the same way. In learning techniques for using words, one is acquiring concepts and so learning how things must be. The normativity of our practices involves non-causal necessity.

In developing this line of argument in Wittgenstein, I will contrast Wittgenstein's indeterminacy arguments with Quine's indeterminacy arguments with respect to translation and reference. Precisely because there are important affinities between their views, the comparison highlights more strikingly just where Wittgenstein and Quine diverge in their respective conceptions of language. The most important of these differences concerns the place of theorizing in language use and acquisition. Where Quine, in virtue of his scientific naturalism, identifies theorizing as essential to language use, Wittgenstein focuses on the normativity of the language-game that, he argues, any form of theorizing presupposes.

1. THE PROBLEM OF NORMATIVE SIMILARITY

Wittgenstein objects to certain traditional philosophical pictures of categorization and rule-following. In both cases, part of his concern is to show that no object is inherently representational or normative.[1] An object, whether a commonplace everyday object like an apple or a post in the road, or something less substantial like a mental image, has representational and normative properties only within a context of actual use and against a background of cognitive skills. Fundamental to skills of application are those for judging sameness, sameness of kind and sameness of action.

For Wittgenstein an investigation into our judgments of sameness implicates how we learn to make these judgments. So, in his early examination of the denotational theory of meaning, Wittgenstein attacks this theory by undermining its companion picture of how language is acquired. The picture of language acquisition is a simple one: adults point to an object in the child's immediate environment and name it. The child then associates the name with the object and henceforth uses that name for all similar objects. The effectiveness of the ostensive definition presupposes the pupil's capacity to grasp that the baptismal object is an exemplar that functions as the standard for correct application of the term uttered. Wittgenstein challenges the adequacy of this picture to explain what he is after, namely, the normativity of language itself. Naming cannot in general fix meaning because it is itself a semantically sophisticated act that presupposes a great deal of conceptual stage-setting and language mastery: "only someone who already knows how to do something with it can significantly ask a name" (*PI* §31). If that background understanding is eliminated, then ostensive definition cannot succeed, for it is always indeterminate in

---

[1] This disjunction suggests that the two expressions "representational" and "normative" can be used interchangeably. This really is not correct. Normative is the more basic and general of the two expressions. Representations are one kind of norm, but not the only.

itself. There is no such thing as absolute similarity, only similarity relative to some description or aspect. Thus, the success of ostensive definition depends upon the recipient already having the background and conceptual competence that is required. For ostension to play a role in acquisition of language, it cannot be that of ostensive definition. There must be a way of categorizing that is not a matter of naming.[2]

A related, and equally radical, point is made in connection with rules. A rule qua formula (like the formula "+1" of *PI* §185) is indeterminate unless combined with a method of application. Some have held that the method of application can be supplied by an interpretation of the rule. But Wittgenstein objects that interpretations of rules "hang in the air along with what [they] interpret, and cannot give any support" to how the rule is applied (*PI* §198). Interpretations must be grounded in a kind of rule-following that is not informed by interpretation, but which provides a non-interpretive method of application against which interpretations can be made. Without this, interpretation collapses and with it any normative constraint. The "paradox of interpretation" is that our traditional device for determining correct usage (namely, interpretation of the rule) results in the collapse of the very distinction between correct and incorrect.

Use of interpretation and ostensive definition both presuppose the mastery of normative practices. Being intrinsically indeterminate, both need "stage-setting," a background in virtue of which category judgments can be made, rules cited, concepts applied, derivations completed, and actions performed. The background itself cannot be more of the same—it cannot be more rules, interpretations, or bare pointings. If it were, it would be subject to the same kind of indeterminacy that affects ostensive definition and interpretation when these are seen as fixing

---

[2] Many who recognize that the ostensive definition picture of language acquisition presupposes significant cognitive competence on the part of the child draw a very different conclusion. They take these considerations to support a strong nativist position. The child has an innate array of cognitive capacities, concepts, and theories that enable her to respond appropriately to ostensive definitions. See, for example, J. A. Fodor, *The Language of Thought* (New York: Thomas Y. Crowell, 1975); F. C. Keil, *Concepts, Word Meanings, and Cognitive Development* (Cambridge, Mass.: MIT Press, 1989); Henry M. Wellman, *The Child's Theory of Mind* (Cambridge, Mass.: MIT Press, 1990); and Steven Pinker, *The Language Instinct* (New York: William Morrow, 1994). But Wittgenstein sees the strong nativist solution as explanatorily bankrupt. On his view it engenders an explanatory regress by reproducing in the child the very mastery of norms—epistemic, logical, and conceptual—for which we are seeking an explanation. The nativist psychologist takes the mastery of norms as unproblematic, but that is precisely what Wittgenstein takes to be the key philosophical issue. What is troubling to Wittgenstein is the very idea that the initiate learner can supply all that is required to turn an association between a word and an object into a normative meaning relation.

meaning (that is, providing the identity conditions for the reapplication of a term). Rather, the background is that against which we interpret, name, and justify by appeal to rules. Wittgenstein's task is to provide an account of our background normative practices that eliminates the indeterminacy that affects ostensive definition and interpretation while retaining the normativity of our practices. This is his response to the problem of normative similarity.

There are important affinities between Wittgenstein's two arguments and Quine's arguments for the indeterminacy of translation and the inscrutability of reference. Wittgenstein argues that ostensive definition, in itself, cannot fix reference; and that interpretation, if the only method for using rules, results in the collapse of the very distinction between correct and incorrect. Referring and interpreting both require background stage-setting. Quine argues that different, and incompatible, translation schemes, because they involve different kinds of apparatus of individuation, are fully compatible with all the evidence available to the field linguist, and so reference is inscrutable. There is an ineliminable indeterminacy in what we are referring to, precisely because reference can only be established by way of a background theory. These look like arguments that should lead to similar views of language, reference, and meaning. Nevertheless, the conclusions each draws from his arguments are quite different. This difference in the morals they draw for language is striking for a further reason. Both find language learning philosophically significant, agreeing in important respects in their characterizations of language learning. Both take the holophrastic sentence of early language learning as basic, not the word as a single referring expression; and both reject nativist accounts of language learning in favor of conditioning accounts (broadly conceived). Yet Wittgenstein seeks to show that it is the traditional philosophical theories of meaning and language that are the source of the indeterminacies, not ordinary language itself, whereas Quine endorses indeterminacy as part and parcel of our "home language" even as we "acquiesce in its use." This difference is rooted in their very different pictures of language and the methodologies employed to support these pictures.

Quine's approach to the problem of meaning is to begin with the situation of a field linguist trying to provide a translation of a radically alien language, a language of which the linguist knows nothing. His only resources for translating this language are the verbal and other behaviors of the natives, the environment in which they act, and his own language and sensory experience. These constraints on the evidential and theoretical resources of the linguist are revelatory, on Quine's view, of language and meaning in general. Wherever Quine discusses this situation of radical translation, he also draws parallels between the linguist and the child acquiring its first language. For both linguist and child, observation sentences, namely, those sentences "that are directly and firmly associated with our stimulations," provide "the entering wedge," as Quine puts it, for learning language and translating a language.[3] What Quine sees as common to the linguist and the child is the meager evidential basis each has for constructing a complex language. What supports this description of both the linguist and the child is Quine's fundamental commitment to a scientific naturalism that accords the sciences the prerogative in determining truth. The sciences of behavior, for Quine, are the psychophysiology of the sensory systems and scientific behaviorism, each of which identifies the stimulation of our sensory organs as the interface between ourselves and the world. In consequence of adopting this claim, both linguist and child can only acquire an understanding of the language to which they are exposed using the stimulations to their sensory receptors as their evidentiary starting point.

The only method available to the linguist is to form hypotheses about which of the native's utterances report (or at least correspond to) the presence of publicly salient phenomena. His example is the now famous hypothesis that the native utterance 'Gavagai!' means 'Rabbit!' (or 'Lo, a rabbit!') in English. The only way the linguist can test this hypothesis is by actively questioning the native to see whether he assents to the question 'Gavagai?' when he has been sensorily stimulated by rabbits and dissents when he has not been so stimulated. The success of this hypothesis testing requires that the linguist can correctly identify assent and dissent in the native language and that he can empathetically identify the sensory stimulations of the native. The entire approach takes similarity of sensory stimulations, both for a single individual at different times and between individuals, as the only empirical evidence for constructing translation manuals or acquiring language. Quine's approach to language learning (whether that of the field linguist or the child) takes for granted both the natural similarity of sensory stimulations and their logical interconnections with a growing web of belief.[4] By contrast, Wittgenstein's problem of normative similarity extends precisely to what we can take for granted with respect to similarity in our observations as well as in our inferences.

---

[3] W. V. Quine, *Pursuit of Truth* (Cambridge, Mass.: Harvard University Press, 1990), pp. 3 and 4.

[4] This mixing of physical causal descriptions with logical or normative ones has been pointed out and criticized by many. See, for example, Richard Rorty, *Philosophy and the Mirror of Nature* (Princeton: Princeton University Press, 1979), ch. 4.

Wittgenstein's response to his own indeterminacy arguments reflects a very different approach to language. Its central idea is that of the language game, which he characterizes in three ways: as a methodological tool in examining philosophical theories, as akin to the way in which children learn, and as an explanatory device describing language use in relation to other forms of acting (*PI* §5). Wittgenstein uses language games in all three ways to explore the stage-setting or background involved in ostensive definition and interpretation. The background concerns our capacity for taking a range of objects or properties to be of the same kind and our actions and judgments to be going on in the same way—without their being reducible to sensory stimulation and without our doing so by applying principles of identity or interpretations of rules or hypotheses of use. In other words, for Wittgenstein the problem of normative similarity arises precisely because neither of the resources that Quine draws upon (sensory stimulations and hypothesis formation) characterize our capacity for judging sameness. This can be seen early in the *Investigations* where Wittgenstein discusses the role of ostension both in learning and in fixing the meaning of words (*PI* §§1–38). Wittgenstein contrasts ostensive definition, which uses an object as an exemplar to fix the meaning of a word, and ostensive teaching, which effects an association between a word and an object (*PI* §6). Ostensive teaching does not fix meaning, even if it is an important part (as both Wittgenstein and Quine believe) of initiate language learning. This distinction is one that Quine completely overlooks, and it is for this reason that he misunderstands, and so underestimates, Wittgenstein's critique of ostensive definition.

Quine takes Wittgenstein's argument to be that ostensive definition requires the use of a kind term or sortal.[5] This he rejects on the ground that our innate sensory capabilities are such that we can be conditioned to respond to a particular property, say, a color like red, without the explicit use of the sortal expression "color." Indeed, for Quine, such basic conditioned associations between natural properties and words are the basis for all subsequent language acquisition. They provide the foundation from which we bootstrap ourselves up to higher levels of linguistic competence. There are passages in Wittgenstein that support a similar picture, but with the following important difference. Ostensive teaching is not simply a kind of stimulus-response conditioning. Rather it effects an association in a *normatively* structured setting. Or, as Wittgenstein puts it:

---

[5] See W. V. Quine, "Ontological Relativity," in his *Ontological Relativity and Other Essays* (New York: Columbia University Press, 1969), p. 31.

Don't you understand the call "Slab!" if you act upon it in such-and-such a
way?—Doubtless the ostensive teaching helped to bring this about, but only
together with a particular training. With different training the same ostensive
teaching of these words would have effected a quite different understanding.
(*PI* §6)

By the use of the word "training," Wittgenstein means to draw attention to the practice within which ostensive teaching occurs. Different
training involving the same association of a word and object would
effect a "quite different understanding." It is not that Quine ignores the
importance of the social setting within which conditioning occurs, but
that he seems not to accept the significance that Wittgenstein attributes
to this. Where Wittgenstein and Quine agree is in holding that we are
endowed with an array of natural reactions to certain kinds of situations and training. Quine seeks to identify these in terms of stimulations
to our sensory receptors while Wittgenstein identifies them in terms of
our behaviors in response to certain situations.

The normativity of the ostensive training of the novice is provided by
society in the form of the teacher. Such training does not fix the meaning of the words (for their meaning determines the nature of the training), but it does endow the novice with the skills for using the words
appropriately. Such training could occur, as Quine maintains, without
the explicit use of sortals in the teaching itself.[6] Ostensive definition, on
the other hand, does fix meaning in the sense that it supplies an exemplar or paradigm. But to know *how* to take the exemplar on the basis
of its presentation does require a sortal to differentiate which property
is the relevant one. This kind of explanation requires that the recipient
be a competent language user and that a sortal be used if the definition
is to succeed. So, Quine's quick dismissal of Wittgenstein's view of
ostensive definition misses the point by conflating ostensive teaching
and ostensive definition. Training draws on our natural reactions which
are tied to the forms of sensory experience available to us, but these natural reactions are not based upon the sensory stimulations to our perceptual organs in the way that Quine maintains. Ostensive training
does not provide meager evidence, not even meager evidence presented
in an orderly fashion by the teacher, nor does it fix meaning. It is not a
matter of evidence at all but of exploiting the natural reactions of the
novice in initiating that person into a practice or language-game.

Parallel to this contrast between ostensive training and ostensive

---

[6] Consider Wittgenstein's discussion of the various ways in which the rules of chess
can be learned (*PI* §31).

definition, but developed much more fully, is Wittgenstein's contrast between the role of interpretation or hypothesis in understanding a rule and what he calls our "blindly obeying" a custom in which we act as a matter of course[7]—that is, as we were trained to do. A mark of that blind obedience within a practice is the harmonious agreement and certainty among practitioners concerning what is the same, whether this concerns categorization or rule-governed action. It is a shared sense of the obvious that is acquired paradigmatically in initiate learning, in the grasping of rules and concepts through the acquisition and exercise of skills and techniques. And this shared, unquestioned, and certain sense of the obvious is normative. It can be objected that characterizing blind obedience as normative is to conflate automatic individual behavior and normative collective practice. It suggests that the normativity of our language games is a function of individually acquired automatic behavior.

But this would be to misunderstand Wittgenstein's point in appealing to our blindly obeying a rule as a response to the indeterminacy arguments raised in connection with rule-following. It is a misunderstanding because it presupposes an oversimplified conception of normativity. Just as ostensive teaching is a means that we humans have in associating word and object without that association fixing the meaning of the word, so blind obedience is that automatic and unthinking judgment distinctive of the obvious without that automatic response constituting the standard, as it were, of sameness. Both ostensive teaching and blind obedience occur within a language-game, that is, within a social temporally extended practice. As the discussion of ostensive definition leads to an examination of the philosophical notion of reference, so the discussion of blind obedience within a practice leads to an investigation into the nature of logical necessity. We cannot understand the normativity of our practices without understanding how necessity, broadly considered, is an integral part of all normative practices. Our bedrock "blind" judgments and actions concerning normative similarity are part of that background without which rule-following, interpretation, and theorizing are impossible. So, to understand our "blind" judgments and actions is to understand how normativity enters and infuses human life. Wittgenstein's task thus can be seen as providing an account of the normative dimension of human life that eliminates indeterminacy. To do this requires showing the place of non-causal necessity in our practices.

---

[7] Cf. *PI* §219.

2. NORMATIVE SIMILARITY AND BACKGROUND TECHNIQUE

The notion of a background against which, or in virtue of which, the foreground is made salient or possible is familiar. It is now (virtually) the conventional wisdom of philosophy. We can distinguish several such notions. Knowledge and theoretical claims presuppose background theory and methodology. Beliefs, perceptual and otherwise, are embedded within a network of beliefs and other intentional states. Perceptual saliency presupposes a perceptual background. Words have meaning only in the context of a sentence. Insofar as meaning is use, the use of words must occur only in the context of ongoing practices. So, appeal to a background is closely associated with holistic approaches to knowledge, mind, and language—or, if not holistic, at least anti-atomistic theories. This is certainly true of both Wittgenstein and Quine.

As a first step in better understanding Wittgenstein's characterization of the background, which includes the obvious, I shall look to Part VI of the *Remarks on the Foundations of Mathematics*.[8] This part concerns the acquisition (or adoption, as Wittgenstein puts it) of concepts, and in particular mathematical concepts. He thinks that how we learn these has profound implications for our philosophical understanding of the special justificatory status of proof and its grounding in our background judgments of what is obviously the same. He proposes providing what he calls "radical explanations" for the justificatory status of proofs by appeal to how we are trained in the mastery of mathematical techniques. The effect of such training is to see the hardness of the logical "must" as a "lesson . . . drawn from the scene."

Wittgenstein opens with a characterization of mathematical proofs as that which "give propositions an order. They organize them" (*RFM* VI.1). He spells this out in a Kantian manner: "The concept of a formal test presupposes the concept of a transformation-rule, and hence of a technique" (*RFM* VI.2). A proof is a pattern of propositions, a way of "organizing propositions." But no such organized set of propositions can be grasped as a proof, or indeed be a proof (and Wittgenstein puts

---

[8] Part VI was written during the period (1941–44) just before Wittgenstein completed Part I of the *Investigations* (1945). It is important to note that of all the *Nachlass* material collected together in the revised edition of *RFM*, only Parts I and VI are presented complete as Wittgenstein wrote them without editorial revision or rearrangement. All the other parts have been subject to varying degrees of editorial revision. I want to thank David Stern for drawing this to my attention. See Michael Biggs and Alois Pichler, *Wittgenstein: Two Source Catalogues and a Bibliography*, Working Papers from the Wittgenstein Archives at the University of Bergen No. 7 (Bergen, 1993), pp. 60–9.

the point in both the cognitive and ontological ways), unless it is subject to transformation rules. For Wittgenstein, this requires a method of using the rules to transform the propositions. The point is clear. No particular pattern of propositions, considered in isolation from rules showing how the propositions are related to one another, can be a mathematical proof. There must be rules of transformation. This, however, threatens to start a regress. For, if a proof presupposes transformation rules in order to be a proof, the transformation rules themselves, in order to be rules, must presuppose rules of application. Wittgenstein rejects any attempt to stop this regress of rules by appeal to a rule that is self-interpreting or in some other way carries its application within itself. Instead Wittgenstein stops the threatened regress by embedding the transformation rules within a practice of application, which provides the background against which the proof can be constructed. This is what Wittgenstein here calls a "technique." It is a skilled activity, not a further set of rules.

To make these general remarks more concrete, let us take as an example of a proof and its relation to transformation rules Euclid's proof for the infinity of prime numbers.[9] This proof justifies the proposition that the prime numbers are infinite. Here it is:[10]

---

[9] It is a proof that Wittgenstein cites in *RFM* VI.6 where he draws attention to an important affinity between instances or examples of finding a prime number $> p$ and the algebraic proof: "It will now be said that the algebraic proof is stricter than the one by way of examples, because it is, so to speak, the extract of the effective principle of these examples. But, after all, even the algebraic proof is not quite naked. Understanding—I might say—is needed for both."

[10] Euclid, *The Thirteen Books of the Elements*, vol. 2, trans. Thomas L. Heath (New York: Dover, 1956), p. 413. Let me enter two caveats to my use of Euclid's proof. First, Wittgenstein's interpretation of Euclid's proof is in fact more complicated than is indicated in the text of this paper. I want to highlight certain points which would only be lost if all the complications of a full explication were introduced. The most important of these complications is that Euclid's proof is an indirect proof by contradiction—a reductio ad absurdum. It involves a conspicuous use of the law of excluded middle. Many interpret Wittgenstein as endorsing an intuitionist mathematics and so as rejecting the use of indirect proof by contradiction and of course denying the validity of the law of excluded middle. See Crispin Wright, *Wittgenstein on the Foundations of Mathematics* (Cambridge, Mass.: Harvard University Press, 1980), esp. Part Two; and S. G. Shanker, *Wittgenstein and the Turning Point in the Philosophy of Mathematics* (Albany, N.Y.: SUNY Press, 1987), esp. chs. 2–3. This is an important issue, but, for the purposes of this paper, the proof could be reconstructed to avoid this. What is crucial is that the proof constitutes a set of instructions for finding a new prime number for any finite set of prime numbers. The second caveat concerns treating Euclid's proof as a constructive proof. The modern proof for the infinity of prime numbers is not a constructivist proof. Again, this is a matter I do not want to take on in this paper. What is important is that Wittgenstein did take it to be a constructive proof and that taking it as such helps elucidate Wittgenstein's notion of background technique.

Let *a*, *b*, *c*, . . . *k* be any prime numbers
Take the product *abc* . . . *k* and add unity.
Then (*abc* . . . *k*+1) is either a prime number or not a prime number.
(1) If it *is*, we have added another prime number to those given.
(2) If it is *not*, it must be measured by some prime number, say *p*.

Now *p* cannot be identical with any of the prime numbers *a*, *b*, *c*, . . . *k*.
For, if it is, it will divide *abc* . . . *k*.
Therefore, since it divides (*abc* . . . *k*+1) also, it will measure the difference,
or unity: which is impossible.
Therefore in any case we have obtained one fresh prime number.
And the process can be carried on to any extent.

To offer this proof as a formal test for the infinity of prime numbers requires the ordered use of transformation rules such that for any finite set of prime numbers, a new prime number can be constructed. The transformation rules include certain rules of logic (like modus ponens and assumption introduction) and rules of calculation (add 1 to the product of the prime numbers).[11]

Using this proof as our blueprint or set of instructions for how to order our use of transformation rules, "we have obtained one fresh prime number. And the process can be carried on to any extent." To construct this proof requires that we can use transformation rules of logic and of calculation. These transformation rules themselves presuppose techniques of inference and calculation. Using modus ponens or assumption introduction involves techniques for identifying premises, drawing conclusions, and constraining options. Adding, multiplying,

---

[11] If one performs the formal test by actually applying the transformation rules step by step, it becomes quite clear that, as Wittgenstein says, the concept of a proof presupposes the concept of transformation rules. We will follow Euclid in specifying a set of prime numbers as the total set. This is the hypothesis that will generate the required contradiction.

Let 2, 3, and 5 be the prime numbers.
Take the product of 2, 3, and 5, and add 1.
$2 \cdot 3 \cdot 5 = 30 + 1 = 31$.
Then 31 is either a prime number or not a prime number.
If it is, we have added another prime number to the list of prime numbers, and so it was not complete.
If it is not, 31 must be divisible by some prime number, *p*.
Now, if *p* is identical with any of the prime numbers 2, 3, 5, it will (evenly) divide 30. Since *p* is also to (evenly) divide 30 + 1, then *p* must evenly divide 1, which is impossible.
Thus we get the contradiction that *p* divides 31 evenly and that *p* does not divide 31 evenly.

On the basis of this contradiction, we reject the hypothesis we began with (that 2, 3, 5 are the only prime numbers) as the source of the problem.

dividing involve techniques for manipulating numerals to maintain equivalencies. The proof itself is a recipe for using these techniques in an ordered fashion to create the desired result as stated by the mathematical proposition that the number of primes is infinite. The meaning of that mathematical proposition is given by its proof. It is not a metaphysical proof concerning the totality of prime numbers. Rather, it expresses the fact that for any finite set of prime numbers, it is always possible to construct another, and this process is indefinitely repeatable.

Wittgenstein explicates the close relation among mathematical proposition, proof, and transformation rules as a conceptual or grammatical connection. A proof is an organized pattern of propositions that provides a "picture" of the proposition that the number of primes is infinite. But the background techniques involved in calculating or drawing inferences are activities, ways of applying the rules in the actual construction of a formal test. The foundational questions concern issues of application and so the production of regularities. For Wittgenstein, issues concerning application can only be explained in terms of the techniques of rule use. Mastery of techniques, as developed and judged in training contexts, just constitutes what it is to go on in the same way.

There are two important features of Wittgenstein's notion of a technique:

[O]nly through a technique can we *grasp* a regularity.

The technique is external to the pattern of the proof. One might have a perfectly accurate view of the proof, yet not understand it as a transformation according to such-and-such rules. (*RFM* VI.2)

His first point is that we cannot recognize a regularity unless we have some way of applying or implementing a rule. In other words, we can recognize regularities in nature, in society, in mathematics only to the extent that we can regularize our own behavior.[12] Using a technique is engaging in self-regulating behavior in certain contexts. The regularities (and so similarities) of nature are not forced upon us by some kind of natural resemblance or causal necessity alone; nor are they available to us by way of some principle or ideal of identity. This repetitive and self-regulating behavior that marks the mastery of technique is the basis for what counts as the same. Judgments of sameness are a function of our own repetitive regulated behavior in virtue of which we can grasp other

---

[12] David Pears makes this point in *The False Prison*, vol. 2 (Oxford: Clarendon Press, 1988), p. 371, when he states that "We discover the regularities in nature's behaviour only by first establishing regularities in our own behaviour."

regularities. Self-regulated behavior is constrained behavior, not in virtue of being an instance of a physical law but in virtue of the subject being trained in techniques. Constraint, repetitive regular behavior, and normative judgment of sameness go together.[13]

The second feature of technique states that "the technique is external to the pattern of proof" (*RFM* VI.2). There are no propositions that are part of the pattern that describe the technique for applying the transformation rules without which the pattern is not a proof.[14] So one might see the proof written out and yet not be able to "understand it as a transformation according to such-and-such rules" (*RFM* VI.2). This is the situation of one who has not studied mathematics or logic and sees a proof or derivation written down, but does not understand how or why the successive lines of the proof or derivation are introduced. That individual cannot see a proof in the pattern of propositions, for he does not see it as an organized pattern in which the conclusion must be what it is. The pattern which is there cannot be recognized as such until the subject has mastered the techniques for using the rules through the actual repetition of constrained behavior. It is against the mastery of the background techniques that a proof is differentiated from a mere series of sentences.[15] We mark that difference syntactically: a proof is stated non-temporally, whereas the activity of proving a mathematical proposition is temporally bounded.[16] Wittgenstein is interested in precisely this move we make from taking the activity of testing to be "so to

[13] This is an oversimplified account of the relation between self-regulation and judgments of sameness. There are many cases of rule-following, even quite simple cases, that are not repetitive in the way that has been emphasized here. Teaching children to share is teaching a rule, but one that can be realized in a variety of ways, from sharing toys by dividing them up to sharing a swing by waiting in line. I owe this point and example to John Deigh. The mathematical example is useful precisely because so many of the techniques involved are not multifaceted in this way. Even if there is more than one technique for, say, adding or multiplying, whichever technique is used, its mastery is mastery of addition.

[14] Wittgenstein is particularly drawn to Euclidean proofs in geometry precisely because geometry is, as it is said, "the mathematics of all plane figures constructible with a straight edge and compass." Euclidean proofs are recipes for constructing geometric figures.

[15] This will have implications for how Wittgenstein sees the relation between behavior and an intentionally describable action. Behavior itself can be seen and isolated from the background against which it is intelligible as an intentional action. This is one of the points of analogy between psychology and mathematics.

[16] Wittgenstein develops this point as follows in *RFM* VI.2:

How do you test for a contrapuntal property? You transform it according to *this* rule, you put it together with another one in *this* way; and the like. In this way you get a definite result. You get it, as you would also get it by means of an experiment. So far what you are doing may even have been an experiment. The word "get" is here used temporally; you got the result at three o'clock.—In the mathe-

speak, experimental" to taking it as a proof for a mathematical proposition. The distinction that Wittgenstein is drawing can perhaps be made more intuitively appealing by relating it to the everyday contrast we draw between rote learning and understanding concepts. In rote learning, the pupil can produce the formulae or propositions but cannot use them to do anything. With understanding, the pupil can use the proof as a recipe for generating new prime numbers from any given finite set of primes. A list of sentences is no more a proof than a list of objects is a description of a state of affairs.[17] Structure or organization must be added to both. Normative similarity judgments, involving the mastery of techniques, are part of that structuring.

We can draw a contrast, then, between the idea of a network of beliefs (and other intentional states) and the idea of the background techniques or know-how. This contrast brings out an important difference between Wittgenstein's two indeterminacy arguments. The stage-setting that Wittgenstein argues successful ostensive definition requires is a network of beliefs that prepares the place for introducing the new term. The paradox of interpretation argument, on the other hand, shows the need for something other than more of the same (more beliefs or propositions or sentences). It shows the need for background technique. Because background technique cannot be captured in any description or set of rules, it can only be shown in the context of a language-game. The place where it is best shown is the place where it is acquired—in the context of the initiate learner. How we learn these techniques is constitutive of what we learn precisely because what we learn cannot be separated from the context of use. What this also shows is that, echoing Plato, denotational theories of meaning are twice removed from linguistic reality: ostension, as fixing meaning, presupposes a system of beliefs, which in turn presupposes background techniques of sign use.

So, techniques of use are the source of our bedrock judgments of sameness. Linguistic competence consists, in large part, in the mastery

---

matical proposition which I then frame the verb ("get", "yields" etc.) is used non-temporally.

The activity of testing produced such and such a result.

So up to now the testing was, so to speak, experimental. Now it is taken as a proof. And the proof is the *picture* of a test.

[17] In putting the matter this way, I intend to draw attention to the similarity in what Wittgenstein says about objects and states of affairs in the *Tractatus* and propositions and proofs in *RFM*. As Wittgenstein tells us in the *Tractatus*, the world is all that is the case, that is, the totality of states of affairs, not the totality of objects. Similarly mathematics, and by extension any rule-governed practice, is the domain of proofs and not propositions.

of such techniques. Wittgenstein's very method itself of investigating theories of language by using language-games of a familiar sort undermines the point of trying to separate language from language use. The kind of holism that Wittgenstein is endorsing here is *heterogeneous*, involving, as we have seen, not only the idea of a network of beliefs but also the idea of a background of techniques acquired over time in first-language learning. As these techniques can only be demonstrated, their justification (or "radical explanation," as Wittgenstein puts it in *RFM* VI.14 and 23) lies with an appeal to how we learn, that is, to how we come to see that "matters must be like that." This is the topic of the next section, but first I need to bring out how Quine's position differs on these matters.

An intimate connection between what language is and how we acquire it is also found in Quine's writings. But, as we know, his account is governed by a very different method of inquiry into language, namely, that of the field linguist trying to translate the radically alien language of an unknown people. Part of what supports this approach is Quine's sense of a deep affinity between the position of the radical translator and the child. Both must develop complex theories using sensory experience as their sole, but meager, evidential base. As a result of assimilating first language acquisition to radical translation in this way, Quine concludes that the indeterminacy of reference revealed by his thought experiment is an ineliminable feature of all language use:

On deeper reflection, radical translation begins at home . . . Our usual domestic rule of translation is indeed the homophonic one, which simply carries each string of phonemes into itself.[18]

So, in the end, our similarity judgments derive from a limited natural resemblance (similarity within the quality space of each sensory system) and indeterminate theorizing, indeterminate precisely because natural similarity in perceptual quality space (such as a rabbity pattern of retinal stimulation) is compatible with rival ontological theories. The holism that Quine draws upon to support this is a *homogeneous* holism. All is assimilated into the network of beliefs, which for Quine is a network of interconnected sentences, a network which includes even the laws of logic and rules of inference. The only background, in the sense in which I have been contrasting network and background, is the physiology of our various sensory systems.

A second way in which the views of Wittgenstein and Quine diverge in how they construe their respective indeterminacy arguments con-

---

[18] Quine, *Ontological Relativity and Other Essays*, p. 46.

cerns the derivative semantic status of words, and so reference. Both agree that reference cannot be semantically basic. This can look like their both agreeing (minimally) with Frege's context principle that the meaning of the individual word is a function of its role in a sentence (especially, an assertoric sentence). While this is true of Quine's view, it can only distort Wittgenstein's position. For Quine, the holophrastic observation sentence used by the radical interpreter and the child is the entering wedge into language. But, for Wittgenstein, the entering wedge for the child is participation in a primitive language-game just as the entering wedge, methodologically, for understanding what language is, is the primitive language-game. When, after a period of gathering evidence, Quine's linguist hears 'Gavagai!', he hears 'Lo, a rabbit!' When Wittgenstein's builder, who is trained in the building game, hears 'Slab!', he hears a call to action.[19] This difference reflects Quine's conception of language as an interconnected set of theories and Wittgenstein's conception of language as ongoing regulated activities involving the coordination and cooperation of the participants.

A final point of contrast will take us to the next stage of the argument. Quine's indeterminacy arguments are part of his ongoing attack on the analytic-synthetic distinction and the idea of non-causal necessity. The language of necessity, for Quine, belongs to the realm of pragmatic considerations, indicating our reluctance to revise or give up certain claims. For Wittgenstein, however, the indeterminacy arguments show the inadequacies or incoherence of certain philosophical theories of language and meaning. Wittgenstein retains the contrast between the conceptual and the empirical, and with that distinction, a place for necessity. What must be is not just what we are loathe to give up, but what stands fast for us as obvious. Indeed, what Wittgenstein is arguing is that unless something stands fast for us, we can't even be in the position to be loathe to give anything up.

3. NORMATIVITY AND "PSYCHOLOGIZED" NECESSITY

What the non-temporal marker indicates, according to Wittgenstein, is the *normative role* played by both the proof and the proposition it

---

[19] Even the use of the exclamation point by each of them differs. For Quine, it indicates that the linguist is making a report on the current state of affairs (rather than a question). For Wittgenstein, it indicates a command to do something.

supports. The proof is not the entry to a realm of eternal verities.[20] The proposition that there is an infinite number of primes is, for Wittgenstein, a rule and the proof "a *blue-print* for the employment of a rule" (*RFM* VI.3). As such, it "stands behind the rule as a picture that justifies the rule" (*RFM* VI.3). So, a proof justifies a rule not by deducing certain eternal features of numbers which the metaphysical proposition describes. Nor does it provide inductively based evidence for extrapolating a mathematical generalization. Rather, the proof justifies the rule by showing how the rule is to be used. Euclid's proof for the infinity of primes is a blueprint or recipe for constructing a new prime number for any given finite number of primes. It "teaches us a technique of finding a prime number between p and $p! + 1$. And we become convinced that this technique must always lead to a prime number $> p$. Or that we have miscalculated if it doesn't" (*RFM* VI.6). The proof, then, as a picture that justifies the rule, is not a representation, that is, it does not show how things are, but how to produce what must be. In other words, the elements of the picture are not isomorphic to some possible state of affairs, but are instructions for creating an isomorphism between a (normative) proposition and what actually occurs:

III.30 A proof leads me to say: this *must* be like this . . . What does 'it *must* be like this' mean here in contrast with 'it is like this'? . . .

I want to say that the *must* corresponds to a track which I lay down in language. (*RFM*, pp. 165–6)

If we grant Wittgenstein his thesis that proofs and mathematical propositions (or certain of them) are special because they are normative rather than because they are metaphysical truths, we need to understand better this normativity and the necessity it imposes. This requires rethinking the modalities of necessity, contingency, and possibility in terms of normativity rather than metaphysical reality. His account of necessity is not restricted to the case of mathematical propositions. It applies much more broadly, with the mathematical case providing the prototype for his account of the necessity of the grammatical propositions of the *Investigations*[21] and the propositions that hold fast of *On Certainty*.[22] As such, it can be seen as an account of "conceptual truth,"

---

[20] See Shanker, *Wittgenstein and the Turning Point in the Philosophy of Mathematics*, esp. ch. 7, who argues for a similar interpretation.

[21] Examples include "Only you can know if you had that intention" (*PI* §247), "Every rod has a length" (*PI* §251), "One plays patience by oneself" (*PI* §248), and "Another person can't have my pains" (*PI* §253).

[22] Examples from *On Certainty* include "Here is a hand" (*OC* §1ff), "The earth has existed since long before my birth" (*OC* §84ff), and "Every human being has two human parents" (*OC* §239ff).

though that is a misnomer for Wittgenstein. Not because there are no such things for him as propositions that are *conceptually* constraining but because there are no such things as conceptual *truths*. Grammatical propositions and propositions that hold fast are no more truths (whether metaphysical truths or truths by virtue of meaning) than is the mathematical proposition that the number of primes is infinite. Like that mathematical proposition, they are not truths at all, but norms. As we know, in all three of his major critiques, Wittgenstein argues that no object is inherently normative; and that the individual mind cannot be the source of those norms without generating an explanatory regress. So, Wittgenstein is looking for a way of describing normativity, one that does not attempt to explain "the determination of a concept," as he puts it in the *Remarks*, in terms of either the powers of the individual mind or the object denoted by a concept. We can see that this revival of a contrast between conceptual (or grammatical) propositions and empirical propositions runs counter to Quine's central thesis that no such distinction can be made. However, Wittgenstein's way of drawing the distinction does not run afoul of Quine's objections, as it is not a distinction between kinds of truths but between norms of a game and moves within the game.

The expression "the determination of a concept" combines two elements that Wittgenstein sees as two sides to the same coin. The first element concerns the logical space created by the word and its background techniques of application and the second concerns the prescriptive role of concepts and rules. The logical space of a concept is, to a large extent, a function of the background techniques of application, techniques which I have argued elsewhere cannot themselves be understood as a set of rules, but are intersubjectively shared social practices.[23] The logical space created by a concept or rule is realized in the normatively shaped behavior of the participants in the language-game. Participants, through a process of training, come to see that things "must be like that" (*RFM* VI.7). The justification that proofs afford their rules is due to the normative role played by the proof as a blueprint or recipe for getting the desired result. It shows how to obtain the results one ought to get if one has grasped the concept or rule. It does not, however, predict what will happen. If I don't follow the proof or I get distracted in the middle of things or if I think "who cares?" or if any other of an

---

[23] See Meredith Williams, "Rules, Community and the Individual," in Klaus Puhl, ed., *Meaning-Scepticism* (New York: De Gruyter, 1991) and "The Philosophical Significance of Learning in the Later Wittgenstein," *Canadian Journal of Philosophy* 24 (March 1994): 173–204.

indefinite range of contingencies occur, I won't construct a prime number. This underscores the fact that "what I derive from the picture is only a rule. And this rule does not stand to the picture as an empirical proposition stands to reality.—The picture does not shew that such-and-such happens. It only shews that what does happen can be taken in this way" (*RFM* VI.5), namely, as following the rule correctly or not. The range of possibilities, the range of possible uses, is thus a matter of how in fact we make judgments and draw inferences. What we find obvious and what we find must be the case gives us the differentiation required for the creation of the logical space of possibilities.

In short, the actual use of an expression creates the space for the concept. This reverses the usual explanatory relation between concept and use. Wittgenstein approaches this same issue from another direction as well, by looking at the special way in which a proof justifies a rule. A proof justifies its rule by showing the order in which various techniques are to be used to produce the predetermined outcome (as specified by the rule). The series of prime numbers must be infinite. The answer to 9 times 8 must be 72. The "must" expresses a normative necessity that is not captured by the classical characterization of necessity in terms of truth, as that for which a contradiction results from its denial. Rather, it expresses the fact that the result one gets in going by the rule "is, so to speak, *overdetermined*. Overdetermined by the fact that the result of the operation is defined to be the criterion that this operation has been carried out" (*RFM* VI.16). In other words, "'It must be so' means that this outcome has been defined to be essential to this process" (*RFM* VI.7). Some commentators have preferred to express this as stating that the relation between a rule and its correct application is internal.[24] Their point is to emphasize that these propositions cannot be empirical propositions, subject to substantiation by experience. The rule is a way of judging what is done, not describing what is done. Getting that particular result is itself a criterion for having followed the rule.[25]

Clearly this contrasts with Quine's insistence that the result one gets in going by the rule is underdetermined, if not indeterminate. For Quine, the very features that make room for normativity—that neither natural causation nor rational interpretation determines techniques of use—provide the grounds for claiming the indeterminacy of our concepts. How can Wittgenstein then see in these same features of rule-following practices an *over*determination of acceptable results? For

---

[24] Baker and Hacker, for instance, prefer this way of characterizing the relation between rule and its application. See G. Baker and P. M. S. Hacker, *Scepticism, Rules and Language* (Oxford: Blackwell, 1984).

[25] Cf. *RFM* VII.61, esp. pp. 424–5.

Quine, propositions like "The number of primes is infinite" (or a Wittgensteinian example like "Every human being has two human parents") are embedded in a network of sentences like any other sentence, such as "Roses don't flourish in Illinois summers." The only difference is in how extensively the sentences are connected to other sentences in the web. They express empirical propositions and as such are underdetermined by the evidence available to us and indeterminate as to their reference. That is not to say that we won't believe them with certainty, but that certainty is not derived from the epistemic warrant that is available. The certainty is psychological and to be justified, if at all, pragmatically. How can Wittgenstein, who would agree that the inductively available evidence for these claims is meager, maintain that getting these results is nonetheless overdetermined by the rule? The explanation comes in connection with how we learn these rules.

This introduces the second element in the determination of a concept, the prescriptive role of concepts and rules. This is a function of how we acquire the relevant background techniques and their associated world pictures through initiate training. It is through the acquisition of such bedrock practices that we grasp the obvious and the necessary. Initiate learning is marked by the same blind acceptance of ways of going on that Wittgenstein appeals to in his reaction against the paradox of interpretation. Quine's failure to eliminate indeterminacy is explained by his misunderstanding of the conditions that must be met for language use, namely, the mastery of bedrock practices that provide the background of shared judgments of the obvious, of normative similarity. This leads to his mistaken assimilation of language learning to the situation of radical translation. But, for Wittgenstein, grasping a normative necessity is to be explained in terms of "signif[ying] that the learner has gone in a circle," not in terms of the learner's having rationally intuited the number system or tested various hypotheses concerning the use of words. So, to understand Wittgenstein's account of grasping a necessity, which is to engage in normative rule-following, we need to identify the learning circle to which Wittgenstein appeals.

The learning circle is temporally bounded. It is the actual process of teaching a pupil how to multiply, for example. The pupil begins and ends with the same mundane activity of getting a mathematical result. Something as simple as the activity of multiplying 8 by 9 to get 72 can be both the start and the end of the learning circle. Nothing is different in the expression of the arithmetic proposition. At the beginning of learning and at the end of learning (when the pupil sees that 8 times 9 must result in getting 72), the same expression is inscribed "$8 \cdot 9 = 72$." What differs is the normative status of that proposition for the pupil.

The vehicle for that change in status is the mastery of a cognitive skill or technique through training. These skills are modes of behavioral self-regulation that create the space for going on in the same way by constituting a set of regularities (mathematics) or by revealing certain natural regularities (categorization). These techniques, as we have seen, cannot be fully specified in propositional form (for then the threatened regress re-emerges), but are acted out in our reactions and actions that have been shaped by our initiate training.[26] It is precisely the fact that these techniques cannot be specified propositionally that Quine identifies, wrongly on a Wittgensteinian view, as grounds for claiming indeterminacy. But, for Wittgenstein, these techniques constitute the obvious ways to go on or continue in virtue of which judgments of sameness are made possible. The notion of what is obvious is normative.

Judgments of sameness, then, are not grounded solely in natural resemblances in the world to which our sensory systems are sensitive, but in our shared sense of the obvious or the obvious way to go on. An isomorphism is created between the techniques we have acquired through training and certain natural regularities. But it is the set of techniques (in part) that determine what natural regularities are salient for us (color, shape, size). Nor could Quinean hypothesis formation replace or do the work that training in techniques does. Neither simple conditioning nor rational interpretation determines techniques. It is precisely this that makes room for the normative dimension of rules and concepts. What overcomes the abstract problem of indeterminacy of ostension and interpretation is that we can be, and are, trained in certain ways. Quine mistakes the possibility of alternative principles of individuation for the indeterminacy of our actual judgments because he holds that both background theory and background individuating apparatus are presupposed, must be involved, in our actual judgments of the obvious. But Wittgenstein's point is that the background required is that of mastery of techniques, not the application of principles of individuation or theory.

Developing techniques of use creates the regularities necessary for judgments of similarity or sameness without which language or any rule-governed enterprise is impossible. As Wittgenstein puts this point

---

[26] This is what leads Merrill B. Hintikka and Jaakko Hintikka, *Investigating Wittgenstein* (Oxford: Blackwell, 1986) to maintain that central to Wittgenstein's philosophy is "the ineffability of the semantic." They pursue this idea by characterizing "the role of language-games as the basic semantical links between language and reality" (p. 212). They are certainly onto something correct in Wittgenstein. Though the techniques cannot be described, they can be shown. It is in this way that the doctrine of showing survives.

in *RFM*: "the phenomenon of language is based on regularity, on agreement in action" (VI.39). In the learning situation, regularity is guaranteed because no alternative way of responding is permitted. The role of the teacher is crucial here, for the resources available to the pupil are not simply his sensory stimulations but an environment shaped by the teacher. The learning circle moves from the experimental activity of testing in which the pupil's reactions are shaped by the teacher, creating the sense of the obvious, to the activity of testing in which the result is seen as necessary, as what must be:

It is as if we had hardened the empirical proposition into a rule. And now we have, not an hypothesis that gets tested by experience, but a paradigm with which experience is compared and judged. And so a new kind of judgment. (*RFM* VI.22)

Effecting this kind of change is the result of the learning circle. What is involved in adopting a concept reveals a strong link between the process of learning and what is learned, for the training itself is constitutive of the concept acquired. To adopt the concept is to acquire the technique, and technique can only be shown and practiced. The training we get is a part of what we learn.

Explaining necessity in terms of the normative role that rules and concepts play after appropriate training looks in some ways like a revival of psychologism, the thesis that norms describe our de facto psychology. On this view, mathematical principles and laws of logic, insofar as they are laws at all, are empirical generalizations about how we think (or associate ideas) as a matter of fact.[27] In this way, logical or conceptual necessity is reduced to the psychological, a variant on the Humean idea that necessity is psychological compulsion. Logical or metaphysical necessity is thus a projection of how we are psychologically determined to think. But Wittgenstein does not revive this crude version of psychologism or the projectivism to which it naturally leads. He does indeed hold that our use of language, concepts, and rules is grounded in our shared natural history. He emphasizes that if certain general facts of nature were different, then our concepts and language-games would be different.[28] To this extent, he agrees with the empiricist that our "necessary truths" are contingent, and so he rejects the rationalist idea that necessity goes all the way down, as it were, to metaphysical necessity. Yet he is not reductionist in his account of the

---

[27] See J. S. Mill, *A System of Logic* (London: Longman, 1873), of course. And for a contemporary version, see Patricia Churchland, *Neurophilosophy* (Cambridge, Mass.: MIT Press, 1986).

[28] See, for example, *PI* §80, *PI* II.xii; *RFM* I.5.

relation between language and any of these general facts of nature. The philosophical problems involved are not to be solved by engaging in an empirical investigation:

If the formation of concepts can be explained by facts of nature, should we not be interested, not in grammar, but rather in that in nature which is the basis of grammar?—Our interest certainly includes the correspondence between concepts and very general facts of nature . . . But our interest does not fall back upon these possible causes of the formation of concepts; we are not doing natural science. (*PI* II.xii)

The necessity expressed in mathematical propositions or grammatical propositions in general is not the physical necessity expressed by laws of nature or laws of psychology. This is the mistake of classical psychologism, which takes mathematical and grammatical propositions to be empirical propositions. Wittgenstein argues that these propositions look as though they are fact-stating. This is what has led philosophers to treat them as either metaphysical truths or empirical generalizations. They are neither. Their necessity resides in the fact that they are normative propositions. Their normative functioning lies in the background techniques and world pictures which create the logical space for our judgments and actions concerning what is obviously the same and what must be so. These techniques are socially engendered and sustained.

So Wittgenstein's "psychologism," if it can be called that, arises in a different way.[29] First, though these propositions are necessary in virtue of the normative role they play in our practices, it is a contingent fact that such practices exist and that we can engage in them. To underscore this point, Wittgenstein asks us to consider changes in certain general facts of nature:

[I]f anyone believes that certain concepts are absolutely the correct ones, and that having different ones would mean not realizing something that we realize—then let him imagine certain very general facts of nature to be different from what we are used to, and the formation of concepts different from the usual ones will become intelligible to him. (*PI* II.xii)

Second, the prescriptive role in our lives of mathematical, logical, and other grammatical propositions is a function of how we acquire the relevant background techniques and their associated world pictures through initiate training. It is through the acquisition of such bedrock

---

[29] Historically, Wittgenstein can be seen to reject Frege's strong distinction between the logical and the psychological, but not by a return to the old forms of psychologism represented by J. S. Mill in the nineteenth century.

practices that we grasp the obvious and necessary. Only by taking an object or test or whatever, not as the particular object or inscription that it is, but as a standard by which behavior is shaped, can the pupil come to the view that things must be a certain way, and only by coming to hold that things must be this way can a pupil acquire concepts or the use of rules at all.

It is tempting at this point to say that Wittgenstein's account of necessity and possibility requires distinguishing between what is internal to a practice and what is external to that practice. For he seems to be saying that rules that are constitutive of a practice create necessities within that practice, but external to the practice the rules are contingent and so could be replaced by alternative practices or language games. This idea of what is external and internal to a practice has been endorsed by philosophers as diverse as Carnap and Foucault.[30] Wittgenstein himself struggled with this problem in the *Tractatus* in his attempt to find the limits of what can be thought. And it is tempting to interpret his notion of language games as involving such an idea. However, to apply this distinction straightforwardly either to his use of language games or to his account of necessity and rules in his later writings is a mistake.

It is a mistake, I think, for two important reasons. The first is that it suggests that there are alternatives to the necessities that inform our actual bedrock practices. This is a mistake for Wittgenstein because the very notion of alternative possibilities can only be made with respect to available concepts. The logical space for alternative possibilities requires some practice which constitutes the bedrock of certainty against which possibility is defined. Yet these practices and their constitutive judgments exist contingently both as practices and insofar as any individual participates. They are contingent without realizing a preexistent possibility. Possibilities, like simplicity, can be judged only relative to a normative practice. There is no way to make sense of the idea of possibilities independently of the contrasts that we can draw and their embeddedness in our shared judgments of what is obviously the same.[31] Wittgenstein's account of initiate learning concerns what it is for an individual's behavior to become normatively guided. That is, by

---

[30] See R. Carnap, "Empiricism, Ontology and Semantics," in Leonard Linsky, ed., *Semantics and the Philosophy of Language* (Urbana: University of Illinois Press, 1952); Carnap, *Meaning and Necessity* (Chicago: University of Chicago Press, 1947); and M. Foucault, *The Archaeology of Knowledge* (New York: Pantheon, 1972).

[31] There is this much to the anti-realist interpretation of Wittgenstein. It is part of Wittgenstein's rejection of the idea of logical form, of an eternally given range of possibilities within which all contingencies occur.

the adoption of concepts, which involves taking certain results as necessary.

The second reason for applying the Carnapian picture of internal and external issues to Wittgensteinian bedrock practices is that these constitute our human form of life. There is no perspective outside of this. For ordinary games, like chess or football, there is no difficulty in applying the Carnapian picture. One can change the rules of a game in virtue of considerations that are external to the game. In football the goal posts were moved from the zero-yard line to the back of the end-zone. This was done for external reasons, to make kicking a field goal more difficult. Though Wittgenstein uses the game of chess to introduce his notion of a language-game, our bedrock practices are unlike chess in certain crucial respects. Where chess may or may not be played in a society, naming objects, following rules, experiencing pains, anticipating the future are not optional practices that may or may not be in place. Wittgenstein is concerned with those aspects of our form of life that are not optional, that we cannot imagine doing without or changing for reasons external to these practices. The logical connective tissue of our system of beliefs, our interactions with ordinary objects and other people, our memories of the past and hopes for the future all implicate propositions that hold fast and ways of going on that cannot be jeopardized without inducing madness. This is not a transcendental argument for the necessity of our form of life. It is rather an argument, or perhaps observation, that we cannot but start *in medias res*.

The only "justification" we have for what is obviously the same is a description of how we were trained in the acquisition of concepts and rules. That training itself occurs in the context of a way of living, a custom (cf. *RFM* VI.34)—a context in which "we talk and act. That is already presupposed in everything that I am saying" (*RFM* VI.17). On Wittgenstein's view, we have no better or deeper explanation of sameness than that we are trained to judge in conformity with others. No philosophical theory of identity, no physical or physiological account of natural similarity, and no psychological theory of sameness is sufficient to ground these judgments. Justification for these bedrock judgments of sameness is provided by radical explanations in terms of the social training the initiate learner undergoes. The sense of the obvious is mastered by the initiate learner who unquestioningly (this is redundant since the initiate learner is precisely the one without the resources for questioning or knowing) acquires—through training—a second "linguistic" nature, that is, dispositions for using words in connection with objects and as part of actions. Without a bedrock of the obvious, there could be no practices, no norms, no rules.

We can see that Wittgenstein is not opting for the elimination of (non-causal) necessity but for a different understanding of necessity, one that makes the contrast between necessary propositions and empirical propositions fundamental rather than that between necessary truths and contingent truths. *Pace* Quine, meaning and reference cannot be radically indeterminate while language nonetheless flourishes.[32]

4. CONCLUSION: INDETERMINACY OF MEANING OR BLIND OBEDIENCE?

Broadly speaking, both Wittgenstein and Quine develop indeterminacy arguments from which the problem of normative similarity arises. Both Wittgenstein and Quine reject the transparency of reference and with it denotational and atomistic theories of meaning. Yet despite this apparent overlap in arguments and philosophical views, there are striking dissimilarities. In particular, Quine holds that indeterminacy is an ineliminable aspect of language use whereas for Wittgenstein the bedrock similarity judgments we make blindly or as a matter of course are determinate. That this is a hand is as obvious as that '5' must follow '4' when we are counting. The certainty of these judgments is immune to Quine's scruples about reference and meaning, but Quine's scruples are not immune to Wittgenstein's arguments.

Quine's picture of language is such that the only point of contact with the world is the observation sentence and the sensory stimulation that is the sentence's stimulus meaning. The acquisition of language as well as any revisions to the interconnected network of sentences that constitutes our web of belief turns on this single point of contact with reality. This is his scientific naturalism at work. It prepares the ground for the universality of the indeterminacy argument, but, if indeterminacy is genuinely universal, it undermines Quine's own account of belief formation and change. Crucial to Quine's conception of revising the web of belief is the idea of recalcitrant experience that is at odds with existing beliefs and that forces changes within the network of accepted sentences. Recalcitrant experience is recurrent sensory stimulation that elicits assent to the corresponding occasion sentence even if that forces

---

[32] This needs some elaboration as there are places where Quine seems to be saying something quite similar to this. In "Ontological Relativity," p. 49, he says that "in practice we end the regress of background languages, in discussion of reference, by acquiescing in our mother tongue and taking its words at face value."

change elsewhere in the web of belief. The problem of normative similarity applies to the role that Quine assigns the recalcitrant experience. If all is indeterminate, there can be no notion of recalcitrance. The idea of a recalcitrant experience carries with it both the idea of the violation of some expectation and the idea of some kind of necessary connection among beliefs. We must have expectations about what is the same recalcitrant experience and we must use some necessary inferential connections. Quine insists that nothing in the web of belief is immune to revision. He also holds that in the face of recalcitrant experience, the web or total theory must be revised. The notion of revising our total theory requires that we have some way of understanding in what the inferential connections among sentences consist. This is the point at which difficulties arise. Dummett has made the argument quite forcefully:

Quine's thesis involves . . . that the principles governing deductive connections themselves form part of the total theory which, as a whole, confronts experience . . . [W]e must recognize the total theory as comprising rules of inference as well as logical laws . . . But in that case, there is nothing for the inferential links between sentences to consist in.[33]

Quine's picture of language is thus subject to the problem of normative similarity both with respect to categorization and rule-following, and hasn't the resources for avoiding it. How can we have a recalcitrant experience unless we have expectations about what would be the same experience and about how the sentences of our total language are interconnected? Quine's picture of language as a total theory resting on a slight foundation of sensory stimulations collapses if indeed all is indeterminate.

Wittgenstein, on the other hand, rejects both Quine's picture of language and his interpretation of the child's socialization into the linguistic community. For Wittgenstein, the proper picture of language is that of the language-game in which words and actions in context cannot be isolated from one another. An important feature of a language-game is the lack of hesitancy or disagreement among the participants. What strikes Wittgenstein is not the meager point of contact between participants at the level of sensory stimulations but the considerable commonality in the judgments and reactions of the participants. These judgments and reactions are made as a matter of course and are justified, if at all, by appeal to the training in which the relevant techniques

---

[33] Michael Dummett, *Frege: Philosophy of Language* (London: Duckworth, 1973), p. 596.

were acquired. Indeterminacy is eliminated, or rather simply does not occur, through the acquisition of techniques of application. The process of learning techniques is thus constitutive of what is learned. What is so learned are not metaphysical truths or analytic truths but normative rules which fix what is the same and so what is necessary.

3

The Sense Is Where You Find It

Lars Hertzberg

I. For many philosophers, particularly among those who have found their inspiration in Wittgenstein's later work, appeals to the distinction between what does and does not make sense seem to be an important part of philosophical method. Wittgenstein himself said that his aim was to teach his readers to pass from disguised nonsense to patent nonsense (*Philosophical Investigations*, §464), and he gave numerous examples of the use of this method. I shall try to argue, however, that it is not clear precisely how invocations of nonsense in philosophy are to be understood. My aim in this essay is to try to clarify the role or status of such invocations. I shall do so through a discussion of the reading of Wittgenstein's view of nonsense put forward by Cora Diamond.

In her essay "What Nonsense Might Be,"[1] Cora Diamond discusses different ways of understanding the concept of nonsense. She defines and criticizes what she calls a 'natural' view of nonsense, and points to the possibility of a different view, which she says is the one to be found in Frege, and also in the *Tractatus* as well as in *Philosophical Investigations*. Let me briefly recapture her argument. Consider the sentences

(M) Scott kept a runcible at Abbotsford

and

(C) Caesar is a prime number.

On the natural view, the reason (M) is nonsense is that the word 'runcible' has not been given a meaning, and hence the resulting sentence has, as it were, a blank in it. In (C), on the other hand, all the words have a meaning, only the meaning is 'wrong': the words just cannot be brought together in this way to make a meaningful sentence. Sentence (M) has too little meaning, as it were, (C) has too much. Cora Diamond

---

[1] Originally published in *Philosophy* 56 (1981), repr. in *The Realistic Spirit: Wittgenstein, Philosophy, and the Mind* (Cambridge, Mass.: MIT Press, 1991), pp. 95–114. In what follows, references are to the reprinted version.

rejects the latter part of this claim, that is, as it applies to (C). It is due, she argues, to overlooking Frege's principle that we cannot discuss the meaning of a word in isolation. Only as it occurs in a sentence does a word have logical properties. When the words 'Caesar' and 'prime number' are combined in the way they are in (C), this shows that either the word 'Caesar' cannot have the logical properties it has in the sentence "Caesar crossed the Rubicon," that is, it cannot be the proper name of a person, or the words "prime number" cannot have the meaning they have in the sentence "53 is a prime number," that is, they cannot be arithmetical terms. The sentence succeeds neither in making a historical assertion, nor in formulating a purported truth of arithmetic. But this means that this sentence too has a blank in it, unless we are familiar with some other use of these words that might be relevant in this connection, say, a use of the word 'Caesar' as an expression for a number, or a use of the words 'prime number' as a political term.[2]

I should like to express Cora Diamond's point by means of a metaphor: the sentential context, as it were, pushes out any meaning of a word that would make the sentence incongruous, and the sentence homes in on any meaning, if available, that would make sense of it.

The reason we are inclined to overlook this point, she says, is that we fail to take seriously another of Frege's strictures, that of always distinguishing between the psychological and the logical. From the fact that in hearing (C) most of us will automatically think about the founder of Imperial Rome it does not follow that this is what the word 'Caesar' must refer to in this sentence. What the word means there depends on how it is used in the sentence, not on what anyone happens to be thinking about.

Cora Diamond then goes on to say:

In Wittgenstein this view of nonsense is in fact developed much more than it is in Frege, and you could put it this way: for Wittgenstein there is *no* kind of nonsense which is nonsense on account of what the terms composing it mean— there is as it were no 'positive' nonsense. *Anything* that is nonsense is so merely because some determination of meaning has *not* been made; it is not nonsense as a result of determinations that *have* been made. (p. 106)

I should claim that [this] view of nonsense is one that was consistently held to by Wittgenstein throughout his writings, from the period before the *Tractatus* was written and onwards. (p. 107)

In support of this claim with respect to *Philosophical Investigations*, she quotes §500:

[2] Ibid. pp. 97ff.

When a sentence is called senseless it is not as it were its sense that is senseless. But a combination of words is being excluded from the language, withdrawn from circulation. (p. 106)

II. I find Cora Diamond's discussion interesting and highly suggestive. The question I wish to raise concerns its application in Wittgenstein's later thought. It seems to me that there is both something right and something wrong in her suggestion that the view which she attributes (rightly, I am sure) to the Wittgenstein of the *Tractatus* is also to be found in *Philosophical Investigations*. What I would contend, roughly speaking, is that an analogous insight applies there too, but that it has to be expressed in different terms, terms that actually make a great deal of difference.

After that, I wish to take a look at the nature of philosophical invocations of nonsense from the point of view of Wittgenstein's later philosophy, using as an example Stanley Cavell's discussion of skepticism.

It seems to me that considerations analogous to those that might persuade one to reject the natural view of nonsense should also make one doubtful about the possibility of asking whether a *sentence*, taken by itself, does or does not make sense. Cora Diamond says: "it is . . . not obvious that the first word in 'Caesar is a prime number' means what it does in 'When did Caesar cross the Rubicon?'" (p. 99). Thus she evidently takes it for granted that the latter sentence *is* a way of picking out a determinate use of the word 'Caesar'. But there seems to be no reason to suppose that it is. After all, the sentence "Caesar crossed the Rubicon" might as well describe, say, the dealings between a Mafia operator, Caesar, and a crime syndicate known as the Rubicon.[3]

Again, if my son has a pet turtle, called Caesar, and I suddenly ask him "Did you know that Caesar crossed the Rubicon?" he is very likely to think that I am talking gibberish.

Or let us, on the other hand, imagine the following conversation between two judges at a dog show:

---

[3] Part of what makes us overlook this may be a peculiarity of the example. Julius Caesar is one of those individuals, like Napoleon or Shakespeare, or phenomena like the weather, that one can bring up at the start of a conversation almost anywhere and at any time without having to prepare the ground for it. If the example had been instead, "Smith is a prime number," the dependence of what was being said on the context would be more immediately striking. Wittgenstein speaks, in *Philosophical Investigations*, §117, about the mistake of regarding the sense of the word as an atmosphere that it carries with it into every kind of application. In these terms, it might be said that a name like 'Caesar' comes as close as any word can to carrying its context with it like an atmosphere.

A: What are the prime contenders in this class?
B: Well, Caesar is a prime number.
A: Which one is that?
B: It's number 53.
A: Yes, you're right, of course, 53 really is a prime number.

The example, perhaps, is a little strained, but what it seems to give us is a case in which, on the one hand, (C) makes good sense, while on the other hand, "53 is a prime number" is not used as an assertion in arithmetic.

The point is that a sentence considered by itself may seem to carry a determinate sense, yet in a given context may turn out to carry a different sense, or the sense may be lost. Or a sequence of words that looks as if it did not make sense by itself might turn out to make sense, etc.

In fact, there seems to be no more reason for saying that the word sequence "Caesar crossed the Rubicon," by itself, constitutes an historical assertion, than there is for saying that the word 'Caesar', taken by itself, refers to the founder of Imperial Rome, or for saying, for instance, that the English word 'hand', taken by itself, is a noun rather than a verb. In all these cases, we probably would respond to these linguistic items by classifying them in this way if we encountered them in isolation, but in no case does this fact seem to have anything other than a *psychological* significance.[4]

It seems natural to apply Frege's stricture once more on this level, and say that we cannot speak about the logical properties of a sentence in isolation, but only as it is uttered by a speaker in a context. There is a hint, however, that Cora Diamond would reject this response, by invoking a distinction between the perceptible sentence and the sentence considered as expressing a particular thought (p. 110). Thus, the perceptible sentence "Caesar crossed the Rubicon" would be expressing different thoughts in the case in which it referred to the founder of Imperial Rome and in the case in which it referred to dealings within the Mafia. And what carries the sense is not the perceptible sentence, but rather the sentence-as-expressing-a-particular-thought.

---

[4] What would be meant by saying that our responses in such a case have merely psychological significance, I take it, is that calling a response to a word encountered apart from a context right or wrong would be arbitrary (e.g. it would usually be neither 'right' nor 'wrong' for me to think about the Roman statesman if my eye happens to fall on the word 'Caesar' on a slip of paper lying around somewhere). In other words, nothing would hang on our responding one way or the other, the way something will normally hang on the way we respond to a remark made in the course of an actual conversation. (I am inclined to regard this as a tautology. A context, one might say, is precisely that in light of which it matters how someone responds to what is said.)

I am not sure whether the passage in which Cora Diamond makes this suggestion represents her own recommendation or is just her interpretation of Frege. In any case, this expedient would not resolve the problem at hand, since it would still be true that, as long as the context is not given, one and the same sequence of words might be thought to express any number of thoughts.

III. Wittgenstein says, in *Philosophical Investigations*, §117:

You say to me: 'You understand this expression, don't you? Well then—I am using it in the sense you are familiar with.'—As if the sense were an atmosphere accompanying the word, which it carried with it into every kind of application.

Here, Wittgenstein is evidently drawing attention to the kind of temptation that is involved in thinking of meaning as something psychological. Then he goes on to say:

If, for example, someone says that the sentence 'This is here' (saying which he points to an object in front of him) makes sense to him, then he should ask himself in what special circumstances this sentence is actually used. There it does make sense.[5]

Evidently, Wittgenstein is not contrasting single words with sentences here, but words and sentences on the one hand with particular uses of sentences on the other hand.

Consider an example similar to Wittgenstein's. I once overheard the following conversation opener: someone sitting down at a table asked the person seated opposite to him, "Where are you?" and got the answer, "I'm here." Taken in isolation, this may sound like a bit of dialogue from a Marx Brothers film, but we get a different view of the matter when we are told that the setting was a philosophy conference with participants from various institutions, and that the interlocutors had not met before. What the questioner meant was "Where do you teach?" and the answer was one out of a range of possible answers: "I teach at this place," rather than, say, at Swansea, or Edinburgh, or Illinois.

What makes it the case that this is what the speakers' words meant?[6] One popular move at this point is to invoke one of Paul Grice's conversational maxims, which enjoins speakers to be as informative as the

---

[5] "In diesen hat er *dann* Sinn."(My italics.)

[6] Of course, in view of the description given above, the questioner might have meant any number of things. It is hard to describe a situation in such a way that no ambiguity remains. In an actual conversation, the interlocutors will not normally worry whether they understand each other as long as the talk goes along smoothly. What matters to our present purposes, however, is that it was clear in the context that the questioner was not, for instance, trying to *find* the person he was addressing.

situation requires. To tell someone whom you know to have normal powers of vision, and who is looking at you in broad daylight, that at this moment you are seated at the table opposite him, would be to violate this maxim (and so, presumably, it would be for that other person to request such information). This is not how we converse. Therefore, when someone utters these words, you must look round for some other way of understanding them.

On this type of view it is true that you *could* have meant the words "I'm here" as a report of your current whereabouts, and in this case too, you would have managed to say something true. (It *is there* to be said, it will be claimed, even if no one would ever actually *say* it.) Perhaps it will even be claimed that this was what your words 'literally' meant. Now it is true, the argument continues, that if you *had* said this and meant it in the latter way, your interlocutor would be likely to misunderstand you, since he would have expected you to follow the conversational maxims commonly accepted, and hence he would have been on the look-out for some other way of understanding your words. But this does not alter this fact about the meaning of the utterance.

Now I find this sort of move rather suspect. It seems to be connected with the inclination some philosophers have to distinguish between language as it really is and language as it enters into human intercourse. This distinction in turn is bound up with the philosophical idea of language as a formal system. Obviously Grice's conversational maxims have the effect of protecting the idea of the language system from challenges involving an appeal to the ways in which language is actually used, by suggesting a way of squaring the fact that we would never actually speak in certain ways with the fact that a powerful philosophical picture of language entails that it should be *correct* to speak in those ways.[7]

In fact, there appears to be a deep rift in philosophy between those who are inclined by temperament to argue along such lines and those who are inclined to reject this line of argument.[8]

Actually, I would contend, this line of thought depends on the same failure to distinguish questions of meaning from questions of psychology which underlay the natural view of nonsense criticized by Cora Diamond. By *thinking* of a certain application of his words, on this view, the speaker can, the actual context notwithstanding, *make* them

---

[7] For an incisive criticism of this view of language, see Pär Segerdahl's *Language Use: A Philosophical Investigation into the Basic Notions of Pragmatics* (Houndmills: Macmillan, 1996).

[8] Cp. Paul Grice, "Prolegomena," in his *Studies in the Way of Words* (Cambridge, Mass.: Harvard University Press, 1989), esp. p. 17.

mean what they would mean if they were uttered in a different context. But this of course is absurd. Doing this is no more possible than saying "Bububu" and meaning, "If it doesn't rain I'll go for a walk," to use an example of Wittgenstein's (*Philosophical Investigations*, p. 18).

I think this can be seen the most clearly if we think about the view of truthfulness that a Gricean account seems to entail. Consider the following case: a man is to be fined for a traffic violation. In Finland, the amount of a fine is determined on the basis of the combined incomes of spouses. When the highway patrolman asks him whether his wife is working, he tells him she is not—which of course (given that these claims are not routinely checked) brings down the amount of the fine—justifying this lie to himself by pretending that the question meant: "Is she at work right now?"[9] On the Gricean account the man is speaking the truth since he is thinking the truth, he is simply violating a conversational maxim. (This brings to mind the doctrine of mental reservation said to have been adopted by Jesuits.)

Now this seems clearly wrong: rather than excusing the reply, this subterfuge could be considered an aggravating circumstance, since it combines the lie with a fraudulent admission of the demand for truthfulness (the man lies to himself as well as to the police).[10]

The only way out for a defender of the literalist view of language, it seems, is to claim that the notion of truth used here has no direct connection with *speaking* the truth. But this response would reinforce the impression that the philosophical idea of language as a formal system is an artifact which is not intended to have the power to illuminate the human use of language (although Grice, for instance, claimed that that was what he wanted to do).

Now, by a line of argument *analogous* to that adopted by Cora Diamond, it could be said that the circumstances, in the exchange imagined above, exclude taking the remark "I'm here" as a way of letting

---

[9] Again, of course, our description of the example does not exclude the possibility that that was what the policeman was actually asking about, and hence the man may have been speaking the truth. My point is simply that he cannot make his assertion true simply by *thinking* of a context in which those words could be used to make a true assertion.

[10] It is an interesting aspect of our attitude to language that we should be open to this kind of self-deception, i.e. in the case of a lie we may think it an extenuating circumstance that our words could, given the right sort of context, have been construed as true. We are, it might be said, inclined to give the form of words an importance of its own (consider, too, the use of language in making up riddles, which often rely on taking words in an outrageously 'literal' sense). Obviously, the fact that we relate to language in this and similar ways provides the soil for the philosophical idea of a dichotomy between language as a system and language as actually used.

the other person know where one is seated. And in the same way, the situation in which a traffic citation is being written out, in conjunction with the Finnish penal system, excludes taking the question, "Is your wife working?" as an inquiry about her activity at the moment of speaking. Using the image I suggested before, we could say that the irrelevant interpretation is 'pushed out' by the circumstances.

It should be emphasized that these are clear and unambiguous observations pertaining to the linguistic character of the utterances as made in the situations we have imagined. They are not just points of psychology, speculations about the associations speakers might be inclined to get from various utterances in various contexts. In fact the shoe is on the other foot: as we saw, it is only by taking a psychological view of meaning that we could hold on to the notion that the meaning of what we say is, or could be, independent of context, as it is taken to be on the 'literalist' view.

If this line of argument is acceptable, then, it means that questions about the sense of a sentence are only to be asked about sentences as used by particular speakers on particular occasions. Where does this leave philosophers' appeals to what does and does not make sense?

IV. I wish to approach this question in a roundabout way, by taking a look at a discussion about skepticism involving Wittgenstein, Stanley Cavell, and Marie McGinn.

Marie McGinn, in her book *Sense and Certainty*, quotes the following remark from *On Certainty*:

I know there is a sick man lying here? Nonsense! I am sitting at his bedside, I am looking attentively at his face.—So I *don't know* it, then, that there is a sick man lying here? Neither the question nor the assertion makes sense. Any more than the assertion "I am here," which I might yet use at any moment, if suitable occasion presented itself . . . And "I know there is a sick man lying here," used in an *unsuitable* situation, seems not to be nonsense but rather seems matter-of-course, only because one can fairly easily imagine a situation to fit it.[11]

McGinn takes Wittgenstein's point to be this: utterances like "(I know) there's a sick man lying here" or "I'm here" may sometimes be used to convey genuine information and sometimes not. They fail to convey genuine information in cases in which what they say is obvious. In these cases, uttering these sentences is nonsense. She says that Wittgenstein uses this point as an argument against the skeptic, taking it to show that

[11] Marie McGinn, *Sense and Certainty: A Dissolution of Scepticism* (Oxford: Blackwell, 1989), p. 108. The remark quoted is §10 in *On Certainty*. I follow McGinn's translation. The first italics are mine.

what the skeptic is concerned to deny are claims that could not even be meaningfully made.

However, she does not consider this a good argument. For it is open to the skeptic to retort that "the implication that one is saying something that could, in the context, be genuinely informative is one that can be cancelled without any misuse of the language."[12]

On this score, she claims to disagree with Stanley Cavell, who in her view lays too much stress on such an appeal to the obvious in his discussion of Wittgenstein and skepticism in *The Claim of Reason*.[13]

It seems clear to me, however, that this is not the only way in which Wittgenstein's remark can be read. What makes a situation suitable or unsuitable for saying "I'm here" is not necessarily a matter of what is *obvious*. Sometimes (as in the conversation described a little while ago) the words "I'm here" are used to exclude some other alternative (say, "I teach at Illinois," or, "I'm sitting over there in the back," telling someone where I have reserved a seat in the refectory). But even in the cases in which they are not used to exclude any alternative, they may still make sense. Thus, if I see a friend scouting the refectory for where I'm sitting, I may call out, "I'm over *here*." Or, having hurried to the opera where my wife is waiting impatiently with the tickets, I may call out to her, "*Now* I'm here." Or, having gone through a long story about my narrow escape from death in a serious illness, I may conclude by saying, "Well, here I am today."

In none of these latter cases could the words convey any information to an audience. They are not used here to exclude an alternative. If we tried to unpack the sentence "I'm here" by comparing it with other sentences in which these words occur, what we would come up with might be something like, "The person who is now speaking is now at the place at which he is speaking." Such a sequence of words, of course, could *never* convey *information*, since in order to avail themselves of what it is saying the audience would already have to know what it is trying to tell them. And yet what we would be doing in producing these utterances in these situations may clearly be intelligible. Perhaps it could be said that in all these cases we are *drawing attention* to a fact, though the significance of doing that, in turn, is dependent on the particular circumstances in each case. In other words, the situations we have imagined are what Wittgenstein might have called suitable situations for

[12] McGinn, *Sense and Certainty*, p. 108.

[13] Stanley Cavell, *The Claim of Reason: Wittgenstein, Skepticism, Morality, and Tragedy* (New York: Oxford University Press, 1979), esp. pp. 204–21. It should be mentioned that Cavell is not discussing *On Certainty*.

uttering the words "I'm here," but what makes them suitable is not the fact that what is being said is not, as it were, obvious.

V. In fact, for Wittgenstein to have made the point that to say "I'm here" in an unsuitable situation is meaningless because obvious would not have been wrong so much as incoherent. In order to judge that a certain claim is obvious, I should evidently have to understand the claim. The paradox is this: it appears that we should have to understand what the speaker is saying in order to realize that we don't understand what he is saying. Of course, if an utterance makes no sense, there is nothing there *to* understand, nothing that could be either obvious or not obvious. We are constantly tempted to overlook the remark by Wittgenstein that Cora Diamond quotes: "When a sentence is called senseless it is not as it were its sense that is senseless."[14]

Marie McGinn, as we saw, regards such a move as central to Cavell's discussion of skepticism.[15] She is right in rejecting it, but I am not sure whether she is right in attributing it to Cavell. (I should point out, however, that McGinn is very subtle and that there are many strands to her argument. I hope I am not doing her injustice.) She argues that Cavell avoids the difficulty of having to say that an utterance may be senseless and obvious at one and the same time by appealing to a distinction between what a sentence means and what the speaker means in uttering it. Thus for a speaker to say, "I'm here" or "This is a hand" may be senseless because there is no point he could reasonably achieve by uttering it, and yet his words may make sense as a statement that is obviously true. However, this is precisely the sort of distinction I criticized in discussing Grice.

Now Cavell sometimes expresses himself as though this were what he was saying, but the way I read his argument it is not actually dependent on his taking this line. Let me try to explain.

We are inclined to think about the sense or senselessness of an utterance as a matter of its falling inside or outside the bounds of language. If certain conditions are fulfilled, it makes sense, if not, it lies beyond the limit of meaningful expression. These conditions have often been narrowly conceived. This is a characteristic of mainstream analytical philosophy, where they have been taken to involve some such thing as the syntax of the sentence uttered, the categorial compatibility of the words, the reality of the entities referred to, the verifiability of the resulting statement, or the like. In other cases, they have been thought

[14] Wittgenstein, *Philosophical Investigations*, §500, quoted in Diamond, "What Nonsense Might Be," p. 106.
[15] *Sense and Certainty*, pp. 93–4.

of more widely, as involving, say, the fact that an utterance succeeds in making a point, or the fact that some rational goal can be achieved by means of it. (This last seems to be Marie McGinn's reading of Cavell.) On either view, the meaningful use of language is surrounded, as it were, by a huge sea of gibberish, that is, possible but meaningless combinations of words: depending on one's philosophical convictions these would either be ill-formed formulae, category mistakes, remarks about unreal objects, unverifiable assertions, or pointless utterances.

Now I do not believe that this picture is involved in the point Cavell is making. What follows from the *obviousness* of what someone is saying (or maybe we should rather say: from its obviousness being obvious to all parties concerned) is not that it makes no sense, but simply that it cannot be understood as a way of *telling* anybody anything, that is, as an attempt to convey information otherwise not available to an audience.[16] No suggestion is being made here about the utterance falling outside the bounds of *language*; it is simply that, whatever the speaker may be doing with his words, it must at any rate be something other than *this*. Once more we see an application for Cora Diamond's point: this way of taking the utterance is 'pushed out' by the circumstances. Whether we know how to take it or not, *this* is not a way in which it *can* be taken.

In other words, when Wittgenstein suggests that the circumstances are not 'suitable' to the uttering of certain words, what he ought rather to have said is that they exclude taking the words in a certain way. The point is not that this utterance ought to have been made in another context, but that it cannot be made here *as* the kind of utterance it might have been if it had been made in that other context. (In fact, Wittgenstein's way of formulating the point at *Philosophical Investigations*, §117 is superior in this respect.)

Actually, it is only to the extent that we understand how someone's utterance is to be taken that we can tell how the words contained in it are to be understood. Thus, the context of the utterance "I'm here" will show whether the word 'here' is being used to exclude some alternative place or not. Perhaps we could say: until we know what kind of utterance has been made we do not even really know what sentence has been uttered.

VI. Another way of putting this point is to say that it is not so clear in what sense there could be counterexamples to a philosopher's claim that a certain type of utterance does not make sense. It would, I believe,

---

[16] See *The Claim of Reason*, pp. 208ff.

be a misunderstanding to suppose that, if we encounter someone who is using words in what the philosopher claims is a meaningless way, then either the philosopher must be wrong or the speaker must be violating some rule of language. In this connection we might think about Wittgenstein's remark in *Zettel* (§320):

if you follow other rules than those of chess you are *playing another game*; and if you follow grammatical rules other than such and such ones, that does not mean that you are saying something wrong, no, you are speaking of something else.

When someone, in a philosophically innocent context, utters words that we find bewildering, the utterance *was* actually made, nevertheless; the situation now is one in which those words have been uttered, and *this* is the situation we have to deal with if we wish to understand what was going on. The speaker may just have been trying to make conversation, or he may have been ironic, or may have been repeating to himself a turn of phrase he had just picked up, or maybe on the other hand he was mispronouncing a word, or was under some kind of misapprehension, and so on. Then again, maybe he was not really speaking at all, just mechanically coming out with words, or maybe he was insane and thus a speaker only in some attenuated sense. However, we do not reckon his just having violated the rules of language as one possible description of what he had been doing alongside the others, as though that would relieve us from having to deal with what was said.

I am tempted to turn this into a tautology, and to say: unless the speaker was doing *something* in uttering his words, that is, unless there was *some* way of making sense of what he was saying, then he was not actually *using words* in the first place, hence he was not flaunting the rules of language either.

Now the philosopher, of course, is not the judge of actual conversations; rather, in philosophy, we discuss imaginary ones. However, it would be a misunderstanding of the philosopher's task to suppose that we should be trying to establish 'what can be said' and 'what cannot be said'. What we may end up saying, at most, is things like, "You can't say this and mean that," or, "If you say this here, it will come out as something quite different from what you mean to be saying," or maybe even just, "*I* wouldn't say that if I wanted to make that kind of point in this situation." The temptation to give this point the form, "That wouldn't make sense," on the other hand, is a mark of philosophical impatience.[17]

---

[17] We may note, in this connection, that many of the invocations of nonsense in *Philosophical Investigations* are tentative or conditional.

If the philosopher is successful in convincing her opponent, what she succeeds in bringing about, accordingly, is not the realization that there are certain things one is prohibited from saying, but rather that one is no longer *tempted* to say them. Such a result will always, in a sense, be ad hominem.

This appears to be Cavell's position too:

I am in no way hoping, nor would I wish, to convince anyone that certain statements cannot be made or ought not be made. My interest in statements is in what they do mean and imply. If 'cannot' and 'ought' are to come in here at all, then I confess to urging that you cannot say something, *relying on what is ordinarily meant in saying it*, and mean something other than would ordinarily be meant.[18]

To judge by her more recent writings, there is reason to think that Cora Diamond would not disagree with the view that has been put forward here. In her introduction to *The Realistic Spirit*, she speaks about "a dramatic shift" that is central to Wittgenstein's later work, one that

went with a profound criticism of the *Tractatus*, . . . a rejection . . . of a Kantian spirit which lays down . . . internal conditions of language's being language, of thought's being thought. The notion in the later philosophy of philosophy as liberating is thus tied to an ability to look at the use without imposing on it what one thinks must already be there in it. The notion of use itself and what is meant by giving and presenting it thus also changes: an expression is not presented timelessly—its use is not given—by the general form of the propositions it characterizes; use can be seen only as belonging to the spatial, temporal phenomenon of language.[19]

And, in a discussion elsewhere about the private language argument, she writes: "Wittgenstein's argument is designed to let us see that there is not anything we want . . . [This] does not show that *something* is 'logically impossible' or 'conceptually impossible' . . .; it shows us that there was not anything at all that we were imagining."[20]

Now if I understand these passages correctly, they involve a rejection of the idea that, from the point of view of Wittgenstein's later work, it could be a task of philosophy to decide under what conditions a sentence makes sense. This would be misguided, as I have tried to argue, for two reasons: first, because it is a mistake to suppose that we can discuss the meaning of a sentence apart from its use, and second, because

[18] *The Claim of Reason*, p. 212.
[19] *The Realistic Spirit*, pp. 32–3.
[20] "Rules: Looking in the Right Place," in D. Z. Phillips and Peter Winch, eds., *Wittgenstein: Attention to Particulars* (Houndmills: Macmillan, 1989), p. 21.

it is a mistake to believe that philosophy can place limits on the possible uses of language. If that is how these passages by Cora Diamond are to be read, they constitute an implicit rejection of part of her own position in "What Nonsense Might Be." But even if I concur in her rejection of it, I still think a great deal is to be learnt from that essay.[21]

[21] I wish to thank Markus Heinimaa, Logi Gunnarsson, and Sean Stidd for their comments on an earlier version of this essay.

4

How Long Is the Standard Meter in Paris?

Cora Diamond

In his lectures on "Naming and Necessity,"[1] Saul Kripke raises questions about §50 of *Philosophical Investigations*, a long and complex section. He picks out and criticizes this pair of sentences:

There is *one* thing of which one can say neither that it is one metre long, nor that it is not one metre long, and that is the standard metre in Paris.—But this is, of course, not to ascribe any extraordinary property to it, but only to mark its peculiar role in the language-game of measuring with a metre-rule.

I shall look at the relation between Kripke's reading and criticism of that pair of sentences and his reading of Wittgenstein on rules.[2] I want to put Kripke-on-Wittgenstein-on-rules into a wider context of Kripke-in-disagreement-with-Wittgenstein.

I. KRIPKE ON WITTGENSTEIN AND THE STANDARD METER

In this section I summarize what Kripke has to say about Wittgenstein on the standard meter.

Kripke first rejects Wittgenstein's statement that one isn't ascribing some extraordinary property to the standard meter in Paris, if one says

This paper is dedicated to the memory of Peter Winch, and I would like to use his own words of appreciation for Wittgenstein to express my appreciation for him: my attitude to Peter's work "has always been one of gratitude for the help it has given me in seeing what are the important questions, and what kinds of questions they are."

[1] Saul Kripke, "Naming and Necessity," in D. Davidson and G. Harman, eds., *Semantics of Natural Language* (Dordrecht: Reidel, 1972). Page number references are given in parentheses in the text.

[2] Kripke, *Wittgenstein on Rules and Private Language* (Cambridge, Mass.: Harvard University Press, 1982).

that it can't be said of it that it is one meter long or that it is not one meter long. Kripke disagrees; he says that that would indeed be a very extraordinary property, and that Wittgenstein must be wrong (p. 274). If we measure the meter rod with a footrule, and it comes out 39.37 inches, then why *isn't* it a meter long? He then uses the example of the length of the meter rod in developing his own ideas: he wants to explain why he denies that the statement that the rod is one meter long *is a necessary truth*. In order to explain why he denies this, he first describes how we can allow for the fact that the length of the rod varies. We could, he says, make a more precise definition of the meter length by specifying that a meter is the length of stick S at some particular time t_0 (ibid.).

Here we might note that this now supposedly more precise definition shows how far Kripke's approach is from Wittgenstein's. Wittgenstein is thinking of a language-game in which there is comparison of various objects with the meter rod in Paris; the reader knows what it is like to compare a measuring rod with something else, and that knowledge is needed if we are to see the point of Wittgenstein's remark. If, however, we suggest, as Kripke does, that how long something is is determined, not by comparison with the rod in Paris, but by comparison with the length which it had at some particular time, it is now much less clear what language-game is being played. How am I to compare some object I *now* want to measure with the length the rod in Paris had five years ago? My point is not that there is no way to answer that question; there are certainly ways, involving the use of whatever theories, in which we could make such comparisons. The point is rather that, from Wittgenstein's perspective, talk of a length used as a standard (a length, that is, with which we make comparisons) hangs in the air unless there is some context, either one that actually exists or one that we can imagine, in which we can see what is to count as making comparisons with the standard length. Kripke's supposedly more precise definition of one meter is actually a definition which assumes that a standard length can be defined completely in advance and independently of our engaging in some activity of carrying out comparisons of lengths. (As Kripke sees the case, our activities of determining the length of things are not relevant to what it is we are referring to by "one meter," hence needn't be mentioned in discussing how reference is fixed. Nor is use in a language-game relevant to what it is to refer to something, on Kripke's view; there is an implicit reliance on what is here an unexamined idea of reference. These comments of mine involve a refusal to go along with Kripke's way of separating what he thinks of as epistemological issues from metaphysical ones, including the metaphysics of reference, and so it could be argued that they beg questions against him; but my point here is merely that we are, without comment by Kripke, shifted into a mode of discussion which takes a particular conception of the issues for granted.) Kripke's move towards a more precise definition should be seen as exemplifying what Stanley Cavell has called (in writing about Kripke on rules) "philosophy's drastic desire to underestimate or to evade the ordinary."[3] Not that there need be anything un-ordinary about fixing a standard of length more precisely; what, in particular, indicates the philosophical move away from the ordinary is the willingness simply to ignore the connection between having a standard of length and having a way of telling how long things are (the willingness to ignore the connection with criteria which 'articulate the ordinary'— see the quotation from Cavell in note 3).[4]

Anyway, Kripke now has a more precise definition: a meter is the length of stick S at t_0. Is it then, he asks, a necessary truth that S is one meter long at t_0? No, he says, because the person giving the definition may have as his intention the fixing of reference of the term "one meter." The person wants to refer to *a certain length*, which he picks out by an *accidental* property of stick S, the property of having that length at t_0. It is easy to see that the stick did not have to have that property; it might have been heated at t_0, and if it had it would have been longer: it would not in those conditions have had the length it had in the actual conditions. That S was *that* long at t_0 is certainly not necessary. So, if we pick out a particular length by saying that it is the length that S had at t_0, and if we say that a meter is by definition *that length*, then (this is Kripke's argument) it is not a necessary truth that S is a meter long, because it is not necessary that it had, at t_0, *that length*, the length we are referring to henceforward as "one meter" (p. 274).

(Here is another way of making Kripke's point. Suppose that S had been heated at t_0, and that we had defined the length *one meter* as the length that it had then. The result would be that we would have had a somewhat *greater length* as our standard meter. So although we would still have *said* that the length of S at t_0 was the standard meter length,

---

[3] Cavell, "The Argument of the Ordinary," in *Conditions Handsome and Unhandsome* (Chicago: University of Chicago Press, 1990), p. 68. The sentence from which the quoted phrase comes is: "I will simply say, starting out, that Kripke's account, in drastically underestimating, or evading Wittgenstein's preoccupation with the ordinary (hence with 'our criteria,' which articulate the ordinary), evades Wittgenstein's preoccupation with philosophy's drastic desire to underestimate or to evade the ordinary."

[4] For Wittgenstein on some of the issues in this paragraph, see *Philosophical Investigations*, p. 225; also, *Remarks on the Philosophy of Psychology*, vol. 1, §§632 and 1109.

the length meant (referred to) by "one meter" would be a different and greater length.

Case 1. S is 39.37 inches long at t_0. We define "one meter" as its length at t_0.

Case 2. S is 40 inches long at t_0. We define "one meter" as its length at t_0.

If we define "one meter" by the length S has in the Case 1 scenario at t_0, then it is not a necessary truth that it has *that length*, since, in the Case 2 scenario, it has a different length.)

Kripke goes on (p. 275) to use the example to explain how he wants to distinguish between a priori statements and necessary ones. This is tied for him to the distinction between the epistemological status of a statement and its metaphysical status. If I fix the reference of the term "one meter" via the length which S has at t_0, then I can know the truth of "S is one meter long at t_0" a priori, "without further investigation," that is, without measuring it. But, as we have seen, S might perfectly well have had some other length at t_0; it might not have had *that* length which we defined as the meter length. So it is not necessary that S have been one meter long at t_0, any more than it is necessary that S have been 39.37 inches long at t_0. Of *no* length is it necessary that S have been *that* long at t_0.

There are connections between defining a standard of length (something that is a measure of length) and having rules determining how length is measured. It would be possible to examine the relation between Kripke on the standard meter and Kripke on Wittgenstein on rules by starting with the implications of Kripke's treatment of the standard meter for the question what it is for something to be a measure, and how that does or doesn't involve rules. But I take an alternative route; and I shall not reach until Part 7 Kripke's treatment of rules and of Wittgenstein on rules.

2. WITTGENSTEIN ON THE LENGTH OF THE STANDARD METER: CONTEXT AND CONNECTIONS

One thing that may strike us, reading Kripke on Wittgenstein on the standard meter, is the contrast with his treatment of Wittgenstein on rules. Whatever one thinks of his interpretation of Wittgenstein on rules, Kripke clearly spent much time thinking about it and discussing it; whereas in the case of Wittgenstein on the meter rod, he appears to have taken Wittgenstein's view to be not worth pondering—it is simply something Wittgenstein got wrong; it is useful merely as an example, and there is no suggestion that Kripke spent any time thinking about what was going on in the passage which he quotes and criticizes.[5]

In fact a great deal is going on in that passage. It is part of Wittgenstein's extended discussion of philosophical ideas about names: names of simple elements, such that *what is the case* is the combination of such elements. So language *describes* what is the case by compounds of the simple names. What the names supposedly name is things, then, that cannot be said either to *be* or not to *be*. Wittgenstein's argument in this extended passage is that that conception, which he utilized in the *Tractatus*, is the result of misunderstanding the role of samples in our language-game.

The passage has connections with other important ideas in Wittgenstein's early and later work. At its heart is the analogy between describing something and *measuring*; and the use of measurement analogies runs through Wittgenstein's thought from the *Tractatus* onward.[6] In the English translation of the passage, another connection emerges, between measures and rules. The Latin word *regula*, which gives us "rule," has a group of earlier concrete meanings: a ruler for drawing lines, a footrule for measuring; in Latin and Italian also a pattern, a model, a sample or example. So the notion of a measure, the tool for measuring, the *sample* meter, connects with a whole group of central ideas in Wittgenstein's philosophy. In lectures Wittgenstein made explicit connections between the use of rules and the use of measuring rods;[7] I will get back to these in Part 6.

---

[5] I have quoted Kripke's remark that Wittgenstein simply got things wrong in §50; and it is clear that Kripke reads both the sentences about the standard meter, quoted above, to express Wittgenstein's own view; that is, Kripke does not take either or both of them to be spoken by an 'interlocutor', whose views Wittgenstein would take to be subject to criticism. Heather Gert interprets *PI* §50 so that it is not Wittgenstein's own view that the standard meter cannot be said to be either one meter long or not one meter long. See her "The Standard Meter by Any Name Is Still a Meter Long," forthcoming in *Philosophy and Phenomenological Research*. In what follows I focus on what Wittgenstein took to be the role of the meter rod in measuring; what ways of speaking of that role may show confusion will emerge in the discussion.

[6] For an important passage from the years between the *Tractatus* and the *Investigations*, see *Philosophical Remarks*, p. 72, in which the application of language to reality is metaphorically expressed as the application of a yardstick to what is measured by it: Wittgenstein speaks of the application of the yardstick of language.

[7] *Wittgenstein's Lectures on the Foundations of Mathematics, Cambridge, 1939*, ed. Cora Diamond (Ithaca, N.Y.: Cornell University Press, 1976), pp. 104–6; cf. also other references to putting a calculation into the archives in Paris, pp. 112, 114.

The topics of *PI* §50 had been important for Wittgenstein from the early 1930s onward. An earlier discussion in which connections with Kripke's ideas can be seen is in *Philosophical Remarks* (p. 72), in a passage immediately after the passage quoted in note 6, where the application of a yardstick to an object is treated as an analogy for the application of language to the world. He says there that what he once called "objects," simples, were simply what could be referred to without any risk of their possible non-existence. With that conception in view, he asks:

What if someone said to me "I expect three knocks on the door" and I replied "How do you know that there *is: three knocks*?"—Wouldn't that be just like the question "How do you know there is: six feet?" after someone has said "I believe A is 6 feet tall"?[8]

Here we see the idea that, if we can speak truly or falsely of A's being 6 feet tall, there must be the length to which we refer, the length which coincides with A's height or fails to do so. An object which is actually used as a measure can exist or not exist, and so it may seem as if, in measuring, we are comparing the measured object with the actual measuring rod only as a way of comparing with a *length*. The actual rod, we may think, has a particular length, and it is that length which is the real measure.[9]

Immediately after the sentences in §50 which Kripke criticizes, Wittgenstein makes a further comparison, between having a standard meter in Paris, and having a standard in Paris fixing the color *sepia*. "Sepia" will mean the color of the hermetically sealed sample in Paris; and Wittgenstein says that it will make no sense to say of the sample that it has that color or that it hasn't. Kripke would presumably also take Wittgenstein to be wrong about this. He might express disagreement by saying that the sample in Paris has a particular color. It is a plain contingent fact about that piece of dyed cloth (or whatever it is) that it has that particular color. So, if that color is now to be called *sepia*, then surely it is a contingent fact that the sample itself is sepia.

A crucial part of the argument that I have put into Kripke's mouth is

---

[8] The published English translation uses the plural verb "exist" with "three knocks" and with "six feet." To say that six feet exist is to say that there are six feet, but the question with which Wittgenstein is concerned is not whether there are six feet, but whether there is *the length* six feet. In the German version of the question, what is asked is whether *six foot* exists, a form like that in which we speak of a six-foot length. I am grateful to James Conant for help with the translation here.

[9] I am grateful to Thomas Ricketts for critical discussion of the issue of how Kripke's views are related to those with which Wittgenstein is concerned in *PI* §50.

the claim that *the sample has a particular color;*[10] and that sort of claim gets a great deal of attention from Wittgenstein in the 1930s, especially in Part II of the *Brown Book*. I have included in an Appendix to this section some material from the *Brown Book* discussion of sentences in which we say that something *has a particular such-and-such.*[11] Wittgenstein draws attention there to a contrast between two uses such sentences can have, which I shall illustrate here by a pair of examples, not Wittgenstein's.

"This rod has a particular length, namely 39.37 inches."

"This rod has a particular length," said, for example, when one is concentrating on the thing's length, and not going on to specify the length or to compare it in length with anything else.

The first sentence goes on from "This rod has a particular length," to specify the length, to describe the rod by relating it to *something else*; and Wittgenstein calls that sort of use of such sentences the transitive use. The contrast is with saying such things as "This rod has a particular length" while attending to the thing's own length, without any further specification or comparison. That use of "has a particular such-and-such" Wittgenstein calls intransitive. In this second case, though, we may seem to ourselves to be comparing the length of the rod with a prototype, but, if we were to point to anything to explain what length we meant when we said it had a particular length, we would point to the rod itself. Wittgenstein is concerned with the potentiality for philosophical confusion in the latter sort of case; the potentiality for confusion when we treat the concentrating-your-attention use of "It has a particular such-and-such" as a special reflexive case of the transitive use. (See, for example, his discussion, quoted in the Appendix below, of contemplating a drawing of a face, and saying of it: "It has a particular expression," thinking of the expression as something distinct from the face, as though having got hold of the expression that the face has were getting hold of the prototype to which the drawn face corresponds.) The issues with which he is concerned in these *Brown Book* discussions can be traced back into the *Tractatus*, where he discusses the nonsense-sentence "Socrates is identical" (5.473, 5.4733). He doesn't say why he

[10] Although I have put these words into Kripke's mouth, they run very close to his use of "a certain length" in connection with the standard meter.
[11] In the parallel material in *Eine Philosophische Betrachtung*, ed. Rush Rhees, in *Schriften*, vol. 5 (Frankfurt am Main: Suhrkamp, 1970), Wittgenstein uses the words "besonder" and "bestimmt" virtually interchangeably, e.g. in speaking of the idea that the name of a color comes in a particular way, on pp. 231–2.

chooses that example of nonsense; the example is meant to bear on the philosophical confusion of treating self-identity as a property things have. The word "identical" has two uses parallel to the two uses of expressions like "has a particular such-and-such." Identification of a thing can be expressed in a sentence of the form "A is identical with B," where two different expressions replace "A" and "B," and we could call these identity statements transitive. We can, however, also concentrate our attention on a thing, and we might then want to say that it is identical with something, namely itself, and this is one source of the idea of self-identity as a property everything has. That idea is treated in the *Tractatus* as a kind of delusion; the implied diagnosis of the delusion is parallel to the diagnosis given in the *Brown Book* of cases in which we take ourselves to be making a kind of comparison between a thing and something about it which we explain by pointing to the thing itself, that is, in which an 'intransitive' use is taken to be a reflexive case of the transitive use. (The connection between the *Brown Book* discussion and the *Tractatus* view of identity surfaces in *PI* §216.) There is a further important connection in the *Brown Book* between the cases discussed there and misunderstandings about names and reference, in particular with the idea that we can concentrate on something and give it a name, without at the same time committing ourselves in any way about the use of the name.

I return to these issues in Part 5; I have wanted here only to bring out that Wittgenstein's remarks about the standard meter are tied to a range of subjects which are central for his thought.

Appendix to Part 2

From *Brown Book*, p. 158:

The troubles which we have been turning over since §7 were all closely connected with the use of the word "particular". We have been inclined to say that seeing familiar objects we have a particular feeling, that the word "red" came in a particular way when we recognized the colour as red, that we had a particular experience when we acted voluntarily.

Now the use of the word "particular" is apt to produce a kind of delusion and roughly speaking this delusion is produced by the double usage of this word. On the one hand, we may say, it is used preliminary to a specification, description, comparison; on the other hand, as what one might describe as an emphasis. The first usage I shall call the transitive one, the second the intransitive one.

The contrast Wittgenstein means comes out sharply, he says, if we consider "peculiar" instead of "particular"; and he explains the contrast with examples that are not connected to philosophical problems. Thus an example of the 'transitive' use of "peculiar" would be "This soap has a peculiar smell—the smell of ground-ivy leaves"; an example of the 'intransitive' use would be "This soap has a quite peculiar smell." In this second case, "peculiar" is not used to introduce a comparison but more or less like "striking" or "out of the ordinary."

The first paragraph below is a condensed version of an example meant to lead into the discussion of how intransitive uses of "particular" are connected with philosophical problems. (The last three-quarters of the paragraph are directly quoted, as are the following two paragraphs. All the material is from pp. 160–1.)[12]

If I say "I have noticed that A comes into the room in a particular way," I might, if asked, specify the way: "He always sticks his head into the room before coming in." [That would be an example of the 'transitive use' of "a particular way."] But suppose I have been observing A as he sits smoking; I want to draw him like this. I am contemplating, studying, his attitude; and as I contemplate it, I might be inclined to say and repeat to myself "He has a particular way of sitting." But the answer to the question "What way?" would be "Well, *this* way," and perhaps one would give it by drawing the characteristic outlines of his attitude. On the other hand, my phrase "He has a particular way . . .," might just have to be translated into "I'm contemplating his attitude." Putting it in this form we have, as it were, straightened out the proposition; whereas in its first form its meaning seems to describe a loop, that is to say, the word "particular" here seems to be used transitively and, more particularly, reflexively, i.e., we are regarding its use as a special case of the transitive use. We are inclined to answer the question "What way do you mean?" by "*This* way," instead of answering: "I didn't refer to any particular feature; I was just contemplating his position." My expression made it appear as though I was pointing out something *about* his way of sitting . . . whereas what makes me use the word "particular" here is that by my attitude towards the phenomenon I am laying an emphasis on it: I am concentrating on it, or retracing it in my mind, or drawing it, etc.

Now this is a characteristic situation to find ourselves in when thinking about philosophical problems. There are many troubles which arise in this way, that a word has a transitive and an intransitive use, and that we regard the latter as a particular case of the former, explaining the word when it is used intransitively by a reflexive construction.

Thus we say, "By 'kilogram' I mean the weight of one litre of water," "By 'A' I mean 'B'," where B is an explanation of A. But there is also the intransitive use: "I said that I was sick of it and meant it." Here again, meaning what you said could be called "retracing it," "laying an emphasis on it." But using

---

[12] I have corrected what appears to be the wrong placing of one pair of quotation marks in the third paragraph.

the word "meaning" in this sentence makes it appear that it must have sense to ask "*What* did you mean?" and to answer "By what I said I meant what I said," treating the case of "I mean what I say" as a special case of "By saying 'A' I mean 'B'" . . . Suppose to the question "What's a kilogram?" I answered, "It is what a litre of water weighs," and someone asked, "Well, what does a litre of water weigh?"

Wittgenstein goes on (§16, p. 162) to discuss the case of a face-drawing, of which we might want to say, as we take in the expression, that "It has a particular expression," but if we were to point to anything to explain what expression we meant, it would be to the drawing itself. "We are . . . under an optical delusion which by some sort of reflection makes us think that there are two objects where there is only one . . . [T]he phrase 'getting hold of the expression of this face' suggests that we are getting hold of a thing which is *in* the face and different from it."

In §15, in connection with the inclination to say that the word "red" came in a particular way when one answered the question "What color is the book there?" by saying "Red," Wittgenstein speaks about the feeling that one could give this way in which the word comes a name, if it hasn't already got one. In the kind of case with which he is concerned, we feel as though we could give a name to the thing on which we are focusing when we say "He has a particular way of sitting," or "The word comes in a particular way," "without at the same time committing ourselves about its use, and in fact without any intention to use it at all" (p. 159).

3. MALCOLM ON KRIPKE ON WITTGENSTEIN AND THE STANDARD METER

Norman Malcolm has criticized Kripke's remarks about Wittgenstein and the standard meter.[13] Although he treats Kripke with respect, nothing in Malcolm resonates with Kripke's views, and the result, I think, is that his treatment is unhelpful. But it may be illuminating to see *why* it doesn't work.

Malcolm begins by explicating Wittgenstein's remark about the standard meter in Paris not being sayably either a meter long or not a meter

---

[13] "Kripke and the Standard Meter," in Norman Malcolm, *Wittgensteinian Themes: Essays 1978–1989*, ed. G. H. Von Wright (Ithaca, N.Y.: Cornell University Press, 1995). Page number references are given in the text.

long. He fills in a possible background to the establishing of the meter standard; then he says that what Wittgenstein meant by the remark about the standard meter is that one cannot say that the standard meter has been *determined by measurement* to be one meter long (p. 58). Well, for sure this is not what Kripke takes Wittgenstein to mean, since Kripke's argument against Wittgenstein essentially depends only on the rod's having a definite length. We refer to that length by the expression "one meter," and the rod can be known to be one meter long *without* measurement, without investigation. (Kripke does refer to the possibility of measuring the meter rod in inches. But his point there is not that we need to measure the rod to determine that it is one meter long. It is rather that, given that we clearly can measure the rod in inches, and that we have previously established a conversion of 39.37 inches to the meter, why can we not say of a rod which is 39.37 inches long that it is one meter long?) Kripke is not denying what Malcolm puts into Wittgenstein's mouth, that the length of the meter rod is not established by measurement. Malcolm's reading of Wittgenstein makes the passage much more verificationist in character than it is; but Kripke is correct in not reading the Wittgenstein passage in a verificationist way. In fact, Wittgenstein's remarks engage much more closely with Kripke's conception than they would on a verificationist reading. Kripke's conception of the meter rod as being one meter long depends upon there being lengths, including the length which we refer to by the term "one meter," which, on his view, can be known a priori to be the length of the rod at t_0. Kripke's idea, if we put it into Wittgenstein's language, is that the 'yardstick of language' laid up against the world gives a *fit* between the expression "one meter" (taken with the referential relation to a definite length, established for it) and the meter rod, a fit which is not determined by any empirical measurement. Such a conception of the 'yardstick of language' takes the capacity of the yardstick to measure to lie in the referential relations of its terms to such non-empirical objects as lengths. Kripke's idea that the rod has some definite length, a length to which we refer through the rod's having it, but which is only accidentally exemplified by this rod, has complex connections to the ideas with which Wittgenstein is concerned in the passages quoted from *Philosophical Investigations* and *Philosophical Remarks*.

After Malcolm explains Wittgenstein's remarks about the meter rod, he turns to direct criticism of Kripke's idea that the definition of the meter length as the length of the rod in Paris *fixes the reference* of the expression "one meter," makes it refer to *a certain length*, the length which Kripke says it is not necessary that the rod in Paris has. If the people fixing the meter standard had had in mind some particular length *before* they decided to use the particular rod which they fixed on as a standard, and if they chose that particular rod because it had the particular length which they already had in mind, then, Malcolm says, it would make sense to say that these people establishing the standard wanted to mark out a certain length and picked a rod accordingly.[14] But if they did not already have in mind *any* particular length, and, as we can imagine, simply picked out at random a stick S from a heap of sticks of different lengths, and stipulated that *one meter* was by definition the length of S, then it cannot be said that the definers wanted to mark out *a certain length*. *Whatever* length S had, that would be established as one meter; and, that being so, Malcolm concludes, there is nothing contingent about S being one meter long. The only contingency around would be the contingency of the use of S as opposed to some other stick (pp. 59–60).

Malcolm rejects Kripke's claim that, in defining the meter length, we are *fixing the reference* of the expression "one meter." He finds this way of talking obscure, but would have no serious objection to it if, by *fixing the reference of "one meter"* were meant only fixing it that "one meter" is to mean the length of S; what he rejects is the idea that, by the definition, the words "one meter" come to have as their reference an object, *a certain length*, a length which S contingently has. He has two objections to that idea.

First, he objects to talking of "one meter" as referring to or naming or designating *an object* (p. 63).[15] The second and more worked-out objection is that, if we were to go along with Kripke in this way of talking, the 'object' referred to by "one meter" would simply be *whatever*

---

[14] The case of the previously fixed-on length is somewhat closer to the original 1799 proceedings than is the case, central for Wittgenstein, Kripke, and Malcolm, in which no previously fixed-on length is used in picking a rod to keep as a standard. The latter sort of case does approximate to the situation after the discovery that the length fixed on in 1799 had been miscalculated, and before the redefinition of the meter in 1960 using atomic theory. During Wittgenstein's life, the meter was not in fact defined by the length of a rod but by the distance between two scratches on a metal bar in Sèvres.

[15] It should be noted that this use of length expressions as designating objects can unobjectionably go with talking about lengths in this sort of way: "The length five yards is greater than the length four meters." This kind of non-temporal talk about lengths is alluded to by Wittgenstein in connection with comparable talk of colors. In addition to reporting on the colors of bodies, we can state the relationship of colors, as for example "Blue is darker than white." Wittgenstein says that that is a different language-game (*Remarks on Colour*, ed. G. E. M. Anscombe, trans. Linda L. McAlister and Margaret Schättle (Berkeley: University of California Press, 1984), p. 34). Malcolm's remarks, unlike Wittgenstein's, do suggest that non-temporal talk of the relation of lengths to each other or of colors to each other is inherently suspect. See also Wittgenstein's earlier treatment of this kind of case, which is closer to Malcolm's, in *Remarks on the Foundations of Mathematics*, original and revised editions, Part I, §105.

S's length is. The object has no identity independent of whatever S's length is. If S's length had been different, the standard length, one meter, would be *that* length. We then still have a coincidence between the length *one meter* and the length of S. There is no counterfactual situation in which the length *one meter* and the length of S come apart, since the identity of the length referred to depends on the length of S (pp. 63–4).[16] And Malcolm then returns to the idea that the only way to drive apart and treat as contingent the relation between the meter length and the length of S is by taking for granted a case in which the standard-setters have some specific length in mind *before* they pick on S to use as the standard.

The argument by Malcolm that there is no way to drive apart the length *one meter* and the length of S is a bad argument in the first place, and also makes it impossible for Malcolm to see clearly what understanding of the situation grips Kripke. In Part 4, I show what is the matter with Malcolm's argument.

4. HOW LONG MIGHT THE STANDARD METER HAVE BEEN?

Let us imagine that we do not yet measure things against any standard measure, but that we have a practice of comparison of lengths. We can say of A and B that A is longer than B, or shorter, or the same length. We can also imagine comparisons of length which we do not actually carry out. I might draw a picture of a comparison, perhaps of the height of two children, a comparison which I have not made but might go on to make. Or I might draw a picture of a comparison which I could have made but didn't, say a comparison of the height of Susan as she was two years ago with Robert as he was two years ago. My picture shows what it would have looked like if I had compared them.

I can also draw a picture of a comparison between Susan's height now and Susan's height as I imagine it will be in two years' time. I cannot actually put the Susans alongside each other, as they are in the picture, but I can draw them alongside each other. "You will be half a head

---

[16] Here Malcolm is rejecting the idea of "one meter" as what Kripke calls a rigid designator. My discussion of the dispute between Kripke and Malcolm does not depend on the introduction of that term. I return to questions about the metaphysical implications of the term in Part 9; my argument there reinforces my claim in Part 4 that Malcolm rejects too much of Kripke's account.

FIGURE 1

taller," I tell Susan as I show her the picture. I can also compare in imagination Susan's height as it is with Susan's height as it would have been if she had taken more vitamins. I can draw this comparison too; see Figure 1. She would have been taller if she had taken those vitamins. So it is contingent that she is the height she is; this says no more than we have already said.[17]

Suppose that we had agreed a year ago: whatever height Susan is a year from now, we shall define that as *one meter*. So we can add to our picture of Susan-compared-to-what-she-would-have-been-if-she-had-taken-her-vitamins an indication that Susan as she is defines our meter. But we can also go on and add more. In Figure 2 the present meter is drawn in and so also is what we would have called a meter if Susan had taken her vitamins and grown taller over the past year. We have drawn a situation in which, although Susan's height is what is called a meter in that situation, her height is greater than what we have in fact fixed on as a meter. This is meant to show what is wrong with Malcolm's

FIGURE 2

---

[17] The claim about contingency could be spelled out with scope indicators; I should say that that makes it no clearer than by using pictures.

argument that we cannot drive apart, even in a counterfactual situation, the length of S and the standard meter length. That argument rests on the false idea that we cannot describe the counterfactual situation in terms of our own meter length. The important point in the Susan example is that we can use Susan as she is and make a comparison between her and Susan as she would have been. We are not adding anything problematic if we go on to call her a measuring rod and if we measure with that measuring rod, in imagination, Susan as she would have been. Even if we imagine her to have been used also in that counterfactual situation as a measuring rod, we can still compare in imagination Susan as she is with Susan as she would have been, the measuring rod we have, compared in imagination with the measuring rod we would have had.[18] Malcolm rules out that kind of comparison, because he doesn't allow us to say that, if S had been heated at t_0, it would have been longer than one meter in length. It is, on his view, necessarily one meter in length; and this "necessarily" is the ruling out of the kind of comparison I have drawn. Malcolm is not simply trying to make the point that whatever length S is, or whatever height Susan is, we shall call that *one meter*. That it is not meant to be simply *that* point comes out in his remark that we cannot identify the object, the meter length, except via whatever length S has. But that is exactly what we can do in imagination; and here I am following Wittgenstein's advice to connect our use of "we can imagine it" with "we can draw it." (See e.g. *Blue Book*, p. 4.)

Malcolm's argument interferes with Kripke's doing something quite legitimate; it thus stops us from reaching the point at which he does something genuinely problematic.

5. COMPARING THE METER ROD WITH ITSELF

I have argued that there is nothing wrong with the last picture, in which we compare Susan's height in the counterfactual situation with Susan's height as it is. But now suppose we think along these lines. In the counterfactual situation, we have Susan as she would have been if she had taken her vitamins measured by our own standard of one meter: Susan as she is. In the actual situation, Susan herself could equally, we think, be compared with the length that we have fixed on as our measure: and

[18] Compare Kripke's discussion (p. 288) of the use of the distance between King Henry's fingertip and his nose to define the yard length. As Kripke notes, if certain accidents had befallen the king, the distance between his fingertip and his nose would have been rather shorter than one yard.

so we get the next picture, Figure 3 below. Here we are thinking of the difference between the counterfactual situation, on the right in Figure 3, and our actual situation, on the left, in terms of the different results we get in the two situations using Susan's actual height as our standard length. She *has* a certain height. The difference between the two situations is then that, using that height as our standard Susan-meter, she is (and could a priori be known to be) one standard Susan-meter in height in the actual case, while she is considerably taller than one meter in the counterfactual case.

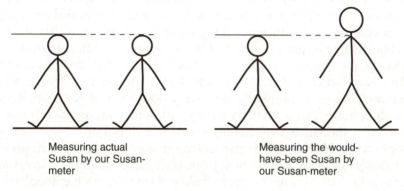

Measuring actual
Susan by our Susan-
meter

Measuring the would-
have-been Susan by
our Susan-meter

FIGURE 3

The picture we now have might not lead into any philosophical confusion: it might be merely a picturesque way of representing what the previous two pictures represent, namely that Susan (like other people) would have been bigger had she taken her vitamins. But the representation of Susan's actual situation could be misleading. It is an example of the kind of representation Wittgenstein speaks of as 'reflexive'. We are considering Susan's height, but not, in this picture, considering it in comparison with anything else; but we nevertheless regard this case as a special case of a comparison. We are not comparing her height with that of another child, or with what her height will be, or with what it might have been; we are, as it were, reading her height off her, and seeing her as fitting it: she is *just that height*. We compare her with her height; they fit exactly.

In *PI* §279 Wittgenstein says: "Imagine someone saying 'I do know how tall I am!' and showing it by laying his hand on top of his head!" The case is not changed if the person who says this also says that his height defines a new unit of length, the W, and that he is exactly one W tall. This match between him and the length one W is not the result of a comparison made within some practice of comparing the heights of people with that of other people and with other things. Kripke's idea of the a priori knowability of the statement that stick S is one meter long at t_0 is parallel to the a priori knowability of the boy's being one W tall, and that case is like the absurd case of laying one's hand on top of one's head to give one's height.

We have arrived by a roundabout route at something not very far from the point Malcolm made right at the beginning of his discussion. Malcolm says that Wittgenstein's claim that the meter rod cannot be said to be one meter long or not one meter long means that it has no length *determined by measurement*. And the point we have reached is that there is a difference between using Susan's height in real and imagined comparisons with other things, and saying of Susan that she has 'some definite height', thinking of her as compared with, and matching exactly, the height which we have read off her, that 'definite height'. This is a non-comparison represented as a comparison. "How tall is Susan?" is here answered by laying a hand on top of her head. There needn't, however, be anything wrong with representing a non-comparison as a special case of a comparison; if it does lead to some philosophical problem it will be particularly important not to try to get rid of the problem by simply ruling out such representations. Here I am criticizing Malcolm for failing to follow Wittgenstein's methodological precept that one has to untie a philosophical knot by philosophy which is as complicated as the knot it is trying to undo. (What I have tried to do is to show the 'disguised nonsense' of Kripke's remarks about the a priori knowability of the length of stick S at t_0 by connecting those remarks with the patent nonsense of the boy's idea that he can show you how tall he is by laying his hand on his head; see *PI* §§464 and 524. Kripke's remarks are in fact somewhat more hedged than the boy's: in the first place he says only that *there is a sense* in which we can speak of the a priori knowability of the rod's being one meter long, and in the second place he denies that a claim to know that the rod is one meter long is a claim to have got hold of a piece of contingent information, even though on his own view it is contingent that the rod is one meter long at t_0; see pp. 275, 346–7. I do not think that these hedgings affect the issues here.)

The argument I have given does not imply that there is any kind of problem in describing a case in which the meter rod has changed its length.[19] We can easily imagine a situation in which we wake up one morning and find that the rod that we have been using as a standard

---

[19] The discussion of this case, and of the issues in the next paragraph, owes much to questions asked by Gary Ebbs and Gary Hatfield.

appears to have become longer or shorter. Even if we had defined "one meter" as the length of that rod, we might now say that the rod was not a meter long, and so in the imagined case we have separated the length of the rod from the length 'one meter'. We can indeed make comparisons between the length of any rod, including our standard, and the length of the same rod as we remember it to have been the day before; making the rod into our standard hardly precludes such comparisons. Or, again, we can use our knowledge of natural laws to infer that, the temperature having changed by so much, the rod we were using as our standard has expanded to such-and-such degree; or our evidence may let us determine that it has not changed. The account which I have given of confusions that may be reflected in talk of a rod's having a particular length doesn't imply that our treatment of our standards of measurement cannot take seriously possible changes in the length of the standard itself. We may or may not need to control carefully for such changes, depending on the purposes for which we measure. (There is, however, nothing in principle the matter with having a standard that varies somewhat in length, or with having in circulation many standards, of somewhat various lengths; indeed, things were somewhat like that when the human foot was used as a measure, and what was roughly as long as a man's foot could be called a foot long. The purposes for which measuring is used may not make it worth bothering with to have some way of settling apparent discrepancies.)

When we control for changes in the length of the standard, we make use of physical laws which provide us with conditions in which such-and-such physical properties of such-and-such objects are constant; and such constancies may be used directly to define a standard of measurement, instead of being used simply to enable us to fix conditions in which some standard object itself will remain unchanged. The physical laws, together with other natural laws, give us reproducible procedures the results of which will always be the same (unless, of course, they are not, because, e.g., we have failed to control something we thought we were controlling). We can express the relevant constancies by saying such things as "There is a certain length, which is the wave length of so-and-so, under such-and-such conditions," but the expression "a certain length," if used in expressing a constancy or functional relation which is taken as the basis of our system of measurements, is thereby being given a reflexive, not a transitive, use. Physics gives us constancies; whether our descriptions of these use "a particular length," "a particular weight," or related sorts of phrase in a transitive or in a reflexive way isn't for *physics* to say. Our ways of thinking about physical constancies may, though, make it natural for us to read an intransitive use as if it were a special case of a transitive use. On the case of standards defined directly through physical constancies, see Wittgenstein's remarks on the definition of the kilogram, quoted in the Appendix to Part 2 above. When Wittgenstein asks us to imagine the question "Well, what does a liter of water weigh?" as a response to "A kilogram is the weight of a liter of water," he means to draw to our attention that, if one were to say that a liter of water in such-and-such conditions always has a particular weight, the statement would be grammatically unlike "There is a particular weight that all the tomatoes from this plant have when they are ripe." "Particular" in the latter case is transitive; but the question how much a liter of water weighs brings out that, in the sort of context Wittgenstein was considering, "There is a particular weight that a liter of water always has" contains an intransitive use of "particular." The point here is not that there is some kind of rule that you can't say that what a liter of water weighs is a kilogram; it is rather to make clear what you are doing if you do say that. The possibilities for philosophical confusion are at least as great in the case of theory-based definitions of standard units of measurement as they are in that of definitions using a standard object like the rod in Paris. More would need to be said about these matters if my topic were measurement, but it is the relation between Kripke's views and Wittgenstein's, and Kripke himself focuses on the kind of case in which a single standard object like the meter rod is used to fix the unit of length. It should, however, be clear that the issue of the different ways of using "particular" does not arise simply because of the kind of case that Kripke himself discusses.

I began my criticism of Malcolm in Part 4 by imagining a practice of comparing the height of people with each other and with other things. In the background here is our actual practice, in which we learn such things as that one mustn't stand on tiptoe when being compared in height with someone else, in which we learn that a ruler placed flat on the head of someone to compare that person's height with that of someone else must go parallel to the floor, in which we put the two people back to back, and so on. In the example I used, we gradually detach our idea of measuring height from that background of practice; we reach a point at which we think of Susan simply as 'having a certain height', and we begin to think of this as a matter of her fitting that height which we have read off her. This picture can lead into philosophical confusion through its seeming to illustrate a kind of measurement which is totally independent of the whole business of actually putting objects alongside each other, reading properly off instruments, and so on. It can begin to seem as if what we are doing if we do use Susan as a measuring rod is really comparing other objects, not with Susan (who is after all pretty continuously changing in height, and who sometimes stands up tall and sometimes slouches), but with that length which she herself fitted at the time we fixed our standard. And when we consider, not the Susan-meter, but the meter defined in terms of the wavelength of the light given off by krypton in certain conditions, or some other such physical constancy, the idea of the unit of measurement as detachable from our actual modes of comparison of objects to each other may be far more compelling. This issue of detachment from the language-game is important; before returning to it I shall consider further Wittgenstein's use of the idea of keeping something in Paris.

6. WITTGENSTEIN AND THE ARCHIVES IN PARIS

In the section of *Philosophical Investigations* in which he mentions the standard meter rod in Paris, Wittgenstein also imagines a case in which we keep standard color-swatches, like the standard sepia, in Paris too. This idea of 'keeping a standard in the archives in Paris' he gives a further extended use in his lectures on the foundations of mathematics. What we will keep in the archives in Paris will be whatever exactly turns out to be necessary for us to use in some language-game if some range of comparisons is to be made in that game. Thus, let us say that people reporting on colors are uncertain quite how close a match to the sample in Paris is necessary if they are to describe something as sepia. It might then be useful for them to have also a group of sepia-like shades kept in the archive with the standard sepia; these shades are sorted into sepia and non-sepia, so the shade-samples, with their labels, make plain how far from the standard sepia a color can be and still be called sepia. (Compare Quine on the use of 'foils' in comparisons: things "that deviate just barely too much to be counted" as belonging to the kind in question.)[20] But a language-game with color-reports and requests for objects of a certain color and so on might in fact be played without a degree-of-match guide. When Wittgenstein explains his ideas about 'keeping something in the archives' in his lectures, he notes that, if we settle on a particular rod as a standard of length and put it into the archives, we might still be unclear how to make comparisons with the rod, and so we might want to deposit in the archives also a

[20] W. V. Quine, "Natural Kinds," in Stephen P. Schwartz, ed., *Naming, Necessity, and Natural Kinds* (Ithaca, N.Y.: Cornell University Press, 1977), p. 159. (First published in Nicholas Rescher et al., eds., *Essays in Honor of Carl G. Hempel* (Dordrecht: Kluwer, 1969).)

description or picture of the method of use of the standard rod. The picture might be of one or two examples of uses of the rod. That might be all we needed in order to go on with the language-game.

The notion of 'depositing something in the archives', depositing it among the samples or paradigms with which comparison is made, is important for Wittgenstein's philosophy of mathematics, for his treatment of the character of mathematics (and its relation to logic), and in particular for his treatment of calculation and of proof. A calculation is something we could lay down in the archive of measurements as a standard of comparison, something by which we can describe what actually happens in an experiment; a proof also is described by Wittgenstein as something that can be laid down among the paradigms of language, the samples used in making comparisons.[21] In *Lectures on the Foundations of Mathematics*, Wittgenstein's extended discussion of the idea of the archives (pp. 105–6) focuses on the establishing of rules of multiplication. He develops an analogy between such rules and standards of measurement like the meter rod. We could, he suggests, take a calculation, say the multiplication of 465 by 159, and put that in the archives in Paris. *This* is to be the standard for multiplication: "Do it like this."

Turing raised an objection to Wittgenstein's idea: the trouble, he said, is that you cannot put *all* multiplications into the archive but only a finite number of them. So what if I do a multiplication not in the archive?

Wittgenstein emphasized in his reply that the number of multiplications being infinite is entirely irrelevant to the way things in the archive establish what we are to do. Suppose there were people who only ever multiplied up to three-digit numbers, and whose entire set of multiplications, up to 999 times 999, were in the archives. There might nevertheless be some problem for them how this table was to be applied in particular cases. Having *all* the multiplications in the archives might for them not be enough to enable them to go on. Conversely, having only one or two might be perfectly enough. In our own case, we might simply put into the archives the multiplication table or a single sample multiplication—and that might be enough, "if everyone knew from it how to multiply in other cases." So an important part of Wittgenstein's reply to Turing is that what we need to have in the archives is whatever in our practice can be used as a standard without trouble. A single example can be the standard we need for an unlimitedly large number of multiplications.

---

[21] See *LFM*, pp. 104–14, and *RFM*, orig. edn., Part I, §§32, 164; much of the rest of Part I is relevant.

Wittgenstein conceives of the archives in Paris as a storehouse of instruments used in various language-games. Just as a meter rod made of platinum and iridium and kept near Paris was in 1939 an instrument used in measurement, so multiplication tables are instruments used in a great variety of linguistic activities. These are instruments with which comparison is made, which we are trained to use; we *do* pick up the training and use them as standards, without trouble, in a vast number of cases. So, for example, if people with appropriate training can tell how to construct their own one-meter samples if they are given a statement defining the meter in terms of such-and-such physical constancy, and if people who use the samples thus constructed get on fine and don't run into discrepancies, we might put a statement of the definition and a physics textbook into the archives, just as we might have in the archives a multiplication table.[22]

Let us now go back to Kripke and to the move he makes early in his discussion of the standard meter, shifting from its definition via the length of S to its definition via the length of S at a particular time.

7. KRIPKE, MEASURES, AND RULES

As I mentioned in Part 1, Kripke's discussion of the more precise definition of the meter, in terms of the length of a stick at a particular time, abstracts entirely from the actual use of the newly defined meter length in measuring things. It is plain that, if this new definition is to be applied in actual measurements, we shall use the stick in question plus some formula for calculating its difference from the length it was at t_0. This matter isn't in view at all in Kripke's discussion as something

---

[22] I have heard it argued that the difference between the definition of the meter using a stick and the case of a definition using atomic theory is that in one case what we are comparing with when we measure things is a stick and in the other case we are genuinely comparing with a length, the length to which we have access through the theory-based definition. In the latter case, or so it is argued, reference to *a certain length* is not introduced merely through a philosophical gloss. A full discussion of this argument would be beyond the scope of this essay; but here I want only to note that the discussion might involve drawing attention to the multiplicity of kinds of linguistic instruments that we may put into the archives, including not only sticks and multiplication tables, but statements like "A meter is by definition so-and-so many times the length of such-and-such under such-and-so conditions." The ideas we have of referential connections to a thing (to 'a length') abstract from the uses to which we are in fact able to put the instruments in the archives; and some of the discussion here would parallel points made in Part 7, in connection with Kripke's account of the definition of the meter in terms of the length of a stick at a particular time, which also abstracts from the application of the standard.

relevant to the definition being a definition of length. Kripke's idea is that, in virtue of the definition, we have fixed on a particular length, which is therefore in definite relations to the lengths of whatever objects we might wish to measure. How we actually go about discovering the relation between the fixed-on length and actual objects is not relevant to our having fixed on the length, not relevant to our being able to refer to it. (Kripke's argument about reference is tied to his conception of the separability of metaphysics and epistemology, to which I shall return.) The length of the rod is intrinsically, in being a particular length, already a measure, already capable of being compared with measurable objects, including stick S at t_0. So now we are back with the case we were considering in Part 5, the meter rod compared with itself. When we think of the case in which the rod is not actually being compared with anything *else* as a special reflexive case of a comparison, when we think of it as compared with the length which we read off it, we are taking it that the capacity of *that length* to *be* a measure is independent of any actual activity of measuring things using sticks or whatnot. The idea of our having reached a particular length with our words "one meter" is the idea of *what* we have named as having internal to it the possibility of use as measure. What it is for a thing to be or not to be that length is fixed by the length itself. (Malcolm was indeed objecting to this conception when he insisted that the length *one meter* has no identity distinct from that of the length of the stick S at t_0, but I hope to have shown that his argument fails as an argument and doesn't reach to the source of the problem.) What gives strength to the idea that the essential thing in measuring is the comparison with a definite length, conceived as 'fitting' the stick used in measuring, is that the stick itself is just a piece of wood or metal; we might say of it, Wittgenstein notes, that in itself it is dead; *it* cannot say that the body measured is of such-and-such length (*PI* §430). The stick appears as a mere means through which we reach something that is intrinsically a measure. And so, in our philosophical view of the workings of the language of measurement, what appears central is establishing the referential connection to the 'definite length'; the actual practice of using words and sticks of wood or metal rods in measuring things disappears from view.

Wittgenstein's idea that we might want to say that the *stick* can't say that the body to be measured is of such-and-such length connects most directly not with Kripke on the meter rod, but with Kripke on rules. When Kripke discusses Wittgenstein on rules, he considers the example of doing the sum 68 + 57, which he imagines to be a sum which he was not explicitly taught, and which he has not done in his past arithmetical practice. The problem here, the problem to which Wittgenstein draws our attention, is, Kripke thinks, that in such a case there is *nothing that tells him* that the answer he should give to "How much is 68 + 57?" is 125 not 5.[23] This account of the problem shows that, as he is conceiving the situation, any table which he has used, any examples which he has worked over, are, as it were, *dead and inert*. They are silent; they don't tell him that 125 agrees with them, and that 5 is inconsistent with them. The Wittgensteinian paradox, as Kripke explains it, is essentially an elaboration of this 'inertness' of our examples and rule formulations (written, spoken, or in our minds). They can be interpreted in various ways; they cannot themselves tell us how to go on when we are confronted with 68 + 57.[24] They are (that is) like the meter rod, when it appears a mere dead piece of wood or metal, incapable itself of saying that a body is of such-and-such a length. When we consider the metal rod or piece of wood in abstraction from the context of the language-game, its only role appears to be that of allowing us to reach via our linguistic intentions *its length*, the particular length which it has, which is what will enable us to measure. And here we should think of Wittgenstein's description of the idea that, when a rule is communicated to another person by examples, the fundamental thing which is communicated is something *beyond* what is actually presented to the other person; any explanation given via examples or tables merely uses the examples or tables to enable the other person to reach the something else which is essential (*PI* §§209–10; *RFM*, 3rd edn., pp. 320–2).

Wittgenstein's image of the archives is meant to bring out that, although indeed no piece of wood or metal, no mathematical table or set of examples, looked at apart from practice, is as it were *a live measure*, we are as a matter of fact able to use pieces of wood or metal as standards of comparison, as measures; similarly, we can be shown examples of multiplication or addition and go on to compare *with them*, and to treat departures from them as *adding wrong*. There is such

---

[23] See esp. pp. 21–2.

[24] As Kripke's discussion on p. 52 makes clear, the issue as he sees it (and as he understands Wittgenstein's view of it) is not the finitude of the number of cases of addition; for even if I had given myself explicit instructions about the case of 68 + 57, there would remain a question as to what those instructions tell me to do *now*, now that I actually have to do the sum. And even if I played myself a little tape-recording of the instructions I earlier gave myself, the argument would be that the instructions don't say what it is to follow them. It becomes clear at this point that the complaint that nothing tells me what answer to give to "How much is 68 + 57?" is, in a sense, mis-stated. For the complaint is rather that whatever tells me what answer to give (and many things, like a tape-recording, might tell me) doesn't really tell me what answer to give. I have lost any hold I had on what I mean by "telling me what answer to give"; and it now appears very obscure what I mean by saying that the earlier addition sums I did, or the explicit formulations of a rule, do not tell me what to do now. I have no idea what it is that they don't do.

a thing as adding wrong, within the context in which we have no problems distinguishing what is in accord with the examples we have started from, or what is in accord with the tables, from what is inconsistent
with those examples or with the tables. The metaphor of placing those
sample calculations in the archives represents the fact that among us, in
our practice, these *do* to fix what is correct arithmetic and what is
incorrect, just as the platinum-iridium bar does (or did until 1960) to fix
measurement. In 1960 we needed something else for some highly specialized purposes. The archives represent the fact that what instruments
we need in a linguistic activity depends on all sorts of things in the circumstances of those engaging in the activity. The things in the archives
are then our live measures; they are there precisely because *they* are
what we need; we don't need something beyond them to tell us what is
in agreement with them and what is inconsistent with them. If in a particular case we did, we would put it into the archives.

The archives, then, provide a means of representing a fundamental
idea in Wittgenstein's later thought: that of 'rotating' our philosophical
examination, rotating it around the fixed point of our real need (*PI*
§108). We need, for example, to carry out multiplications and to distinguish doing them right from doing them wrong. What standard can we
use? What standard will, in our use of it, tell us "Do it so!" Kripke
works with the idea that we need something that is not silent, that will
tell us what to do; and he is right, we do. But we need then to be able
to turn our attention to the instruments of language that do tell us what
to do, in the sense in which the multiplication table which the child
copies and memorizes tells the child what to do when she is asked to do
a multiplication which perhaps she has never done before.

Several reviewers of Kripke's book mention his failure to see an
important feature of Wittgenstein's argument. When Wittgenstein
speaks about the 'paradox' that nothing appears to fix what is in accord
with a rule, he treats the *appearance* of paradox as the result of our
own philosophical misunderstandings. Warren Goldfarb puts the point
this way: the 'paradox-monger' is presented by Wittgenstein as someone who "has assumed some notion of accord with a rule, but has
divested it of the ways we go about taking things to be in accord or
not." *That's* what makes it possible for the paradox to appear.[25]

I have been arguing that a related kind of characterization applies
also to Kripke on the standard meter. If we ignore the fact that the standard meter, the metal rod in Paris, is there in the archives because it is

---

[25] Goldfarb, "Kripke on Wittgenstein on Rules," *Journal of Philosophy* 82 (1985):
471–88, at p. 488.

for us a useful instrument of language, an instrument of comparison, it may seem merely a stick by which we become able to denote a particular length, where *that length* is a measure both of the meter rod and of anything else we might wish to measure. That idea parallels closely Kripke's understanding of what following an arithmetical rule would be like if there were no Wittgensteinian paradox, what he thinks it does seem to us it is like, before we see the paradox. Just as the stick S supposedly puts us into a position to denote a particular length by the words "one meter," our practice with examples of addition-sums *we think* puts us into a position to denote by a word or symbol, say the plus sign, an *arithmetical function. That function* by its nature can stand as 'measure' of whatever I may go on to do in adding. If, when I am confronted with "68 + 57" I say "125," what I say, 'measured' by the function which I denote by the plus sign, is correct. The parallel between Kripke's understanding of measurement and his understanding of rules includes this further point: the standard meter in Paris, stick S, is itself thought of as compared with the length one meter: measured by that length, the stick (through which we came to be able to refer to the length) is one meter long; and similarly the original set of examples of addition sums, through which we came to be able to refer to the addition function, can be thought of as compared with the function. It provides the standard for judging them, as for judging any other putative addition; measured by it, they are correct additions.[26] The Wittgensteinian paradox then fits into this Kripkean scheme as essentially an interference with our capacity, the capacity we think we have, to connect with the function. The paradox makes clear that anything I attempt to use as a means to connect with some particular arithmetical function connects *as well* with an infinite number of other functions. The addition examples I use thus get me nowhere. If we step out of the Kripkean understanding and look at the situation as Wittgenstein does, the diagnosis will be that Kripke has given to the arithmetical examples the role which we give to the metal rod when we consider it abstracted from connection with our actual practice of measuring, and find it to be 'dead'.

[26] The parallel between the two cases is closer still. The definition of the standard meter, as Kripke understands it, connects "one meter" with a certain length, but it could equally be thought of, given his treatment, as connecting "one meter" with a particular function from any measurable item and time to a number, a function the value of which for S at t_0 is knowable a priori to be 1. Just as the addition function is (or is thought to be, prior to our grasp of the Wittgensteinian paradox) the standard for our additions, so the meter-length function is the standard for our actual measurings (unless we think that here too the Wittgensteinian paradox interferes). Cf. *Zettel*, §141 for some discussion of how the specification of a single standard length can be taken to fix a system of measurement in various ways.

The fundamental question, in Kripke's account of his own central example, is whether by the word "plus" he has meant the plus function. He had, supposedly, always thought he had meant plus by the word "plus," but the Wittgensteinian argument is then supposed to show that that is doubtful. But now what is this that he is supposed to have thought, before the paradox? We can here raise a question whether the sentence giving what he is supposed to have thought, "By the word 'plus' I meant the plus function," is what it looks as if it may be, namely a 'reflexive' use of a kind of sentence which has an unproblematic 'transitive' use. Sentences of the form "By 'A' I meant B," where the expression replacing "A" is different from that replacing "B," would be transitive uses of the kind of sentence in question. (See the Appendix to Part 2, above, for Wittgenstein's discussion of sentences of the form "By such-and-such I meant so-and-so.") One can frequently clear up an ambiguity in what one said by giving a different expression and saying that that is what one meant. We have seen that, in other cases of intransitive uses of sentences which have both transitive and intransitive uses, it is possible to slide into philosophical confusion by treating the intransitive cases as special reflexive cases of the transitive use. Or, at any rate, this is what Wittgenstein tried to show. We saw such a movement in connection with the case of the meter length. We moved there from cases in which we can say of a thing that it has a particular length, 1.3 meters, say, by comparing it with the rod in the archives, to the idea that the rod in the archives has a particular length; and we think of it as in a sense measurable by that length, its length. We read its length off it, and it and that length match. I tried earlier to show how the movement to the reflexive use is aided by thinking of the counterfactual case, in which we have a different instrument of measurement, alongside our actual case: the counterfactual Susan-measure and the actual Susan both thought of as measured by Susan's actual height. The same kind of movement to a reflexive use is involved in reaching Kripke's understanding of our supposed pre-paradox belief. Here too the movement to a reflexive use is aided by thinking of counterfactual cases. By the word "plus" we might indeed have meant something different from what we do mean, say minus; this counterfactual may help us move towards thinking of the statement that by "plus" I mean plus as both not necessary and as nevertheless a priori knowable. In the case of the word "plus," we have in the archives, we may suppose, some examples of additions, as, in the measurement case, we had a metal rod. The arithmetic examples are sample uses of expressions of the form "a plus b," as the rod was the sample for "one meter." In the reflexive treatment of the meter rod, we think of ourselves as denoting by "one meter" the length we have read off the measuring instrument itself; the instrument is, contingently it seems, that long. In the reflexive treatment of meaning, we take the function which we have read off the examples, we denote it by "plus," and we see the examples and the function as matching, as wouldn't be the case if we compare the function with examples we might have used to fix a different meaning for the word "plus."

Wittgenstein's slogan "Don't look for the meaning, look for the use" has various applications. One of them is in connection with the wish to make a reflexive use of the word "meaning." I might have meant something else; I do mean what I mean; at least I think I do before I hear from Kripke about Wittgenstein's paradox. As Kripke conceives the situation before we hear about the paradox, if we take ourselves to mean something by the word "plus," the important thing for us will be the connection with that which we mean, the particular function; the examples and training and practice with the word in a sense fall away except as the means through which the connection is established. So anything that seems to show that such a connection is *not* established is seen as profoundly paradoxical. On this view of what it is to mean something by one's words, any genuine 'straight' solution to the paradox would involve showing that, contrary to the kind of consideration adduced by the paradox-monger, we are able to establish a connection between our words or symbols and a particular function; we are able to denote a function, are able to mean plus by "plus." This is why Kripke thinks that, had Wittgenstein stated his views straightforwardly, it would have been clear that he was committed to a "sceptical denial of our ordinary assertions" about what we mean (pp. 69–70). (Here I should want to emphasize the point that the conditions for a 'straight' solution to the supposed paradox are given through a reflexive use of language. Kripke's description of *what Wittgenstein allegedly shows us that there isn't* is also given through a reflexive use of language. There is no fact of my, or anyone's, having meant plus by "plus.") For there to be a fact of our meaning addition by "plus" is for there to be a connection between our words and something capable of a normative or 'measuring' role, independently of any activity of ours. And that is entirely parallel to what Kripke himself takes for granted is available in his own treatment of the measuring rod and its length.

In much contemporary philosophy of language, 'reflexive' examples are treated as if they were not themselves possible indications of philosophical fishiness. By "Schnee," we say, the Germans mean snow, by "snow" we mean snow. A transitive use is put first to make our intransitive use appear like a special case of the transitive use. Or we have: "Schnee ist weiss" is true-in-German if and only if snow is white, and "Snow is white" is true-in-English if and only if snow is white. My argument in this part of the paper has been that we should bethink ourselves of the similarity between saying "I know what the sentence 'Snow is white' means, it means that snow is white" and saying "I know how tall I am, *this* tall!" while laying one's hand on one's head. The emphasis on "*this* tall" doesn't make the words and gesture give one's knowledge of one's height; mental concentration on white snow (or anything else) doesn't make the words "It means that snow is white" state something about meaning that one knows. My height can be used to give you someone else's height, an English sentence to give you the meaning of a German one, or of another English sentence, but repeating a sentence and taking its quotes off is putting your hand on your own head.

8. KRIPKE, WINCH, AND WITTGENSTEIN'S DEVIOUSNESS

This section is about Kripke's claim that Wittgenstein is not straightforward; if he were, it would be clear, Kripke argues, that he is committed to the impossibility of genuinely true attributions of meaning (pp. 69-78). Kripke's claim that Wittgenstein is really denying what we usually believe depends on the distinction between, on the one hand, what we are entitled to assert (entitled in some language-game to *call* true) and, on the other, what is true because it asserts that such-and-such fact obtains, and that fact does obtain. According to Kripke, Wittgenstein denies that the fact that would make our attributions of meaning true ever does obtain, but holds that we are nevertheless entitled in our language-games to make such attributions and indeed to speak of them as true (pp. 70-8, 86). In his criticism of Kripke on this matter, Peter Winch asks what we are to understand by a *genuine fact*, if not what is stated by a statement we take to be true. He says that Kripke gives no alternative acceptable explanation of what the genuine fact that supposedly isn't there would be.[27] My aim in this section is to show how Winch's objection would appear, from Kripke's point of view, to share the kind of deviousness that he sees in Wittgenstein's own approach. And so I must first show what sort of answer Kripke could take to be available to Winch's question as to what the genuine fact is supposed to be.

[27] "Facts and Superfacts," in his *Trying to Make Sense* (Oxford: Blackwell, 1987), p. 62.

I approach the issues here by turning again to the analogy with the case of the meter rod in Paris, thought of by Kripke as having a certain length, which we denote by the words "one meter," and which can be thought of as a measure of the rod itself at t_0. The analogy is then with the idea of the word "plus" as denoting, we think, a certain function, a function which stands as measure of any additions we may perform, including any examples which are in the archive. In both cases, what is taken to be the genuine 'measure' is conceived as something intrinsically capable of use as standard, independently of any proceedings in a language-game, and indeed as capable also of indicating what ways of playing any language-games of ours would be improvements on what we have been doing. There is a further point. If the arithmetical function, addition, is conceived in this way as measure of actual calculations, then the truth of statements about whether someone had intended to add, or had meant addition by the use of some sign, is itself properly tested or 'measured' by whether there was an intentional connection with the addition function. If the function is the measure of our additions, then the truth test, or 'measure', of the statement that someone *meant addition* is that there is intentional connection with that function.

Winch's question as to what we are to understand as a genuine fact, if not what is stated by a statement which we take to be true, is then apparently answerable from Kripke's point of view: a statement about someone's meaning addition might be assertible in a language-game, but what it states is understandable via the notion of the addition function as itself a non-arbitrary measure of additions, and as something which may or may not be what the person had specifically intended as measure. (Compare the case of measuring with the meter rod. On a Kripkean account of measuring, the intention to measure the length in meters of something is the intention to make a comparison with a certain length; hence there is no intention to measure unless the intention reaches to the particular length; hence any language-game of describing people as measuring either takes seriously the need to establish a connection with some definite length or ignores that need and simply sets up assertion conditions for ascription of measurement of length. Thus the activity I described in Part 5, in which "a foot long" has a use but does not refer to any one definite length, might be said to have mere assertion conditions for something's being a foot long, for, on this view, there is no fact of the matter of a thing's being a foot long, since no definite length is referred to by "one foot.") Kripke's conception of what it is for us to have a non-arbitrary standard against which to compare our additions is connected quite directly with precisely that distinction between assertion conditions and truth conditions that Winch questioned. If the samples and sticks and tables and formulae which we keep in the archives are conceived to be, not in themselves standards, but means by which we hope to be able to denote genuine standards, then Wittgenstein's approach will indeed appear to leave room for ascriptions of meaning to be assertible even when they are not true. Winch does indeed make clear that Kripke's distinction between assertion conditions and truth conditions is inseparable from Kripke's underlying philosophical views; my point here is that it has a direct connection with the 'reflexive' understanding of measurement which we see in Kripke's discussion of the standard meter.[28] (This issue of 'reflexive' use comes up briefly in Winch's discussion of Wittgenstein on the word "fit," p. 59.) The reflexive conception of measurement, of standards, goes with a conception of what it is for the mind to be in contact with a genuine standard or measure: such contact cannot be seen in our familiar dealings with sticks and swatches and multiplication tables. And so any argument like Winch's, which insists that there is no access to truth conditions apart from an understanding of what counts as establishing when the truth conditions are satisfied, will appear to share Wittgenstein's deviousness: for it asks us to look precisely at the ways in which people's dealings with sticks and swatches and multiplication tables are used in determining what we can say they mean.

9. MY DEVIOUSNESS; AND CONNECTIONS WITH PUTNAM

In Part 4, I took Kripke's side against Malcolm, on whether the standard meter in Paris might have been longer than one meter. But my treatment of that question contains what Kripke might well take to be a kind of Wittgensteinian deviousness. In this final section I explain why; and I show some connections with Hilary Putnam on Kripke[29] and with Kripke on identity.

I have not used the expression "rigid designator" in discussing Kripke's views on the standard meter, although Kripke himself was actually arguing that the expression "one meter" is a rigid designator of a certain length. In his discussion of Kripke's ideas, Putnam points out

---

[28] I should perhaps make clear that I don't intend any general claims about the possibility of a distinction between assertion conditions and truth conditions.

[29] Putnam, "Is Water Necessarily H$_2$O?" in his *Realism with a Human Face* (Cambridge, Mass.: Harvard University Press, 1990), pp. 54–79.

that what Kripke describes in terms of rigid designators can be explained in terms of the ways in which a cluster of natural laws typically enables us to determine the reference of terms which we use in describing hypothetical situations. So, when we consider the hypothetical situation of the meter rod having been heated before the determination of the length one meter, we describe that situation as one in which the meter length defined *within* the hypothetical situation is greater in length than *one meter*; and our account, using *our* measure of one meter, rests on a cluster of laws. In the case of our hypothetically having heated the rod at t_0 prior to defining "one meter" as the length of the rod at t_0, we could, for example, use our laws to give a value for gravitational acceleration, measured in the hypothetical meter units, a value derived via our knowledge of how the rod would expand if heated one degree Centigrade, say.

Putnam's discussion is meant to enable us to separate Kripke's notion of a rigid designator from the metaphysics to which it is attached in Kripke's thought; and Putnam's metaphysically purified notion relies on the very un-Kripkean idea of sortal identity. I too have been implicitly appealing to that same notion. When I described the counterfactual case in which Susan had taken her vitamins, I simply took it that Susan would still be Susan if she had taken those vitamins and grown taller. Kripke would hold that there is a justification for that: namely, the identity of Susan is independent of how much she grows. And that is not, for him, a matter of *our* criteria for identifying someone as the same human being, which is what I was implicitly relying on.

Let us consider here another sort of counterfactual. Take, for example, the idea that, if the being who is now Susan had in an earlier life committed some act of violence, she would have been reborn as a rat, and not as the human being that she is. Kripke's view about this counterfactual might be that in no possible world is something a rat which in our world is Susan. There is no such counterfactual situation; and, further, the fact that there isn't does not merely reflect our criteria or our concepts. Identity is identity; the identity of the being we call Susan is independent of *our* recognition of it as a human being, and independent of how *we* establish identity. Even if we actually only had a word for sortal identity, we could, on Kripke's view *introduce* a word "schmidentity" for *that relation which every object has only to itself*.[30] The

---

[30] Kripke introduces the relation *schmidentity* in response to a different objection. See "Naming and Necessity," p. 310, also p. 350 n. 50. For Kripke's views, I am also indebted to Putnam's discussion, referring to Kripke's Cornell Lectures on "Time and Necessity"; see Putnam, "Is Water Necessarily H_2O?" pp. 64–7.

schmidentity of the thing then determines whether a name attached to it on some one occasion refers on some other occasion or in some hypothetical circumstances *to the same thing*. The schmidentity of a thing depends on its nature, and is as independent of the criteria we use to establish sameness as any length is of the ways in which we actually establish how long something is.

Although earlier I expressed agreement with Kripke in allowing the kind of case, represented in Figure 2, which Malcolm rejects, Kripke would find my implicit reliance there on our concept of a human being a kind of Wittgensteinian deviousness, a kind of evasiveness, evasion of the distinction between on the one hand how we establish reference and on the other what it is we are referring to, and what its nature is, what *can* be the same as it. For, as I meant it, the notion of a human being was itself something in the archives, something alive in our thought and practices, our recognitions, our narratives, our imaginative treatments of what might happen or might have happened to a person. In *PI* §377, Wittgenstein says "Perhaps a logician will think: The same is the same—how identity is established is a psychological question." The 'logician' referred to there insists on the distinction which is central for Kripke, between identity itself and how it is investigated and established. For the logician of §377, Wittgensteinian deviousness would be a matter of identifying psychological questions with logical ones. For Kripke, the deviousness would lie in identifying epistemological questions with metaphysical ones, in treating questions from one domain of philosophy as if they lay in another. Kripke explains this division into domains in "Identity and Necessity,"[31] but it is in view in "Naming and Necessity"; similar divisions of philosophy into its 'domains', and criticisms of philosophers who seem not to appreciate the boundaries, appear frequently in contemporary philosophy (although the emphasis is sometimes on the distinction between the domain of the theory of meaning and that of epistemology). The problem with the division into domains is that it looks as if it could be seen from somewhere above the level of philosophical dispute or discussion, as if philosophical disputes and discussions went on (at any rate when philosophers weren't confused about the borders of the domains) within the various domains discernible from above, each with its own subject matter, the essence of things over here, and our knowledge of them, our access to them, over there. The apparent unquestionableness of this division into domains means that *it* is not seen as itself philosophical. The obviousness and

---

[31] Kripke, "Identity and Necessity," in Schwartz, ed., *Naming, Necessity, and Natural Kinds*; see esp. pp. 84–5. (First published in Milton K. Munitz, ed., *Identity and Individuation* (New York: New York University Press, 1971).)

near-inevitability that the division may have reflects, from a different point of view, what Cavell spoke of, in the passage I quoted in Part 1, as philosophy's drastic desire to underestimate or to evade the ordinary; for the division supposes ideas of mind and meaning (ideas of the reach of mind to what it means) purified from the exchanges, the recognitions and failures, the doubts and certainties, of ordinary life.[32] In the remarks of Cavell's from which my quotation came, he described Kripke as underestimating or evading Wittgenstein's preoccupation with the ordinary, with philosophy's desire to underestimate or evade it. Wittgenstein's attempt to turn attention to the ordinary, to alter the philosophical will to evade it, is an attempt to let us see the significance of the shapings of thought within our lives (the shapings we give to thought), which he speaks of as grammar. The uses to which he puts the notion of grammar can, that is, be seen as responses to the modes of thought, the evasions of the ordinary, that are expressed in the division of philosophy into domains. He says that *essence* is expressed by grammar, and that what kind of object something is, grammar says (*PI*, from §§371, 373). He isn't saying there: "We cannot get hold of *what we mean*, and think about its essence, when we separate it from the ways in which we share words, share modes of thought and action." That way of putting the point about essence and grammar suggests some clear idea of something that we cannot do. The aim of his philosophizing isn't to make us see that there is something we can't do (which is what Kripke takes him to be trying to do), but to change our understanding of what we had taken ourselves to be in search of. (A fundamental analogy for the understanding aimed at by philosophy, as Wittgenstein conceives it, is the understanding we achieve through a classic impossibility proof like that of the trisection of the angle, as Wittgenstein conceives *that*. See Juliet Floyd's discussions of the latter case and of the analogy with the understanding aimed at by philosophy.)[33]

---

[32] Thus, in the case of the metaphysics of identity, the move away from the ordinary is at one stage in Kripke's argument mediated through the introduction of the new term "schmidentity" for that relation everything has to itself. Here the question "What do I know of what it is to *mean* a relation?" is implicitly answered by turning right away from whatever I do with relations in ordinary life, whatever I know of them *there*. The general method Kripke there appeals to, in response to an account of the ways our concepts actually do work, is that of describing a hypothetical language, the operation of which is detached from ordinary life.

[33] Floyd, "On Saying What You Really Want To Say: Wittgenstein, Gödel, and the Trisection of the Angle," in J. Hintikka, ed., *From Dedekind to Gödel: The Foundations of Mathematics in the Early Twentieth Century* (Dordrecht: Kluwer, 1995); Floyd, "Wittgenstein, Mathematics and Philosophy," in Alice Crary and Rupert Read, eds., *The New Wittgenstein* (London: Routledge, 2000).

Putnam's criticisms of Kripke, and the particular issue which he picks
out, namely the contrast between appeal to sortal identity and appeal
to an absolute notion of identity, lead us into the centre of the disagreement between Wittgenstein and Kripke. I have portrayed that
disagreement as concerned with our conception of philosophy itself, its
aims and methods. But, as the Putnam criticism brings out, there is a
particular concept which plays a special role in the disagreement.[34]
Right at the centre of Kripke's thinking is his idea of identity as a relation everything has to itself, and his idea of the law of identity, a law of
logic, which he takes to be a substantial law, a law with content and
with metaphysical implications. The notion of identity had for
Wittgenstein too a special significance. He was convinced early in his
life that the law of identity could only by a kind of illusion be taken to
be a substantial law, a law with content and with metaphysical implications; he was convinced too that the idea of identity as a relation is
confused.[35] The special significance that identity has for Wittgenstein in
his later thought emerges in his placing of two remarks about identity
in the middle of his treatment of rules in *Philosophical Investigations*;
the connection between the topic of rules and that of identity lies in the
idea of a rule as providing a standard with which we can make a comparison, something which enables us to see what it is to go on in the
same way. The remarks on identity at *PI* §§215–16 immediately follow
Wittgenstein's discussion of following the rule always to write the *same*
number: "2, 2, 2, 2, ..." They also connect the treatment of identity
(and thereby also the treatment of rules) with the discussion (in *The
Brown Book*) of transitive and intransitive uses of words. The connection with *The Brown Book* comes out in *PI* §216:

"A thing is identical with itself."—There is no finer example of a useless proposition, which yet is connected with a certain play of the imagination. It is as if
in imagination we put a thing into its own shape and saw that it fitted.

We might also say: "Every thing fits into itself." Or again: "Every thing fits
into its own shape." At the same time we look at a thing and imagine that there
was a blank left for it, and that now it fits into it exactly . . .

[34] Putnam's criticisms imply that another particular concept also has a special role in
the disagreement, that of reference. And indeed the differences between Kripke and
Wittgenstein on reference, on what it is for our thought or our words to reach this or
that, a length, a function, or whatever it may be, run through the various issues discussed
in my essay.
[35] See Roger White, "Wittgenstein on Identity," *Proceedings of the Aristotelian
Society* 78 (1977–8): 157–74, for a discussion of the *Tractatus* treatment of identity. See
also Burton Dreben and Juliet Floyd, "Tautology: How Not To Use a Word," *Synthese*
87 (1991): 23–50.

"Every coloured patch fits exactly into its surrounding" is a rather specialized form of the law of identity.

When Wittgenstein speaks of the law of identity as connected with a certain 'play of the imagination', what he has in mind is the same kind of movement of thought described in the passages from the *Brown Book* that I have discussed.[36] The left-hand part of Figure 3 (in Part 5 above), where we take Susan to 'fit' the length we have read off her, illustrates the sort of imaginative movement Wittgenstein meant. (The idea to which Wittgenstein gives voice in *PI* §215, that if you are seeing a thing you are seeing identity, is parallel to the idea—not Kripke's idea but a closely related idea of Nathan Salmon's—that if you are observing a thing, you are observing its length, you are in a cognitive relation to *a particular length*: just by looking at the object and its length, you can know of the length that the object has that length.[37] There a play of the imagination becomes philosophical theory.)

Identity, Wittgenstein said in 1913, is the very devil, and "*immensely important.*" He added that it hangs—like everything else—directly together with the most fundamental questions, especially with the questions concerning the occurrence of the SAME argument in different places of a function. Well, it certainly is a devil, one of the devils, a devil which is certainly with us still. And it still hangs together with the most fundamental questions, including questions concerning the occurrence of the same argument in different places of a function. (For when contemporary philosophers try to explain it, they appeal to the idea of a relation which holds between a thing and itself, taking for granted the practices in which we use ordinary-language variables like "a thing" and "itself.") I cannot here go into the issue of Kripke and Wittgenstein on identity; I have wanted in this final section only to show how the issue of Wittgensteinian deviousness can lead us first to questions about the division of philosophy into 'domains' and further to the issue of identity and its significance for Kripke and Wittgenstein.[38]

---

[36] See also §19 of Part II of the *Brown Book*.

[37] See Nathan Salmon, "How To Measure the Standard Metre," *Proceedings of the Aristotelian Society* 88 (1987–8): 193–217, at p. 205.

[38] I am very grateful to have had the chance to present this paper at the Conference on Wittgenstein in America at the University of Illinois in Urbana-Champaign in 1995, and also for discussion of the paper at the University of Pennsylvania, the University of Bergen, and Vanderbilt University. I want to thank also James Conant, Thomas Ricketts, Gary Ebbs, Gary Hatfield, and Thomas Maier for comments and questions

5
Was Wittgenstein *Really* an Anti-realist about Mathematics?

Hilary Putnam

It seems clear that we understand the meaning of the question: "Does the sequence 7777 occur in the development of π?" It is an English sentence; it can be shown what it means for 415 to occur in the development of π; and similar things. Well, our understanding of that question reaches just so far, one may say, as such explanations reach.

Philosophical Investigations, §516

It is widely assumed that Wittgenstein was an "anti-realist" about mathematics, and this assumption then undergirds claims by philosophers as different in other respects as Michael Dummett, Paul Horwich, Saul Kripke, and Richard Rorty that Wittgenstein was an anti-realist across the board. Indeed, very often this is not recognized to be an assumption; the secondary literature often takes it to be self-evident. My aim in this essay is to challenge this assumption, not by presenting a lengthy textual analysis of Wittgenstein's extensive writing on the foundations of mathematics, but by offering a reaction of my own to the "realism" problem which is built on recognizably Wittgensteinian materials, and which does not smack of any sort of "anti-realism." To be sure, even if I can bring this off, it will not show that a more realist (or less "anti-realist") reading is the only possible reading that can be given to Wittgenstein's text; for it will be claimed that one can also build a case for an anti-realist position out of Wittgensteinian materials, and this is what Michael Dummett, Saul Kripke, and Paul Horwich claim to have done (Rorty does not cite texts, but simply tells us what Wittgenstein allegedly thought). Moreover, as late as the last sections of *Remarks on the Foundations of Mathematics* (1944),[1] Wittgenstein *was*,

---

[1] But not necessarily as late as January 1945! For the quotation from Wittgenstein which serves as the epigraph to this paper is compatible with the line I suggest below as the one Wittgenstein should have taken, and is silent on the claim that even "omnisci-

I believe, attracted to the idea that mathematical propositions which are not humanly decidable[2] *lack* a truth-value[3]—an idea which I find deeply problematic, for reasons which will be explained. However, by showing how Wittgenstein's work as a whole—not just the *Remarks on the Foundations of Mathematics*—can support a very different view, I hope to encourage us to take a second look at these *Remarks* themselves, and to ask whether even this view—which is usually taken to be "anti-realist" almost by definition—may not have sprung from very different considerations.

The plausibility of the "anti-realist" readings of Wittgenstein's later philosophy rest on the existence in Wittgenstein's work of what look like "verificationist" ideas. Indeed, Wittgenstein was attracted to such ideas in the early and mid-nineteen-thirties, although not, I believe, when he wrote *Philosophical Investigations* (which is not to deny that he found some insights in verificationism even in the last writing).[4] In addition, the idea that changes in mathematical method—at least when they are as radical as the change from, say, proving a proposition in geometry by classical geometrical means and proving the "same" proposition by means of group theory—constitute a change in the very identity of the proposition being proved attracted Wittgenstein early and late.[5] And this idea can be *seen* as an expression of verificationism.

ence" cannot know if a pattern occurs in the decimal expansion of π if there is no humanly available calculation to show that there is—a claim that is central to the discussion of the law of the excluded middle in Part IV of the original edition of *Remarks on the Foundations of Mathematics*. It is very important that Wittgenstein *published* the *Investigations* and that the material the editors have put together as *RFM* is unpublished.

   [2] For an explanation of what I mean by "humanly" decidable see the Appendix.

   [3] In *RFM*, he writes, "Suppose people go on and on calculating the expansion of π. So God, who knows everything, knows whether they will have reached '777' by the end of the world. But can his *omniscience* decide whether they *would* have reached it after the end of the world? It cannot. I want to say: even God can determine something mathematical only by mathematics. Even for him the mere rule of expansion cannot decide anything that it does not decide for us" (orig. edn., Part V, §34; this remark dates from 1944); but see n. 1. To say that *omniscience* cannot decide a question is, I believe, Wittgenstein's way of saying that there is no answer to be known, i.e. it is an illusion that there must be a right answer.

   [4] Cora Diamond, "Realism and the Realistic Spirit," in *The Realistic Spirit* (Cambridge, Mass.: MIT Press, 1991). See also my "Pragmatism," *Proceedings of the Aristotelian Society* 95.3 (1995): 291–306.

   [5] See Juliet Floyd, "On Saying What You Really Want To Say: Wittgenstein, Gödel, and the Trisection of the Angle," in J. Hintikka, ed., *From Dedekind to Gödel: The Foundations of Mathematics in the Early Twentieth Century* (Dordrecht: Kluwer, 1995). Although Floyd denies that this is what Wittgenstein means, the very passages she cites (e.g. "A question only makes sense in a calculus which gives us a method for its solution," quoted on p. 387), and the repeated insistence, which she documents very well, that "try to find a proof" is not a "method" in the required sense, support my claim.

In addition, there are Wittgenstein's remarks on the law of the excluded middle in mathematics (in *RFM*, orig. edn., Part IV), which, although they are clearly not as "revisionist" as Brouwer's views, have sometimes been seen as expressing quasi-intuitionist sentiments. But I have already said that my concern in this essay is not with this sort of textual question. To repeat, I shall be quite content if I can show that there is *a* way of looking at the questions in the philosophy of mathematics (in particular, a way of trying to dissolve the "realism problem") which is not "anti-realist," but which is "Wittgensteinian."

In seeking such a way, I shall be guided by Cora Diamond's interpretation of the "rule-following" discussion in *Philosophical Investigations*. She has shown that this famous discussion can be read in a way that is neither metaphysically realist nor "anti-realist,"[6] and that way of reading the "rule-following" discussion is one of my guides in my present enterprise.

Secondly, there is an attitude toward the philosophy of mathematics which is widely shared, and to which I myself contributed, according to which the problems in question are so hard that one should despair of seeing any way at all of resolving them. (In fact, I once wrote a report on the present state of the philosophy of mathematics with the subtitle "Why Nothing Works.")[7] The second idea that will guide the present discussion is that *that* view—the view that the problems in the philosophy of mathematics are entirely *sui generis*, and add up to something close to an antinomy of reason—cannot be right. In the end, I shall try to show, the conundrums that bother us in the philosophy of mathematics are intimately connected with, and have precisely the same roots

---

Wittgenstein continues to talk this way in notes which run to almost the very end of *RFM*, but he also suggests a different view, e.g. in *RFM*, orig. edn., Part V, §7:

> Now how about this—ought I to say that the same sense can only have *one* proof? Or that when a proof is found the sense alters?
>
> Of course some people would oppose this and say: "Then the proof of a proposition cannot ever be found, for if it has been found then it is not a proof of *this* proposition." But to say this is so far to say nothing at all.
>
> It all depends *what* settles the sense of a proposition, what we choose to say settles its sense. The use of the signs must settle it; but what do we count as the use?—
>
> That these proofs prove the same proposition means, e.g.: both demonstrate it as a suitable instrument for the same purposes.

This last remark is quite compatible with saying that the same proposition can have both, e.g. an "elementary" proof and an "analytic" proof, which is what I claim the early Wittgenstein would have denied.

⁶ Diamond, "Realism and the Realistic Spirit."

⁷ "Philosophy of Mathematics: Why Nothing Works," in my *Words and Life* (Cambridge, Mass.: Harvard University Press, 1994).

as, familiar conundrums about the indeterminacy of reference, familiar conundrums about the objectivity of value judgments, etc., etc., etc. Of course, the fact that the difficulties are in a sense the same does not mean that they do not require special treatment in each case. It is a feature of philosophical difficulties that each time a difficulty arises anew it seems to be in some way more serious, more real, more intractable, than it seemed before, and that appearance is always connected with particular aspects of the particular form that the difficulty takes, aspects that have to be carefully analyzed in each case. It would be profoundly contrary to the spirit of Wittgenstein to suppose that there is some one magic wand—called, as it might be, "the resolution of the realism/anti-realism problem"—which one can wave to make all the protean forms of that difficulty vanish with a "Poof!" Nevertheless, it seems to me that what we eventually have to reach as we work through the difficulties in the philosophy of mathematics is a standpoint from which the problems here will seem not mysterious and charming but *boring*.

I must also mention a third idea that will guide me in the present essay, and that is that *before* one attempts to dissolve the difficulties, one must give the difficulties a chance to be *felt*; and that means that I will have to try to understand the position of someone for whom those difficulties seem real and intolerable (and that is not hard for me to do, since that is the position I occupied myself for so many years).

WITTGENSTEIN ON FOLLOWING A RULE

We are all acquainted with analyses of Wittgenstein's text according to which the point of Wittgenstein's discussion of rules is that the notion of following a rule, or the normativity of rule-following, is in one way or another to be explained in terms of the notion of conforming to the standards of a community.[8] Such a view may strike one as entailing a profound change in some of the things we think about rules, especially in mathematics, and indeed it does have startling (Kripke would call

---

[8] Cf. Saul Kripke, *Wittgenstein on Rules and Private Language* (Cambridge, Mass.: Harvard University Press, 1982). In "Wittgenstein and Kripke on the Nature of Meaning," *Mind and Language* 2 (1990): 105–21, Paul Horwich also defends such a reading, although he criticizes Kripke's notion of a "fact" and Kripke's description of the position as "skeptical." On Horwich's view I understand a word correctly if I assign degrees of assertibility to sentences containing the word in a way which accords with community standards. Rorty's remarks on Wittgenstein in *Contingency, Irony, Solidarity* (Cambridge: Cambridge University Press, 1989) presuppose a similar interpretation.

them "skeptical") consequences. For example (although Wittgenstein himself *never* says any such thing), it is a consequence of these interpretations that the notion of one individual following a rule in isolation from any linguistic community makes no sense (or in Kripke's version, unless we—in our imagination—"take him into our community" and apply our notions of rule-following to him).[9]

If, however, we actually look at the discussion of following a rule in *Philosophical Investigations* (e.g. §§143–242), it is striking that we find no hint of this claim. The closest Wittgenstein comes to addressing the question whether one individual in isolation could follow a rule, is to ask (§199) "Is what we call 'obeying a rule' something that it would be possible for only *one* person to do, and to do only *once* in his life?" and to answer (he describes this as "a note on the grammar of the expression 'to obey a rule'"):[10]

It is not possible that there should have been only one occasion on which a person obeyed a rule. It is not possible that there should have been only one occasion on which a report was made, an order given or understood, and so on.—To obey a rule, to make a report, to give an order, to play a game of chess are *customs* (uses, institutions).

Now, if Wittgenstein had meant "It is not possible that one person in isolation could obey a rule *period*," then would he not have said so? One wonders why Wittgenstein would have made such a weak statement if what he thought was so much stronger.[11]

(Compare the question Wittgenstein puts to himself in *RFM*, orig. edn., Part II, §67: "But what about this consensus—doesn't it mean that *one* human being by himself could not calculate? Well *one* human being could at any rate not calculate just *once* in his life." Here too he refuses to simply answer "Yes"!)

In defense of the "community standards interpretation," it might be argued that Wittgenstein's use of the word "institution" implies the existence of a community. But it remains the case that, first, the explicit point of §199 is only to rule out the "possibility" that it should happen exactly once that a rule is obeyed, or an order given, and so on, and not to say that a community is necessary; second, the discussion that follows connects the notion of rule-following not with "institutions" in

---

[9] Kripke, *Wittgenstein on Rules and Private Language*, p. 110.

[10] I have retranslated the German.

[11] Compare the question Wittgenstein puts to himself (and the answer he gives!) in *RFM*, orig. edn., Part II, §67. "But what about this consensus—doesn't it mean that *one* human being by himself could not calculate? Well *one* human being could at any rate not calculate just *once* in his life."

the sociological sense, but with the notion of a "practice" and then with the notion of a "regularity," and certainly it is possible for there to be regularities in what one individual human or animal does. One individual can certainly make it a *custom* to do something whether or not his community does (the German word here is "Gepflogenheit," by the way—a word which normally describes the way an individual is in the habit of doing something, unlike the English word "custom," which does normally refer to a communal practice.) Does the whole textual evidence for this astounding interpretation rest, then, on the fact that Wittgenstein included "institutions" in his *parentheses*?

Moreover, the context makes it quite clear why Wittgenstein made the statement just quoted. Although he certainly does not claim that we can *define* "rule" in terms of "regularity," or reduce the notion of a rule to the notion of a regularity, Wittgenstein does argue that following a rule is a practice, and that practices presuppose regularities. A world in which no one even thought of the notion of a rule or of following a rule except for one isolated individual, and that isolated individual had the concepts for just one brief moment and followed a rule for just that moment—if, contrary to Wittgenstein's "grammatical point" there could be such a world—would be a world in which for one moment there was a rule even though none of the regularities in linguistic and extra-linguistic behavior which give content to "rule" talk were ever in place. *That* is the supposition that Wittgenstein thinks is senseless, and it requires no commitment to any astounding philosophical views (no "philosophical revisionism") to accept what Wittgenstein said *here*.

Nor are the doubts and rejoinders that Wittgenstein anticipates in response to what he writes in §§199–207 the ones he should have anticipated if the claim in §199 were so radical. Having stated a condition for talk of rules to make sense (a condition which uses the notion of a regularity), what Wittgenstein quite sensibly worries about is that someone might suppose that even the notion of a regularity (*Regelmässigkeit*) already presupposes the notion of a rule (*Regel*), and thus what Wittgenstein has said is simply *circular*. Section 208: "Then am I defining 'order' and 'rule' by means of 'regularity'?—How do I explain the meaning of 'regular', 'uniform', 'same' to anyone?"

Let me now quote Wittgenstein's response to *this* question in full:

I shall explain these words to someone who, say, only speaks French by means of the corresponding French words. But if a person has not yet got the *concepts*, I shall teach him to use the words by means of *examples* and by *practice*.—And when I do this I do not communicate less to him than I know myself.

In the course of this teaching I shall show him the same colors, the same lengths, the same shapes, I shall make him find them and produce them, and so on. I shall, for instance, get him to continue an ornamental pattern uniformly when told to do so.—And also to continue progressions. And so, for example, when given . .. ... to go on ....

I do it, he does it after me; and I influence him by expressions of agreement, rejection, expectation, encouragement. I let him go his way, or hold him back; and so on.

Imagine witnessing such teaching. None of the words would be explained by means of itself; *there would be no logical circle.* [Emphasis added.]

Wittgenstein makes two principal points in this passage. First, he makes the point that we all know how to explain these notions, and he gives examples of the different ways in which we do explain them—all, notice, perfectly *ordinary* ways, that is, not philosophical ways, ways which presuppose "Platonism" or "mentalism" or any other philosophical account of the real nature of rule-following. And secondly, he adds quite categorically "and when I do this [teach the notions in this way] I do not communicate less to [the student] than I know myself." That is, Wittgenstein denies that there is some other kind of explanation of the notions involved in following a rule (notions of doing the "same" thing, of "continuing" a progression in "the same" way, of behaving "uniformly," of doing such-and-such "ad infinitum" (which is also mentioned in §208), and even the notion "and so on") which one is in possession of either by virtue of being a philosopher or by virtue of having direct acquaintance with something ineffable.

Cora Diamond[12] has pointed out that the target Wittgenstein has in mind is no straw man. F. P. Ramsey, Wittgenstein's friend and interlocutor for several years, believed that, although indeed there is no other *explanation* that one can give of what one does when one follows a rule than the ordinary one (the "banal" one, so to speak), nevertheless following a rule consists in following "psychological laws"—not laws of theoretical psychology, but laws of which each of us has (and can only have) implicit knowledge. This view combines a very special brand of mentalism about the nature of rule-following with the idea of incommunicable knowledge which is a well-known target of the *Investigations.* Thus it makes perfect sense that Wittgenstein would reject that view here, as well as contrast the ordinary teaching of the concept of rule-following with the various mentalist and Platonist accounts that he has discussed before.

What I am suggesting is the following: if the discussion of rule-following in *Philosophical Investigations* expresses skepticism at all, the

---

[12] "Realism and the Realistic Spirit," pp. 59ff.

"skepticism" is directed at *philosophical accounts* of rule-following, and not at rule-following itself. What readers like Kripke and Horwich have done is to take Wittgenstein to oppose not only *metaphysical* realism about rule-following but also our commonsense realism about rule-following, when what Wittgenstein actually doubts is the need for and the possibility of a philosophical *explanation* of rule-following that will justify the commonsense things we say (e.g. our talk of "right" and "wrong" ways to follow rules), and the ways in which we actually teach people to follow rules. Indeed, the point of §208 is that even the concept of a *regularity* does not have or need a philosophical *explanation* in this sense.

Why don't we need a non-commonsensical account? What is wrong with explanations of rule-following in terms of special powers of "grasping concepts," etc., etc.? The answer to this question is, of course, the whole of the discussion in the *Investigations* itself (which is, perhaps, the whole of the *Investigations*). I don't intend to repeat that, but let us recall certain features of the discussion.

Wittgenstein repeatedly tries to show that when philosophers offer accounts of rule-following—accounts which are supposed to explain the possibility of rule-following or to tell us the metaphysical nature of rule-following—while the words used in these explanations may sometimes be in place—may sometimes hit it off, in the sense of giving us a description of an impression we have when we follow a certain kind of rule, a description of the "phenomenology," one might say, of following a rule—the minute we take them seriously as *explanations*, the minute we suppose that some *entity* has been introduced whose *existence* clarifies the supposed question as to How We Are Able To Follow Rules, then we slip into thinking that we have discovered a "supermechanism";[13] moreover, if we try to take the supposed supermechanism seriously, we fall into all sorts of absurdities. At certain points, Wittgenstein indicates the general character of such "explanations" by putting forward parodistic proposals, for example, the proposal that what happens when we follow a rule is that the mind is guided by invisible train tracks (§218), "lines along which [the rule] is to be followed through the whole of space" (§219).

---

[13] Jerry Fodor's talk of "nomic connections" as what enable us to have concepts may be a present-day example of this. According to Fodor, what enables me to refer to things which may not exist, and which may not even be objects of any science—e.g. witches—are *nomic connections to the property of being an object of the kind in question*. (Cf. Fodor, *A Theory of Content and Other Essays* (Cambridge, Mass.: MIT Press, 1992), pp. 100ff.) A nomic connection to the property of being a witch? Talk about supermechanisms!

Even this proposal, please note, may be right as a description of the
"phenomenology" on at least some occasions. If I am computing the
sine of a number that I have never computed before, or taking the
square root of a number, then perhaps it will seem to me as if I am being
"taken" to a series of "new places" quite automatically, as if I am arriving at a series of train stations that I have never visited before while sitting in a train as it continues on its predetermined route. Wittgenstein
remarks that my description only made sense if it was to be understood
symbolically—that is, metaphorically—"I should have said: *This is how
it strikes me*" (§219). But what if people were to believe that the existence of invisible train tracks and the mind's going along like a train
from one station to the next is the *explanation* of what it is to follow a
rule? It would be as if they confused the grammar of a myth with the
grammar of a scientific explanation. ("My symbolical expression was
really a mythological description of the use of a rule," §221.)

Of course, the answer to the question, "Well, what is wrong with
wanting to supplement the ordinary account of rule-following with
another account?" is that there is nothing wrong if it is simply a desire
to understand the empirical facts, to know, for example, what are the
causal preconditions—cultural, biological, psychological, or what have
you—of following this, that, or the other sort of rule. But that isn't the
question the philosopher tries to investigate. What bothers Kripke, for
example, is really the question: how can we grasp rules which do not in
themselves contain any errors, with our finite and all too fallible brains
which inevitably do make errors? And the trouble with that question is
that, in general, it seems genuinely pressing only because one supposes
what is not the case, that a fallible brain could understand an infallible
rule only by being connected with a mechanism (a *super*mechanism)
which was itself infallible. Of course, most philosophers will protest
that such a mechanism is not what they are seeking at all, but at that
point, I believe, Wittgenstein's strategy is to show that they cannot say
what it is they are seeking; that in the end they have a desire for *they
know not what*.

I do not mean to suggest that Wittgenstein's discussion ends here.
Stanley Cavell has reminded us that Wittgenstein has a deep interest in
what in us—I have heard Cavell call it our "perversity"—drives us to
seek answers that cannot make sense to questions that have no clear
sense. My purpose here has been more limited; to remind us that what
Wittgenstein is trying to bring us back to is a standpoint from which
notions like "learning to add two," "understanding the rule keep
adding two," "knowing what it means to add two" do not seem problematic at all. At least as a first step in his investigations, he wants to

make it seem problematic that these notions have become problematic; rather than wondering how it is that we can add two, we should be wondering at the fact that it can come to seem to us the most puzzling thing in the word that we can add two. In the same way, at the end of my discussion I want to be able to say that what is puzzling in the philosophy of mathematics is not that we are able to use and learn and understand and acquire the concepts of, say, number theory, but that it has come to seem to so many philosophers the most puzzling thing in the world that we should be able to do this. Unfortunately, there is a large gap between commonsense realism about adding two and anything that could be called "commonsense realism" about *number theory*. We still have a number of issues to discuss in this connection. One of them is the so-called "ontological question."

DO THE QUANTIFIERS IN MATHEMATICS RANGE OVER "INTANGIBLE OBJECTS"?

For Willard V. Quine, the quantifiers—that is, the logical particles "every" and "some" (or "there exist")—are our way of talking about objects; since we use them in mathematics, mathematics too consists of generalizations about *objects*. "The words 'five' and 'twelve'," Quine writes, "name two intangible objects, numbers, which are *sizes* of sets of apples and the like."[14]

This attitude raises two broad questions. One question, the question that Quine himself has focused on almost exclusively in his writing on the philosophy of mathematics, is the epistemological question: what *justification* is there for positing the existence of these "intangible objects"? Quine's answer (as is well known) is that the justification is analogous to the justification for positing the existence of electrons and other such unobservable entities in physics: such posits[15] increase our ability to predict observation conditionals and generalized observation conditionals, statements of the form "If A then B," where A and B are observation sentences, and sentences of the form "At any place and any time, if A then B," where A and B are observation predicates. The other

---

[14] "Success and the Limits of Mathematization," in Quine's *Theories and Things* (Cambridge, Mass.: Harvard University Press, 1981), p. 149.

[15] This talk of "posits" was employed by Quine in his celebrated essay on the ontological question, "On What There Is," in his *From a Logical Point of View* (Cambridge, Mass.: Harvard University Press, 1953), pp. 1–19.

question—which has been in the foreground of discussion since the publication of Paul Benacerraf's famous paper "Mathematical Truth"[16]—is the semantic question. It is widely accepted in analytic philosophy nowadays that reference to objects presupposes that those objects are ones that we can observe or otherwise causally interact with, or at least describe in terms of properties and objects with which we can causally interact. We describe quarks, for example, in terms of their charge, their "charm," etc.; and we have access to charge and "charm" because these are magnitudes which determine the outcomes of physical interactions: quarks, like photons and electrons, are the quanta of fields with which we interact. But we do not have physical interactions with numbers, and the properties in terms of which we describe numbers and sets—say, being the successor of a number, or containing certain sets or numbers—are not properties which characterize physical objects or fields. Mathematical objects, if there be such, are causally inert. But then how can we so much as refer to them?

The attitude Wittgenstein expresses, for example, in his *Lectures on the Philosophy of Mathematics* is very different.[17] He clearly poohpoohs the idea that talk of numbers—either ordinary numbers or the so-called "transfinite numbers"—is in any way analogous to talk of objects. If we think that way, then of course we will think that set theory has discovered (or posited the existence of) not just objects, and not just intangible objects, but an *enormous*—an *unprecedentedly* large— quantity of intangible objects. And the very vastness of the universe which set theory appears to have opened up for our intellectual gaze will then be part of its charm; but Wittgenstein thinks that this reason for being charmed is a bad one. Wittgenstein believes—and I think he is right—that it does not make the slightest sense to think that in pure mathematics we are talking about objects. The difference between the use of the quantifiers here and the use of the quantifiers when we are literally formulating generalizations about (what we ordinarily call) objects is just too great. In *RFM* (orig. edn., IV, §16) he is equally scornful:

The comparison with alchemy suggests itself. We might speak of a kind of alchemy in mathematics.

It is the earmark of this mathematical alchemy that mathematical proposi-

---

[16] "Mathematical Truth," in P. Benacerraf and H. Putnam, eds., *Philosophy of Mathematics: Selected Readings*, 2nd edn. (Cambridge: Cambridge University Press, 1983).
[17] Cf. Lectures XXV and XXVI, particularly pp. 251–6.

tions are regarded as statements about mathematical objects,—and so mathematics is the exploration of these objects?[18]

To be sure, someone might argue that there is no real opposition between Wittgenstein's view and Quine's view. One might claim that Quine and Wittgenstein are both trying to show the senselessness of metaphysical realism with respect to mathematics; Wittgenstein shows it by means of a certain sort of philosophical therapy while Quine shows it by means of what one might call philosophical irony. Quine has reinterpreted the statement that in mathematics we are talking about objects in a way that totally robs it of its supposed metaphysical significance. Although the subject of this essay is Wittgenstein's philosophy of mathematics and not Quine's, I should like to make a couple of remarks about this as a possible interpretation of Quine's doctrine of ontological commitment.

First, even if it were correct—and I shall say in a moment why I don't think it is—it clearly does not represent the way in which realistically inclined philosophers of mathematics have understood Quine's criterion of ontological commitment. The paper by Paul Benacerraf I cited, for example, clearly assumes that if we take the quantifiers in classical mathematics to be "objectual" quantifications in Quine's sense,[19] then we are committed to regarding them as ranging over objects in a sense perfectly analogous to the sense in which quantifiers over the books in my office range over objects. It is even more obvious that the recent work on the philosophy of mathematics by Benacerraf's colleague at Princeton, David Lewis,[20] takes the idea that the quantifiers of classical mathematics need to be interpreted as ranging over some *stuff*, some *things* or other, perfectly seriously. But—and this is my second point—Quine himself is clearly not free of the tendency to think of "abstract objects" as perfectly analogous to physical objects, as his epistemology of mathematics shows.

Still, one might ask, what is wrong with speaking of anything that *exists* as an object? And what better criterion have we for deciding

---

[18] Of course, if one wants to simply *extend* the notion of "object" by speaking of "mathematical objects" in connection with mathematical propositions, that is something different; but then the application of "intangible" makes no sense, since the tangible/intangible distinction goes with the ordinary, unextended, use. On the idea that we continually do extend the use of "object," see my "Sense, Nonsense, and the Senses: An Inquiry into the Powers of the Human Mind" (the 1994 Dewey Lectures), *Journal of Philosophy* 91.9 (1994): 445–517.

[19] "Substitutional" quantifiers are interpreted in terms of the notion of truth of substitution instances of open sentences, rather than in terms of (non-linguistic) "objects."

[20] David Lewis, *Parts of Classes* (Oxford: Blackwell, 1991).

whether talk genuinely commits us to the *existence* of something than
how that talk looks when "regimented" in the notation of symbolic
logic?[21] My answer would be that there are two different attitudes that
one can have towards mathematical logic. One can think of symbolic
logic as the skeleton of an *ideal* language—this is the view that drives
Quine's philosophy[22]—and, of course, it is part of the ideal language
view that the real standard for what *any* sentence means is its translation (or, as Quine says, its "regimentation") in the ideal language. But
one can also think of symbolic logic as simply a useful canon of rules
of inference, and of formalization as simply a technique of *idealiza-
tion*[23] that facilitates the statement of those rules, their representation
as (recursive) calculating procedures, and so on. Indeed, as Wittgenstein
reminds us in *Philosophical Investigations*, the word "ideal" is problematic here. "We are dazzled by the ideal," he writes (§100), criticizing
our tendency to think that "we are *striving after* an ideal, as if our ordinary vague sentences had not yet got a quite unexceptionable sense, and
a perfect language awaited construction by us" (§98).[24] In a formal language, the relation "B is a deductive consequence of A" has a *syntactic
representation*, in the sense of being coextensive with a relation which
is definable in syntactic (in fact, in computational) terms; but that does

---

[21] At times Quine plays down the significance of symbolic logic as such, writing e.g.
"The artificial notion '∃x' of existential quantification is explained merely as a symbolic rendering of the words 'there is something x such that'. So whatever more one may
care to say about being or existence, what there are taken to be are assuredly just what
are taken to qualify as values of 'x' in quantification. The point is thus trivial and obvious." ("Trivial and obvious" if one assumes that the ordinary language (?) expression
"there is an x such that" has just one use.) "Ontology and Ideology Revisited," *Journal
of Philosophy* 80 (1983): 499. At other times, he seems to deny that ordinary language
has ontological commitments, e.g. in "Facts of the Matter" (in R. W. Shahan and K. R.
Merrill, eds., *American Philosophy from Edwards to Quine* (Norman: University of
Oklahoma Press, 1977)), he writes: "It is only our somewhat regimented and sophisticated language of science that has evolved in such a way as really to raise ontological
questions" (p. 183), and "The ontological question for such a language [one with certain
kinds of 'foreign notations'], *as for ordinary language generally*, makes sense only relative to agreed translations into ontologically regimented notation . . . *Translation of
ordinary language into the regimented idiom is not determinate*" (pp. 185–6, emphasis
added).
[22] Cf. my "Convention: A Theme in Philosophy," *Philosophical Papers*, vol. 3:
Realism and Reason (Cambridge: Cambridge University Press, 1992), for an analysis of
Quine's scientism (particularly pp. 182–3). Note that my reading of Wittgenstein has
changed, however, since that paper was written.
[23] A classic statement of this view was Ernest Nagel's "Logic Without Ontology," in
his *Logic Without Metaphysics* (Glencoe, Ill.: Free Press, 1959).
[24] Compare §103: "The ideal, as we think of it, is unshakable. You can never get outside of it; you must always turn back. There is no outside; outside you cannot breathe.—
Where does this idea come from? It is like a pair of glasses on our nose through which
we see whatever we look at. It never occurs to us to take them off."

not mean that a formal language is in some way a "better" language than a natural language.

I believe that the second of these attitudes is the reasonable one. But if we refuse to allow ourselves to think of symbolic logic as "sublime," it becomes difficult to see why we should take seriously the idea that every statement whose symbolization involves the symbol "∃" implies the existence of an object, in some univocal sense of "object" and some univocal sense of "existence." Indeed, there are also purely mathematical reasons *not* to think this. Quine himself has pointed out that existential quantification can be interpreted in at least two different ways, the ways he calls "substitutional" and "objectual." He argues that if one accepts the classical theory of real numbers at face value—that is, without intuitionist or other constructivist reinterpretation of some kind—then one cannot construe *its* quantifiers as "substitutional," and so he concludes that they must be "objectual"; but, as we shall see shortly, there are still other *known* interpretations of the quantifiers over and beyond the objectual and the substitutional. The axioms of first-order logic are simply not categorical in the sense of determining a *unique* interpretation of the quantifiers themselves. There is thus no *mathematical* reason to think that there is some one thing that we must be saying whenever we use the symbol "∃".

DOES REJECTING THE NOTION OF "ONTOLOGICAL COMMITMENT" RESOLVE THE REALISM/ ANTI-REALISM PROBLEM?

So far I have ascribed two attitudes to the later Wittgenstein: common-sense realism about rule-following and contempt for the idea that mathematics presupposes an "ontology," that is, contempt for the idea that any branch of mathematics is literally a description of the behavior of objects of some kind. But I don't wish to suggest that these two attitudes by themselves suffice to give clear content to the notion of commonsense realism with respect to, say, number theory. And even though at the end of the day we hope to arrive at a standpoint from which the "realism problem" does not genuinely arise with respect to, say, number theory,[25] it is clear that many bright people have tried and failed to

---

[25] When I speak of "mathematics" in this essay, I shall be thinking of number theory and analysis (calculus, theory of functions, etc.), *not* of set theory. Set theory depends on a concept ("set") which is itself a neologism introduced by Cantor; and I argue in my

find such a standpoint—too many to encourage the idea that it is easy
to find; and I said at the outset that one of my guiding thoughts will be
that we have to see why the problems in the philosophy of mathematics seem so *hard*—that we have to do justice to the sense that they may
actually be insoluble before we can begin to unravel them. In this connection, it is particularly important to understand why the problems
look so much *worse* after Gödel's theorem.

Entertain, for the moment, the fantasy that Gödel's theorem has not
been proved, and imagine that we all believe (as Hilbert did) that it is
or will in the future be possible to find axioms of mathematics that are
complete; that is, that every sentence in, for example, properly axiom-
atized number theory is either a theorem or else its negation is a theorem, if not in number theory itself, then in a suitable extension of
number theory. In that case, truth in number theory would be coextensive with provability in that extension; and to be provable in a formal
system, we know, is just to be a sentence which is obtainable as the last
line of a longer or shorter proof (or as the bottom of a larger or smaller proof tree) by following certain rules. Now, our commonsense realism with respect to rules (which I have already seen Wittgenstein as
defending) could be seen as implying commonsense realism about provability;[26] and if truth can be identified with provability in a suitable
sense of "provability," then it seems that we have an easy way of being
commonsense realists about mathematical (number-theoretic) truth.

Another advantage to this way of thinking is that it bypasses the
whole question as to the "objectual" or "substitutional" character of
the quantifiers in analysis. For, if analysis is complete, or some extension of analysis is complete with respect to the propositions of analysis
(as Hilbert also believed, or, better, hoped), then we can explain the
truth of whole sentences in analysis in the same way, by identifying it
with their provability in an appropriate formal system. And we can
then argue that even if the quantifiers in analysis are not substitutional,
still, that does not mean that they do have to be understood in terms of
intangible objects. To understand the quantifiers, we could say (speaking, at this point, like good Fregeans, even if he would have been horri-
fied at the view we were defending)—or, indeed, to understand any
symbol in analysis—is just to understand the contribution that those

Tarski lectures, which appeared in Gila Sher and Charles Tieszen, eds., *Between Logic
and Intuition: Essays in Honor of Charles Parsons* (Cambridge: Cambridge University
Press, 2000), that it poses quite special problems, problems which do not arise in
connection with number theory or analysis. As Wittgenstein says, "mathematics is a
motley."

[26] But see the criticism of this idea in the Appendix.

symbols make to the truth-value of whole claims; and we understand the contribution that the various symbols make to the truth-value of whole claims in analysis by understanding the *proof procedure* of analysis. (We would then have a nice example of the way in which a quantifier may be neither objectual nor substitutional.)

But alas! Gödel did prove his theorem, and we do know that there are undecidable sentences in number theory and that some of them will remain undecidable no matter how we consistently extend number theory and analysis. What are we to do?

One possibility would be to try to hold on to the line just suggested, and to take the existence of undecidable sentences in number theory as showing that there are sentences in number theory which are neither true nor false. To be sure, some of those sentences become provable and others become disprovable if we add further axioms to number theory—for example, if we add the sentence expressing the formal consistency of the given system of number theory as an additional axiom to obtain a stronger system, then, in particular, that very sentence CON(NT),[27] which was undecidable in the original system, becomes decidable in the extended system, and hence *true in the extended system*. We could say—even if it seems a most unattractive thing to say at first blush—that we have here a case of *ambiguity*; that CON(NT) was one statement (and was neither true nor false) in the original system NT and is a different statement in the extended system, and is moreover true in the extended system. (This is the line that Wittgenstein entertained in his famous (or notorious) remarks about the Gödel theorem.[28] In the Appendix to this essay I shall try to show that this does *not* mean that Wittgenstein accepted the rest of the anti-realist story—e.g. that he believed, as Michael Dummett does, that understanding mathematical propositions is just a matter of understanding the proof procedures connected with them.)

But this move flies in the face of another Wittgensteinian insight—one which Cora Diamond has written about so beautifully[29]—that it is a fundamental feature of our mathematical lives that we do not

---

[27] CON(NT) is here used to stand for the particular number-theoretic proposition of which Gödel proved that (1) number theory is consistent if and only if that proposition is true; and (2) if number theory is consistent, then that proposition cannot be proved in it.

[28] *RFM*, orig. edn., Part I, Appendix I, §§8–19. [Added November 19, 2000: I no longer think this is a correct reading of Wittgenstein's remarks about the Gödel theorem. My present reading of those remarks is in my paper with Juliet Floyd, "A Note on Wittgenstein's 'Notorious Paragraph' about the Gödel Theorem," *Journal of Philosophy* 97.11 (Nov. 2000): 624–32.]

[29] See "The Face of Necessity," in Diamond's *The Realistic Spirit*, esp. pp. 246–9.

experience every change in our mathematical language-games as a change in the very meaning of the sentences.[30] As Diamond puts it, we sometimes "see the face" of one mathematical language-game in another mathematical language-game. What was wrong with the line that Wittgenstein was tempted by in 1937 in connection with the Gödel theorem is that every mathematician in the world sees the face of number theory based on Peano's axioms in number theory based on Peano's axioms plus CON(NT).[31]

Still, even if CON(NT) is not provable in Peano arithmetic, it *is* provable by metamathematical reflection *on* number theory, as Gentzen showed. Can we identify truth in number theory with the disjunction of formal provability and—however vague the notion may be—provability by metamathematical reflection on number theory? But we have no reason to think that every sentence of number theory is decidable even by metamathematical reflection. What reason is there to think that, for example, the number-theoretic sentence expressing the consistency of Zermelo-Fraenkel set theory is decidable by metamathematical reflection?[32]

Following Michael Dummett, one might *propose a revision in the logic of classical mathematics itself*; in particular, to adopt *intuitionist logic*. This *is* compatible with identifying truth in mathematics with (informal) provability; the logic was motivated by that very identification. And since we would no longer accept the law p v ~p, we would no longer be required to assert

CON(ZF) v ~CON(ZF)

—indeed, for any sentence S of number theory, we would assert S v ~S when and only when we had succeeded in proving S or in proving ~S.

Alternatively, if we do want to preserve the formula

(1) p v ~p

we can do that too. For it was pointed out by Gödel[33] that there is a

[30] Wittgenstein's remark (cited in n. 5) "that these proofs prove the same proposition means, e.g.: both demonstrate it as a suitable instrument for the same purposes" explicitly allows that we *can* see two different proofs as proving the "same" mathematical proposition, contrary to many interpretations of Wittgenstein.

[31] Wittgenstein's example (in the Appendix to Part I of the original edition of *RFM*) was a different one: Russell's *Principia*, and Principia + CON(*Principia*). But the same rejoinder applies.

[32] Indeed, to date all attempts to find a Gentzen-style proof for the consistency of even *ramified analysis* have been utter failures.

[33] Kurt Gödel, "On Intuitionistic Arithmetic and Number Theory," in Martin Davis, ed., *The Undecidable* (New York; Raven, 1965), and in *Kurt Gödel: Collected Works*,

"translation" of classical first-order number theory into intuitionist first-order number theory under which all of the laws of classical logic and first-order number theory are intuitionistically valid. The formula p ∨ ~p, for example, gets "translated" as ¬ (¬p . ¬¬p), where "¬" is intuitionist negation—thus one gets (1) above as a theorem, though not, of course, under its classical interpretation.

In short, if one distinguishes between the validity of (1) with respect to number theory and the semantic principle that every sentence of number theory has a determinate truth value (the law of the excluded middle), then we may say that *syntactically speaking*, under Gödel's "conjunction-negation translation" of classical number theory into intuitionist number theory we end up retaining (or, if you prefer, regaining) the law (1) of propositional calculus without thereby committing ourselves to the law of the excluded middle understood as "bivalence."

In addition, under Gödel's translation, the existential quantifier "∃x" of classical number theory gets "translated" as "¬∀x¬", where "∀" is the *intuitionist* universal quantifier. This is, by the way, the example I promised a little while ago of yet another interpretation of the existential quantifier (over and beyond the substitutional and objectual interpretations that Quine mentions). Unfortunately, however, intuitionism is not the way out of our perplexities.

A LOGICIST INSIGHT

It is a logicist insight that part of the problem is to understand how mathematical statements function as part of science, and not just to understand talk about proofs and theorems. Science isn't separable into a part which is empirical and free of all mathematical concepts, and a part which is the mathematics and free of all empirical content. Empirical science itself contains "mixed statements," statements which are empirical but which speak of, for example, functions and their derivatives as well as of physical entities.

Even as simple a statement as Newton's law of gravitation is "mixed." That law, of course, asserts that there is a force f_{ab} exerted by any body *a* on any other body *b*. The direction of the force f_{ab} is towards *a*, and its magnitude F is given by

vol. 1, ed. S. Feferman, J. W. Dawson, Jr., W. Goldfarb, C. Parsons, and R. Solovay (Oxford: Oxford University Press, 1986), pp. 282–95.

$$F = \frac{gM_aM_b}{d^2}$$

where g is a universal constant, M_a is the mass of a, M_b is the mass of b, and d is the distance which separates a and b. The law presupposes the existence of real numbers corresponding to forces, distances, and masses, and the operations of multiplication and division of real numbers. A "regimented" version of the law would thus require quantifiers over real numbers, or at the very least over rational numbers.[34]

Philosophical accounts of our mathematical concepts face the challenge of explaining how we are able to assign a truth value to such mixed statements. If our account of mathematical language is intuitionist—that is to say, if the only notion of "truth" we have in connection with mathematical statements is the notion of provability (and a restricted kind of provability at that)[35]—while our physical language is incompatible with the assumption that truth coincides with verifiability,[36] then the problem of interpreting the mixed statements seems unsolvable. On the one hand, their interpretation has to be realistic, or at least not anti-realistic, if we are to derive from them empirical statements which are themselves understood realistically; but on the other hand, they contain concepts whose *only* meaning was supposed to be in terms of the contribution they make to the provability of statements.

In some cases this problem can, indeed, be finessed, and in a way that Wittgenstein might well have approved of. If I say that a stick is three feet long (where it is clear from the context that what is meant is three feet ± the inherent inaccuracy of some measurement procedure), then I can reformulate this as "If the stick is correctly measured, the result will be '3'"; and this does not assume that there are logically necessary and sufficient conditions for a measurement's being correct stateable in "observation terms."[37] Similarly, if I say that a certain formula gives the position of the moon at any time, up to a given accuracy, nothing about

---

[34] For a detailed discussion, see "Philosophy of Logic," in my *Philosophical Papers*, vol. 1: *Mathematics, Matter and Method* (Cambridge: Cambridge University Press, 1975), pp. 337–41 (but see also p. 347).

[35] Intuitionists reject non-constructive proofs of existence and impredicatively defined sets, for example.

[36] Cf. my "Sense, Nonsense, and the Senses" in connection with the issue of verificationism.

[37] The idea that the use of such a notion as "correct" measurement does not commit us to a necessary and sufficient condition for the notion is connected with Cavell's insistence that "criteria," in the sense in which Wittgenstein uses the term, are not necessary and sufficient conditions: Cavell, *The Claim of Reason: Wittgenstein, Skepticism, Morality, and Tragedy* (New York: Oxford University Press, 1979).

the way we understand that statement commits us to a notion of mathematical truth that outruns calculability. But the case I describe above cannot be finessed in this way.

I believe that Wittgenstein failed to see the seriousness of this problem, precisely because his examples of the empirical application of mathematics are limited to *calculation*, and to comparing the results of calculations to experiments. (It is important to recall that Wittgenstein was trained as an *engineer*.) Thus he may well have thought that the mixed statements of physics all have the form: the values of such-and-such parameters can be *calculated* in such-and-such a way given such-and-such initial data. But this is simply not the case.

Here is an example which may help to bring out the problem. In mathematical physics, the value of a physical magnitude generally depends on the solution of one or another differential equation—say, for example, the wave equation. But those solutions may in certain cases *not be recursively calculable*, even if the initial conditions are recursively describable[38]—and in such a case, we may very well not be able to *prove* that the solution to the differential equation in question is such-and-such, even to a finite number of decimal places' worth of accuracy. Yet, if we take our physics seriously, there *is* an answer to the question as to what the solution of the differential equation is to such-and-such a number of decimal places.

One way out, Dummett's, is to widen the notion of provability, to interpret the logical connectives[39] not in terms of mathematical provability alone but in terms of the wider notion of *verifiability*, and to collapse the notions of truth and verifiability for empirical statements as well as for mathematical statements. But not only for metaphysical realists but even for commonsense realists, for all of us who are anti-anti-realists, that way out is unacceptable.[40]

---

[38] Marian Boykan Pour-El and Ian Richards, "The Wave Equation with Computable Initial Data such that Its Unique Solution Is Not Computable," *Advances in Mathematics* 39 (1981): 215–39. It is not known whether the Newtonian three-body problem is such a case; there may not be, in general, any way to determine recursively whether the bodies will *collide* or not.

[39] I speak of "interpreting the logical connectives" because that is one way in which intuitionism is frequently presented; e.g. it may be said that for intuitionists, p.q means "p is (constructively) proved and q is (constructively) proved," p ∨ q means "There is a (constructive) proof of p or there is a (constructive) proof of q, and a way of determining which of the two statements is proved," p ⇒ q means "There is a construction which applied to a hypothetical (constructive) proof of p would yield a constructive proof of q," etc.

[40] A position similar to Dummett's but not committed to an atomistic conception of verification is also possible. My position in *Reason, Truth and History* (Cambridge: Cambridge University Press, 1981) was of this kind.

Of course, if we construe mathematical quantifiers (in purely mathematical statements and mixed statements alike) as expressing generalizations about intangible objects ("abstract entities"), and at the same
time construe truth for all three kinds of statements—statements which
do not quantify over any abstract entities, pure mathematical statements, and mixed statements—as verification-transcendent, then we
can preserve our realism with respect to the statements of the first class,
but at the cost of endorsing a form of metaphysical realism for the pure
mathematical and the mixed statements, and thereby having to face the
familiar epistemological and semantic problems. This is the situation
that Paul Benacerraf described so well in the paper I referred to.

Indeed, the epistemological and semantic problems may not even be
the most serious difficulties for this sort of metaphysical realism.
Consider, for example, the form of metaphysical realism in the philosophy of mathematics recently developed by David Lewis.[41] Lewis proposes that we postulate that reality contains not only the matter we
know about in this world, and similar matter in other logically possible
worlds,[42] but that it contains also a vast amount of additional stuff—
stuff which need not be material, and which need not be thought of as
causally interacting in any way with matter, but which need only be
"atomless"[43] and multitudinous—that is, there has to be a *lot* of this
stuff, so much that the number of its parts is a very large cardinal (a cardinal *so* large that one doesn't need to suppose that there are any more
sets than *that* even in Cantor's paradise).

If the atomless stuff is that multitudinous, then, Lewis shows, one
can reinterpret the notion of a set and the notion of membership in a
set in terms of mereology (in terms of the notions of part and whole) in
such a way that one obtains what amounts to a standard model for set
theory. At first blush, this form of metaphysical realism might seem to
provide us with a way of understanding mathematics fully realistically
without postulating any sort of supermechanism. After all, the role of
the atomless stuff in Lewis's philosophy of mathematics is not to act
upon us in any way, or to act on our minds in any way, or to be perceived by us in any way; it is only to provide an "interpretation" of the
sentences of set theory (including the mixed sentences) which is, in a
suitable sense, "standard."[44] So the problem with Lewis's metaphysics

---

[41] Cf. David Lewis, *Parts of Classes*.

[42] Lewis is notorious for his "realism" about possible worlds.

[43] "Atomless" means: every part of the "stuff" has proper parts in turn.

[44] The model must be one that a Platonistically inclined set theorist like Gödel could
regard as making the same sentences true as the sentences he believes are true "in the
universe of sets."

cannot be that he is somehow confusing conceptual and causal questions, because he does not introduce anything that even resembles causality into his story. There need not be any cause and effect connections at all involving the atomless stuff.

This very causal inertness of the atomless stuff brings to light another problem[45]—one which, I believe, affects all forms of metaphysical realism in the philosophy of mathematics, though not as transparently. Suppose Lewis is wrong, and his atomless stuff actually does not exist (supposing, for the sake of the argument, that it makes sense to suppose either that it exists or that it doesn't). *Would mathematics fail to work?*[46] Since the success or failure of mathematics in any of its real-world applications only depends on how the empirical objects behave, and that would not be any different if the atomless stuff did not exist (since by hypothesis it exerts no causal influences on the ordinary empirical objects), it follows that if the mysterious extraphysical "atomless stuff" did not exist at all, then *mathematics would work exactly as it actually does*. Doesn't this already show that postulating immaterial objects to account for the success of mathematics is a useless shuffle?

It is, I think, because we philosophers of mathematics have a tendency to rehearse precisely the sort of dialectic that I have just laid out before us (with, of course, our own individual variations), that we suffer from the occupational disease of tending to believe that at the end of the day the problems must be both *sui generis* and hopeless. After all, haven't the arguments I laid before you shown that commonsense realism about rule-following does not suffice to yield the desired commonsense realism about even the elementary theory of numbers? And anti-realism and metaphysical realism likewise don't work. So, in short, neither the opposing metaphysical positions nor the Wittgensteinian therapy designed to rid us of the problem are successful—or, at any

---

[45] I am indebted to Jody Azzouni for the idea for the argument which follows, if not to its precise form. See his stimulating *Metaphysical Myths, Mathematical Practice* (Cambridge: Cambridge University Press, 1994).

[46] David Lewis would doubtless respond that this counterfactual makes no sense, given his own theory of counterfactuals. *Tant pis* for that theory of counterfactuals! The counterfactual: "If Lewis's atomless stuff did not exist, still everything we observe in our world—including the success of mathematics!—would still occur" is what I have called a *strict* counterfactual (see *Renewing Philosophy* (Cambridge, Mass.; Harvard University Press, 1991), pp. 51–2), that is, one in which the consequent is a *logical consequence* of the antecedent, and such counterfactuals ought to be true in any adequate theory of counterfactuals. (Note also that even if the antecedent is "metaphysically impossible" in Lewis's sense—if it is a sense—still it is not *logically contradictory*. There is nothing degenerate about this particular strict counterfactual.)

rate, that is how it can look to one. Is there another way to look at these problems?[47]

A REVISITING OF THE "COMMONSENSE REALISM ABOUT RULES" ISSUE

I said that it was an insight of the logicists (one inherited by Wittgenstein and Quine) that an adequate account of our mathematical practice must include the whole of that practice, and that means in particular the application of mathematics, the way in which mathematics is used in accounting, in measuring, in empirical science, and so on. I went on to argue that, in particular, anti-realist and formalist interpretations of pure mathematics do not fit well with commonsense realism—or just anti-anti-realism—with respect to, for example, empirical science. But this argument may have another consequence, one less welcome for the position I wish to defend, namely that I was wrong to praise Wittgenstein for what I described as his defense of commonsense realism with respect to rule-following. The problem with commonsense realism, it may seem, is not that commonsense realism is a *wrong*, or bad, or incoherent philosophical position, but that it isn't a philosophical position at all. Of course, Wittgensteinians will agree that this is the case; it is a part of most if not all interpretations of Wittgenstein's later work that it was not his *intention* to put forward a "philosophical position" in any conventional sense of that term, and this is something he himself tells us. Still, analytic philosophers of a more conventional mindset will ask (and indeed do ask) whether Wittgensteinians are not too *complacent* about this state of affairs. After all, not having a phil-

---

[47] I have intentionally not discussed Hartry Field's nominalism (see his *Science Without Numbers* (Princeton: Princeton University Press, 1980)). Although it was an important contribution to the discussion, it is widely realized that it did not work. Unfortunately, most of the critics have directed their fire solely to the mathematical errors in that work. In my own view, the more serious problems with Field's nominalism are philosophical, and these remain even when the mathematical errors are repaired. In particular, (1) Field's position requires that we be realists about the classical space-time continuum. If we do not take the non-denumerable infinity of that continuum seriously as a *physical* hypothesis, then the construction immediately collapses. (2) Even if we waive this objection, the construction is not "robust"; it does not apply to quantum mechanics, for example, not even to as classical and "realist" a version of quantum mechanics as Bohm's hidden variable theory, nor to theories in which space-time is discrete. But the success of mathematics surely does not depend on the particular Newtonian form of empirical science which Field considers. (Would mathematics stop working if Bohm's theory were true? Or if space-time were discrete?)

osophical position may be just another name for refusing to acknowledge a real problem. And isn't that what is going on here?

I have been arguing that it does not help to suppose that what makes the sentences of number theory true is some bunch of objects, some *stuff*. In the same vein, I suggested that Wittgenstein argued against the very *intelligibility* of the view that what makes it the case that one is following a rule correctly, when one is, is some special relation that one has to some intangible objects, be they mental or Platonic. Doesn't that at once raise the question "Then what *does* make these sorts of claims true?" Isn't that quite obviously a *real* question? And am I not praising Wittgenstein for denying that a real question is a real question?

What exactly *is* the "real question" that Wittgenstein is supposed to have swept under the rug? The formulation suggests that the question is this: what *makes* the statements of mathematics true? For that matter, what *makes true* the statement that such-and-such is the correct way to follow the rule "Add two"? ("Remember that when the last digit is a nine you have to change it to a zero and carry one.") But one does not need to be a "Wittgensteinian" to find that question suspect. The question, after all, rests on a particular picture of truth: truth is what results when a statement stands in a particular relation (it "is made true by," or more simply, it "corresponds to") something else, say a "reality." But, while that picture may fit *some* statements, for example, the statement that a sofa is green may "correspond" to a certain green sofa on a particular occasion—it doesn't seem to fit other equally familiar statements without intolerable strain. Consider ordinary negative existentials. What makes the statement that there is no red book in this room true? The "negative fact" that there are no red books in this room?[48] There is an ancient metaphysical problem about the existence or non-existence of "negative facts." Indeed, are "facts" objects, entities that makes propositions true? Today many, perhaps most, philosophers would say that "It is a fact that there is nothing red in this room" is just a syntactic and semantic variant of "It's true that there is nothing red in this room" (compare "It is the case that there is nothing red in this room"—why has no one proposed an "ontology" of *cases*?). To speak of the fact that there is nothing red in this room is not to cite an object which stands in a mystery relation called "making true" to the statement that there is nothing red in this room; it is simply to refer to

[48] Cf. Wittgenstein, *Lectures on the Foundations of Mathematics*, p. 248: "We have certain words such that if we were asked, 'What is the reality which corresponds?' we should all point to the same thing—for example 'sofa', 'green', etc." And (p. 247), "If you say, 'Something corresponds to the word "red," namely the colour'—how does it correspond if you say (truly) 'There's nothing red in this room'?"

the *truth* of the claim that there is nothing red in the room. Indeed, if we are going to think of the statement "There's nothing red in this room" as being made true by an object, why not take that object to be "the truth" of the statement that there is nothing red in the room? Or, why not just say that the statement is true *because* there is nothing red in the room? This last, at least, has the virtue of being trivially true.

But is it an explanation? Is "The statement 'p' is true because p" an *explanation*?

Of course, we could *deny* that speaking of "the fact that there is nothing red in this room" is just a reformulation of "It is true that there is nothing red in this room."[49] Certain philosophers would say that there are such "entities" (i.e. intangible objects) as facts, and that facts *make* statements true. But one does not need to be a positivist to point out that positing ghostly counterparts of sentences to explain the truth of statements is mere verbiage. Such talk meets none of the standards that we require a serious explanation to meet in everyday life. As an explanation of anything, the idea that "facts" are literally intangible objects is in infinitely bad shape.

The emptiness of this particular explanation of the truth of the statement that there is nothing red in a certain room, namely that it is "made true by a negative fact," is especially easy to see. Once we have broken free of the grip of the particular picture that if a statement is true there must be a *something* which "makes" it true, then we can also see how that picture is responsible for the feeling that there is a "deep problem" whose existence Wittgenstein is somehow refusing to face. The fact that Wittgenstein does, however, use such homely examples as the words "sofa" and "green" and the sentence "There's nothing red in this room"[50] illustrates very well, I think, the fact that he is not at all trying to sweep a genuine problem under the rug; what he is rather trying to do is see just what picture "holds us captive"—that is, to find the roots of our conviction that we *have* a genuine problem, and to enable us to see that when we try to state clearly what the genuine problem is, it turns out to be a nonsense problem. "The results of [Wittgenstein's] philosophy are the uncovering of one or another piece of plain nonsense and of bumps that the understanding has got by running its head up against the limits of language. These bumps make us see the value of the discovery."[51]

[49] I prescind from the fact that the most common use of the locution "It is a fact that" is *epistemic* and not ontological at all. "It is a fact that" has much the same force as "It is quite certain that," in this use.

[50] See n. 48.

[51] *PI* §119.

KRIPKE'S INTERPRETATION OF WITTGENSTEIN AGAIN

This is, I believe, a good point at which to say something about Saul Kripke's brilliant attempt to state a supposed genuine problem in this area, one to which he thinks (mistakenly, as I already indicated) Wittgenstein offered a "skeptical solution."

In order to explain what I think is wrong with Kripke's interpretation of Wittgenstein, I need first to say more than I did above about the nature of what I have been calling "commonsense realism." It is a feature of commonsense realism (as opposed to metaphysical realism) that it always seems to ignore (or beg) the philosophical problem rather than respond to it. Consider, for example, commonsense realism about perception. The commonsense answer to a question like "How do you know that Joan has a new car?" might well be "I saw it." But when John Austin writes that the fact that we hear a bird and recognize the bird "by its booming"[52] is sufficient reason for saying that we know that there is a bittern at the bottom of the garden (or if I say that the fact that we saw it is sufficient reason for saying that we know that our neighbor has a new car), the objection is always that the response has entirely ignored the "problem," namely, that perception, after all, only gives us "direct" acquaintance with our own "sensations" (and that "the real problem" is how we are justified in so much as speaking of perceiving material objects, when all we have directly or immediately before the mind is the sensations). And indeed commonsense realism by itself isn't a metaphysical position, or even an anti-metaphysical position. The philosophical work that Austin does and that Wittgenstein also does of undermining the picture on which the supposed difficulty rests, the picture of experience as consisting of "sensations" in a private mental theater, still has to be done. But notice the nature of the strategy that I am attributing to both Austin and Wittgenstein, and that I have discussed at more length elsewhere.[53] The strategy is not to *counterpoise* an alternative thesis to the various theses of the traditional epistemologists, be they realist theses or idealist theses or empiricist theses or whatever. It consists rather in, first, taking perfectly seriously our ordinary claims to know about the existence of birds and automobiles and what Austin referred to as "middle-sized dry goods," and our ordinary explanations of how we know those things, and, secondly, in meeting the objection that these ordinary claims simply ignore a

---

[52] "Other Minds," in his *Philosophical Papers*, 2nd edn. (Oxford: Oxford University Press, 1970), p. 79.

[53] See my "Sense, Nonsense, and the Senses," esp. Lectures II and III.

philosophical problem by challenging the very intelligibility of the supposed problem. If there is a "program" here at all, it is the program of
"uncovering of one or another piece of plain nonsense and of bumps
that the understanding has got by running its head up against the limits of language. These bumps make us see the value of the discovery."[54]

With this now in mind, let us consider what the parallel dialectic
about following a rule might be. Kripke defines a function "quus" by
the stipulation that *a* quus *b* (where *a* and *b* are whole numbers) is 5
when either *a* or *b* is greater than or equal to 57, and is equal to *a* plus
b otherwise. And he asks us how we can know that we ourselves did
not in the past mean "quus" when we said or thought "plus." (His
ultimate aim is to cast doubt on my confidence that I *now* mean anything when I say or think "plus.")

Well, if someone were to ask me how I know that someone—call her
Joan—doesn't mean "quus" by "plus," my response would be that the
questioner is using the question as a ploy to start a philosophical discussion. (All the more so if the question is not about someone else but
about my own past self!) If Joan were an intelligent adult and a fluent
speaker of English, I would be at a loss what to say. Perhaps I would
just say, "She speaks English." And this seems unresponsive to the
philosophical problem, since of course Kripke doesn't deny that in *some*
sense that is the right answer to give.

But let me pretend that the question is a serious one. Then I may say
that the "hypothesis" that Joan means "quus" by "plus" is one that
can, in fact, be empirically refuted, by asking Joan what 2 + 57 is.[55] To
be sure, it is "logically possible" that Joan would still answer the question "What is 2 + 57?" by saying "59" rather than by giving the answer
which is correct on the "quus" interpretation of "plus," namely "5,"
since Joan might make a mistake in "quaddition." The inference from
the response "2 + 57 = 59" to "Joan does not mean 'quus' by 'plus'" is
not a *deductive* inference. So what? As Austin famously reminded us,
"Enough is enough: it doesn't mean everything."[56]

Kripke's problem is deeper. Even if we can rule out the particular
hypothesis that Joan means "quus" by "plus," we cannot in the same
way rule out every possible hypothesis of this kind. Thus, for each *n*
define a function quus$_n$ as follows:

$$a \text{ quus}_n b = a + b \text{ if } a,b < n$$
$$a \text{ quus}_n b = 5 \text{ if } a \text{ or } b \geq n$$

---

[54] *PI* §119.

[55] The "right" answer, on the hypothesis that Joan means "quus" by "plus," is, of
course, "5."

[56] Austin, "Other Minds," p. 84.

If what Joan means by "plus" is quus$_n$, for some very large N, Joan's response to the sums we actually encounter will be "normal." Still, if she is mathematically sophisticated, could we not ask her "Is there a number N such that a 'plus' b = 5 whenever either a or b is $\geq$ N?" If Joan answers "No," does this not show[57] that, whatever Joan may mean by "plus," she *doesn't* mean "quus$_n$," for any n whatsoever? At this point we encounter the really *deep* move in Kripke's argument.

Joan, Kripke tells us, might not only understand "plus" in a different way from the rest of us; she might conceivably understand almost every word in the language differently, but in such a way that she speaks exactly like the rest of us in all actual circumstances. She would speak differently from the rest of us if we could utter or write down the number N in decimal notation and ask her "What is 2 + N?" or some such question. But suppose the number N is so large that it is *physically impossible* to write it down?[58] Then there might be no *physically possible* situation in which Joan would speak differently from the rest of us, and yet she would "mean something different" from the rest of us by "plus."

Kripke is right to think that this is a possibility that Wittgenstein would dismiss as unintelligible. The idea that someone might mean something different by a word although the supposed difference in meaning does not show up in any behavior at all, indeed in any possible behavior, linguistic or extralinguistic, is a "possibility" that Wittgenstein would reject. But must Wittgenstein's rejection be based on a community-standards view of what correctness in rule-following consists in? (This is close to Wittgenstein's supposed "skeptical solution," as Kripke interprets him.)

Here I wish to bring out the *distance* between what we know

---

[57] Someone might object that I have misunderstood Kripke's problem, that the problem is just this: the underdetermination of, say, a hypothesis about quarks by laboratory evidence is not a problem for us because we grant that there are *facts* about quarks ("considered in isolation," if you please), but that the underdetermination of the supposed "fact" that Joan means *plus* by her speech dispositions is an underdetermination by "all the facts" that there *are*. This is, of course, just Quine's problem of "the underdetermination of reference"; and perhaps Kripke fails to see that it is only because he thinks Quine's problem turns on behaviorist assumptions rather than on the notion of a "fact of the matter." (See his remarks about Quine on p. 57 of *Wittgenstein on Rules and Private Language*.) However, Kripke's emphasis on the fact that the plus function is defined for infinitely many cases, so that it is (supposedly) puzzling how my "finite mind" can hold it all, introduces a different and more interesting line of argument, even if in the end that line, too, turns on the notion of a "fact," and it is that line of argument that I have tried to reconstruct here.

[58] It would also suffice to suppose that N is so large that it is physically impossible for someone with a human brain to calculate with it.

Wittgenstein thought and what Kripke says he thought. All interpreters agree that we know that Wittgenstein thought that we can speak of understanding a word (or of understanding a word one way rather than another) only against the background of a whole system of uses of words, and we know, moreover, that when Wittgenstein speaks of the "use" of words he means also the actions and events with which those uses of words are interwoven. Descriptions of language and descriptions of the world, including what speakers do in the world, are interwoven in Wittgensteinian accounts. Moreover, we know that Wittgenstein thinks that this observation—that the notion of simply understanding a word in isolation from anything one might do with the word, or from the presence of an appropriate background of other uses and actions, makes no sense—is itself a "grammatical" one, that is, in some sense a conceptual observation.

According to Kripke, however, Wittgenstein has much more radical beliefs and much more metaphysical beliefs, in addition to these. Specifically, Kripke's Wittgenstein, Kripkenstein, holds that the only condition we possess[59] for the truth of the claim that someone understands a word the way the other members of the relevant linguistic community do is that that someone be disposed to correctly answer certain specific questions, or, more broadly, to give certain specific linguistic responses in certain situations. Giving those responses in those situations, and the other members of the community then saying that he or she has the concept, itself constitutes a kind of metalinguistic language-game, which Kripke calls the "concept attributing game."

In addition, Kripke ascribes to Wittgenstein a certain concept of a "fact": *there are no facts about "a person considered in isolation" except (1) physicalistic facts, that is, facts about his or her brain-states, and other such materialistic facts, and (2) (possibly) mentalistic facts, that is, facts about his or her sensations, mental images, etc. (described without reference to any intentional content we might ascribe to them).*[60] In short, Kripke assumes—or rather Kripkenstein assumes—

---

[59] However, even this condition—the only one we possess—may not actually determine that the claim *is* true, but only that we agree in calling it true: at *Wittgenstein on Rules and Private Language*, pp. 111–12, Kripke would have Wittgenstein deny that the community's responses determine the truth of *any* sentence, and say that *all* that the facts about the community's responses determine is that the community does not doubt certain sentences (e.g. does not doubt that $a + b \neq c$). On this interpretation of Wittgenstein there is no fact of the matter as to whether *any* sentence in the language is true or false; and yet Wittgenstein still thinks he is able to employ the notion of a fact.

[60] Kripkenstein (pp. 52–4) does consider the possibility that there are other sorts of mentalistic facts, but argues that a mental state that determined the value of the plus function in infinitely many cases would be a "finite object" (because we have "finite

that either materialism or a certain limited form of dualism is the only possible account of what a "fact" is. Given this view of what a "fact" is, Kripkenstein goes on to argue that there are no "facts about a person considered in isolation" which *constitute* the fact that that person understands a word the way other people in the community do. Of course, there is no textual basis at all for attributing these views about facts, or even for attributing the concept of "a fact about a person considered in isolation," to Wittgenstein as opposed to Kripkenstein.

Now suppose Joan uses the word "plus" and the other arithmetical words and mathematical signs the way the rest of us do. (I don't just mean that Joan gives the same answer to questions of the syntactic form "What does *a + b* equal?" that the rest of us do, but that she talks *about* addition the way the rest of us do, and that she talks and behaves the way normal people do about matters which involve the *application* of addition. If you are worried about certain science fiction possibilities, assume also that there are no funny "molecular" facts about Joan which would cast the "sincerity" of any of these responses into question—for example, funny facts about her polygraph results, her blood pressure, her brain waves, etc.[61] If you are worried about the possibility that Joan might be able to conceal her true thoughts even from the polygraph, suppose—with Kripke—that there are no funny facts about her interior monologue as well.) The grammatical remark I ascribe to Wittgenstein is that we cannot understand talk of "meaning something different" by a piece of language when there is no connection between the alleged difference in meaning and anything the person to whom the difference in meaning is ascribed does or says or undergoes or would do or say or undergo. It follows from that "grammatical" observation that in such a case we shouldn't be able to make head or tail of the suggestion that Joan *really* means something other than plus by the word "plus" or the sign "+". The thesis Kripke ascribes to Wittgenstein, in

---

minds") that could not determine the value of the plus function "in an infinity of cases." I leave it to the reader to judge if this argument, with its image of the mind as a finite space and its picture of mental states as objects, is Wittgensteinian at all.

[61] I take *PI* §270, "Let us now imagine a use for the entry of the sign S in my diary. I discover that whenever I have a particular sensation a manometer shews that my blood pressure rises . . .," not only to go against the view that, for Wittgenstein, only "criterial" behavior is relevant to the occurrence or non-occurrence of sensations, and, more generally, of propositional attitudes, but also explicitly to allow the (possible) relevance of scientific facts about a person (facts about so-called "molecular" behavior). These issues were, of course, much discussed during the controversies about logical behaviorism which took place in the 1950s and 1960s. See, on the latter, my "Brains and Behavior," in *Philosophical Papers*, vol. 2: *Mind, Language and Reality* (Cambridge: Cambridge University Press, 1975).

contrast, is that there are no *facts that determine* that an arbitrary sentence S's being true under particular circumstances is incompatible with the meaning the community assigns to the words except the verdicts the community actually renders or would actually render in the "concept attributing game."

Note that this is a *general* thesis—not only a thesis about the word "plus," but a thesis about every word in the language. Let us consider what Wittgenstein would be committed to if he held that thesis. Let us begin with mathematical examples and move to non-mathematical ones.

First, let *a*, *b*, and *c* be three numbers too large (and too "complicated" considered as sequences of digits) for human beings to actually add, say, strings of more than 2^{64} more or less random digits. Then there will be *no fact that determines that one particular answer to the question "Is it the case that a + b = c?" is correct*, on Kripke's interpretation. Our communal understanding of the words *is* just our disposition to give certain responses to certain questions, plus the relation of that disposition to the dispositions of the community. Those dispositions *may*, of course, determine that it is *wrong* to say $a + b = c$, even for very large *a*, *b*, *c*. For example, if we are told that the numbers *a* and *b* end with, respectively, 2 and 3, and that the number *c* does not end with 5, then no matter *how* long *a*, *b*, and *c* are, we can say that $a + b \neq c$. But these negative tests (tests by which we can say on the basis of a limited amount of information about the numbers that $a + b \neq c$) will not suffice to justify a positive statement to the effect that $a + b = c$ (or to employ such a statement in considering whether or not a speaker passes the "concept attributing game" in connection with the sign "+"); indeed, nothing will ever justify such a statement if *a*, *b*, *c* are very long numbers which are not given as values of functional expressions which are short enough to be written down and understood and that we can prove theorems about. For infinitely many triples of numbers *a*, *b*, and *c*, there will be no "fact" as to whether we understand the word "plus" in such a way that *a* plus *b* equals *c*, on Kripke's interpretation of Wittgenstein.[62]

---

[62] I mentioned at the beginning of this essay that Wittgenstein was attracted to the idea that undecidable propositions lack a truth value at various times. Does this not support Kripke's interpretation here? No, for several reasons. First of all, Kripke is interpreting *Philosophical Investigations* (in fact, just the "rule-following discussion" in *Philosophical Investigations*). His interpretation is not supposed to depend on evidence from unpublished writings (Kripke subtitles his book "An Elementary Exposition"). But, as pointed out in n. 1 above, *Philosophical Investigations* refrains from mentioning any controversial views Wittgenstein may have held on undecidable statements in math-

Of course, Kripkenstein's view doesn't imply that we can't *say* things like "No matter how long the numbers *a* and *b* are, there is a number *c* such that *c* is the sum of *a* and *b*." Kripkenstein would say that it is part of the language-game we play that we *do* say things like that. But, I think that Kripkenstein would have to say that when we say "There is a number *c* such that $a + b = c$," what we say doesn't necessarily imply that there is a *fact* as to *which* number *c* is such that, as a matter of "fact," "$a + b = c$" is true.

Just to make this clear: the point I am making is not just the point (which indeed follows immediately from what Kripke writes) that there is nothing about the understanding of any individual considered in isolation that determines the correct answer to all addition problems. It is that when we consider the necessary finiteness of the responses *of a whole community*, Kripkenstein's argument yields the result that *there is no fact about the whole community* which determines the answer to *all* the indefinitely many possible addition problems.

Consider a non-mathematical kind of case which Wittgenstein himself discusses in *Philosophical Investigations*. It can happen that there are disagreements that we are unable to resolve—that is, that the community is unable to resolve—concerning the genuineness of people's expressions of their feelings.[63] I feel that someone's expression of emotion is genuine, but I cannot convince other people. Yet all of us pass the relevant concept-ascribing tests. If the disagreement is about whether someone's avowal of love is sincere, then in the typical case no one would say that some of us lack the concept, or at least no one would say this on the basis of Kripkean criteria. (Of course we do in fact ask whether people really know what love is, but this sort of discussion is one for which Kripke's view seems to leave no room—or perhaps Kripke would say that this is simply a metaphorical way of talking.)

Now Wittgenstein explicitly says that such judgments, judgments on which the community does not come into agreement, are judgments which nevertheless may be right. There are people who are better *Menschenkenner*, people who are better at understanding people, and such people can make "correct judgments." It is true that Wittgenstein says that these better *Menschenkenner* are also, in general, better at making prognoses; but there is nothing in Wittgenstein's text which implies that *each individual correct judgment* of the genuineness of an

---

ematics. Moreover, as I go on to argue above, other discussions in *Philosophical Investigations* are inconsistent with the views Kripke attributes to Wittgenstein.

[63] *PI* II. xi. See my *Pragmatism* (Oxford: Blackwell, 1995), ch. 2, for a discussion.

emotion will eventually be confirmed behaviorally in a way which will command the assent of the whole community. This would be an extraordinary view for Wittgenstein to hold, writing as he does in the same pages, that such judgments are typically made on the basis of "imponderable evidence."

Of course, Kripke has a possible answer here. Kripke ascribes a deflationist account of truth to Wittgenstein, and no doubt he would reply, "Of course, one can say that my judgment or anyone else's judgment of an emotion is correct, or, for that matter, that a judgment concerning the sum of two huge numbers is correct, *meaning by that* simply to endorse, or repeat, the judgment in question. To say that someone is a superior *Menschenkenner* is, thus, simply to endorse that person's verdicts, but it is not to say that there is a fact about that person considered in isolation which is the fact that he is a better *Menschenkenner* than others, and, for that matter, if the community doesn't agree that he is a better *Menschenkenner*, then there isn't even a fact about the community as a whole—or indeed a fact about the universe as a whole— which is the *fact* that the person is a better *Menschenkenner*." In short, Kripkenstein's view is a combination of a "deflationist" account of truth and a metaphysical realist account of fact.[64]

What could have led Kripke to attribute such an extraordinary combination of views to Wittgenstein? One hypothesis—which I am sure is wrong—would be that Kripke himself believes that there are only the two sorts of fact that I mentioned, and that this seems so self-evident to Kripke that he cannot but believe that Wittgenstein thinks this too. I am sure that this is wrong, because it is quite clear that Kripke himself believes that there is another kind of fact about a person considered in

---

[64] It is here that Paul Horwich, who agrees with Kripke in ascribing deflationism about truth to Wittgenstein—and whose view of what constitutes understanding, like Kripke's, implies that there is no determinate right answer to the question *Is p true?* in cases in which the community's standards do not require that one say "Yes" or "No"— parts company with Kripke. (For references, see my discussion of Horwich's views in "Sense, Nonsense, and the Senses," Lecture III.) Horwich's Wittgenstein is an anti-realist about both truth *and* fact. Given the views that Horwich ascribes him, if the community says "There is a number c such that c is the sum of a and b" but the community's standards do not require that one say that any *particular* c is the sum of a and b, then— rather than say that there is such a c but no *fact* as to which it is (the position that I claim Kripkenstein should hold, given the views ascribed to him by his creator)—Horwichstein should say that there is some particular c (which we cannot know) such that $a + b = c$ is true, but no c such that $a + b = c$ is *determinately true*. (The idea that statements can be "indeterminately" true—whatever that means!—is introduced by Horwich in *Truth* (Oxford: Blackwell, 1990), cf. e.g. p. 114.) For a criticism of Horwich's deflationism see "Sense, Nonsense, and the Senses," pp. 497ff. For a criticism of Horwich and Kripke's identification of Wittgenstein's view of truth with contemporary versions of deflationism, see ibid. pp. 510–16.

isolation, namely, the fact that the person *grasps a certain concept*.[65] What makes Kripke think that Wittgenstein would *deny* that it can be a fact about someone ("considered in isolation") that he or she grasps the concept of addition?

I think that the answer must lie in a peculiar ambiguity in Kripke's cumbersome phrase "a fact about a person considered in isolation." Consider the two statements:

(1) Susan means by "plus" what most English speakers mean by the word.
(2) Susan has the concept of addition.

Now, on *any* view, philosophical or non-philosophical, (1) does not express "a fact about Susan considered in isolation." What it says is that there is a certain *relation* between Susan's understanding of a word and a particular linguistic community's understanding of that word. But since the fact that there is no fact *about Susan considered in isolation* which is the fact that she grasps the concept "plus" is supposed to be a shocking thesis (Kripke calls it a "skeptical" thesis, and compares it to Hume's celebrated theses about causation, etc.), this cannot be what Kripke means to point out. Evidently, Kripke, or rather Kripkenstein, means to make the surprising claim that (2) is not a fact about Susan considered in isolation. But it is not clear why not, *even on Kripkenstein's view of what is involved in having a concept*.

To see why not, let us suppose that Susan does have those speech dispositions which enable her to pass the "concept attributing game" when the concept ascribed is the concept of addition, or more specifically *plus*, and the people playing the game are the members of the English-speaking linguistic community. Now, that Susan is disposed to make such-and-such responses under particular circumstances would appear to be as much a fact about "Susan considered in isolation" as any dispositional fact about her—say, the fact that she is fond of sweets, or the fact that she despises Erich Segal's *Love Story*, or whatever. It is true that English speakers wouldn't express that particular fact about Susan by saying that she has the concept of addition if *their* concept of addition were different; but it is equally true that the fact that Susan likes sweets wouldn't be described by English speakers in those words if our concept of *liking sweets* were different.

---

[65] On p. 67 of *Wittgenstein on Rules and Private Language*, Kripke confesses that "Personally I can only report that in spite of Wittgenstein's assurances, the 'primitive' interpretation ['that looks for something in my present mental state to differentiate between my meaning addition or quaddition'] often sounds rather good to me."

One might wonder why Kripke chose to express his view in this puzzling way, rather than by saying—what he might straightforwardly have said—that, on his interpretation, what Wittgenstein thinks is that having a concept—*addition*, or any other concept—is simply having those linguistic dispositions that enable a speaker to pass the appropriate concept attributing game. Of course, if he had put his interpretation that way, then the interpretation would not have been called a "skeptical" interpretation. Rather, it would have been called a *behaviorist* interpretation. For it amounts to saying that possessing a concept is just possessing a certain behavioral disposition; which disposition being determined by the appropriate concept attributing game.[66]

I do not mean to suggest that it was just for "packaging" purposes that Kripke expressed his interpretation in the way he did. I think that, rather, the way in which Kripke chose to express his interpretation is an indication of what Kripke's own view must be. On Kripke's own view, I suspect, that I grasp the concept of addition isn't *just* "a fact about me considered in isolation," but it is a very special kind of fact, a fact that is not reducible to facts about my behavior dispositions, or my behavior dispositions cum bodily states, or the sameness and difference of the foregoing from the behavior dispositions and bodily states of others. Kripke, I believe, sees Wittgenstein as *denying that*.

Yet even this isn't enough to explain what is going on here, because it is pretty easy to see that Wittgenstein would not wish to deny that, say, I, or Susan, possess the concept of addition, or understand the word "plus"; and many have seen that Wittgenstein is anti-reductionist, that he would not wish in any way to reduce the statement that I understand the concept *plus* to any set of statements about my behavior dispositions. Kripke, of course, knows this; so why, in the end, does he—if not in those very words—ascribe to Wittgenstein a view which makes having a concept come to no more than possessing certain behavior dispositions? Or alternatively:[67] a view which implies that there is no such fact as the fact that anyone has a concept, it is just that we sometimes talk that way?

The answer, I think, must be this. While Kripke knows that Wittgenstein was concerned to deny being a behaviorist or a reductionist about the possession of concepts, he finds these denials somehow

---

[66] Kripke does argue that (on his interpretation of Wittgenstein) our behavior dispositions do not determine the *truth* and *falsity* of our mathematical claims; but that is because *there is no fact as to their truth or falsity on this interpretation* (see n. 62 above). This does not show that (on the same interpretation) having a concept is either more or less than being able to pass the concept-attributing tests.

[67] Cf. n. 59 for an explanation of this alternative reading of Kripke's argument.

unsatisfying. They don't come, as it were, with the right metaphysical emphasis. To have the right metaphysical emphasis, Wittgenstein would have to say that the fact that I grasp a certain concept is a fact about me somehow on the same metaphysical *plane*, one which possesses the same metaphysical *reality*, as the fact that my neurons do such-and-such, or the fact that I have such-and-such a mental image when I think of chocolate ice cream. *That's* what Wittgenstein must be denying. If my guess is right, Kripke speaks of "facts about a person considered in isolation" not because of anything in *Wittgenstein's* writings, but because that is a description of what *Kripke* himself believes in, and because he sees himself as having a disagreement with Wittgenstein.[68]

At the same time, Kripke is obviously honest in telling us that Wittgenstein created a problem for him. This comes out in a remarkable misreading of §195 of the *Investigations* on p. 52 of Kripke's book. Kripke writes, "Yet (§195) 'in a *queer* way' each such case [of the addition table] is in some sense already present." And after ruminating on how 'mysterious' a supposed mental state of understanding would have to be (on p. 54 he writes that it would be a "finite object" which contained an infinite amount of information), Kripke quotes "the protest in §195 more fully," namely, "But I don't mean that what I do now (in grasping a sense) determines the future use *causally* and as a matter of *experience*, but that in a *queer* way the use is itself somehow present." Not a hint in this that this sentence is set off in quotes in Wittgenstein's text (i.e. that the voice is the voice of an interlocutor), much less a hint of Wittgenstein's brusque response: "Really all that is wrong with what you say is the expression 'in a queer way'. The rest is all right; and the sentence only seems queer when one imagines a different language-game for it from the one in which we actually use it." In short, Kripke takes the voice of the interlocutor to be Wittgenstein's voice, and he cannot hear Wittgenstein's response at all.

It is because he sees Wittgenstein as showing that it is "queer" that we can understand a rule, that Kripke is virtually forced to see him as a skeptic. If we grant that this is a misreading, then what is it that Wittgenstein fails to do, that Kripke would have him do, other than, as it might be, pound the table when he says that we do grasp concepts and follow rules?

---

[68] I know that Kripke insists that it is not his purpose to talk about his agreement or disagreement with Wittgenstein, but on p. 65 he openly ridicules Wittgenstein's claim that the 'primitive' interpretation (see the preceding note) is a philosopher's imposition, writing, "Personally I think that such philosophical claims are almost invariably suspect. What the claimant calls a 'misleading philosophical construal' of an ordinary statement is probably the natural and correct understanding."

If grasping concepts is (as Kripke hints that he thinks)[69] a matter of special "facts about a person considered in isolation," then we need to be told more about what the causal or other powers of "facts about a person considered in isolation" are supposed to be. It is striking that the alternative to Wittgenstein's view turns out to be *no clear alternative at all*. Indeed, I suspect that it must consist in saying what practically all of us, including Wittgenstein, would wish to say, but with a special stamp of the foot ("It's *something more* than physical facts and mental imagery" versus "The statement that someone grasps a concept is not replaceable by a set of statements about physical facts and mental imagery"—but what does "something more" add?).

MATHEMATICS

Almost everything that I have said so far (which is to say, most of this essay) is preliminary to discussing my announced topic—to discussing the case of mathematics, or rather the case of number theory, which is the only part of mathematics I wish to discuss here.[70] And I have to begin this final section with yet another "preliminary": for if we are to find an analogue to our commonsense realism about tables and chairs, and our commonsense realism about rule-following, in this mathematical case, it will be necessary first to understand what one is to mean by the "ordinary use" of mathematical notions.

Here I am guided by a remark of Stanley Cavell's,[71] that the notion of the ordinary in Wittgenstein has nothing to do with the distinction between the vernacular and technical language, or the language of the "man (or woman) on the street" and scientific language, or anything like that. The notion of the ordinary in Wittgenstein's later philosophy is meant only to contrast with the philosophical. In this sense of "ordinary," for example, a mathematician who proves a theorem about the zeros of the Riemann zeta function is employing *ordinary language*. Nor is the ordinary use of mathematical language confined to *proof* (here one must remember Wittgenstein's remark that "mathematics is a motley"). Mathematicians not only prove theorems, they also make

---

[69] Is this not the "primitive interpretation" that "looks rather good" to Kripke?

[70] It seems appropriate that this is the case, since, in a sense, Wittgenstein's philosophy always consists of "preliminaries."

[71] This is a remark he has made in a course he and I co-teach on Wittgenstein's later philosophy.

conjectures, they apply the theorems that have been proved both inside and outside of mathematics proper, and so on.

An interesting case is the following. Wittgenstein imagines[72] that a mathematician gives a non-constructive proof that the pattern 777 exists somewhere in the decimal expansion of π, where the non-constructivity of the proof resides precisely in the fact that the proof gives no indication *where* in the decimal expansion of π the pattern occurs.

Let us now imagine that a mathematician living at the time Wittgenstein wrote these remarks offered the following probabilistic argument (such arguments are a commonplace in number theory, and often guide research). As far as we know, the decimal expansion of π passes all of the standard statistical tests for randomness. But if that is so, and the digits occur with equiprobability (as they appear to), then, with a probability greater than .95, we should expect the pattern 777 to occur by such-and-such a place in the expansion.

We can imagine (indeed, I have been told that this is the case) that with the development of the computer this conjecture is later confirmed by carrying out the expansion that far.

I want to say that although such a probabilistic argument is not a proof, nevertheless giving such arguments and applying them is a part of the present-day activity of mathematics, although it was probably not a part of the activity of mathematics one hundred or two hundred years ago, and the technique by which we (informally, of course) assign a "probability" to certain mathematical assertions gives a sense to saying things like "It is probable that 777 occurs in the expansion of π before such-and-such a place."

The application I wish to make of this remark is the following. Consider a mathematical conjecture that we have not succeeded in deciding, for example, the celebrated conjecture that there are infinitely many pairs of twin primes (pairs of numbers p, p+2 which are both primes). A great deal of the discussion in the philosophy of mathematics has centered on the question whether in the case of such a statement—one which is undecided and, for all we know, possibly undecidable—it makes sense to say that the statement is either true or

---

[72] *RFM*, orig. edn., Part IV, §27: "A proof that 777 occurs in the expansion of π, without showing where, would have to look at this expansion from a totally new point of view, so that it showed e.g. properties of regions of the expansion about which we knew only that they lay very far out. Only the picture floats before one's mind of having to assume as it were a dark zone of indeterminate length very far on in π, where we can no longer rely on our devices for calculating; and then still further out a zone where in a *different* way we can once more see something."

false. If someone says that it is either true or false that there are infinitely many twin primes, then I think that what a Wittgensteinian philosopher should ask is, "In what context does the assertion occur?" If it occurs in the context of a philosophical discussion as to whether undecided propositions are "really" true or false, then a Wittgensteinian may well doubt that it makes any sense, because of the peculiar metaphysical emphasis that has been put on the notion of being *really* true or false. But if it occurs as a part of a mathematical argument, then it would be regarded as a perfectly trivial remark. If there is—in that context—a commonsense answer to the question, "But how do you *know* that it must be either true or false?" it would be the rhetorical question, "What other possibility is there?"

In short, I want to suggest that, just as Wittgenstein points out that there is a perfectly ordinary way of learning the concepts "Do so-and-so *ad infinitum,*" "Keep doing the *same* thing," "Do this *uniformly,*" ". . ." (as in "Do A, B, C, . . ."), so there is an ordinary way of learning the use of such expressions as "Either S is true or S is false" in mathematics; and just as I take the point of Wittgenstein's discussion of rule-following not to be the expression of skepticism of any kind about *rule-following*, but rather the expression of a "skepticism" about philosophical discussions of rule-following (or, better, the expression of a conviction that such discussions contain a great deal of nonsense), so I would urge that a Wittgensteinian attitude towards the use of the law of the excluded middle in mathematics would involve not a skepticism about the applications of that law within mathematics, but a "skepticism" about the very *sense* of the "positions" in the philosophy of mathematics—logicism, formalism, intuitionism, Platonism, nominalism, and so on.

(I would like to remind us at this point that, as I said at the beginning, that my aim is not to produce Wittgenstein's own view (although I believe he would agree with what I have just written), but to produce a view that builds on genuinely Wittgensteinian materials. I do find the things Wittgenstein says about the law of the excluded middle in the *Remarks on the Foundations of Mathematics* troubling.)

At any rate, to shift from the Twin Prime Conjecture to an example that Wittgenstein actually uses (*RFM*, orig. edn., IV, §9)—contrary to what Wittgenstein writes about the question (he calls it "queer"), I think we should regard the question whether 770 (note that Wittgenstein shifts from "777" to "770" here!) ever occurs in the expansion of π as a perfectly sensible mathematical question. For example, if mathematicians were to make the conjecture that this is the case, try to prove this conjecture in various ways, and so on, they would be doing something that makes perfect sense. What Wittgenstein should have said is that the mathematicians do understand the question whether 770 ever occurs in the decimal expansion of π, and that they have learned to understand such questions by learning to do number theory; and that something that they have also learned by learning to do number theory is that either 770 will occur in the expansion or 770 will never occur in the expansion. (Indeed, this seems to be what Wittgenstein *does* say in *Philosophical Investigations* §516—the paragraph I chose as the epigraph to this paper.)

Of course, objections to what I have just proposed as a "Wittgensteinian" strategy (even if it is not Wittgenstein's strategy in *RFM*) will come from supporters of all the traditional positions: from metaphysical realists, from anti-realists of all varieties, from intuitionists, formalists, and so on. The previous discussion of how one answers these sorts of objections in the case of rule-following is meant to indicate the general strategy to be pursued in responding to each of these objections, although, of course, even to begin to carry it out in detail would require a work as long as Wittgenstein's *Remarks on the Foundations of Mathematics* (which is itself, as we know, not a "work" but a selection of material from Wittgenstein's *Nachlass*). In particular, the question will be raised—both by metaphysical realists and by a certain sort of anti-realist: well, if you say "Either it is true that 770 will occur in the decimal expansion of π or it is true that 770 will never occur in the decimal expansion of π," then you must be doing one of two things. Either (1), by saying that this assertion is perfectly alright (provided it is not meant as a "philosophical" assertion), you merely mean that we can utter the *words* "Either it is true that 770 will occur in the decimal expansion of π or it is true that 770 will never occur in the decimal expansion of π" in the context of a mathematical argument, while leaving the *philosophical interpretation* of those words entirely open—which is something that no philosopher denies; or (2) you are claiming that the mathematician is entitled to say that one of the two disjuncts is *determinately* true. But if one of the two statements is determinately true, then there must be some *fact* that makes one of those statements true; and since the true disjunct may be undecidable, that fact is not (or is not necessarily) any fact about the existence of a proof. But what sort of a fact could this be?

Once again, exactly as in the above discussion of rule-following, a number of suspect philosophical moves are being made here, for example, the distinction between its being the case that either A is true or B is true and its being the case that one of the two propositions is *determinately* true has been assumed, and, more importantly, it is being assumed that if a proposition is true then there is something that *makes* it true (we have already discussed *that* one).

(One might also consider a different objection, which I shall not identify with a person or position, and that is this: "Isn't mathematical truth supposed to be in some way *conceptual* truth?[73] Now, if all mathematical truths were provable, then it would be clear (or at least *clearer*) in what way all mathematical truths were conceptual truths; but after the Gödel theorem it seems that we are stuck with the idea that some number-theoretic propositions are true even though they have no proof (if we are willing to take mathematical instances of the law of the excluded middle as plain mathematical common sense, in the way you are recommending). But then, what sort of thing *is* this 'mathematical truth'? If there is anything that Wittgenstein insists upon, it is that it is not empirical truth, and if it is not conceptual truth either, then what is it?"

Again, in this case, a special philosophical idea, in fact a dichotomy, is in play; the dichotomy between *empirical* and *conceptual* truth is being given a metaphysical emphasis. And we know that this metaphysically emphasized dichotomy is vulnerable to both Quinean and Wittgensteinian criticisms. The right answer to "What sort of truth is it?" is, of course, "*A mathematical truth.*" And that really is a "grammatical" remark.)

Of course, we might say that what "makes" it true (if it is true), that the pattern 770 occurs in the decimal expansion of π is that there is a number n such that the nth, $n+1$st, and $n+2$nd places in the expansion are 7, 7, and 0, respectively, just as what makes it true that snow is white is that snow *is* white—but, of course, this wouldn't be to give an *informative* answer to the question, what "makes" either statement true, but to reject the metaphysical picture of statements as being "made true" by . . . (what, intangible objects?).

---

[73] Indeed, Wittgenstein does say (in *LFM*, p. 251) that "2 + 2 = 4" is a *grammatical* truth. For an account of what this might mean see my "Mathematical Necessity Reconsidered," in my *Words and Life* (Cambridge, Mass.: Harvard University Press, 1994). Wittgenstein's frequent observation that we use (established) mathematical assertions as *rules* (e.g. for determining the coherence or incoherence of empirical statements containing numerical expressions) is often taken to constitute an *explanation* of mathematical truth; it should be evident that if the present essay is on the right track it is no such thing. Wittgenstein is simply describing certain plain facts about the use of these assertions, not advancing a theory of mathematical truth. I am indebted to Yemima ben Menahem's "Explanation and Description: Wittgenstein on Convention," *Synthese* 115 (1998): 99–130, which employs the distinction between reading the passages in question as *descriptions of our practices* and reading them as *explanations* to shed light on Wittgenstein's discussions.

It may be objected: *isn't* the statement that snow is white like the statement that the sofa is green? Even if he didn't use the language of "making true," Wittgenstein was willing to say (in *LFM*) that "green" and "sofa" "correspond" to "realities." Couldn't we say that that white stuff that we see falling from the sky (and have seen through the ages) is the reality that the statement that snow is white corresponds to?

But there is a problem. "Snow is white" is, after all, a universal generalization logically equivalent to the negative existential "There does not exist snow that isn't white." And Wittgenstein was unwilling to extend the language of "realities" corresponding to statements so far as to introduce *negative realities* for negative existentials to correspond to. (Here I am repeating a point made above, of course.) But the objector might respond, "OK, but even if you don't accept negative facts or negative realities (or universal facts or universal realities) one could say that the statement that there is no yellow book in this room corresponds not to 'a reality' but simply to *reality*; that is, *it says something about reality*. Does the statement that 770 never occurs in the decimal expansion of π, if true, correspond to reality as a whole?"

In this connection, I should like to remind you of Wittgenstein's remarks (in *LFM*) on Hardy's (supposed) claim that "To mathematical propositions there corresponds—in some sense, however sophisticated—a reality."[74]

We have here a thing which constantly happens. The words in our language have all sorts of uses; some very ordinary uses which come into one's mind immediately, and then again they have uses which are more and more remote . . . A word has one or more nuclei of uses which come into everyone's mind first.

So if you forget where the expression "a reality corresponds to" is really at home—

What is "reality"? We think of "reality" as something we can *point* to. It is *this*, *that*.

Professor Hardy is comparing mathematical propositions to propositions of physics. This is extremely misleading.[75]

Wittgenstein is not forbidding us *ever* to use the expression "corresponds to reality" in connection with mathematics;[76] on the contrary,

---

[74] Wittgenstein, *LFM*, p. 239. What Godfrey Hardy actually wrote in the article Wittgenstein mentions is that mathematical theorems are "theorems concerning reality." Hardy does not speak of a *correspondence* to reality anywhere in the article ("Mathematical Proof," *Mind* 38 (1929): 1–25).

[75] *LFM*, pp. 239–40.

[76] This represents a change in my reading of this passage from the shorter version of this essay published as "On Wittgenstein's Philosophy of Mathematics I," *Proceedings*

Wittgenstein devotes the next few lectures to exploring different things that one might mean by expressions of the form "statements of such-and-such type correspond to—or are responsible to—a reality," when this expression is applied to mathematical statements and when it is applied to other sorts of statements. Wittgenstein's point is, rather, that Hardy is unable to free himself from the illusion that when he speaks this way he is still employing the expression in a way that is closely akin to its paradigmatic use, as if mathematical expressions were *descriptions* of a region of reality, only not an ordinary region. As Jim Conant has recently put it,[77] "the use to which Hardy attempts to put the expression is to be seen in the end as a confused attempt to amalgamate several of these possibilities of use in such a way as to fail in the end to be saying anything at all."

In addition, the idea that each true mathematical statement has to *describe* reality is in tension with the fact that mathematical truths are not *contingent*. If mathematical statements *describe* an exotic reality, must they not *depend* on that reality for their truth? And if so, doesn't that mean that *they would be false if reality were otherwise*? From as early as 1913 (as Burton Dreben and Juliet Floyd have pointed out),[78] Wittgenstein resolutely opposed the idea that any statement could simultaneously be *about* reality and yet true independently of how reality is; this is, indeed, what lay behind his insistence that logical truths are "tautologous." Of course, if we could make sense of Kant's "synthetic a priori" we might be able to understand how a statement could correspond to reality and yet not be in any way *contingent*. But even the German idealists had trouble in making sense of that notion.

What of Benacerraf's question in the famous "Mathematical Truth" paper? Am I saying that there is a kind of "realist semantics" for the language of classical mathematics which is part of the activity of classical mathematics itself? And if so, how do I account for the notion of reference involved in that semantics? Is the causal theory of reference false for mathematical entities, etc., etc., etc.?

Again, what one needs to do is to take these questions apart patiently. As Jamie Tappenden once remarked to me in conversation, "Benacerraf's paper showed so well why this way of posing the question leads to an impasse, that it should really have been the *end* of that

of the *Aristotelian Society*, Suppl. Vol. 70 (1996): 243–64. Jim Conant's response (see the next note) convinced me that my former reading was wrong.

[77] James Conant, "On Wittgenstein's Philosophy of Mathematics II," *Proceedings of the Aristotelian Society* 97.2 (1997): 195–222.

[78] Burton Dreben and Juliet Floyd, "Tautology: How Not To Use a Word," *Synthese* 87 (1991): 23–49.

discussion rather than leading people to put additional epicycles on views that don't work."

When people speak of a "semantics" for a piece of language, whether they be linguists or philosophers, all they give us (and all they *can* give us) is a formalism which is ultimately interpreted in *ordinary* language. In the sense of having a translation into ordinary language, of course mathematics has a semantics—a "realist semantics," if you please. Or rather, mathematics as it is actually done, "unregimented" mathematics, already *is* in ordinary language. On the other hand, if a "semantics" is something like a metaphysical relation of "correspondence," then I would say that it is wholly unclear what a "semantics" is, or why the alternative to having a semantics in that sense has to be anti-realism.[79] I am beginning to repeat points that I have already made—not, however, unintentionally, but because I wish to emphasize that the assumption that the notion "semantics" has already been given a special philosophical sense that we all, of course, understand is like the assumption that we understand (and have to accept) the claim that if a statement is true there is "something" that makes it true.

WHY THE PROBLEMS IN THE PHILOSOPHY OF MATHEMATICS ARE NOT *SUI GENERIS*

One thing that makes our understanding of mathematical notions seem paradoxical is that not only do we tend to be attracted to the metaphysical realist picture—in fact, it is only since Quine's talk of "ontological commitment" has become so accepted that that has become a very popular picture—but we are attracted also to a formalist picture in which understanding mathematical concepts is something like "internalizing" rules for syntactic manipulation. We have a tendency to think that somehow (unconsciously perhaps) what we are doing—and all we are doing—when we do elementary number theory is deriving formulas from other formulas, that we have, as it were, a proof procedure in our brains for doing that, and the *syntactic* capacity to operate that proof procedure is what constitutes our *understanding* of number theory; and then we encounter the Gödel theorem, and we are all at sea. But *that* picture is already inadequate as a picture of what our understanding of

---

[79] For a fuller discussion of the idea that commonsense realism does not depend on a mystery relation of "correspondence" see my "Sense, Nonsense, and the Senses," particularly Lecture III.

first-order logic consists in. As I pointed out above, it is just not the case that our understanding of first-order logic is correctly described as our having a set of axioms in our brains and a technique for deriving the valid sentences of first-order logic from those axioms. The *interpretation* of the quantifiers themselves is not simply exhausted by the axioms and rules of derivation. The problem is an instance of a more general problem, which one might call the problem of *reductionism*. On the one hand, our understanding of our concepts, and our employment of them in our richly conceptually structured lives, is not a mystery transaction with intangible objects, a transaction with something *over and above* the objects that make up our bodies and our environments; yet as soon as one tries to take a normative notion like the understanding of a concept or Wittgenstein's notion of the use of a word, and equate that notion with some notion from stimulus-response psychology ("being disposed to make certain responses to certain stimuli"), or a notion from computational psychology, or a notion from the physiology of the brain, then the normativity disappears, and hence the concept itself disappears. Cora Diamond's very lovely example[80] of the picture faces is, I think, a useful one here. The smile in a picture face isn't an "object" over and above the charcoal and the paper before us, but that doesn't mean that statements about picture faces are simply reducible to statements about molecules of carbon and molecules of paper. The expression is something we see *in* the charcoal and paper; it isn't the charcoal and paper, and it isn't something "beside" the charcoal and paper. In the same way, we understand, say, the notion of truth, the logical connectives, the notions of number theory, and so on. That understanding isn't something "immaterial" in the sense of being something "over and above" the systems in our brains, the stimuli and our reactions to them, and so on; but it is something we see *in* the practices of certain of the embodied beings that we are. "If you want to understand what it means 'to follow a rule', you have already to be able to follow a rule," Wittgenstein reminds us (*RFM*, orig. edn., V, §32). And if you want to understand what it means "to grasp generalizations about the natural numbers" you have to be able to grasp generalizations about the natural numbers.

At the beginning of this essay I said that one of my goals would be to show that the problems in the philosophy of mathematics are not as *sui generis* as they appear; and in closing I wish to say a little more about why that is the case. Consider, for purposes of comparison, the "problem of the indeterminacy of translation." The problem, as Quine

---

[80] The example is used by Cora Diamond in *The Realistic Spirit*, p. 249.

poses it, is precisely that we cannot point to trajectories of particles (or of fields) which make it true that A is the correct interpretation of a certain discourse, even when we all agree that A is; and Quine concludes from this that "there is no fact of the matter" as to whether A is the correct interpretation. Or consider the so-called "realism" problem about ethical statements, which is again that one cannot point to causal processes or physical objects which make it true that something is good. The discussion that we have just reviewed in the philosophy of mathematics is not, fundamentally, a different discussion. The problem in all of these cases—as, indeed, Simon Blackburn has seen,[81] although I believe that he has taken exactly the wrong view—is that we wish to impose a *pattern* of what it is to be true, a pattern derived largely from the successes of physical science, on all of our discourse. We believe that there is such a phenomenon as magnetism, and it is also the case that our best explanation of the experiences that have led us to believe this involves an appeal to the theory of (electro)magnetism. Magnetism causally, scientifically, *explains* those experiences. But what on earth, one might ask, does this have to do with a discussion of "value judgments," or a discussion of "translation," or a discussion of mathematical truth?

For a certain kind of "scientific realist," the answer is, "Everything." For "scientific realism" is scientific imperialism. *Any* belief which claims "objectivity" must conform to this pattern—the pattern of causal explanation in a natural science. But that is not how scientific realists see themselves.

The reason that scientific realists do not see that what they are doing is simply trying to force all belief which claims to be objective into a single Procrustean bed is that they have prestructured each of these debates in such a way that one *must* choose between two options: in the metaethical case, either concede that "value judgments" possess "only the illusion of objectivity," or produce metaphysical objects standing behind value judgments and guaranteeing their objectivity; in the semantic case, either concede that judgments concerning the correctness of a translation possess only the illusion of objectivity, or defend "the museum myth of meaning"; in the philosophy of mathematics, either concede that mathematical statements possess a truth value only when they are decidable, or defend the existence of a Platonic realm of mathematical objects. Either there are "intangible objects" corresponding to value terms, to interpretations, to mathematical statements—objects

---

[81] Simon Blackburn, *Spreading the Word* (Oxford: Oxford University Press, 1984).

which are causally efficacious, in the way in which magnetism is causally efficacious—or else value judgments, interpretations, undecidable mathematical conjectures are (if taken to have a truth value) as misguided as belief in *ghosts*. In contrast, the Wittgensteinian strategy, I believe, is to argue that while there is such a thing as correctness in ethics, in interpretation, in mathematics, the way to understand that is not by trying to model it on the ways in which we get things right in physics, but by trying to understand the life we lead with our concepts in each of these distinct areas. The problems in the philosophy of mathematics are not simply the *same* as the problems in metaethics or the problems about the indeterminacy of translation, because the way the concepts work is not the same in these different areas; but what drives the sense that there is a problem—a problem which calls for either a "skeptical solution" or an absurd metaphysics—are usually the very same preconceptions about what "genuine" truth, or "genuine" objectivity, or "genuine" reference must look like.[82]

Appendix

In the preceding essay, I said that I do not believe that Wittgenstein's *Remarks on the Foundations of Mathematics* spring from an anti-realist philosophy. That doesn't mean that there are no problems with Wittgenstein's remarks, and I understand perfectly well why some of them would seem to invite an anti-realist reading. In particular, it does seem that Wittgenstein thought, when he wrote the material that the editors have collected under this title, that a mathematical proposition cannot be true unless we can decide that it is true on the basis of a proof or calculation of some kind.[83] Not only is this quite explicit in his 1937 remarks about the Gödel theorem, but the view appears as late as the 1944 remark that even God's *omniscience* cannot decide whether people would have reached 777 in the decimal expansion of π "after the end of the world."[84] How can such a view *not* spring from "anti-realism"?

Here I use "anti-realism" as a name for the family of (different) views of truth today defended by, for example, Michael Dummett, Crispin

---

[82] My thanks to Warren Goldfarb for helpful suggestions.

[83] But see n. 1 in which I contrast what Wittgenstein *published* on this question—*PI* §516—with the unpublished material collected as *RFM*.

[84] *RFM*, orig. edn., Part V, §34. I quote the paragraphs in question later in this Appendix; it can be found in n. 2 as well.

Wright, and Neil Tennant as well as (in Wittgenstein's day) Brouwer. One could, of course, decide to call *any* view in the philosophy of mathematics which identifies mathematical truth with provability "anti-realist," regardless of the *reasons* for the view; but this seems to me a mistake. The point I wish to make in this Appendix is that Wittgenstein's reasons for this identification (which I do believe he made) are, at bottom, totally different from the reasons which move the "anti-realists," and that when we grasp those reasons, we can see how they amount, in fact, to a species of mathematical *realism*.

What I want to say, in brief, is that the inadequacies that I find in *some* (by no means most) of Wittgenstein's *Remarks on the Foundations of Mathematics* represent a peculiar combination of genuine insight with an inadequate knowledge of actual mathematical practice and of sciences which depend on mathematical practice, in particular mathematical physics.

To me, the most striking fact about the *Remarks on the Foundations of Mathematics* is that in spite of the philosophical importance that Wittgenstein himself attaches to the application of mathematics outside of mathematics, the *examples* of such application are remarkably trivial. Apart from applications of arithmetic to results of counting, and a few scattered examples of applications of geometry, there are very few examples of applications in *RFM*. In particular, I tried to show in the preceding essay that crucial difficulties for the view that mathematical truth can be identified with (or is at any rate co-extensive with) provability can be raised from an examination of the ways in which mathematics is used in mathematical physics. But apart from a couple of examples from engineering,[85] the *only* example which might even be regarded as an application in mathematical physics in the whole of *RFM* that I was able to find is a trivial application to the orbit of a comet.[86]

In a way, of course, this is not surprising: Wittgenstein was trained as an engineer; and, indeed, one gets the feeling that he imagines that the application of mathematics to empirical material consists in reading off geometrical relations from pictures and comparing the results of calculations with the results of counting and measurement. These are

---

[85] Examples from engineering in *RFM* can be found (in the original edition) at Part III, §49 and Part V, §51.

[86] *RFM*, orig. edn., Part IV, §23 refers to the proposition that a comet describes a parabola. I do not count the example of the attractive force exerted on something by "an endless row of marbles of such and such a kind" in Part IV, §8, and in the same section, the weight of a pillar composed of "as many slabs as there are cardinal numbers" as applications in *physics*, but rather as bits of pure mathematics.

exactly the ways in which an engineer applies mathematics. I don't mean to suggest that Wittgenstein did not know that there are much more *complicated* uses of mathematics than these in mathematical physics. What I think likely is that he had no idea of the detailed nature of those applications, and that he assumed that while they might, indeed, be more complicated than the trivial ones that he used as examples, that is, indeed, all they are—more "complicated"; that is to say that nothing of *philosophical* interest could be lost by confining attention to the few and trivial applications that he does discuss. If so, I believe that he made a significant error; but an error that doesn't flow from a metaphysical position.

I said, however, that Wittgenstein's position involves some genuine insights as well—insights which combined with a better appreciation of what mathematics and its application are really like could have led Wittgenstein to a more correct and more perspicuous account of what is going on in mathematics. I shall begin by describing two of these insights.

TWO WITTGENSTEINIAN INSIGHTS

(1) *Mathematical propositions wouldn't be* propositions—that is, *meaningful statements—if mathematics were not applied* outside *of mathematics.* (Note that this does not mean that every single mathematical proposition need have such applications.)

If mathematics were not applied outside of mathematics, then there would be no reason to view it as more than a game (one in which, for example, we are allowed to write certain marks on paper when the marks are "axioms" or when other players have written certain other marks on paper—or in a "solitaire" version of the game, when we ourselves have written certain other marks on paper). The question of the "truth" of anything that is produced in the course of the game would be as silly as the question of whether a move in a chess game is "true." This insight is, of course, one that Wittgenstein inherits from logicism. Russell and Frege stressed, for example, the importance of the fact that numbers can be used to *count* things, and for that reason number words occur constantly in *empirical* statements.[87]

---

[87] The logicists had other insights as well: they stressed the importance of the fact that one can count "abstract entities," e.g. numbers and equations, as well as emperors and cabbages, and also stresed that the things counted need not be adjacent in space or time

This is the reason that, in the preceding essay, I said that it would be a mistake to think that Wittgenstein believed, as Michael Dummett sometimes seems to suggest, that understanding mathematical propositions is just a matter of understanding the proof procedures by which we verify them. Indeed, at one point Wittgenstein suggests that a mathematical "proposition" might have a proof but no real meaning, precisely because we would have no idea of how to *apply* it.[88]

(2) *Commonsense realism with respect to rule-following*—which, I argued in the preceding paper, Wittgenstein defends—*does not, in and of itself, commit us to views about infinity (i.e. about just the sort of problem that motivates Kripke's discussion).*[89]

Kripke's "skeptical problem" is initially formulated as the question, how can our understanding of a rule determine what is true in infinitely many cases—and so in more cases than it is physically possible for human beings to "get to." But Wittgenstein is quite clear that when someone, say a child, learns to follow the rule "Add two," he learns to follow a practice which it is possible for human beings to engage in; but such a practice is not one which extends to infinitely many cases, because human beings cannot—not really—add two to infinitely many numbers.

Consider what Wittgenstein says about a child's understanding of infinity (*RFM*, orig. edn., IV, §14):

or even exist in the lifetime of the person doing the counting; hence counting and forming sums of things counted are not physical operations. Wittgenstein's attacks on Russell's *Principia* in *RFM* are attacks on the significance Russell attached to symbolic logic, not on *these* insights. I would also like to say that one thing I like about *RFM* is that Wittgenstein treats empiricist views with a certain respect. It is true that, like Frege, he finds such views in the end completely inadequate, but he is willing to let us see the *appeal* of such views. He doesn't treat an empiricist view as simply a *dumb* view, as Frege does. On the contrary, empiricist views (and also finitist views) are treated as views to which one is naturally led by a desire for clarity, although Wittgenstein does agree with Frege that coming to see their inadequacy is an essential step to any further progress with the questions.

[88] *RFM*, orig. edn., Part IV, §25. I find this remark wrong, by the way, because it seems to me to forget something Wittgenstein himself elsewhere points out, which is that mathematical propositions also have applications *within* mathematics. Wittgenstein himself seems to connect having an application with having a *constructive* proof here, but this is unjustified, unless one thinks of a very limited sort of application. Nevertheless, the fact that Wittgenstein made the remark shows that much more than the mastery of proof procedures is involved in the understanding of mathematical assertions, in his view.

[89] I realize that it is an anachronism to refer to Kripke in explaining one of Wittgenstein's insights, but the anachronism may help a present-day reader.

Suppose children are taught that the earth is an infinite flat surface; or that God created an infinite number of stars; or that a star keeps on moving uniformly in a straight line, without ever stopping.

Queer, when one takes something of this kind as a matter of course, as it were in one's stride, it loses its whole paradoxical aspect. It is as if I were to be told: don't worry, this series, or movement, goes on without ever stopping. We are as it were excused the labor of thinking of an end.

'We won't bother about an end.'

It might also be said: 'for us the series is infinite'.

'We won't worry about an end to this series; for us it is always beyond our ken.'

It is significant that Wittgenstein says "Suppose *children* are taught"; that is to say, this last quotation is not a comment on how a sophisticated mathematician might understand these statements, but about how a child might understand the statement that a series (e.g. the series 1, 2, 3 . . .) is infinite, or that it "has no end."[90]

The point Wittgenstein makes here can be put this way: that when we speak of a human being as being able to follow a rule, in the ordinary applications of that concept we are not required to ascribe to the person (in this case, the children) the mathematical notion of infinity, or the notion that the rule *determines* what it is correct to say in cases that it is not actually possible to get to, and so on.

Kripke, on the other hand, runs together two different questions: the question how our understanding of a rule determines what we count as correct in actual human practice, and the question of *what the mathematical consequences of the rule are*. In posing his "skeptical problem," Kripke takes it as evident that an arbitrary sum is correct if the sum is *determined by the rule*; but this is a way of thinking that Wittgenstein criticizes from the very beginning of *RFM*. As Wittgenstein makes clear,[91] to criticize this is not to say that one cannot introduce a *mathematical* sense of "determine" in which, if we take the "rule" of addition to be, for example, the definition of addition by primitive recursion, we can say that "every correct sum is *determined* by the rule." But to say this is to make a *mathematical* comment about addition; it is not to speak to any of the philosophical problems, because just the notion that puzzled us, the notion of mathematical correctness, has been simply taken for granted.

---

[90] I am not sure that the mathematical notion of the infinite *is* completely absent in the child's grasp that "you can always go on counting." Wittgenstein's discomfort with mathematical talk about what happens in infinite sequences may be influencing his perceptions here.

[91] See *PI* §189 for the distinction between these two uses of "determine."

Thus, we might respond to Kripke as follows: "Professor Kripke, we propose to use the expression *A is determined as the correct answer by the rule R* only when it is possible for human beings to *actually* calculate A by using the rule R; and in all other cases we will use the different expression *A is a mathematical consequence of the rule R*. Now, one of the problems you raised, namely, "How does a rule that we grasp manage to determine what is correct in infinitely many cases?" simply does not arise; for if 'determine' means what we have just proposed it ought to mean, then a rule does *not* determine what it is correct to say in infinitely many cases (although it is 'always beyond our ken' just where we will cease to be able actually to apply it, and hence where it ceases to determine an answer). And if you reformulate your puzzle, by saying 'How can a finite rule have infinitely many different *mathematical consequences*?' then that seems to be a mathematical question, and one whose answer is trivial." I do not mean to say, of course, that this response completely "defuses" Kripke's worries—as we say, those worries have complex sources—but at least one strain in Kripke's complex argument does seem to depend on conflating these two senses of "determine."

One last remark in this connection: in the preceding essay, I suggested that if one accepts what I described as Wittgenstein's defense of our "commonsense realism about rule-following," then one could be led to suppose that the notion of being *provable* is an unproblematical notion, because "to be provable in a formal system, we know, is just to be a sentence which is obtainable as the last line of a longer or shorter proof (or as the bottom of a larger or smaller proof tree) by following certain rules." But we can now see that that was too simple. In addition to what was argued in the preceding essay, that there are decisive objections to taking the truths of mathematics to be coextensive with the provable sentences of mathematics, we can also object that Wittgenstein's commonsense realism about rule-following cannot give us the *mathematical* notion of "provability"; at best it can give us the ordinary empirical notion of "provability." (Of course in daily life we sometimes quite legitimately use the word "provable" in one way and sometimes in the other.) When I said in the essay that Wittgenstein thinks that a necessary condition for a mathematical statement to have a truth value is that it be "humanly decidable," I meant the modifier "humanly" to indicate that I was not talking about the *mathematical* sense of "decidability"; for to say that a necessary condition is that the statement be "decidable" in the mathematical sense—the sense in which it might be decidable even though the shortest proof or disproof was longer than the number of elementary particles in the universe—would be open to the objection that I just made against Saul Kripke, the objection that to understand *that* notion of decidability (or of provability or of disprovability) is already to be able to understand the sort of mathematical notion whose intelligibility Kripke's "skeptic" wishes (initially at least) to call into question.

WHERE WITTGENSTEIN WENT ASTRAY

It remains now to say how, given what I have been calling "commonsense realism about rule-following," a commonsense realism which, we have just seen, does not in and of itself involve one in the sorts of problems that Kripke raises, because it does not require a notion of infinity beyond the notion Wittgenstein says a child might have ("for us the end is always out of reach"), and given a robust insistence on the fact that mathematical propositions are statements with sense only because mathematical concepts have applications in the realm of the *non-mathematical*—given that these are both genuine insights *and* genuinely commonsensical, how Wittgenstein can have been led to the extremely *un*commonsensical view that provability (in what I called the "ordinary" sense) is a necessary condition for mathematical truth.

Michael Dummett[92] has urged that Wittgenstein actually held an even *more* counterintuitive view, namely, that *actually being proved* is a necessary condition for mathematical truth. But even though here and there in Wittgenstein's *Nachlass* one can turn up a note that shows that Wittgenstein "played with the idea" at certain moments in his life, I do not find anything in *RFM* which should be construed as *committing* Wittgenstein to such a radical view. For example, let us pay close attention to what Wittgenstein says in the passage written in 1944 (*RFM*, orig. edn., V, §34) that I mentioned at the beginning of this Appendix:

Suppose that people go on and on calculating the expansion of π. So God, who knows everything, knows whether they will have reached "777" by the end of the world. But can his *omniscience* decide whether they *would* have reached it after the end of the world? It cannot. I want to say: Even God can determine something mathematical only by mathematics. Even for him the rule of expansion cannot decide anything that it does not decide for us.

Of course, human beings cannot possibly calculate at all "after the

---

[92] See Michael Dummett, "Wittgenstein on Necessity: Some Reflections," in Peter Clark and Bob Hale, eds., *Reading Putnam* (Oxford: Blackwell, 1994).

end of the world"—especially if, as is reasonable to suppose, the "end of the world" means the end of space and time. The passage could, of course, be read in another way: there is a Last Judgment in time, and that is "the end of the world," and there is still more time available for calculation after the Last Judgment—but then why should not human beings go on calculating in eternity? The most reasonable interpretation is that we are to suppose that human beings go on calculating to the very limits of physical possibility. (This is not a remark about *religion*, after all.) That is, Wittgenstein is not here—contrary to Dummett's interpretation—saying that not even God could know what human beings *would* count as a correct calculation prior to their actually accepting it as correct (which would involve attributing a strongly "anti-realist" attitude toward counterfactuals to Wittgenstein, on little evidence that I can see); he is saying—as he goes on to make clear—that not even God can decide whether the pattern does or does not occur in the expansion of π except by a calculation which is *actually*—not just "mathematically"—possible. (However, notice the much less problematic statement about this sort of mathematical proposition that Wittgenstein actually *published*, and that I used as the epigraph to the paper.)

Thus, even if this paragraph is not evidence *against* Dummett's interpretation, I take it to be at least compatible with a reading in which mathematical propositions can be provable—and hence true—even though, for quite contingent reasons, human beings don't happen to find the proof.

I think that, if one makes the mistake of supposing that the sorts of examples of the applications of mathematics outside of mathematics that Wittgenstein gives in *RFM* exhaust the *philosophically relevant* sorts of examples there are, then the position I have ascribed to Wittgenstein can appear quite attractive; for there is nothing in these sorts of applications that would require us to suppose that *humanly* unprovable mathematical propositions can have a truth value. The notion that a humanly[93] unprovable mathematical proposition can have a truth value can then appear (as I believe it did appear to Wittgenstein) just as a piece of metaphysical fabulation. The situation is quite different,

---

[93] The fact that Wittgenstein is willing to consider the thought-experiment of imagining that humans go on and on calculating until "the end of the world" may also indicate that he is willing to allow us to idealize human abilities to calculate to the uttermost limits of physical possibility. (So that the relevant line here is not between what *humans* can calculate as opposed to what, say, Martians might be able to calculate, but between what it is within physical possibility to calculate and mere "mathematical possibility" of calculation. If so, this would go even more strongly against Dummett's reading.)

however, when we consider the sorts of applications that I discussed in the foregoing essay.

When we say that a physical system obeys a certain equation—one which is correct according to our best current physical theory—for example, when we say that the state-vector of a physical system obeys the Dirac equation, or, in Newtonian physics, when we say that gravitational forces obey the Newtonian law of gravitation, or even when we say that a certain phenomenon obeys the wave equation, what is the situation? As long as we accept the correctness of Newton's law of gravity, for example, we are committed to the statement that the evolution of an N-body system will be in accordance with the solutions to the appropriate system of differential equations; and it is to this day quite unknown whether the solutions to those equations are recursively calculable even when N = 3.[94] (And, as I mentioned in the foregoing paper, there are cases in which it has been proved that the solutions to the *wave equation* are not recursively calculable, even given recursive initial data.) Indeed, we do not even know whether the values of physical magnitudes at specified future times are, in general, effectively calculable to, say, five decimal places when those magnitudes obey these equations.

"What Wittgenstein would have said" if this had been called to his attention is something I would not even venture to conjecture; but what seems clear is that, short of adopting a wholesale instrumentalist attitude toward mathematical physics—a way out that I myself find utterly unacceptable—one cannot really sustain the identification of mathematical correctness with provability and with calculation that seems not so much argued for as taken for granted throughout the whole of Wittgenstein's *Remarks on the Foundations of Mathematics*.[95]

---

[94] At Gabriel Stolzenberg's suggestion, I emphasize that this is connected with the (possible) undecidability of the question whether the bodies will or will not collide. The phenomenon of "chaos" provides an additional reason to think that the time-evolutions of some physical systems may not be calculable by human beings even when their behavior is governed by deterministic laws.

[95] My thanks to Crispin Wright for helpful suggestions in connection with this Appendix.

6

The Expression of Belief*

Peter Winch

There is indeed an immense gulf, which hardly anyone can fail to see, between Wittgenstein's conception of philosophy and that of the mainstream. Indeed, his method of argument diverges from what is familiar so drastically, that some fail to see that there is any argument there at all. He himself, in his bleak Preface to *Philosophical Investigations,* says his book "is really only an album" and laments that he has been unable to produce the "good book" that he would have liked. There is no reason to doubt that he was sincerely dissatisfied with the work as it stood; but I think there is overwhelming reason not to accept at its face value his description of it as "only an album." Even the paragraph of the Preface that ostensibly is to justify that designation hardly does so in fact. Indeed, in the previous sentence he speaks of it as "a picture of a landscape" and one constructed according to definite principles.

In any case, anyone who reads the book with care—and it is a waste of time to read it in any other way—will soon realize that the structure of argument is very tight. It is, to be sure, a structure of a different sort from that commonly met with in philosophical argument, but the difference is certainly not a matter of lower degree of rigor or connectedness. Rather, the discussion introduces new conceptions of what these argumentative virtues can amount to.

The divergence from the mainstream is nowhere more evident than in Wittgenstein's treatment of the concept of belief, both in *Tractatus* (Propositions 5.54–5.5423) and in *Philosophical Investigations,* Part II,

* [This essay was originally delivered as a presidential address to the American Philosophical Association. At the occasion of its delivery, Winch prefaced the paper with the following remarks: "I usually decline, if only on grounds of incompetence, requests to offer generalizations about the current condition of Anglo-American philosophy. However, I feel fairly confident in saying that the works of Ludwig Wittgenstein are not the favorite reading of most contemporary philosophical professionals. And that is one of the many reasons for my surprise at finding myself here today, since I suppose that those who so flatteringly elected me must have had some inkling of my philosophical predilections."—eds.]

sections x and xi. His discussion is not focused on the kind of question we meet in most of the literature: "What is belief? Is it a state, a process, an activity, a disposition, or what? Is it something psychological or something physiological, or does it partake of both? How are different kinds of belief to be classified?"—and so on. Where he does touch on such questions, he does so as it were glancingly; and this is one reason why little notice has been taken of his discussions by those interested in the concept of belief. But even among those who do take a serious interest in Wittgenstein's work, his treatment of belief is seldom given a central place. I myself think that what he writes about this is both of great importance in itself and also absolutely central to the main thrust of his philosophizing; and so I am devoting this paper to it.

I spoke of the "main thrust" of his philosophizing. The full title of the *Tractatus Logico-Philosophicus* expresses this fairly unequivocally. It is a *philosophical* treatment of *logic*: not primarily directed at the construction of a logical system, but rather at elucidating what it is for a system to be a 'logical' system. I should say that the main aim of *Philosophical Investigations* is the same: though by this time his conception of how this question should be expressed and treated is so different that it may seem—and has seemed to many—that Wittgenstein has by now changed the subject.

The concept of belief becomes a subject for discussion in both the early and the late works because it seems to introduce certain anomalies into the discussion of the nature of logic. In the *Tractatus* the anomaly represented by "certain propositional forms of psychology," such as "A believes that p," "A thinks p," and "A says p," is that it appears superficially as though, in them, "one proposition could occur in another" otherwise than as the basis of a truth operation. Putting it differently, in such propositions the truth value of the whole seems *not* to be a logical function of the truth values of its parts. Take the proposition "Bob Dole believes he will be the next President of the United States." That may be true (or false) quite independently of whether or not it is true that Dole actually will be the next President. Since the *Tractatus* essentially treats all propositions as truth functions of elementary propositions, this is an appearance that has to be dissipated.

In *Philosophical Investigations* the anomaly presented by the concept of belief is a closely related one: it is that expressed in what Wittgenstein calls "Moore's Paradox,"[1] namely, that a sentence of the form "p

---

[1] G. E. Moore presented the paradox in a paper he read to the Cambridge Moral Sciences Club on 26 October 1944. It interested Wittgenstein greatly and his notebooks contain numerous references to it and what Wittgenstein took to be its great philosoph-

and I do not believe that p" sounds like nonsense—indeed very much like a self-contradiction—while, on the other hand, it also sounds as if it asserts what may actually be the case. If Bob Dole were to say: "I shall be the next President and I don't believe that I shall be the next President," that would sound like nonsense. And yet it may actually be the case both that Dole will be the next President and that he does not believe it.

There is an enormous contrast between the ways in which these anomalies are addressed in the two works at the extreme ends of Wittgenstein's career. And yet there is a very close parallel as well, to overlook which is to risk missing a great deal. The three short sections numbered 5.542 to 5.5422 in the *Tractatus* offer a way of dealing with the problem (and one that is at first sight astounding insofar as it is intelligible) and a further brief paragraph, 5.5423, laconically compares our understanding of propositions of the (apparent) form "A believes p" to the perception of pictures with multiple aspects like the Necker cube, which can be seen in two quite different ways. The three-page-long section x of *Philosophical Investigations*, Part II, is a sustained discussion of Moore's paradox about the verb "to believe." Section xi, immediately following, thirty-six pages and the longest section in Part II, is a sustained and fascinating discussion of the whole phenomenon of shifting aspects. The last eight pages of the section drift back, so unobtrusively that the significance of this movement has often been missed, into a discussion of what is involved in our experience of the mental life of other people, their feelings, emotions, and beliefs. This movement must be seen as the *culmination* of the discussion of shifting aspects, and not as a rather inconsequential afterthought; furthermore it is clear that the structural parallel with the *Tractatus* discussion of belief is no accident.

I want now to quote the relevant *Tractatus* passage at length.

5.54 In the general propositional form, propositions occur in a proposition only as bases of the truth-operations.

5.541 At first sight it appears as if there were also a different way in which one proposition could occur in another.

Especially in certain propositional forms of psychology, like "A thinks, that p is the case," or "A thinks p," etc.

Here it appears superficially as if the proposition p stood to the object A in a kind of relation.

---

ical importance. For instance: "Moore poked into a philosophical wasp nest with his paradox; & if the wasps did not duly fly out, that's only because they were too listless" (*Culture and Value*, MS 137 120a, 10 December 1948).

(And in modern epistemology (Russell, Moore, etc.) those propositions have been conceived in this way.)

5.542 But it is clear that "A believes that p," "A thinks p," "A says p," are of
the form "'p' says p": and here we have no co-ordination of a fact and
an object, but a co-ordination of facts by means of a co-ordination of
their objects.

5.5421 This shows that there is no such thing as the soul—the subject, etc.—as
it is conceived in contemporary superficial psychology.
A composite soul would not be a soul any longer.

5.5422 The correct explanation of the form of the proposition "A judges p"
must show that it is impossible to judge a nonsense. (Russell's theory
does not satisfy this condition.)

First, to get one possible misunderstanding out of the way,
Wittgenstein is *not* saying that when someone says something like
"Peter Winch thinks that this lecture will go on too long," this is a misuse of ordinary language. He is saying that if such a proposition is subjected to truth-functional analysis, the elementary propositions which
are brought to light will, none of them, have a form that looks like the
original. In particular there will be nothing corresponding to the ordinary-language name "Peter Winch," no reference for instance to a 'soul'
or 'pure subject of thought' who (or which) thinks the thought in question.

Notice that Wittgenstein's formulation of the 'propositions of psychology' under discussion is couched in the third person—"A believes /
thinks / says p." However, I think it is obvious on a little reflection that
he intends *all* expressions of belief, etc., whether in the third, second, or
first person, to be covered by this general formulation; and it seems to
me noteworthy that there is no suggestion here that the first- and third-
person forms have to be dealt with *differently*.

In spite of the fact that Wittgenstein uses a third-person formulation
there are many grounds for believing that it is the first-person form—
"*I* believe / think / say that p"—that is fundamental for understanding
why he treats this matter as he does. In particular: propositions, possible values of p, that is, are conceived in the *Tractatus* not as Fregean
'thoughts'—timeless 'third world' entities, existing (in some sense) quite
independently of being judged or asserted in any particular context. It
is an essential feature of a Tractarian proposition that its sense is completely determinate; and we reach a completely determinate sense only
when we grasp the sign in the concrete circumstances of its application.

3.262 What does not get expressed in the sign is shown by its application.

What the signs conceal, their application declares.

The *Tractatus* is of course short on examples, but we can use an example from *Philosophical Investigations*[2] to illustrate also how Wittgenstein conceived propositions in the earlier work. Consider the sentence, "After he had said this, he left her as he did the day before." Wittgenstein remarks that while I should understand this as part of a narrative,

[i]f it were set down in isolation I should say, I don't know what it's about. But all the same I should know how the sentence might be used; I could myself invent a context for it.

That is, in *Tractatus* terminology, "what does not get expressed in the sign is shown by its application."

Tractatus 5.5422 reads:

The correct explanation of the form of the proposition "A judges p" must show that it is impossible to judge a nonsense. (Russell's theory does not satisfy this condition.)

A corollary of this is that we can say that a judgment has been made, a proposition expressed, only in circumstances in which the words we perceive can be attributed to a human being as their author. If, for instance, I heard the words "After he had said this, he left her as he did the day before" being emitted by one of those machines designed to reproduce electronically the sound of human speech, I should not understand what I hear as a proposition in the sense of the *Tractatus*—unless, that is, I took it as a message left on the machine by a human being at some remove or other. This tempts me to say that, for the *Tractatus,* the value of x in "x believes / thinks / says that p" is always "I"—but, of course, "I" uttered by some particular person or other. This is certainly not an altogether satisfactory way of putting things, but I think it is the best that can be done without going too far outside the framework of the *Tractatus* which, as I have remarked, is silent about the relations between first- and third-person utterances.

Let us then see what can be made of *Tractatus* 5.542 as applied to the *first* person—"I believe (etc.) that p," it is said, has the form "'p' says p." If I want to tell you that I believe my lecture will go on too long, I can, of course, say, "I believe the lecture will go on too long"; or I might even adopt the curious mode of speech favored by candidates for political office in the United States and say "Peter Winch believes the lecture

---

[2] Part I, §525.

will go on too long." But I can just as well express my belief to you by saying simply, "This lecture will go on too long." The utterance of those words in that context constitutes the assertion, or proposition, that this lecture will go on too long; but is also an expression of the belief that this lecture will go on too long. I do not have to prefix those words with "I believe that . . .," and if I do so prefix them, that does not make my utterance any *more* an expression of my belief. As Wittgenstein was to put it much later in *Philosophical Investigations*, II. x:

If however, "I believe it is so" throws light on my state, then so does the asser-tion "it is so". For the sign "I believe" can't do it, can at the most point in that direction.

His point could be put like this: if I say simply "I believe" or "I have a belief" (and no completion concerning what I believe is supplied by the context), I tell my hearer absolutely nothing about my 'state'. Insofar as a description is what is in question at all, it is a description *completely* dependent on the report of *what* I believe.

So far so good. Or at least, so far not so bad. We now have to see what, from this perspective, we are to make of those values of "A believes that p" that actually are couched in the *third* person. For even if we can identify the sense of "I believe that p" with, simply, p, we emphatically can *not* do this with "*He* believes that p." Suppose, then, one of you in the audience recognizes the *words* I am using but does not understand what it is I am saying, what it is I believe or think. You ask the lady sitting next to you: "*What* is Winch saying?" She replies, "Winch is saying that the words 'I believe' are redundant in the sense that they do not transform into an expression of belief an utterance that previously was not one." Her reply relates, and is understood by you to relate, to the words you both heard me utter. The situation is parallel to that in which your neighbor asks you to explain a passage in the writ-ten text of the lecture. "What is he saying here?" is roughly equivalent to "What does this passage mean?"

It will not have escaped the skeptical listener that my last remarks apply specifically to the form "A *says* that p." What about "thinks" and "believes"? The relation between these needs much more extensive treatment than I can give it here; but I want to make some brief remarks which are important for my principal theme.[3] Consider the following from *Tractatus* 3.31:

[3] I have treated this topic much more extensively in "Language, Thought and World in Wittgenstein's *Tractatus*," ch. 2 of my *Trying to Make Sense* (Oxford: Blackwell, 1987).

Every part of a proposition which characterizes its sense I call an expression (a symbol).

(The proposition itself is an expression)

Expressions are everything—essential for the sense of the proposition—that propositions can have in common with one another.

Although the examples of 'expressions' considered in the *Tractatus* are mainly *words,* there are hints that the net ought to be cast much more widely. For instance, 4.002:

Man possesses the capacity of constructing languages in which every sense can be expressed, without having an idea how and what each word means—just as one speaks without knowing how the single sounds are produced.

Colloquial language is a part of the human organism and is not less complicated than it.

From it it is humanly impossible to gather immediately the logic of language.

Language disguises the thought; so that from the external form of the clothes one cannot infer the form of the thought they clothe, because the external form of the clothes is constructed with quite another object than to let the form of the body be recognized.

The silent adjustments to understand colloquial language are enormously complicated.

The *Tractatus* of course makes no attempt to describe these enormously complicated adjustments of the human organism, and assumes that what is logically essential can be characterized without this. That is one of the most important ways in which *Philosophical Investigations* differs from it: Wittgenstein's treatment of logic in the later work *consists* precisely in what he there calls "remarks on the natural history of mankind." If we look back on the *Tractatus* with the hindsight provided by *Philosophical Investigations* we may say the following—in elucidation of the *Tractatus*'s puzzling claim that "A believes that p" has the form "'p' says that p."

Suppose you hear the words "This lecture is going to last too long." It is only if this incident takes place in a certain very familiar kind of context that you will *hear them as* the expression of a belief: not, for instance, if the sound emanates from a tape recorder on which an English lesson is being played. If, on the other hand, the sound has been produced by a worried-looking human being whom you know to be called Winch and whom you know plans to give a lecture directly, you will normally hear it as saying that the lecture that is about to take place will be excessively long. Your interest in this may be of two sorts. You may thereupon resolve not to go to the lecture, since it will probably keep you from a more attractive engagement later in the evening.

In that case you are simply interested in p. On the other hand you may be interested in reassuring me, fearing that my nervousness over the coming lecture's length will prevent me from delivering it intelligibly. Now you are interested, not so much in the proposition that the utterance "p" expresses, as in the fact that what it expresses is my belief. You will now give emphasis to quite different elements in the circumstances of the utterance than in the first case.

The context which serves to determine the sense of a thought or belief may be as far-reaching as you like; it need not be confined to the immediate circumstances. There are cases in which my knowledge of the kind of life a person has had will be what makes me able to understand his or her utterance. This is likely to be the case, for instance, if someone insists that a friend of hers is innocent of a crime of which the evidence seems to show him to be guilty. And this is of course important too for the cases where the 'expression' we are dealing with is not the actual uttering of a sentence. We can see this from the example in hand. My assertion that A believes the accused to be not guilty may be based on all sorts of considerations: my general knowledge of her character and habits of thought, the expression on her face, the tapping of her foot—and so on and so on.

I want to make the proposal that the formula "'p' says p" can be so read that the first occurrence of "'p'" is taken to include such non-linguistic (albeit in a narrow sense) forms of expression. Or, differently put, when I say to you "A believes he is guilty," you are entitled to ask me on what I base this assertion and *any* (serious) answer I may give to this will correspond to the utterance "p."

I come now to the concluding paragraph of the *Tractatus* discussion of "A believes that p" in which the reference to shifting aspects occurs. The second half of 5.542 says of the 'analyzed' form "'p' says p,"

here we have no co-ordination of a fact and an object, but a co-ordination of facts by means of a co-ordination of their objects.

In the third-person case, "A says that p," the two facts in question are the fact stated by the expression "p" and the expression "p" itself. (It is important to remember 3.14: "The propositional sign is a fact.") The 'objects' of which the propositional sign is composed are the 'names' which stand for / mean / represent the objects of which the fact stated is composed. We can now interpret these notions in the liberal way I have just been suggesting. The fact of A's saying that p is composed of / consists of the objects which enter into that fact—everything that make A's utterance the expression that it is. We can concentrate our attention on that fact—if you like, on A's linguistic and other expressive behavior (together with the surroundings essential to their being so expressive). In so doing we are not excluding from consideration altogether the proposition we read this behavior as expressing: otherwise we do not understand the behavior for what it is—the expression of a certain belief. It is because the objects / the 'names' constituting A's expressive behavior are correlated with the objects constituting the fact that A states / thinks / believes that we can see the aspect of saying / thinking / believing in it. We do not grasp what A's behavior is without grasping the fact that it expresses and *in* grasping the fact we grasp the correlations between its 'names' and the 'objects' comprising the fact stated / thought / believed.

This explains the importance of 5.5423:

To perceive a complex means to perceive that its constituents are combined in such and such a way.

This perhaps explains that the figure

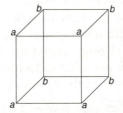

can be seen in two ways as a cube; and all similar phenomena. For we really see two different facts.

It is not *simply* that we perceive the two facts, but rather that we *perceive the one in the other*.

As I have already noted, this analogy reappears, enormously expanded, in *Philosophical Investigations*, Part II, section xi, immediately following the discussion of belief in section x, to which I now want to turn. I said earlier that the subject is here approached from the perspective of Moore's Paradox: that whereas "p and I do not believe that p" sounds like nonsense, it nevertheless also seems to report a combination of facts which could indeed be realized. Putting the matter like this suggests that the paradox rests on the supposition that the first-person form of "to believe" ascribes a state or disposition to its utterer. The section opens with an ironic question designed to call precisely this conception in question:

How did we ever come to use such an expression as "I believe . . .?" Did we at some time become aware of a phenomenon (of belief)?

Did we observe ourselves and other people and so discover belief?

A little later Wittgenstein spells out in more detail a version of the picture he is combating.

This is how I think of it [*Ich denke so*]: Believing is a state of mind. It has duration; and that independently of the duration of its expression in a sentence, for example. So it is a kind of disposition of the believing person. This is shewn me in the case of someone else by his behavior; and by his words. And, to be sure, equally by an utterance of the form "I believe . . ." and by his simple assertion.[4] What about my own case: how do I myself recognize my own disposition?— Here it will have been necessary for me to take notice of myself as others do, to listen to myself talking, to be able to draw conclusions from what I say!

As he notes, it is just at this point that the picture begins to distort, for:

My own relation to my words is wholly different from other people's.

A natural first response is to point out that a frequent use of the first person expression "I believe" is not to make any assertion about myself, but to qualify the force with which I am making the assertion. The qualification is sometimes in the direction of indicating hesitancy, but sometimes also of indicating especial vehemence (perhaps this is characteristic of certain religious contexts). This response is sound enough perhaps, as far as it goes, but unfortunately it does not go very far, as Wittgenstein brings out in the following remark:

Suppose I were to introduce some expression—"I believe," for instance—in this way: it is to be prefixed to reports when they serve to give information about the reporter. (So the expression need not carry with it any suggestion of uncertainty . . .)—"I believe . . ., and it isn't so" would be a contradiction.[5]

Part of the reason for this is a point I have already tried to bring out: that the expression "I believe" can only give you information about my state if it is completed by a clause saying *what* I believe. Or perhaps the matter is better put as follows. Our use of the verb "to believe" is indeed very irregular, at least if we compare it with other verbs like "to walk," "to scream," "to eat." But it would be a mistake to regard the irregularity as a sort of *ambiguity,* in the sense that "believe" is taken to mean something quite different when it is used in the first person from what it means in the third. Our use of the verb has a unity about it, in the sense that what we mean when we use it in the first person is *interdependent* with what we mean when we use it in the third person.

---

    [4] I have modified the published translation here. The German text reads: "Und zwar ebensowohl eine Äußerung 'Ich glaube . . .,' wie seine einfache Behauptung."
    [5] *PI* II.x.

This, I take it, is what Wittgenstein is getting at in the following, very important, passage:

Even in the *supposition* [*Annahme*] the pattern is not what you think.

When you say "Suppose I believe . . ." you are presupposing the whole grammar of the verb "to believe," the ordinary use, of which you are master.— You are not supposing some state of affairs which, so to speak, a picture presents unambiguously to you, so that you can tack on to this supposition something other than the ordinary assertion.—You would not know at all what you were supposing here (what, for example, would follow from such a supposition), if you were not already familiar with the use of "believe."[6]

I remarked earlier that one of the most important changes that take place between the writing of the *Tractatus* and *Philosophical Investigations* is the way in which, in the latter, Wittgenstein places at the center of his discussion a detailed description of what in the *Tractatus* is merely mentioned by the way, almost as an afterthought: namely, "the enormously complicated silent adjustments" which the "human organism" has to make to understand colloquial language. The above is an example of what I mean. Because in the *Tractatus* the unit is simply the form of the 'proposition', "A believes that p," Wittgenstein is there unable to give a perspicuous account of the importance of the relation between, for example, the first-person and the third-person forms of the verb "to believe"; and I, confining myself within the limits imposed by the *Tractatus* discussion, was reduced to the clumsy formulation that, for the *Tractatus,* "A" in this formula in a sense always takes the value "I." I believe, incidentally, that it is something like the same constraints that, in that work, resulted in the remarks about solipsism which have proved so fatally easy to misunderstand. Here in *Philosophical Investigations*, on the other hand, the unit he works with is the whole 'language-game' within which we express our own and discuss each others' beliefs.

Moreover, as is brought out best, perhaps, in the *Remarks on the Philosophy of Psychology*,[7] our use of the verb "to believe" itself varies according to the nature of the wider language-game in the context of which it is being used. So, for instance:

§142. The child that is learning to speak learns the use of the words "having pain," and also learns that one can simulate pain. This belongs to the language-game that it learns.

---

6 *PI* II.x. I have slightly changed the Anscombe translation.
7 These constitute a large part of the manuscript and typescript source material on which Part II of *Philosophical Investigations* was based.

Or again: It doesn't just learn the use of "He has pain" but also that of "I believe he has pain." (But naturally not of "I believe I have pain.")

This brief passage brings out, first, that in the context of talk about one's pains, "to believe" lacks a first-person conjugation; and, second, that in order to understand the significance of this and similar grammatical facts, we need to study (among other things) the phenomenon of simulation.[8] So,

§151. Believing that someone else is in pain, doubting whether he is, are so many natural kinds of behavior towards other human beings; and our language is but an auxiliary and extension of this behavior. (For our *language-game* is a piece of behavior.)

More broadly still, we shall not understand the intricacies of the ways in which we speak of 'believing' without studying the intricacies of the different forms of behavior for which these ways of speaking are "an auxiliary and extension."

Bearing this thought in mind, I want now to consider Moore's Paradox a bit further. The first lesson to be drawn here is to refrain from trying to understand the nature of the anomaly presented by "p and I don't believe that p" in terms of what 'states of affairs' its component sentences report, but rather in terms of the 'language-games' into which reporting and expressing what one believes enter; or, in the phraseology I have already quoted, in terms of "the natural kinds of behavior towards other human beings" of which our language "is but an auxiliary and extension." In these terms it seems to me that Wittgenstein puts the matter most succinctly in the following remark from his *Last Writings on the Philosophy of Psychology*:

§142. "I believe he'll come, but he certainly won't come." If I say that to someone, it tells him that he won't come but that nevertheless I am thoroughly convinced of the opposite, *and will act according to this belief.* However, by the very fact that I am reporting to someone else that he won't come, *I am not acting according to this belief.*[9]

That at least is the language-game we naturally think of when we are presented with the paradox. But, as Wittgenstein points out, it is possible to think of other language-games which would work differently. In *Remarks on the Philosophy of Psychology*, he constructs the following example.

---

[8] This task is executed in considerable detail in the *Last Writings on the Philosophy of Psychology*, vol. 2.

[9] The emphases are mine.

§813. Imagine an observer who, as it were automatically, says what he is observing. Of course he hears himself talk, but, so to speak, he takes no notice of that. He sees that the enemy is approaching and reports it, describes it, but like a machine. What would that be like? Well, he does not act according to his observation. Of him, one might say that he speaks what he sees, but that he does not *believe* it. It does not, so to speak, get inside him.[10]

As Wittgenstein says, there are other, perhaps less artificial, cases where something similar holds: the case, for instance, of a man who "says that God has spoken to him or through his mouth."

§817. The *important* insight is that there is a language-game in which I produce information *automatically*, information which can be treated by other people quite as they treat non-automatic information—only here there will be no question of any 'lying'—information which I myself may receive like that of a third person. The 'automatic' statement, report, etc. might also be called an 'oracle.'—But of course that means that the oracle must not avail itself of the words "I believe."

And then he adds a remark which points straight at the heart of what all this is about.

§818. Where is it said in logic that an assertion cannot be made in a trance?

The disturbing feature of Moore's Paradox was that it gave the impression that there exists some logical obstacle in the way of reporting a state of affairs which may quite well hold. Such an impression already presupposes a certain conception of logic as an existing ideal structure to which our use of language is ultimately answerable.[11] Wittgenstein's mature thinking rejects this conception: if we do indeed have a use for a certain expression, then it is, *logically* speaking, perfectly in order.

Of course this does not rule out the possibility that there are all kinds of *other* objections to its use—political, moral, religious, or professional. One can well imagine (adapting another example of Wittgenstein's)[12] that the railway employee who announces "The five o'clock train will

---

[10] I think here of Lewis White Beck's characteristic anecdote about the general who receives an incredible report from the battlefield: "Well, Colonel, since you saw it with your own eyes, I have to believe it. But by God, Sir, if *I* had seen it with *my* own eyes, I wouldn't have believed it."

[11] Cf. *PI* §81, which I discuss in "Persuasion," *Midwest Studies in Philosophy*, vol. 17: *The Wittgenstein Legacy*, ed. Peter E. French, Theodore E. Uehling, Jr., and Howard K. Wettstein (Notre Dame, Ind.: University of Notre Dame Press, 1992), pp. 123–37.

[12] *RPP* i, §486.

arrive on time," adding in a different tone of voice, "and I don't believe it," will be looking for a new job quite soon; but he has not said anything paradoxical. It may be quite important to be clear precisely what kind of objection is being made in such contexts. I think, for instance, that Sartrean accusations of *mauvaise foi,* however strong their moral justification may or may not have been, gave the impression of being made in the name of pure logic in what seemed, to me at least, a rather unsavory manner.

Be that as it may, there are areas of human life within which the phenomenon Wittgenstein calls that of "two people speaking out of my mouth" is not something pathological or off-beat but of the essence. One of the most striking and important of such areas is the political, where people may hold certain offices in the name of which they speak. We have the English metaphor of 'changing hats', in cases where a single person holds different offices which require conflicting utterances on the part of the office holder. Or there are the cases where the requirements of someone's office conflict with what he or she sees as required by private conscience. Vere's speech to the court-martial in Melville's *Billy Budd* is a classic example.[13]

It is frequently important in cases of conflict of such kinds to be clear about what *sort* of issue we are dealing with. Left-wing politicians, for instance, may be accused of hypocrisy when they avail themselves of social facilities that they are politically committed to abolish—such as private schooling for their children. I don't want to make any general pronouncement either for or against the propriety of such behavior, since I believe that will depend very heavily on the details of particular cases. What I do object to, however, is the widespread tendency to dispense with such examination of details as unnecessary on the grounds that a person who acts like this is obviously contradicting him- or herself by professing a moral principle and failing to act on it. It is fairly easy to see, however, that there is no logical contradiction here; that someone need not be prevented from working wholeheartedly for the abolition of private education by sending his or her children to private schools. (I repeat: I am not claiming a priori that there can be nothing objectionable about such behavior; but the case for that must be made on other grounds.) Hobbes, incidentally, is a classic case of someone who tries to eliminate the possibility of any sort of genuine conflict between the public and the private, through his combination of a

---

[13] See "The Universalizability of Moral Judgments," in my *Ethics and Action* (London: Routledge & Kegan Paul, 1972).

covenant theory of political authority with the contention that breach of a covenant is a form of self-contradiction.[14]

I commented earlier on the striking structural parallel between the *Tractatus* discussion of belief in Propositions 5.54 to 5.5423 and that in *Philosophical Investigations*, Part II, sections x and xi. In both there is a discussion of, and an attempt to resolve, an apparent logical anomaly concerning propositions reporting somebody's belief; and in both, this discussion is followed by a reference to the phenomenon of shifting aspects. There is, however, this big difference. In the earlier work the apparently anomalous status of propositions of the form "A believes that p" appears as a difficulty as it were on the verges of the main argument—it is treated in sections the numbering of which (5.541–5.5423) seems to register a fairly peripheral importance; in *Philosophical Investigations*, on the other hand, sections x and xi are quite pivotal to the argument of Part II as a whole, and indeed to the whole work. And the external contrast between *Tractatus* 5.5423 and *Philosophical Investigations* II.xi could hardly be greater. The former consists of a diagram and about nine characteristically lapidary lines of text; the latter of about sixty pages of text, full of examples all discussed in great detail.

I have spoken of Wittgenstein's contention that in order to understand the intricacies of the ways in which we speak of 'believing' we must study the intricacies of the different forms of behavior for which these ways of speaking are "an auxiliary and extension." *Philosophical Investigations* II.xi is a contribution to such a study. Of course the examples it considers go far beyond simple cases of 'believing that such-and-such is the case'. Wittgenstein's own comment on this is:

In giving all these examples I am not aiming at some kind of completeness, some classification of psychological concepts. They are only meant to enable the reader to shift for himself when he encounters conceptual difficulties.[15]

I do not want by any means to suggest that the only conceptual difficulties Wittgenstein is interested in here are those surrounding the concept of belief. But I do want to stress that many of the points he emphasizes in the course of his discussion have a peculiar relevance to difficulties we have encountered in that area. For instance, in connection with several of his examples he is anxious to distinguish cases of

---

[14] This argument was important to Hobbes. It recurs, with minor variations, in *De Cive* (ch. 3, sect. 3f.), *The Elements of Law* (Part 1, ch. 16, sect. 2f.), and *Leviathan* (Part I, ch. 14, para. 8f.), and is needed to avoid having political obligation collapse into self-interest and/or naked compulsion.

[15] *PI* II.xi.

change of aspect from cases where it never occurs to someone to see what is before him under more than one aspect; and he attaches a special kind of importance to the first kind of case. If we reflect back on the treatment of the 'psychological verbs' both in *Tractatus* and in *Philosophical Investigations* (especially II.xi), we can see that the *change* of aspect cases are indeed especially relevant here: indeed, *Tractatus* 5.5423 already emphasizes this. And the following remarks from *Philosophical Investigations* II.xi reinforce the point.

If you search in a figure (1) for another figure (2), and then find it, you see (1) in a new way. Not only can you give a new kind of description of it, but noticing the second figure was a new visual experience.

And again, slightly earlier in the same section, in his discussion of the duck-rabbit picture and the 'picture-face':

"I saw it quite differently, I should never have recognized it!" Now, that is an exclamation. And there is also a justification for it.

I should never have thought of superimposing the two heads like that, of making this comparison between them. For they suggest a different mode of comparison. Nor has the head seen like *this* the slightest similarity to the head seen like this—although they are congruent.

We might compare this kind of case with a criminal investigation in which a detective is suddenly struck, in listening to the account a witness is giving of a certain incident, not by what her words show about the incident being described, but by what they show about her—the witness. (Various factors might be involved here: e.g. what her words show her to know—which she could perhaps have come to know only in a certain way—what they show about her attitude to someone else involved in the case, and so on.) And again I repeat the point, which is always in the background of Wittgenstein's own discussion of belief, that they have such a significance only to the extent that they are also understood as a description of that other incident.

An interesting example is the long-drawn-out interrogation of Raskolnikov by the police official, Porfiri, in Dostoevsky's *Crime and Punishment*. At the center of the investigation of course is the question: who actually committed the murders? There is a mass of circumstantial evidence some of which points to Raskolnikov's guilt, but not decisively. Porfiri's interrogation ranges over a wide field, probing Raskolnikov's attitudes, political convictions, and so on; its aim is to secure, eventually, a confession from Raskolnikov, but it is important to Porfiri that it should be a *genuine* confession, and one may say that what is at stake for him is at least as much the state of Raskolnikov's soul as the question of who actually did the killing. At the same time, of course, the state of Raskolnikov's soul is inextricably bound up with the question whether he did the killing or not. What Porfiri perceives, as certain aspects dawn on him during the interrogation, is not 'a property of the object' (i.e. Raskolnikov), but 'an internal relation between it and other objects'.[16] A good example comes during the first, 'social', meeting in Porfiri's apartment, prior to Raskolnikov's 'official' interrogation at the police station. The subject of discussion is a neo-Nietzschean article Raskolnikov had recently published concerning the right of 'exceptional' people to remove obstacles to their projects without regard for conventional morality. At first the discussion is purely philosophical; until Porfiri gives expression to "one little idea" that he says he does not want to forget:

What I mean is this: . . . But I really don't know how best to express myself . . . The idea is too strange . . . it belongs to the realm of psychology . . . What I mean is this: when you were writing your article, you must, ha, ha, ha, have thought of yourself too, at least a little bit, as an exceptional human being who has "something new to say," to use your own expression . . . Isn't that so?

Here Raskolnikov's opinions are suddenly put into a quite different context and gain a quite new significance: an 'internal relation'—to use now Wittgenstein's own expression—emerges between Raskolnikov's quasi-philosophical writings and his role in the murder Porfiri is investigating.

A feature of Porfiri's continuing interrogation is his sensitivity to what Wittgenstein calls "fine shades of behavior," and also his recognition that there are always two sides to 'psychological proofs': both ideas of great importance also in *Philosophical Investigations* II.xi. In Wittgenstein's discussion the concept of "fine shades of behavior" comes into prominence in the course of a transitional phase which passes from consideration of different kinds of perceptual—mainly visual—examples of change of aspect, through consideration of sensitivity to aesthetic distinctions and ability to respond to fine shades in the meaning of a word, to ability to fathom the souls of other people. Throughout these discussions the emphasis is on the one hand on the *indeterminateness* of what may be considered as relevant to the making of judgments in these areas and on the other hand on the importance of such judgments.

(Fine shades of behavior.—Why are they *important*? They have important consequences.)

---

[16] I am applying here a remark from *PI* II.xi.

A temptation Wittgenstein is, I think, combating here is to suppose that for issues of such importance it must be possible, at least in principle, to specify firm criteria for distinguishing between correct and incorrect judgments. Consider the following:

"At that word we both thought of him." Let us assume that each of us said the same words to himself—and how can it mean MORE than that?—But wouldn't even those words be only a *germ*? They must surely belong to a language and to a context, in order really to be the expression of the thought of that man.

If God had looked into our minds he would not have been able to see there whom we were speaking of.[17]

That last famous remark reminds me of a line given to Sir Thomas More in the movie version of *A Man For All Seasons*. More, on becoming Lord Chancellor to Henry VIII, has refused to give any political office to one of his hangers-on, Richard Rich (whom, with all too much justification, he does not trust), and recommends him to become a teacher. Rich protests disgustedly that even if one is a good teacher no one will know, so what's the point? More's response (roughly):

Well, you would know; your students would know; and God would know. That's not a bad audience.

My question is, what is added in that reply by the reference to God? There is a picture there, of course, of an all-knowing observer. The picture might even be painted—with God looking down from Heaven with an expression of approval at Rich before his responsive students. However, the question Wittgenstein is always asking is: how is such a picture applied? More's God—the 'God of religion'—is very different from the 'God of the philosophers' toward whom Wittgenstein is ironically gesturing in my last quotation from him. Spelling out the application of the picture would take a long time and take us through territory not all of which could be foreseen in advance. It would depend on what religious difficulties, disagreements, and obscurities would have to be dealt with by the interlocutors. But certainly, so it seems to me, discussion of the role that God's 'all-seeing' plays in the life of a believer, and in his or her attitude to that life, would have to play a prominent part. And issues would arise about which there would almost certainly be considerable, and often perhaps unresolvable, dispute. For instance, confessional differences, concerning the sacrament of confession, might well be relevant. The complex, uncertain, and murky background suggested here is in sharp contrast to the simple

[17] Ibid.

philosophical picture Wittgenstein is combating with his remark—"If God had looked into our minds he would not have been able to see there whom we were speaking of"—suggesting as it does that what gives sense to the obscurities of human discourse is a quite determinate and unambiguous state of affairs ('fact of the matter'). That the background of issues from which More's (apocryphal) remark draws its sense is in this way indeterminate and not always resolvable does not *detract from* the remark's importance. On the contrary! It brings out how much, in human discourse, is rooted in the very uncertain ground of mutual understanding between human beings, a theme which dominates the last few pages of *PI* II.xi. We may be inclined to think that a quasi-aesthetic sensitivity to fine shades of behavior is a luxury we must dispense with if we want to get at the hard facts. It was in that spirit that a well-known Australian philosopher (as I once heard) used to refer disparagingly to the members of his university's English department as "the truth and beauty girls." But, as Wittgenstein remarked of a similar inclination in a very slightly different connection:

> Call it a dream. It does not change anything.[18]

One concluding remark. Throughout his career Wittgenstein thought of philosophy as an activity of clarification, of displaying without distortion or concealment the logic of our thinking. For this reason logic itself must be the instrument of philosophy, for:

> The solutions of logical problems must be neat for they set the standard of neatness.
> Men have always thought that there must be a sphere of questions whose answers—a priori—are symmetrical and united into a closed structure.
> A sphere in which the proposition, simplex sigillum veri, is valid.[19]

The *Tractatus* works with this picture of how things must be and tries to show how it is possible and what are its consequences. The truth-functional reduction of the logical constants is the instrument of this attempt. The so-called 'propositions of psychology' are a problem because they seem to resist this truth-functional reduction. A symptom of this resistance is that theories of judgment like Russell's make it look as though there could be a complex proposition a constituent of which were nonsense.[20] The *Tractatus* offers an account of such propositions based on the insistence that the expression "p" in "A believes that p" expresses a genuine proposition.

---

[18] Ibid.
[20] See *Tractatus* 5.5422.

[19] *Tractatus* 5.4541.

In *Philosophical Investigations*, Wittgenstein continues to strive as passionately as ever for the utmost clarity. The formal systems of logic may be helpful in this aim insofar as they are recognized as objects of comparison, as he puts it[21]—and not thought of as somehow extracted from the nature of things. In contrast to *Tractatus* 5.4541, we read in a note from 1944:

> What's ragged should be left ragged.[22]

His problem in *Philosophical Investigations* is how to combine this aspiration with the aspiration for clarity. It is a problem that comes to a head precisely in II.xi and again, significantly, the so-called 'propositions of psychology' are at the root of the difficulty, this time because of the indeterminateness, or indefiniteness, that is endemic to them:

What is most difficult here is to put this indefiniteness, correctly and unfalsified, into words.

This putting into words, however, will not be a comprehensive theory of such propositions. As Wittgenstein says earlier in the section, his aim is not

some kind of completeness, some classification of psychological concepts. <The wealth of examples rather> are only meant to enable the reader to shift for himself when he encounters conceptual difficulties.[23]

This is in line with the remark from a notebook of 1948:

> Anything the reader can do for himself, leave it to the reader,[24]

and perhaps it helps to explain the resistance Wittgenstein's work continues to encounter.

---

[21] *PI* §81.
[22] *Culture and Value*, MS 128 46, ca. 1944.
[23] *PI* II.xi.
[24] *Culture and Value*, MS 137 134b, 25 December 1948.

7

Wittgenstein's "Plan for the Treatment of Psychological Concepts"

David H. Finkelstein

> Plan for the treatment of psychological concepts.
> Psychological concepts characterized by the fact that the third person of the present is to be verified by observation, the first person not.
> Sentences in the third person of the present: information. In the first person present: expression. ((Not quite right.))
> The first person of the present akin to an expression. (Z §472)

A striking feature of Wittgenstein's later writings is his preoccupation with psychological self-ascriptions—that is, with statements such as "I am afraid," "I am expecting an explosion," and "I'm in pain." This preoccupation is evident in the remarkable passage from *Zettel* reproduced above.[1] In what follows, I'll be offering a reading of this passage. My primary aim will be to clarify what Wittgenstein means when he characterizes a psychological sentence in the first person of the present as "akin to an expression." Along the way, I hope to shed light on what a number of his late writings have to say about, first, the relation between an expression and that which it expresses and, second, the authority with which we speak about our own mental goings-on.

I. DETECTIVISM

Let's begin by considering what it is that Wittgenstein rejects in his "Plan for the treatment of psychological concepts." He says that psychological sentences in the first person of the present are not verified by observation. I'm going to call the sort of view that Wittgenstein here and elsewhere opposes *detectivism*. More precisely, I'll use the term

---

[1] This passage also appears at *RPP* 2 §63.

"detectivist" to refer to anyone who thinks that a subject's ability to say what she is thinking or feeling is the result of her somehow *finding out*—whether by observation alone or in conjunction with inference and memory. A detectivist thinks that our ordinary consciousness of at least some significant range of mental states or events is explained by the fact that we are able to detect their presence.

Exactly how we should understand the process by which a person detects the presence of her own mental goings-on is something about which detectivists have held, and continue to hold, a variety of views. Many have been drawn to the idea that we inwardly observe mental items via some kind of "inner sense" or "inner eye." Some, like Bertrand Russell in *The Problems of Philosophy*, have held that the inner sense provides us with direct, infallible knowledge of items that are, in principle, private.[2] Others, many contemporary detectivists among them, have claimed that we know our own states of mind thanks to a more prosaic perceptual mechanism—one understood to be on all fours with the mechanisms that enable us to see and hear, only directed toward states and events that are literally inside our heads.[3]

Not all detectivists posit any sort of *inward* observation. One rather unusual version of detectivism with which Wittgenstein was familiar was put forward by Russell in 1921. In *The Analysis of Mind*,[4] Russell provides an account both of what desires are and of how we come to know our own. According to this account, a desire is any mental occurrence that involves "discomfort"—where what it means for a mental occurrence to involve discomfort is that it causes its subject to engage in "movements tending to produce some more or less definite change involving the cessation of the occurrence."[5] Russell writes:

---

[2] Bertrand Russell, *The Problems of Philosophy* (Oxford: Oxford University Press, 1912), pp. 49–51.

[3] Paul Churchland and Nicholas Humphrey (a neuropsychologist) provide recent statements of this sort of detectivism:

> [S]elf-consciousness . . . is just a species of perception: *self-perception*. It is not perception of one's foot with one's eyes, for example, but is rather the perception of one's internal states with what we may call (largely in ignorance) one's faculty of introspection. Self-consciousness is thus no more (and no less) mysterious than perception generally. It is just directed internally rather than externally. (P. Churchland, *Matter and Consciousness* (Cambridge, Mass.: MIT Press, 1988), p. 74.)

> It is as if I, like every other human being, possess a kind of 'inner eye', which looks in on my brain and tells me why and how I'm acting in the way I am—providing me with what amounts to a plain man's guide to my own mind. (N. Humphrey, *The Inner Eye* (London: Faber & Faber, 1986), p. 68.)

[4] Bertrand Russell, *The Analysis of Mind* (New York: Humanities Press, 1921).

[5] Ibid. p. 71.

The cycle [of restless movements caused by a mental occurrence involving discomfort] ends in a condition of quiescence . . . The state of affairs in which this condition of quiescence is achieved is called the "purpose" of the cycle, and the initial mental occurrence involving discomfort is called a "desire" for the state of affairs that brings quiescence.[6]

When I am hungry, I'm subject to a mental occurrence that causes me to engage in restless movements likely to lead to my eating. That this occurrence is a desire *to eat* consists in the fact that upon eating, my restless activity comes to an end.

Given this analysis of desire, how is it that I am sometimes able to say what it is that I desire? According to Russell, "'Conscious' desire . . . consists of desire in the sense hitherto discussed, together with a true belief as to its 'purpose,' i.e. as to the state of affairs that will bring quiescence with cessation of the discomfort."[7] How, then, do I come to have a true belief concerning what will bring quiescence? Russell writes that "the discovery of our own motives can only be made by the same process by which we discover other people's, namely, the process of observing our actions and inferring the desire which could prompt them."[8] Thus, according to the sort of detectivism that Russell defends in 1921, when I say what it is that I desire, I issue a report that is based on (1) observation of my own restless behavior, and (2) an inference as to what is likely to bring the behavior to an end.

* * *

In *Philosophical Remarks*, we find Wittgenstein criticizing Russell's 1921 analysis of desire:

I believe Russell's theory amounts to the following: if I give someone an order and I am happy with what he then does, then he has carried out my order.

(If I wanted to eat an apple, and someone punched me in the stomach, taking away my appetite, then it was this punch that I originally wanted.) (*PR*, III §22)

Later, in the *Investigations*, Wittgenstein is still preoccupied with the account of desire and self-knowledge that Russell defends in 1921:

Saying "I should like an apple" does not mean: I believe an apple will quell my feeling of nonsatisfaction. *This* proposition is not an expression of a wish but of nonsatisfaction. (*PI* §440)

It's not just *The Analysis of Mind*'s funny sort of detectivism that Wittgenstein is concerned to criticize. His opposition to every sort of

---

[6] Ibid. p. 75.   [7] Ibid. p. 72.
[8] Ibid. p. 31.

detectivism emerges as a theme in his later writings, a theme that is sounded in, for example, the follow passages:

Does it make sense to ask "How do you know that you believe?"—and is the answer: "I know it by introspection"?

In *some* cases it will be possible to say some such thing, in most not. (*PI* §587)

When someone says "I hope he'll come"—is this a *report* about his state of mind . . .?—I can, for example, say it to myself. And surely I am not giving myself a report. (*PI* §585)

But that which is in him, how can I see it? Between his experience and me there is always the expression!

Here is the picture: He sees it immediately, I only mediately. But that's not the way it is. He doesn't see something and describe it to us. (*LaWrPP2*, p. 92)

How does Wittgenstein think we should understand psychological self-ascriptions if not as observation reports? In the next section, I shall discuss an answer to this question that I take to be unsatisfactory—both as a reading of Wittgenstein and as an account of how we should think about psychological self-ascriptions—but which, nonetheless, can easily seem to be the only alternative to detectivism.

2. CONSTITUTIVISM

The position I have in mind might be stated as follows: "Our mental state self-ascriptions are unlike observation reports in that they constitute the very facts to which they refer. There is no need for me to engage in anything like self-observation in order to state, for example, what I intend to do this evening because when I say that I intend to go to bed early, I *make it the case* that this is what I intend. My authority concerning my own states of mind is not epistemic; it is, rather, like that of an army colonel when he declares an area to be off-limits. The colonel needn't be better informed about the area than his soldiers are. His authority consists in the fact that what he says goes. So it is with my authority about my own states of mind. Typically, what I say goes." I shall call a philosopher who holds a view of this sort a *constitutivist*.

It might seem as if we must choose between some form of detectivism and some form of constitutivism (or else, some hybrid position) when we try to make sense of our psychological self-ascriptions. ("Either I discover my state of mind or I, as it were, make it.") If one thinks that detectivism and constitutivism together exhaust the available views of first-person authority, then it will be natural to read Wittgenstein—who often speaks against detectivism—as putting forward some version of constitutivism. This is, as it were, a *negative* reason to read Wittgenstein as a constitutivist: he's not a detectivist, so he must be a constitutivist. But there are also positive reasons to read Wittgenstein as a constitutivist. There are passages in his writings that can look like positive endorsements of some form of constitutivism.

Someone who wanted to read Wittgenstein as a constitutivist might appeal to the following passage from *Zettel* for support:

But how does the person in whom it goes on know which event the process is the expectation of? For he does not seem to be in uncertainty about it. It is not as if he observed a mental or other condition and formed a conjecture about its cause. He may well say: "I don't know whether it is only this expectation that makes me so uneasy today"; but he will not say: "I don't know whether this state of mind, in which I now am, is the expectation of an explosion or of something else."

The statement "I am expecting a bang at any moment" is an *expression* of expectation. This verbal reaction is the movement of the pointer, which shows the object of expectation. (Z §53)

A commentator who took Wittgenstein to be a constitutivist might put the point of this passage as follows: "An expectation is like a pointer in that it is, as it were, aimed at something—its object. Now, how is it that I am able to say at what my expectation is aimed? Many philosophers would claim that when I inwardly observe my expectation, I see the direction in which it points, but Wittgenstein rejects this view. What he is saying in the last sentence of the passage is that when I avow an expectation, I am not reporting on the direction in which my mental state points, but rather, setting or determining the position of the pointer. When I say I am expecting a bang, I make it the case that a bang is what I am expecting."

I think the most lucid proponent of a reading of Wittgenstein along these lines has been Crispin Wright. In the passage that follows, Wright states a view that he himself endorses and that he thinks Wittgenstein might have endorsed:

The authority which our self-ascriptions of meaning, intention, and decision assume is not based on any kind of cognitive advantage, expertise or achievement. Rather it is, as it were, a *concession*, unofficially granted to anyone whom one takes seriously as a rational subject. It is, so to speak, such a subject's right to declare what he intends, what he intended, and what satisfies his intentions; and his possession of this right consists in the conferral upon such declarations, other things being equal, of a constitutive rather than a descriptive role.[9]

Wright's constitutivism falls out of his reading of Wittgenstein's remarks about rule-following. In the next few paragraphs, I'll sketch the connection between what Wright's Wittgenstein has to say about rule-following and what he has to say about psychological self-ascriptions.

Wright states what he takes to be a lesson of Wittgenstein's remarks about rule-following as follows:

It might be preferable, in describing our most basic rule-governed responses, to think of them not as informed by an *intuition* (of the requirements of the rule) but as a kind of *decision*.[10]

It is tempting to say that when someone sets out to follow a rule, she intuits, or perceives, its requirements; she sees what the rule calls for. According to Wright's Wittgenstein, to say this is to commit oneself to a problematic, platonistic conception of rules. On Wright's reading of Wittgenstein, when someone follows a rule, she doesn't perceive its requirements; she decides them. She, as it were, stipulates what the rule calls for.

There is an obvious problem with saying that when someone follows a rule, she decides or stipulates its requirements. This way of putting things suggests that when someone is confronted by a rule, she is free to decide that anything she feels like doing is what the rule calls for. Wright's answer to this problem is to say that it is only our best judgments (i.e. our best *decisions*) about a rule that determine what it requires. One may go wrong in trying to follow a rule because one may act in ways that don't conform to the best judgments about what it calls for.

By virtue of what is some judgment about a rule's requirements a *best* judgment? According to Wright, a best judgment is one that is arrived at under certain ideal conditions—under what he calls "C-conditions." From here, Wright gets to constitutivism in two steps. The first step is to extend the sort of story he wants to tell about rules so that it applies as well to intentions, wishes, and the like. If it is platonistic to think that

[9] Crispin Wright, "On Making Up One's Mind: Wittgenstein on Intention," in Weingartner and Schurz, eds., *Logic, Philosophy of Science and Epistemology* (Kirchberg: Hölder-Pichler-Tempsky, 1987), pp. 400–1.

[10] Crispin Wright, "Wittgenstein's Rule-Following Considerations and the Central Project of Theoretical Linguistics," in A. George, ed., *Reflections on Chomsky* (Oxford: Blackwell, 1989), p. 240; also Crispin Wright, critical notice of Colin McGinn, *Wittgenstein on Meaning, Mind* 98 (1989): 289–305, p. 300.

mere marks on a page can, of themselves, call for one behavior rather than another, then it is also platonistic to think that an intention can, of itself, determine what would fulfill it. According to Wright, the question of what it is that would satisfy an intention is, like the question of what a rule calls for, settled by a judgment made under ideal conditions. Thus, what we might call Wright's *stipulativism* is not restricted to rules or signs; it extends to mental states as well.

The second step on Wright's path from stipulativism about rules to constitutivism about mental content is to claim that under most *ordinary* conditions, when I make a judgment about my own intentional state, it is a best judgment. This is to say, for judgments or opinions that may be expressed in the form of avowals of intention, desire, expectation, and so on, what Wright calls the C-conditions are usually satisfied. Typically, according to Wright, when I say that I intend to φ, I make it the case that φ is what I intend to do.[11] Thus, he ends up with a constitutivist account of intentional state self-ascriptions:

[W]hy is it *a priori* reasonable to believe that, provided Jones has the relevant concepts and is attentive to the matter, he will believe that he intends to φ if and only if he does? . . . [T]he matter will be nicely explained if the concept of intention works in such a way that Jones's opinions, formed under the restricted set of C-conditions, play [an] extension-determining role . . .[12]

Jones is generally right about his own intentions because, under ordinary conditions, his taking himself to have a particular intention fixes it that he does.

* * *

I argue elsewhere that stipulativism neither captures the moral of Wittgenstein's remarks about rule-following nor turns out to be a coherent position in its own right.[13] Thus, I believe that Wright's constitutivism, which grows out of his stipulativism, has its roots in poor soil. I can't begin to argue this point here, however, nor would it really be to my present purpose. For even if you were to grant both that stipulativism is a hopeless strategy for explaining content *and* that Wittgenstein is no stipulativist, you might still be drawn to a constitutivist reading of Wittgenstein, one according to which—although he is

---

[11] Wright notes that this determination is defeasible. What a subject says about his own intentional states is generally allowed to stand, but subsequent events occasionally overturn his judgment.

[12] Wright, "Wittgenstein's Rule-Following Considerations," p. 252.

[13] See my "Wittgenstein on Rules and Platonism," in A. Crary and R. Read, eds., *The New Wittgenstein* (London: Routledge, 2000).

not a stipulativist about content in general—he nonetheless holds that, ordinarily, the avowal of a mental state constitutes, rather than reflects, its subject matter. After all, constitutivism offers a way to explain the special authority that attaches to our mental state avowals without appealing to any sort of privileged epistemic access, and this does seem to be something that Wittgenstein is after.

But is this really what constitutivism offers? Notice that while constitutivism may have some prima facie plausibility when we think about intentions and expectations, it has none when we consider sensations. It would be worse than unsympathetic—it would be *crazy*—to think, for example, that toothache sufferers speak with authority about their pain because their pain is constituted by their avowals of it.[14]

Wright knows better than to attribute this crazy view about pain to Wittgenstein. He endorses constitutivism and reads Wittgenstein as a constitutivist, but *only* about intentional states. Wright contrasts intentional states with what he calls "genuine episodes and processes in consciousness," characterizing the latter as "items which, like headaches, ringing in the ears, and the experience of a patch of blue, may have determinate onset and departure, and whose occurrence makes no demands upon the conceptual resources of the sufferer."[15] He puts the point of contrast as follows:

[N]othing strictly introspectible has, in the case of any of these concepts [meaning, understanding, intending, expecting, wishing, fearing, hoping], the right kind of characteristics. We cannot, honestly, find anything to *be* the intention, etc., when we turn our gaze inward . . .[16]

According to Wright, we do sometimes "turn our gaze inward," and when we do, we find only "episodes of consciousness." Only these headache-like items are "strictly introspectible." Wright avoids saddling Wittgenstein with the crazy view that headaches are constituted by avowals of them by reading him as a constitutivist about expectations and intentions, but not about pains.[17]

---

[14] I'm afraid that I do know of one reader of Wittgenstein—a professor in an English department—who not only attributes this view to Wittgenstein, but endorses it himself. (At least he's not a dentist.)

[15] Wright, "Wittgenstein's Rule-Following Considerations," p. 237.

[16] Ibid.

[17] One problem with this strategy is that, prima facie, constitutivism doesn't seem much more plausible (or sympathetic) as a story about *fear* than as a story about pain. And Wright does suggest that Wittgenstein is a constitutivist about fear as well as expectation and intention (see "Wittgenstein's Rule-Following Considerations," p. 237). (Wright might try to analyze fear into an intentional component and a sensational component. I don't think any such strategy would work, but I won't pursue the point here.)

According to the position that Wright thinks Wittgenstein might have held, a typical self-ascription of expectation has a completely different grammar from a self-ascription of pain; the former constitutes its subject matter while the latter does not. But Wittgenstein's writings tell a different story—one according to which such self-ascriptions *share* something that we must recognize if we are to rid ourselves of philosophical confusion about them. Earlier, I cited a passage from *Zettel* §53 that, I said, might seem to support a constitutivist reading of Wittgenstein. Let's look at part of it again:

> The statement "I am expecting a bang at any moment" is an *expression* of expectation. This verbal reaction is the movement of the pointer, which shows the object of expectation.

Compare that remark about expectation with the following passage about pain:

> [H]ow does a human being learn the meaning of the names of sensations?—Of the word "pain" for example. Here is one possibility: words are connected with the primitive, the natural, expressions of the sensation and used in their place. A child has hurt himself and he cries; and then adults talk to him and teach him exclamations and, later, sentences. They teach the child new pain-behaviour.
> "So you are saying that the word 'pain' really means crying?"—On the contrary: the verbal expression of pain replaces crying and does not describe it. (*PI* §244)[18]

Throughout his late writings, Wittgenstein urges us to view—not only self-ascriptions of expectation, intention, and the like, but also—self-ascriptions of pain and other sensations as, or as akin to, expressions.

If Wittgenstein held the sort of view that Wright sets out, his "Plan for the treatment of psychological concepts" ought to have recommended that we think about self-ascriptions of intention and self-ascriptions of sensation in entirely different ways. But what the "Plan" says is that *psychological* self-ascriptions—that is, sentences in the first person of the present that involve psychological concepts—are "akin to expressions" (and it is clear from what immediately follows this remark that Wittgenstein means to include sensation concepts among those that can be called psychological). Of course, we might read Wittgenstein as a more thoroughgoing constitutivist than Wright suggests we should; we might take him to be a constitutivist about sensations as well as intentional states. But this would be to attribute a crazy view of sensations to him. In what follows, I'll try to provide a reading of Wittgenstein that attributes no crazy views to him but still allows us to

---

[18] See also *LaWrPP*2, p. 92 and Z §§484–7.

make sense of his wanting to compare both avowals of expectation and avowals of sensation to expressions.

According to the constitutivist reading of *Zettel* §53, "the movement of the pointer"—an avowal of expectation—fixes or determines what the expectation is *of*. But the final sentence of *Zettel* §53 does *not* read, "This verbal reaction is the movement of the pointer, which *determines* the object of expectation." The sort of pointer that Wittgenstein has in mind is one that *shows* something—makes something manifest. In *Zettel* §53, Wittgenstein is trying to draw attention to the way in which a psychological self-ascription, like a facial expression, can make someone's mental condition manifest. What *sort* of making manifest is this?

3. THE CEO AND THE CONTEXT PRINCIPLE

Let's compare two ways in which something may be made manifest. Imagine that Joan rolls up her sleeves, whereupon you see that one of her wrists is badly scarred. Such a scar might be the result of an accident, but given what you know about Joan's history, you infer that she has tried to kill herself. We might say that in rolling up her sleeves, Joan makes her scar manifest. We might also say that she makes it manifest to you that she has attempted suicide. Now, when someone's face lights up in a joyful expression, in which of these ways does she make her joy manifest? Is joy, so expressed, analogous to Joan's scar, or to her suicide attempt?

Neither. On the one hand, we are able to understand one another's facial expressions without needing to make inferences. Often, the only way I am able to describe someone's facial expression is as joyous or miserable; I don't typically see a person's smile or wince as a set of psychologically neutral movements and infer from these that she is in this or that mental condition:

> "We see emotion."—As opposed to what?—We do not see facial contortions and make inferences from them (like a doctor framing a diagnosis) to joy, grief, boredom. We describe a face immediately as sad, radiant, bored, even when we are unable to give any other description to the features.—Grief, one would like to say, is personified in the face. (Z §225; see also *PI* §537 and Z §218)

On the other hand, *seeing* that someone is happy or in pain is not quite like seeing that Joan's wrist is scarred. In *Philosophical Remarks*, Wittgenstein registers his dissatisfaction with a view by describing it as follows:

Pain is represented as something we can perceive in the sense in which we perceive a matchbox. (*PR*, p. 94)

Pain isn't the sort of thing we can perceive in the way a matchbox or a scar is perceived. Our thoughts and feelings are not hidden inside us in the way that a matchbox may be hidden in a handkerchief, or a scar inside a shirt-sleeve. If I express my pain by crying out, or my anger by scowling, this isn't like rolling up a sleeve and revealing a scar.[19]

Why not? What's the difference? I want to begin to characterize the difference by turning to a case in which someone speaks with a kind of first-person authority, not about her state of mind, but about the meaning of a word. Imagine a board meeting at which the chief executive officer has this to say about an employee: "Phillips is a real team-player, by which I don't mean that he's a stupid sheep, but rather that he won't help himself at the expense of this company." Now consider the question: How did the CEO find out what she meant by "team-player"? Did she listen to the first half of her sentence and interpret it? If so, why do the other board members attach such weight to *her* interpretation of the remark? Such questions are confused. The confusion may be characterized as follows: the second half of the CEO's sentence is not a *report* on the first half, but rather, an *expression* of its meaning. But now, what does *this* mean?

Part of what it means is that the members of the board hear the whole sentence and understand it as a coherent unit; the two halves of the sentence make sense in light of each other. The second half of the CEO's sentence is as much a part of her assessment of Phillips as the first. To understand what the whole sentence means—to hear what the CEO is saying about Phillips—a listener needs to take in the second half of the sentence together with the first. We can call the second half of the sentence a gloss on, or interpretation of, the first, but it isn't *merely* an interpretation; it's an elaboration, a fleshing out. It makes the CEO's meaning manifest in a way that a listener's interpretation of her remark would not. The weight that the board members accord the second half of her sentence does not reflect the CEO's superior ability to detect

---

[19] I take it that part of the point of the following passage is that in the use of the word "pain" there is no such thing as *exhibiting what one has got* if "exhibiting" is understood to have the grammar that it has when we say that someone exhibited her scar:

> Do not say "one cannot", but say instead: "it doesn't exist in this game". Not: "one can't castle in draughts" but—"there is not castling in draughts"; and instead of "I can't exhibit my sensation"—"in the use of the word 'sensation', there is no such thing as exhibiting what one has got . . .". (Z §134)

features of her own utterances or mental states. It reflects the fact that a sentence is what we might call a unit of intelligibility; the word "team-player" and the CEO's gloss on it are two parts of a single, coherent, intelligible whole.

Consider a variation on our story: At the board meeting, the CEO says, "Phillips is a real team-player," without elaborating on what she means by this. Five years later, her secretary is reading through the minutes of the meeting. He asks her what she meant by "team-player." The CEO remembers neither the meeting nor Phillips. She says, "Well, that's not a word that I often use. I suppose I might have meant it ironically—as a kind of insult to this Phillips." The CEO interprets her own remark as if it were made by someone else; she takes up a third-person perspective on it. Her two remarks, separated by years and forgetting, do not constitute a single unit of intelligibility. The second remark might provide information (or misinformation) about the first, but what we have in this version of the story are two separate remarks, not two parts of something that make sense together. In this version of the story, the CEO's second remark doesn't come with the sort of authority that we saw in the first version. Here, she is not expressing her meaning; she is merely interpreting something that she once said.

There is an analogy between the way the CEO's expression of what she meant by "team-player" is understood to fit coherently into the context of a sentence and the way an expression of, say, anger is understood to fit coherently into a person's behavioral and psychological life. In what remains of this essay, I'll argue that according to Wittgenstein, the way I make my anger manifest when I express it, whether by scowling or by announcing that I'm angry, is akin to the way in which the second half of the CEO's sentence makes the meaning of its first half manifest. Like many of Wittgenstein's views, this one owes something to Frege—specifically, to Frege's context principle.

* * *

In the introduction to *The Foundations of Arithmetic*, Frege writes, "In the enquiry that follows, I have kept to three fundamental principles." The second of these principles is "never to ask for the meaning of a word in isolation, but only in the context of a proposition."[20] Later in the book, he writes, "It is enough if the proposition taken as a whole has a sense; it is this that confers on the parts also their content."[21]

[20] Gottlob Frege, *The Foundations of Arithmetic* (Evanston, Ill.: Northwestern University Press, 1953), p. x.
[21] Ibid. p. 71.

Frege's context principle constitutes a rejection of the view that understanding a sentence requires that one grasp the meanings of independently intelligible sentence-parts. For Frege, the sentence is the primary unit of intelligibility. A part of a sentence—a word, for example—has the meaning that it does only in the context of the whole to which it belongs.

An example of Frege's helps to make the point. Compare the following sentences:

(1) Vienna is the capital of Austria.
(2) Trieste is no Vienna.

The logical role of the word "Vienna" is different in these sentences. In the first sentence, "Vienna" functions as proper name. In the second, it functions, Frege says, as "a concept-word, like 'metropolis.'"[22] It would make sense to say, "Although Trieste is no Vienna, Paris is a Vienna—the only one in France." Imagine that someone who said this also had occasion to say, "Vienna is the capital of Austria." She would not thereby commit herself to the view that the capital of Austria is in France. The word "Vienna" does not mean the same thing in sentences (1) and (2). We come to see what a particular use of a word means only when we consider it in the context of a whole sentence.

I want to suggest that what goes for the word "Vienna" also goes for the word "team-player" in the CEO example. The word "team-player" means what it does only in the context of the whole in which it appears. But in the sentence uttered by the CEO—"Phillips is a real team-player, by which I don't mean that he's a stupid sheep, but rather that he won't help himself at the expense of this company"—we see a special kind of sentential context, one that constitutes a gloss on, or interpretation of, that which it contextualizes. In the sentence "Trieste is no Vienna," the words "Trieste is no" contextualize the word "Vienna," but they do not constitute an interpretation of it. We could say that the CEO speaks with a special authority concerning what she meant by the word "team-player" because she is offering an interpretation of it that is not a *mere* interpretation. Her interpretation contextualizes that which it interprets in a way that an interpretation offered by one of the other board members would not.

* * *

One can hear echoes of Frege's context principle in both the *Tractatus* and the *Investigations*. At *Tractatus* 3.3, Wittgenstein says: "[O]nly in

---

[22] Gottlob Frege, *Translations from the Philosophical Writings of Gottlob Frege* (Totowa, N.J.: Rowman & Littlefield, 1952), p. 50.

the context of a sentence has a name meaning." And in §49 of the *Investigations*, he writes:

We may say: *nothing* has so far been done, when a thing has been named. It has not even *got* a name except in a language-game. This was what Frege meant too, when he said that a word had a meaning only as part of a sentence.

Wittgenstein doesn't merely inherit Frege's context principle; he reshapes it in a number of ways—two of which I'll call to your attention. One of them is signaled by Wittgenstein's use of the term "language-game" in the passage from the *Investigations* just cited. He speaks of language-games where Frege spoke of sentences. However it is that one ought precisely to characterize what Wittgenstein means by "language-game," it is clear that language-games are, as it were, *wider* than sentences. Frege's point—that our words mean what they do only in their contexts—is still present in the *Investigations*, but Wittgenstein has wider contexts in mind. Consider the following passages:

"After he had said this, he left her as he did the day before."—Do I understand this sentence? Do I understand it just as I should if I heard it in the course of a narrative? If it were set down in isolation I should say, I don't know what it's about. (*PI* §525)

The phrase "description of a state of mind" characterizes a certain *game*. And if I just hear the words "I am afraid" I might be able to *guess* which game is being played here (say on the basis of the tone), but I won't really know it until I am aware of the context. (*LaWrPP1* §50)

About the first of these passages, I want to say that there is a sense in which I *do* understand the sentence mentioned, but—and this is Wittgenstein's point—there is another sense in which I don't understand it at all. I have no idea whom the sentence is about or what condition "he" left "her" in the day before. The second passage makes a similar point. What someone is doing when he utters the words "I am afraid" depends on a context that is wider than a sentence. Wittgenstein wants to show us that the functions and meanings that our words have depend on the ways in which they are situated, not just in sentences, but in conversations and stories; in stretches of discourse, thought, and behavior; in spans of human life. We could say that Wittgenstein reshapes Frege's context principle by enlarging the contexts to which it, or some descendant of it, applies.[23]

---

[23] Here, we might consider another variation on the CEO example: Imagine that the CEO says, "Phillips is a real team-player," without glossing what she means by this. Later in the meeting, one of the board members says to the CEO, "A few minutes ago,

So: one way in which Wittgenstein reshapes and extends Frege's context principle is by calling attention to contexts that are wider than sentences.[24] A second way he does this is by bringing out that it is not only linguistic items—words or sentences—that depend for their significance on their surroundings. The following passage concerns the significance of a wordless activity—the placing of a crown on someone's head:

A coronation is the picture of pomp and dignity. Cut one minute of this proceeding out of its surroundings: the crown is being placed on the head of the king in his coronation robes.—But in different surroundings gold is the cheapest of metals, its gleam is thought vulgar. There the fabric of the robe is cheap to produce. A crown is a parody of a respectable hat. And so on. (*PI* §584)

In thinking about such examples, it helps to imagine glimpsing a few seconds out of a movie. Suppose that while channel-surfing, you catch a moment of a film in which a man is slowly closing a door. There is a sense in which you know what you are seeing—a man closing a door—but another sense in which you don't. You don't know the meaning of this activity—this door-closing—because you don't know how it figures in the story. Perhaps if you saw more of the film, you would want to say that in closing the door, the man was breaking off a love affair, or trying to stay hidden, or insulting the butler. The significance of our

---

you remarked that Phillips is a real team-player. I wasn't sure just how you meant that. Were you implying that he's not particularly creative or original?" The CEO replies, "No; I meant that he's good at getting along with people." In this example, the CEO's initial remark about Phillips and her gloss on it are not part of a single sentence. They are, however, part of what we can think of as a somewhat broader and looser unit of intelligibility—the CEO's remarks about Phillips at the board meeting. (The CEO speaks with authority here too, but perhaps not quite the same degree of authority as in the original example. The contextual relation is not so tight here as in the first version of the story.)

[24] I would argue that Wittgenstein's remarks about rule-following should be viewed in light of this point about how he appropriates Frege's context principle. The difference between the way Crispin Wright reads the remarks on rule-following and the way I read them might be summarized as follows. For Wright, a central lesson of Wittgenstein's remarks about rule-following is that since no amount of interpretation can breathe meaning into the noises and ink-marks that constitute our words, they must depend for their meaning on something else—something like stipulation. On my reading, Wittgenstein's point would be better put by saying that the question "What gives meaning to the dead ink-marks and noises we produce?" arises at all only because, in doing philosophy, we're moved to consider words apart from the contexts in which they have their significance (see my "Wittgenstein on Rules and Platonism"). Thus, there's a sense in which Wittgenstein's discussions of rule-following can be viewed—indeed, I think should be viewed—as making a point similar to the one that Frege makes when he warns us not to ask after the meaning of a word apart from its context. The difference is that whereas Frege stresses a word's sentential context, Wittgenstein wants to call attention to the broader context of human activities in which words have their uses and their significance.

activities, both with and without words, depends on how they are situated in our lives:

> Only surrounded by certain normal manifestations of life, is there such a thing as an expression of pain. Only surrounded by an even more far-reaching particular manifestation of life, such a thing as the expression of sorrow or affection. And so on. (Z §534)

The point here is the same as in the coronation passage—only here, the activity at issue is the expressing of a state of mind rather than the placing of a crown on a head. An affectionate glance or touch would not *be* an expression of affection, or of anything else, were it not for the "particular manifestation of life" that surrounds it.

It is not only our words and activities whose significance depends on the "manifestations of life" that surround them. According to Wittgenstein, just as an expression of love depends for its significance on the life in which it is situated, so too does the loving state of mind that it expresses. In the section of the *Investigations* that immediately precedes the coronation passage, Wittgenstein writes:

> Could someone have a feeling of ardent love or hope for the space of one second—*no matter what* preceded or followed this second?——What is happening now has significance—in these surroundings. The surroundings give it its importance. (*PI* §583)

Frege says "never to ask for the meaning of a word in isolation, but only in the context of a proposition." Wittgenstein might have said never to ask after someone's mental condition in isolation, but only in the context of the events in his life:

> "Grief" describes a pattern which recurs, with different variations, in the weave of our life. If a man's bodily expression of sorrow and of joy alternated, say with the ticking of a clock, here we should not have the characteristic formation of the pattern of sorrow or of the pattern of joy.
>
> "For a second he felt violent pain."—Why does it sound queer to say: "For a second he felt deep grief"? Only because it so seldom happens?
>
> But don't you feel grief *now*? ("But are you playing chess *now*?") (*PI*, p. 174)

A person *can* feel grief at a particular moment. But that it is *grief* he feels has to do with what comes before and after that moment. This is not to say that someone's grieving at time t_2 *makes it the case* that he was grieving at t_1 (any more than it is to say that what a person does at t_1 makes it the case that he's grieving at t_2). But we *can* say that at each moment, a person's psychological condition makes sense in light of feelings, behavior, and events that precede and succeed it.

4. WITTGENSTEIN ON PSYCHOLOGICAL SELF-ASCRIPTIONS

Earlier, I claimed that the CEO speaks with authority about what she means by the word "team-player" because her gloss on this word isn't a *mere* interpretation. When she says, "Phillips is a real team-player, by which I don't mean that he's a stupid sheep, but rather that he won't help himself at the expense of this company," she provides both an interpretation of "team-player" and a sentential context for it. I just now claimed that, according to Wittgenstein, a person's psychological condition at a particular moment depends on the surrounding events in her life in something like the way that, according to Frege, a word's meaning depends on its sentential context.

We are now in a position to state a significant point about the character of our mental state self-ascriptions. Just as, in the first version of the CEO story, the CEO's self-interpretation contextualizes that which it interprets and so isn't a mere interpretation, our psychological self-ascriptions contextualize that which they ascribe and so aren't mere ascriptions. Typically, when someone ascribes, for example, an expectation to himself, the ascription is an essential part of the "weave of life" in which his expectation participates and from which it draws its sense. This is part of what Wittgenstein is calling to our attention when he stresses the expressive character of psychological self-ascriptions. An avowal of expectation bears a relation to a person's psychological condition that is akin to the relation the CEO's self-interpretation bears to her use of "team-player."

Consider an example. Wittgenstein writes:

An expectation is embedded in a situation from which it takes its rise. The expectation of an explosion, for example, may arise from a situation in which an explosion is *to be expected*. The man who expects it had heard two people whispering: "Tomorrow at ten o'clock the fuse will be lit". Then he thinks: perhaps someone means to blow up a house here. Towards ten o'clock he becomes uneasy, jumps at every sound, and at last answers the question why he is so tense: "I'm expecting . . .". This answer will e.g. make his behaviour intelligible. It will enable us to fill out the picture of his thoughts and feelings. (Z §67)

On the one hand, the man's expectation isn't suddenly constituted when he expresses it in words. It is, rather, "embedded in a situation from which it takes its rise," a situation in which the man has good reason to expect an explosion and in which his expectation of an explosion is expressed in a variety of ways. On the other hand, when the man described in the passage says, "I'm expecting an explosion," he isn't—

or, anyway, he needn't be—reporting a fact that he has observed. Rather, his avowal of expectation is, like his jumping at every sound, a piece of expectant behavior, an act of expecting. His avowal requires no more inner observation than does his jumpiness. Like his jumpiness and his overhearing talk about a fuse, his psychological self-ascription is an integral part of the situation in which his expectation is embedded and from which it takes its rise. It is because of *this* that it carries a kind of authority that another person's ascription of an expectation to him would not. His authority when he says what he expects derives from the fact that his avowal of expectation helps to contextualize the very thing that it is an avowal of. What's at issue isn't mere ascription; it is something more, something that could be called his expressing his expectation in words.

5. "NOT QUITE RIGHT": THE ASSERTORIC DIMENSION OF PSYCHOLOGICAL SELF-ASCRIPTIONS

We saw that in his "Plan for the treatment of psychological concepts," Wittgenstein writes:

> Sentences in the third person of the present: information. In the first person present: expression. ((Not quite right.))
> The first person of the present akin to an expression. (Z §472)

The "Not quite right" is puzzling. In other passages, Wittgenstein simply asserts that one or another psychological sentence in the first person *is* an expression. (We saw that in *Zettel* §53, he writes, "The statement 'I am expecting a bang at any moment' is an *expression* of expectation.") Why then in *Zettel* §472 does Wittgenstein indicate that it isn't "quite right" to say that psychological sentences in the first person of the present are expressions?

Although I have been drawing attention to what might be called the expressive dimension of psychological self-ascriptions—to the way in which an avowal of, say, desire is like a desirous facial expression—we should not overlook an important difference between an avowal of desire, on the one hand, and a desirous look, on the other. When I avow that I want a bite of your ice cream, I express my desire for a bite, and I *say* that I want a bite. I both show you and tell you what I want. When I stare longingly at your spoon as it moves from the dish to your lips, I express my desire, but I don't thereby assert that I want a bite.

Unlike a bodily expression, a psychological self-ascription asserts the existence of the very state of affairs that it makes manifest. It is for this reason that we are inclined to speak of *authority* in connection with psychological self-ascriptions but not in connection with smiles or desirous looks. If you want to know my psychological condition, you ought to attend both to what I say about myself and to my bodily expressions of emotion, intention, and so on. We speak of authority, however, only in connection with the former because when I say what's on my mind I make a *statement* that has a special claim to truth.

It is easy to get confused here—easy to think that if an utterance of "I'm so happy" is an authoritative assertion or statement, then it must carry the sort of authority that attaches to other kinds of statement. This thought will lead one to assimilate first-person authority either to the authority of an eye-witness or to the authority of the army colonel who declares an area off-limits—either, that is, in the direction of detectivism or in the direction of constitutivism. It might be less confusing if we didn't call expressive avowals *assertions* or *statements* at all. Wittgenstein notes:

> To call the expression of a sensation a *statement* is misleading because 'testing', 'justification', 'confirmation', 'reinforcement' of the statement are connected with the word "statement" in the language-game. (Z §549)

Misleading as it is, however, there is an important respect in which such avowals are like run-of-the-mill statements: they are truth-evaluable. Unlike smiles and winces, they have an assertoric dimension. They are, we might say, assertions of a special sort.

It is very often assumed that when Wittgenstein characterizes psychological self-ascriptions as expressions, he means to be denying that they are assertions.[25] On such a reading, what Wittgenstein has to say about psychological self-ascriptions can seem fairly easy to dismiss. Consider, for example, the following from a paper by David Rosenthal:

> In *Philosophical Investigations* Wittgenstein (1953) seems to have held, roughly, that although one can report that some other person is, for example, in pain, in one's own case one can only express the pain, and not report it as well. If so,

---

[25] Crispin Wright speaks of "the *expressivist* tradition of commentary," which interprets Wittgenstein as "denying that avowals are so much as *assertions*—that they make statements, true or false—proposing to view them rather as *expressions* of the relevant aspects of the subject's psychology" (Wright, "Self-knowledge: The Wittgensteinian Legacy," in C. Wright, B. C. Smith, and C. Macdonald, eds., *Knowing Our Own Minds* (Oxford: Oxford University Press, 1998), p. 34). The present essay arises out of a conviction that we should take seriously (more seriously than, e.g., Wright himself does) Wittgenstein's oft-repeated suggestion that mental state avowals be understood as (or as akin to) expressions, *without* reading him as an expressivist.

sentences like 'I am in pain', which ostensibly report bodily sensations, actually just express them.

But however suggestive this idea may be, it is plainly possible to report explicitly that we are in such states. And it is indisputable that others sometimes assert of us that we are, or are not, in particular mental states, and we sometimes explicitly contradict what they say. It is not just that we undermine what they say, as I might by saying 'ouch' when you say I am not in pain. Rather, we literally deny what others say about us. If we were unable to report on our own states of mind, but could only express them, this direct denial of the ascriptions others make about us would be impossible. If you deny that I am in pain and I simply say 'ouch', we have not thus far contradicted each other.[26]

I want to suggest that when, in his "Plan for the treatment of psychological concepts," Wittgenstein says that it is "Not quite right" to assimilate psychological self-ascriptions to expressions, he is, in effect, rejecting this way of reading what he has to say about such utterances. These utterances aren't *exactly* like facial and bodily expressions: there is a crucial difference, namely, that they have an assertoric dimension. In the end, it is not particularly important whether we say that psychological self-ascriptions *are* expressions or that they are *akin* to them, as long as we keep in view both how they are like winces of pain and how they are unlike them.

I should add that part of what is at issue in the passage from Rosenthal's paper is how to understand Wittgenstein's use of the word "report." Earlier, I quoted (part of) the following from the *Investigations*:

> When someone says "I hope he'll come"—is this a *report* [*Bericht*] about his state of mind, or an *expression* [*Äußerung*] of his hope?—I can, for example, say it to myself. And surely I am not giving myself a report. (*PI* §585; I have departed slightly from Anscombe's translation.)

How should we understand the use of the word "report" that we find here? Should we, following Rosenthal, take "report" to mean, merely, *an assertion—an utterance with truth conditions*? If so, the final sentence of this passage looks mysterious. Why would Wittgenstein think it *obvious* that I cannot be saying something *true* to myself? A better gloss on what he means by "report" would be: *an attempt (or apparent attempt)*[27] *to inform someone of some fact or facts that the speaker has*

---

[26] David Rosenthal, "Thinking That One Thinks," in M. Davies and G. W. Humphreys, eds., *Consciousness* (Oxford: Blackwell, 1993), p. 203. For another reading along these lines, see Robert J. Fogelin, *Wittgenstein* (London: Routledge, 1987), pp. 197–8.

[27] A report may be a lie.

learned. On this understanding of "report," that final sentence makes sense. But notice that on this understanding of "report," it does not follow from a self-ascription's not being a report that it is not an assertion.

6. CONCLUSION

There's a moment in *LaWrPP2* at which Wittgenstein's interlocutor asks, "Can one know what goes on in someone else in the same way he himself knows it?" Many philosophers—for example, Russell in 1912, in *The Problems of Philosophy*—would answer that one cannot. According to Russell in 1912, what goes on in a person is, in principle, accessible only to him. A few philosophers—for example, Russell in 1921, in *The Analysis of Mind*—would answer that one can know what goes on in someone else in the same way he himself knows it, by observing his behavior and inferring his state of mind. Still others, including a number of contemporary philosophers, would answer that although *at present* one cannot know what goes on in someone else in the way he himself knows it, this is a contingent limitation on our powers.[28]

How does Wittgenstein answer his interlocutor's question? He doesn't. Here is the whole passage from *LaWrPP2*:

"Can one know what goes on in someone else in the same way he himself knows it?"——Well, how does he know it? He can express his experience. No doubt within him whether he is really having this experience—analogous to the doubt whether he really has this or that disease—comes into play; and therefore it is wrong to say that he knows what he is experiencing. But someone else can very well doubt whether that person has this experience. Thus doubt does come into play, but, precisely for that reason, it is also possible that there is complete certainty. (p. 92)

According to Wittgenstein, his interlocutor's question presupposes too much, or better—it comes too late. Regardless of whether one answers

---

[28] Thus, David Armstrong writes:

We can conceive being directly hooked up, say by a transmission of waves in some medium, to the body of another. In such a case we might become aware e.g. of the movement of another's limbs, in much the same sort of way that we become aware of the motion of our own limbs. In the same way, it seems an intelligible hypothesis (a logical possibility) that we should enjoy the same sort of awareness we have of what is going on in our own mind. A might be 'introspectively' aware of B's pain, although A does not observe B's behavior.

(D. M. Armstrong and Norman Malcolm, *Consciousness and Causality* (Oxford: Blackwell, 1984), p. 113.)

Yes or No—whether one affirms the privacy of the mental or denies it—
one misses the essential point: that the relation a person bears to his
own experience is not *epistemic*; it is not a matter of his knowing or
failing to know something in this way or that. To get this relation into
view, we must attend to the expressive dimension of mental state self-
ascriptions.[29]

At *PI*, p. 222, Wittgenstein describes the ambition of this region of
his philosophizing as one of condensing a whole cloud of philosophy
into a drop of grammar. My aim in this paper has been twofold: first,
to characterize a cloud of philosophy, one that we might call the dialectic between detectivism and constitutivism; and, second, to show how
Wittgenstein's "Plan for the treatment of psychological concepts" offers
the sketch of a plan for condensing this cloud into a few drops of grammar—drops of grammar such as, "The first person of the present akin
to an expression."[30]

---

[29] On p. 221 of *WNL*, Wittgenstein has just been criticizing the idea that certain inner
goings-on are private, whereupon an interlocutor replies: "But do you really wish to say
they are not private? That one person can see the picture before the other person's eye?"
Wittgenstein would not have us *deny* that inner goings-on are private. *Given* a picture
of the mental according to which inner items appear before the mind's eye, such items
ought to be called private. But it is precisely this picture (and related ones) that
Wittgenstein would have us call into question. He writes:

> The great difficulty here is not to represent the matter as if there were some-
> thing one *couldn't* do. As if there really were an object, from which I derive its
> description, but I were unable to shew it to anyone. (*PI* §374)

[30] I am grateful to James Conant and to John McDowell for illuminating conversations about the topics addressed in this paper.

8

Morality, Human Understanding, and the Limits of Language

Ben Tilghman

It is clear to us now that Wittgenstein's concern in his earlier work was ethical. The *Tractatus* is an ethical document and was written not to expound, but to show the ethical point of view. M. O'C. Drury made a general comment about Wittgenstein's work when he said that alongside his interest in mathematics, logic, and psychology there is an ethical demand.[1] Drury saw this ethical dimension in the drawing of the limits of language that puts ethics in its proper place. He said that to draw the limits of language requires self-denial and a renunciation of a very strong tendency in our nature. I have argued in other places that the *Philosophical Investigations* is also an ethical document. In addition to Drury's point about the ethical demand implicit in drawing the limits of language it has, I think, an additional ethical dimension. I want to explain what that other dimension is and then draw attention to some of the passages in the *Investigations* and *Remarks on the Philosophy of Psychology* as well as *Zettel* where this other dimension meets with the necessity of drawing the limits of language and then show where some of these limits are when we run up against contemporary American materialism.

For many philosophers today ethics is largely a matter of trying to arrive at principles that will guide our actions in dealing with morally sticky public issues such as legal rights, abortion, homosexuality, and social justice. For Wittgenstein ethics was a very personal thing. He was not concerned to formulate principles to guide action nor to present arguments in favor of legislation to promote fairness or to establish a more perfect union. He was, of course, concerned with *acting* on the principles that lay at the heart of his own morality.

My contention that the *Investigations* has an ethical dimension may

---

[1] M. O'C. Drury, "Some Notes on Conversations with Wittgenstein," in Rush Rhees, ed., *Ludwig Wittgenstein: Personal Recollections* (Oxford: Oxford University Press, 1984), p. 81.

seem surprising in the light of the fact that the work contains no explicit mention of ethics at all. The moral dimension of the *Investigations* lies beneath the surface where a concern is to be found about what underlies all ethics and makes moral relations possible. Whatever view you take of the nature of moral relations, it involves relations among people, concern for people, and concern for yourself and your relations to other people. Concern for people presupposes an understanding of other people, and much in the *Investigations* investigates what it is to understand other people and to some extent what it is to understand yourself. It is through this concern that we can see a motive for the attack on the private object picture of the mental, a picture that if taken seriously makes understanding others impossible and, perforce, makes it impossible to enter into any kind of relationship with them. It is here that we find one of the moral dimensions of the *Philosophical Investigations*.

In *PI* II.xi Wittgenstein talks about understanding the thoughts, feelings and intentions of other people. Some of this same ground is covered in *Z* and also *RPP* 2. We can, of course, understand other people. There are no theoretical metaphysical or epistemological difficulties standing in the way, but this understanding can have its difficulties and its limitations. These difficulties and limitations, however, are practical ones. I am thinking of the difficulties we meet when, for example, we don't know another or his situation well enough or are strangers to his cultural background. There are, of course, different kinds of understanding, and understanding another person is not very much like understanding a problem in mathematics or understanding a piece of machinery.

Understanding another involves judgment of his character, actions, and so on. In this connection Wittgenstein talks about agreement in judgments. There is agreement in mathematical judgments. We almost always agree in the results of our calculations, and if our sums do occasionally turn out to be different, we check the addition again. There is also a large measure of agreement in judgments of color. The fact that we agree in these things makes up part of our concepts of both calculation and color. There are, however, other areas where there is often less than general agreement. Aesthetics obviously is one of these. The area that I want to concentrate attention on, however, is in the judgment of the genuineness of expressions of human feeling. While I may be sure that someone is pretending, say, to be in pain or to be pleased with a Christmas present, another person may not be at all. Consider the exchange the Duchess of York has with her grandson about what "crook back'd Richard" had told him:

DUCHESS: Oh, that deceit should steal such gentle shapes,
         And with a virtuous vizard hide foul guile!
         He is my son; yea, and therein my shame;
         Yet from my dugs he drew not this deceit.
BOY: Think you my uncle did dissemble, grandam?
DUCHESS: Ay, boy.
BOY: I cannot think it. (Shakespeare, *Richard III*, II.ii)

Had the boy been privy to certain damning facts about his uncle or had he more experience in the ways of villains he may well have seen things for what they were and agreed with the Duchess.[2] Too often, however, decisive facts are not available to us and we must rely on our own resources for judgment with all their shortcomings of inexperience, bias, and ignorance.

Wittgenstein speaks to such shortcomings in these passages:

Is there such a thing as 'expert judgment' about the genuineness of expressions of feeling?—Even here, there are those whose judgment is 'better' and those whose judgment is 'worse' . . .

Can one learn this knowledge? Yes; some can. Not, however, by taking a course in it, but through '*experience*.'—Can someone else be a man's teacher in this? Certainly. From time to time he gives him the right *tip*.—This is what 'learning' and 'teaching' are like here.—What one acquires is not a technique; one learns correct judgments. There are also rules, but they do not form a system, and only experienced people can apply them right. Unlike calculating rules. (*PI* II.xi)

The voice of his adversary then protests that "The genuineness of an expression cannot be proved; one has to feel it." Well and good, returns Wittgenstein; yet he nevertheless asks, "what does one go on to do with this recognition of genuineness?" He quotes Alceste's comment on Orontes's sonnet from Molière's *Le Misanthrope* (II. ii), "Voilà ce que peut dire un coeur vraiment épris," which I translate freely as "That is a truly passionate heart speaking." Suppose you get someone to agree with you about the genuineness of the passion—"what are the further consequences? Or are there none, and does the game *end* with one person's relishing of what another does not?" In the corresponding passage in the *Remarks on the Philosophy of Psychology* he adds, "In a vague

---

[2] It has been suggested that the boy's response, "I cannot think it," may not mean simply that he does not think it, but rather something more to the effect that he cannot permit himself to think it since his minority has been put into the trust of Richard and he is in his power. The boy must realize that he is in no position to challenge his uncle and must go along with whatever he says. Understood in this way, the situation is another example of a practical difficulty standing in the way of proper judgment. I do not accept this reading, but an examination of the textual evidence is not in order here.

way consequences can be imagined. The other one's attention gets a new direction" (*RPP* 2, §697)

An analogy with aesthetics can be instructive. Some aesthetic issues are merely matters of relish. My friend is decorating her living room and I suggest that this wallpaper would best complement the furniture, but she replies that she prefers the other. The game can well end at that point and remain a matter of relish. It need not, however, end there. I point out certain relations of color and pattern and perhaps even the historical tradition of using that kind of paper in such a room. She may now realize things she had not seen before and her attention may be given a new direction.

If there is no proof of the genuineness of expression, then it can be made to appear as if the matter is purely 'subjective', a matter of 'relish' or a matter of feeling, that is, something akin to a matter of taste—which wallpaper do you like best?—and upon which nothing of any real importance hinges. Wittgenstein rejects that appearance and makes it clear that the game does not end there; it just gets started there. There are consequences to such recognitions.

One can be convinced by evidence that an expression is genuine, but this evidence is often what he calls 'imponderable' evidence that can include 'subtleties of glance, of gesture, of tone'.[3] A judgment formed on the basis of imponderable evidence can at least sometimes be confirmed by 'ponderable' evidence. He then says:

But I may be quite incapable of describing the difference [between the two kinds of evidence]. And this not because the languages I know have no words for it. For why not introduce new words?—If I were a very talented painter I might conceivably represent the genuine and the simulated glance in pictures. (*PI* II.xi)

Very talented painters have represented such things. Think of Giotto's *Kiss of Judas* panel in the Arena Chapel frescoes. Judas kisses Christ on the cheek and Christ looks at his betrayer with an expression that says, "I know exactly what you are doing."

Whether or not imponderable evidence can in principle always be confirmed by ponderable evidence I leave an open question. Someone says that although he was sure she loved him, he now knew it; she told him so. Asked whether he could be sure the declaration was sincere, he replies that the way she said it makes it clear. The presumably confirming evidence may itself partake of the imponderable.

---

[3] It was Kjell S. Johannessen who first called my attention to the importance of the notion of imponderable evidence, especially with respect to aesthetics.

There is no reason to suppose that there cannot be something very much like 'expert judgment' in these things, although there aren't any who have international recognition in the way that, say, Bernard Berenson had as a connoisseur of art. More than one wealthy American collector put himself in the hands of Berenson when it came to buying Florentine painting. Some who had no taste of their own relied on Berenson to cater to their vanity by providing them with the best of the old masters, but there were no doubt others who relied on Berenson to instruct them in matters of taste and appreciation. There are nevertheless interesting analogies between Berenson's expertise in judging art and judging the genuiness of an expression.

Since it would be unseemly to imagine a more obtuse Christ who fails to recognize the dissimulation in the kiss of Judas, let us imagine instead the Mafia godfather who fails to recognize the true nature of the kiss of his scheming *capo*. A loyal associate who realized what was going on may warn him of the danger despite the godfather's never having seen it for himself. When it comes to human relations, however, the important thing is that one be brought to see the expression for oneself. It is one thing for the associate to tell him of the deception, it is another for him to show how it is to be recognized. In like manner Berenson can tell the robber baron that this is a great painting and it is also possible that he can instruct him in how to look at paintings.

An example of the kind of judgment Wittgenstein is talking about is afforded by a passage in Mme de Lafayette's novel of manners and love at the sixteenth-century court of Henri II, *La Princesse de Clèves*. The beautiful young Mlle de Chartres has recently married M. de Clèves, but now as Mme de Clèves she finds herself attracted to a certain M. de Nemours who is generally considered to be one of the greatest ornaments of the court. She tries to conceal her infatuation from him, but is unable to do so. Here is the passage:

Despite the pains that she took to avoid his glance and to speak to him less than to any other, there escaped from her certain things which partook of initiating an approach, which led that prince to judge that he was not indifferent to her. A man of less penetration than he would perhaps not have noticed it; but he had already been the object of love so many times that it was difficult not to know when someone loved him.[4]

While there are no internationally known experts in these matters analogous to a Berenson or a Culbertson, it is nevertheless clear that

[4] Marie-Madeleine Pioche de La Vergne, comtesse de Lafayette, *La Princesse de Clèves* (1678); my translation.

Nemours's judgment in these things is better than many others, and if anyone counts as an expert, he surely should; and doubtless he could be sought out by young aspirants to courtly status. It is a discernment that clearly requires experience; not just experience of people in general, but experience in the particular ways of the French courtly society of that time where love was too often a game of sexual infatuation played in the interstices of marriages of alliance and convenience.

We can imagine a younger and inexperienced Nemours being tutored in these courtly matters. One older and wiser calls his attention to a glance, a gesture, a pattern of studied avoidance and the like and explains the importance of such things in recognizing what passes for love in that rarified context. If we are to think of rules in this kind of case, they are not the kind that define an activity such as "three strikes is out," nor are they really rules of strategy such as "never swing on three and nothing." They are at best but indications and examples of the kinds of thing to look for.

In the *Investigations*, Wittgenstein uses the expression 'imponderable evidence' and contrasts it with 'ponderable' evidence, but in *RPP* 2 he speaks instead of sufficient and insufficient evidence (§614). The material that makes up these two works was written during the same period and it is not clear whether the one distinction was meant as a correction of the other. At any rate, there is a significant difference in the distinction between ponderable and imponderable evidence and that between sufficient and insufficient. This difference can be brought out by the following contrasting examples.

We may agree that there was an uncharacteristic sharpness in the boss's manner this morning and we may wonder whether he is not upset about something; perhaps the impending business deal fell through. We both agree that his manner points to some such thing, but there is not yet sufficient evidence to say that it is the loss of the contract that has in fact upset him. It will take further observation to confirm or disconfirm our hypothesis. Imponderable evidence, however, is a rather different matter. What one person takes as an indication of a feeling, another may take as an indication of something quite other or not take it as anything at all. Mme de Clèves looks away when Nemours glances in her direction. Someone else may suppose she simply doesn't like him or may not even recognize the movement as *averting* her gaze. The idea of imponderable evidence is thus much more interesting than that of merely insufficient evidence and involves us in much subtler and richer aspects of human behavior.

What is the moral significance of Nemours's discernment? Once he divined her interest in him, he found himself attracted to her. He was not, however, altogether successful in hiding his feelings from her, although he tried. Once a number of people were admiring a small portrait of her and Nemours secretly made off with it. Everyone thought that it had got misplaced. Mme de Clèves alone had seen what really happened, but she pretended not to be aware of anything untoward. They never spoke of what was happening to them.

She decided she wanted to live in the country away from the court to avoid the presence of Nemours that was causing her so much inner conflict. This led to strained relations with her husband who knew the necessity of maintaining the influential contacts that only presence at the court could provide. Nemours's passion forced him into several rash expediencies and the result was misfortune for all. M. de Clèves fell ill and his death was attributed to chagrin at what he believed was his wife's faithlessness. Mme de Clèves retreated to a convent and gave herself to charitable works while time eventually extinguished the passion of Nemours.

Nemours's discernment profoundly affected the lives of three people. We can, however, imagine other possible outcomes to the business. Had his discernment not been so acute, he would never have suspected he was an object of her attention and there would have been no response to encourage her to pursue the game further. Or we could imagine him being fully aware of her state of mind and rebuking her for it. He could have told her not to be silly and to remember that she was, after all, a married woman and thus put paid to the affair at the very beginning.

Once entangled in such intimate human relations we are deep into serious moral issues. The philosophical lessons we are to learn from this bring us back to the limits of language and the self-denial that goes with accepting them. We cannot say when imponderable evidence turns into ponderable evidence. It is not like the case of a chemist who can have a hunch that the molecular structure of this stuff is so-and-so, where the worth of that hunch has to be cashed in terms of experimental proof. In human relations, however, there may not be, and need not be, the kind of objective evidence that constitutes definitive confirmation of the 'hunch' of imponderable evidence. The kind of proof available to the chemist is not available when it comes to the recognition of human feeling.

In *RPP* 2 Wittgenstein asks whether we can imagine that what is unprovable to us is provable to other beings and then adds, "Or would that change its nature to the point of its being unrecognizable?" (§698). Here we want to ask what it is that might be imagined and who these other beings might be. A possibility has already been imagined for us and we do not have to look far to find, if not those other beings, at least those who aspire to that condition. We don't have to look for aliens from outer space as we might suppose; rather, we can find them in contemporary materialism. I take Paul M. Churchland and what he says in his *Matter and Consciousness*[5] as my example.

To get Churchland's parade going, it has to be assumed first that our familiar ways of talking about ourselves and other people, what is called in the trade 'folk psychology', is a species of theory, only an inadequate or mistaken one, and secondly that all those thoughts, feelings, and intentions that we have been concerned with are private mental events that we are aware of by introspection.

According to Churchland, materialism holds that 'folk psychology' is either an incomplete representation of our inner natures or it is a complete misrepresentation of them. The reductive materialism of the mind/brain identity theory identifies states of consciousness with brain states and assumes that the vocabulary of 'folk psychology' can be defined in terms of, or reduced to talk about, neural states. Eliminative materialism makes the stronger claim that "*Our common-sense psychological framework is a false and radically misleading conception of the causes of human behavior and the nature of cognitive activity*" (p. 43), and consequently commonsense or folk psychology must be eliminated in favor of the conceptual framework of what is referred to as a 'completed' neuroscience.

Churchland says that as matters now stand we do have some, albeit incomplete, access to our inner states by introspection. This access is incomplete because it does not bring to our awareness the multitude of neurological events that he believes underlie and constitute our consciousness. He identifies this introspective access with self-knowledge and wonders how it can be improved; after all, everyone wants to have more self-knowledge. To explain how this improved self-knowledge might come about he has recourse to a pair of analogies. A trained musician is able to pick out and identify the chords and their interrelations in a piece of music in a way that an untrained ear cannot, and the experienced wine taster is able to make discriminations opaque to ordinary folk. Given appropriate developments, might we not be able to do something like that with our introspective awareness?

Consider then the possibility of learning to describe, conceive, and introspectively apprehend the teeming intricacies of one's inner life within the conceptual framework of a 'completed' neuroscience . . .

---

[5] Paul Churchland, *Matter and Consciousness* (Cambridge, Mass.: MIT Press, 1988). I am indebted to Richard Scheer for calling my attention to the aptness of this work as a target for Wittgenstein's criticism.

Suppose we trained our native mechanisms to make a new and more detailed set of discriminations, a set that corresponded not to the primitive psychological taxonomy of ordinary language, but to some more penetrating taxonomy of states drawn from a 'completed' neuroscience. And suppose we trained ourselves to respond to that reconfigured activity with judgments that were framed, as a matter of habit, in the appropriate concepts from neuroscience. (pp. 179–80)

The confusions in all of this are so deep and many-layered that it is difficult to know where to start to try to untangle them. Only a couple of essays in that direction are possible here. Let us note, to begin with, the incoherence of thinking of our day-to-day descriptions and explanations of people and their behavior as theoretical. In this philosophical world, however, all language turns out to be theory, and this tells us nothing about, pardon the expression, 'folk psychology'. That aside, it should also be noted that looking at our day-to-day dealings with our fellows as theory opens the way for the criticism that it is bad theory, that is, bad science. The response to that, it seems to me, is that it is not theory and not science and doesn't pretend to be, and hence can be neither bad theory nor bad science. The relative relevance of imponderable evidence to judgments of our fellow human beings and to scientific judgments is one clear kind of difference here.

Another point is introspection. The idea that our awareness of our own thoughts, feelings, and so on is the result of something called introspection is a piece of philosophers' nonsense that does not need rehearsing here. The suggestion that we might someday 'introspectively apprehend' the neural processes that constitute our consciousness may strike us as nonsense raised to some power. He says that by analogy with the musician and the wine taster,

Glucose consumption in the forebrain, dopamine levels in the thalamus, the coding vectors in specific neural pathways, resonances in the nth layer of the peristriatal cortex, and countless other neurophysiological and neurofunctional niceties could be moved into the objective focus of our introspective discrimination and conceptual recognition. (p. 180)

To move these things into the objective focus of our conceptual recognition, he thinks, would be analogous to making the discriminations of the musician and wine taster.

Churchland goes on to say that should the possibility of the completed neuroscience envisioned be realized, it would be, in his words, 'a dawning' in which the marvelous intricacies of our psychological states are finally revealed (p. 180). This strongly suggests that once these marvelous intricacies are revealed we will know what our psychological states really are, just as we are now supposed to know that clouds are really water vapor in suspension. And, we must suppose, we would also know without question when any particular state is actually present.

At one point in a discussion of introspection Wittgenstein poses the sample question, "Do I really love her, or am I only pretending to myself?" (*PI* §387). The implication of Churchland's program is that Wittgenstein's question would be immediately answerable under the new instauration in which the marvelous intricacies of our mental sates are revealed, and right off he should be able to distinguish the genuine feeling and its expression from the counterfeit. There is, however, a difficulty. The materialist's program would eliminate our old familiar ways of talking and substitute for them a new conceptual scheme. We could then no longer speak of *love*, and whatever neural processes are revealed to the new and improved introspection would in no way be revelatory of what love really is. What promises to reveal the marvelous intricacies of our psychological states manages only to change the subject. Wittgenstein would then be right in saying that things would have changed their nature to the point of their being unrecognizable.

There is, of course, a role for introspection to play in our lives, for example in achieving self-knowledge, but this familiar notion of introspection is not the introspection of traditional philosophy and nothing like Churchland's conception of it. Churchland's notion of self-knowledge is passing strange. For him it is a matter of becoming aware of the neurological events that make up our awareness. But let us set aside for a moment the confusions in the philosopher's idea of introspection and suppose that by some scientific technique or other we could become aware of the neurological states and processes that are presumably relevant to my love. Would the awareness that there are x, y, z neural events now taking place answer my question about the genuineness of love? Or raise the question about her: Does she really love me? Would knowledge of her neural processes answer the question for me? Wittgenstein speaks to this.

Imagine that people could observe the functioning of the nervous system in others. In that case they would have a sure way of distinguishing genuine and simulated feeling.—Or might they after all doubt in turn whether someone feels anything when these signs are present?—What they see there could at any rate readily be imagined to determine their reaction without having any qualms about it.

And now this can be transferred to outward behaviour.

This observation fully determines their attitude to others and doubt does not occur. (Z §557)

There are two significant points in this passage. It calls attention to the problem of establishing the proper correlation between neural events and particular feelings. There is a certain surface plausibility to supposing that there is a clear distinction between genuine love on the one hand and conscious and deliberate deceit on the other, and hence between the neural states underlying them. But when I am in doubt myself about whether I really love her, I won't know how to classify the current neural events. The neurology that was supposed to settle the matter can't help.

The second point imagines people ignoring the first difficulty and its doubts and going ahead to distinguish the true from the false on the basis of brain states. The result of this is an altogether new practice of talking about feelings and relating to people. It is, in effect, a new way of living. This is a point that is largely ignored by contemporary materialists who tend to put all the emphasis on the language of a revised conceptual scheme without realizing that the language, like any other, must be rooted in a life. A new language has to bring with it a new set of practices and ways of living. Wittgenstein makes clear the consequences of this.

'These men would have nothing human about them.' Why?—We could not possibly make ourselves understood to them. Not even as we can to a dog. We could not find our feet with them. (*RPP* 2, §700)

Things would indeed become unrecognizable.

All of this raises the most serious difficulties for the intelligibility of reductive materialism. Eliminative materialism fares even worse. The reductive version at least tries to keep some connection with our familiar concepts, but the eliminative version dispenses even with that, and we haven't the foggiest notion of what will be expressed by the envisioned neuroscience.

Here it will be useful to remind ourselves of what introspection and its connection with self-knowledge can really be like. After he raised the question about love, Wittgenstein went on to say that "the process of introspection is the calling up of memories; of imagined possible situations, and the feelings that one would have if . . ." We may add that self-knowledge can also involve, among many other things, being fully aware of one's own motives and assessing them morally. To determine the genuineness of my love for her may demand that I make sure I am not seeking her hand out of pity, say, for her fatherless condition or possibly for the prestige that connection with her family can bring. It is difficult to imagine what the moral assessment of dopamine levels in the thalamus would amount to.

For the people in Churchland's new world, those with whom we could not find our feet, identifying whatever is to pass for the feelings of others, and we may suppose of themselves as well, would be more like making scientific measurements or even mathematical calculations than anything we recognize as dealing with our fellows. When Wittgenstein called our attention to the obvious fact that we do agree about the results of mathematical calculations, he made a remark that many doubtless find unsatisfactory: "I have not said *why* mathematicians do not quarrel, but only *that* they do not." We are tempted to demand an explanation why that is so, something perhaps in the special nature of mathematical propositions, but Wittgenstein puts us off by going on to say, "What has to be accepted, the given, is—so one could say—*forms of life*" (*PI* II.xi).

And this is the response that we must give to anyone who finds in the uncertainty of human relations something that science should eventually be able to overcome. Here we must remind ourselves: this is what our life is like and there is nothing to regret about that. To be sure, there are always things to be regretted about this or that episode in our lives and this or that misjudgment of another, but nothing to be regretted about there being a life in which the genuineness of human feeling is judged in the way that it is and a life in which moral consequences follow in the wake of such judgment.

There are uncertainties in our knowledge of both ourselves and other people, and often the evidence upon which our judgments of others are made is what can be called imponderable. There may be no agreement about what a piece of imponderable evidence points to or even that it is evidence at all. The influence of materialism in contemporary philosophy is one thing that makes clear that there is a very strong temptation to suppose that these uncertainties and the lack of agreement in judgments are shortcomings. We must, however, bridle these temptations and recognize when we have run up against the limits of language. That there is only better and worse judgment about the genuineness of human feeling is not a shortcoming, but is a feature of the concept of genuineness. We must remember that it is not merely a fact about mathematics that there is agreement in judgment about the results of calculation, for that agreement is a constituent of our concept of mathematics. If there were no such general agreement, then whatever it is that we are doing with columns of figures would not be what we call adding and subtracting. Similarly, if there were strict procedures to determine the correctness of judgments about other people, then whatever it is that we would be doing in thinking, for example, "I am sure she loves me," is not what we would call judging the genuineness of human feeling. At the edge of materialism we reach one limit of language. Were we to venture beyond that edge our lives would be unrecognizable.[6]

[6] I am indebted to James Hamilton for helpful comments and criticisms.

9

The *Investigations'* Everyday Aesthetics of Itself

Stanley Cavell

We have all, I assume, heard it said that Wittgenstein is a writer of unusual powers. Perhaps that is worth saying just because the powers are so unusual, anyway in a philosopher, and of his time and place. But why is this worth repeating—I assume we have all heard it repeated—since as far as I know no one has denied it? Evidently the repetition expresses an uncertainty about whether Wittgenstein's writing is essential to his philosophizing; whether, or to what extent, the work of the one coincides with the work of the other. If you conceive the work of philosophy as, let's say, argumentation, of some well-understood sort, then it will be as easy to dismiss as to admire the writing—to admire it, perhaps, as a kind of ornament of the contemporary, or near contemporary, scene of professional philosophy, hence as something that lodges no philosophical demand for an accounting. But if you cannot shake an intuition, or illusion, that more is at issue than ornamentation (indeed that the issue of ornamentation is itself quite unclear), and yet you do not wish to deny argumentation, or something of the sort, as internal to philosophy, then a demand for some philosophical accounting of the writing is, awkwardly, hard to lose.

I describe what I am after here as the *Investigations'* everyday aesthetics of itself to register at once that I know of no standing aesthetic theory that suggests its applicability in understanding the literariness of the *Investigations*, I mean the literary conditions of its philosophical aims; and also to suggest the thought that no work will be powerful enough to yield this understanding of its philosophical aims that lacks the power of the *Investigations* itself. Does this mean that I seek an aesthetics within it? I take it to mean, rather, that I do not seek an aesthetic concern of the text that is separate from its central work. My idea here thus joins the idea of an essay of mine on Wittgenstein from 1986, "Declining Decline," which tracks the not unfamiliar sense of moral or religious fervor in the *Investigations* and finds that its moral work is not separate from its philosophical work, that something like the moral has become for it, or become again, pervasive for philosophy.[1] (As Emerson words the idea in "Self-Reliance":[2] "Character teaches above our will. Men imagine that they communicate their virtue or vice only by overt actions, and do not see that virtue or vice emit a breath every moment." "Character" in Emerson always invokes simultaneously a level of the soul, let me say, and the letter of writing. "Emit a breath every moment" suggests the voice in every word. The idea is to open the question of what constitutes the agency, or insistence, or, in a famous term of Emerson, the consistency, of creatures who speak, whose actions communicate the movements of the soul.)

There is something more I want here out of the idea of an ordinary aesthetics. The *Investigations* describes its work, or the form its work takes, as that of perspicuous presentation (*Übersichtliche Darstellung*) (§122), evidently an articulation of a task of writing. And it declares the work of its writing as "lead[ing] words back from their metaphysical to their everyday use" (§116), a philosophically extraordinary commitment not only to judge philosophy by the dispensation of the ordinary, as much as to evaluate the ordinary by the dispensation of philosophy, but to place philosophy's conviction in itself in the hands, or handling, of ordinary words. But we also know that Wittgenstein invokes, indeed harps on, the idea of the perspicuous as internal to the work of formal proofs. Then is his use of the idea, in this one section of the *Investigations* that explicitly invokes the idea, meant to signal an ideal of lucidity and conviction that he cannot literally expect in a work made of returns to ordinary words?—it is indeed an ideal that philosophers characteristically take logic to *show* is not to be expected from ordinary words. Yet Wittgenstein goes on in the next paragraph to insist: "The concept of perspicuous presentation is of fundamental significance for us. It earmarks our form of presentation, how we look at things." So is the idea that the writing of the *Investigations* contains an equivalent, or some analogy or allegory, of proofs? Or that after all it is meant to project arguments of formal rigor, even though its surface form of presentation does not, to say the least, spell them out? How else could we account for the influence of this work, such as it is, in institutions of professional philosophy?

My somewhat different proposal is that Wittgenstein is claiming for

---

[1] "Declining Decline," in my *This New Yet Unapproachable America: Lectures After Emerson After Wittgenstein* (Chicago: University of Chicago Press, 1989).

[2] All references to Emerson are to Ralph Waldo Emerson, *Essays and Lectures*, ed. Joel Laporte (New York: Library of America, 1983).

the ordinary or everyday its own possibility of perspicuousness, as different from that of the mathematical as the experience of an interesting sentence is from the experience of an interesting theorem. But how can this be? Doesn't Wittgenstein's idea of the perspicuous just *mean,* as it were, the look of a formal proof? My proposal is rather to conceive that Wittgenstein once hit off an experience of the convincingness, perhaps of the unity, of a proof, with the concept of perspicuousness; and for some reason, later (or earlier), he hits off an experience of a unity, or a reordering, of ordinary words with the same concept, as if discovering a new manifestation of the concept in discovering something new about the ordinary. He had said, in the section in question: "A perspicuous presentation is a means to just that understanding which consists in 'seeing connections'." Understanding a proof surely requires seeing connections. So does understanding a unity among and within ordinary sentences. Is there an interesting connection here to be seen between these means, as it were, of understanding, call them formal and non-formal, or ordered and ordinary?

I am encouraged to look for a specific manifestation of perspicuousness in the ordinary by the passage in the *Investigations* (§89) in which Wittgenstein asks: "In what sense is logic something sublime?" His answer, as I understand it, expresses one way of seeing his turn from the thoughts of the *Tractatus* to those of the *Investigations*. I almost never allow myself an opinion about the *Tractatus*, in which I do not know my way about. But I cannot avoid just this instance now. The *Investigations* answers: "For there seemed to pertain to logic a peculiar depth. Logic lay, it seemed, at the bottom of all the sciences." And then appears one of those dashes between sentences in this text, which often mark a moment at which a fantasy is allowed to spell itself out. It continues: "For logical investigation explores the essence of all things. It seems to see to the ground of things and is not meant to trouble itself over whether this or that actually happens." Is Wittgenstein fighting the fantasy or granting it? Then a larger dash, and following it: "[Logic] takes its rise, not from an interest in the facts of nature, nor from a need to grasp causal connections; but from a striving to understand the foundation, or essence, of everything empirical." But again, is this good or bad, illusory or practical? Then finally: "Not, however, as if to this end we had to hunt out new facts; it is much more essential for our investigation that we want to learn nothing *new* from it. We want to *understand* something that is already open to view. For *this* is what we seem in some sense not to understand." So something in this philosophical fantasizing turns out to be practical after all, and something that winds up sounding like a self-description of the *Investigations*.

Many such self-descriptions are famously concentrated in the ensuing several dozen sections of the book (§§ 90–133). ("A picture held us captive." "Our investigation . . . seems only to destroy everything interesting, that is, all that is great and important.") Logic, however, drops out—that is, as a formal ideal, not to say as the ultimate formal systematization of the unity of knowledge. But the *aim* of philosophy, expressed by that fantasy of logic, may be said to remain, if transformed, the mark of philosophy's intellectual seriousness. It demands an extraordinary understanding, but not of some new discovery; it is not in that way in competition with science. And the aim is still essence, the ground of everything empirical, but the means to this ground is as open to view, and as ungrasped, as what there is to be grasped essentially. The means is something called the ordinary. And there is no single or final order in which ordinariness and its articulation of essence is to be ordered, or presented, or formed—we might even say, reformed. The new route to the old aim Wittgenstein calls grammatical investigation. What is its form, or order?

Wittgenstein says (§123): "A philosophical problem has the form: 'I'm at a loss.'" I translate "Ich kenne mich nicht aus" so as to bring out my sense, expanded upon elsewhere, of affinity in Wittgenstein's characterization of philosophy here, startling in its apparent casualness, with the loss Dante suffers (loss of way) faced with the dark wood in the middle of life's journey, as he begins to recount the journey. The implication of the affinity, granted its presence, is that Wittgenstein is here marking the beginning of something to which this beginning gives, or from which it is given, a certain form. Religion may call a similar condition, differently placed, perdition. Such a moment marks the place from which Emerson, beginning "Experience," calls out, "Where do we find ourselves?" It is, accordingly, as the philosophical answer to this disorientation that Wittgenstein proposes the idea of a perspicuousness achieved—outside the realm of proof—as a return, a return to what he calls the ordinary, or "home" (I place the quotes to remind ourselves that it is obscure whether we have ever been there). The section that names perspicuous presentation mentions the importance of "intermediate cases," hence suggests that the idea of understanding as "seeing connections" is one of supplying language-games—as in the string of cases of "reading" (§§156–78), or in comparing the grammar of the word "knows" to that of "can" or "in a position to" and also to "understands" (§150), or, more generally, in showing grammatical derivation, as of the grammar of "meaning" in part from "explaining the meaning," or in showing grammatical difference, as between "pointing to an object" and "pointing to the color of an object."

Perspicuous presentation is accordingly the end of a philosophical problem that has *this* form of beginning (loss).

But the methods of language-games, though perhaps the most
famous forms in which the *Investigations* is known, at least outside the
precincts of professional philosophy, put no more literary pressure on
language—they pose no greater problem for aesthetics—than J. L.
Austin's appeal to what we should say when. (Not that Austin's prose
is easy to characterize—I have said something about that recently in
taking up Derrida's treatment of *How To Do Things with Words* in my
Pitch of Philosophy.) I mean, it is not in this region of the perspicuous
that the pressure intensifies to account philosophically for the genius of
this writing. What the provision of language-games requires is apparently no more than the common mastery of a language. (It is a matter
of asking for and providing, for example, the difference between doing
something by accident and by mistake, or between seeing bread and
seeing all the signs of bread, or between knowing the other from his or
her behavior and knowing the other *only* from his or her behavior.) The
genius would come in seeing how this mastery, and equally the loss of
mastery, calls for philosophy. If writing of a certain character is essential to displaying or accounting for what is thus seen, then this writing
is essential to the philosophical work of the *Investigations*. And it, too,
then would have to fall under the concept of perspicuous presentation.

Sometimes the movement from being at a loss to finding oneself happens at a stroke—of a pen, of genius—in any case without the means or
intermediary methods of grammatical investigations. Here I adduce
moments from *Philosophical Investigations* expressed in the words of
such memorable gestures as these: "What is your aim in philosophy?"
"To show the fly the way out of the fly-bottle" (§309); "Why can't my
right hand give my left hand money?" (§268); "We have got on to slip-
pery ice where there is no friction and so in a certain sense the conditions are ideal, but also, just because of that, we are unable to walk"
(§107); "If I have exhausted my grounds I have reached hard rock, and
my spade is turned" (§217); "The human body is the best picture of the
human soul" (II.iv); "If I am inclined to suppose that a mouse has come
into being by spontaneous generation out of grey rags and dust, I shall
do well to examine those rags very closely to see how a mouse may have
hidden in them, how it may have got there and so on . . . But first we
must learn to understand what it is that opposes such an examination
of details in philosophy" (§52); "(Uttering a word is like striking a note
on the keyboard of the imagination)" (§6); "But if you are *certain*, isn't
it that you are shutting your eyes in front of doubt?" "They are shut"
(II.xi). These are patently, all but ostentatiously, "literary" gestures of

the *Investigations*, outstanding in the sense of that work as cultivating its literary grounds. Can we say how precisely?

I note that there is pleasure to be taken in them; and a shock of freedom to be experienced; and an anxiety of exposure (since they treacherously invite false steps of the reader: I have heard the observation about the keyboard of the imagination taken as Wittgenstein's own opinion about words, not as the spelling out of a captive's fantasy); and they are at once plain and sudden, especially in context—let us say they are brilliant. But our question is whether they are essential to the work of the *Investigations*, which is before all to ask whether they represent philosophical work. So if we observe that the pleasure comes in being liberated from an unexpressed, apparently inexpressible, mood—a liberation attributable to the finding or inventing of a specific order of words—then we have to ask whether providing expression, something Freud speaks of as making a construction, is a form of work. The lines or gestures I just cited require a specific talent to compose, one perhaps dangerous to philosophy, or distracting; and they require a matching aesthetic effort to assess: for example, to see whether their pleasure and shock and anxiety are functions of their brilliance. Differences in the work philosophy does and the work that art does need not be slighted if it turns out that they cross paths, even to some extent share paths—for example, where they contest the ground on which the life of another (hence of oneself) is to be examined, call it the ground of therapy.

But is this work to be comprehended by way of the *Investigations'* idea of perspicuous presentation? To capture the pervasiveness and the specificity of the experience in question (the pleasure, shock, anxiety, liberation), it will help to remember that text's recurrence to scenes of pain, especially scenes of what I call inexpressiveness, associated with fears of suffocation or of exposure. This is how I have understood what is at stake in such a moment as Wittgenstein presents beginning, "Yes, but there is *something* there all the same accompanying my cry of pain" (§296). Words suffer fixation in philosophizing. It is such fixation, call it spiritual paralysis, as it were a hallucination of necessity, of some necessary meaning, from which the order of words in the ostentatiously literary gestures cited may be said to offer freedom. As do, but differently, the citing and constructing of language-games. I would like to have a good description of this difference.

I took this line of thinking about the perspicuous in a course I offered with Hilary Putnam in the spring of 1993, prompted by my commitment to the class to go over—something I have rarely done—aspects of my own writing on the *Investigations* in Parts One and Four of *The Claim of Reason*.

In turning to that book of mine with some consecutiveness for the first time in years, I was struck by an air of pathos I found in it—long before the description, near the opening of Part Four, of the fantasy of inexpressive privacy or suffocation—gathering intensity at the close of each of the two chapters that end Part One. There we come across stifled screams in a Hemingway hospital ward; and Keats's mourning for a dead poet; and images of starving or abandoned children. My surprise at these rediscoveries was greeted with certain smiles of recognition from a number of the graduate students present, as though I was tardy in my literary self-observations. Naturally I attributed this pathos to the pathos of the *Investigations* itself, specifically to its portrait of—or its conviction that there is something to be seen as—the human condition, say the human as conditioned by the present stage of history.

Part of my sense of the *Investigations* as a modernist work is that its portrait of the human is recognizable as one of the modern self, or, as we are given to say, the modern subject. Since we are considering a work of philosophy, this portrait will not be unrelated to a classical portrait of the subject of philosophy, say that to be found in Plato's *Republic*, where a human soul finds itself chained in illusion, so estranged from itself and lost to reality that it attacks the one who comes to turn it around and free it by a way of speaking to it, and thus inciting it to seek the pleasures of the clear light of day. A difference of the modern self is that, no longer recognizing itself in Plato's environment, and subject to a hundred daily impertinent interventions, it no longer surmises an elsewhere in which, or from which, to claim its own intelligibility or companionability. So the kind of work proposed in the text of the *Investigations* will at first seem to the one to whom it is addressed—the modern philosophical subject—to be obvious, uninteresting, remote. But if for some reason one or another of us moderns persists in considering the work, we may begin to divine our own voices returning there. Everything depends on the specificity and recognizability with which the portrait of our condition is drawn.

I have begun specifying the portrait in the philosophically recurrent sense—or the recurrence of philosophy in recognizing the sense—of lostness to oneself. This beginning of philosophy is related, I believe, to the feeling of philosophizing as an effort to achieve the indestructible (§55), but at the same time the experience of Wittgensteinian therapy initially as the destruction of everything great and important (§118), as if human self-destructiveness is at war with itself in philosophy. This is equally expressed in the sense that our ideal encloses us, threatens us with suffocation ("There is no outside," §103). I have more than once noted the human sense of disappointment with the human, in the form of a disappointment with the language it is given ("A name ought really to signify a simple" (§39)); this pairs with human perverseness ("Why does it occur to one to want to make precisely this word [the word 'this'] into a name, when it evidently is not a name?—That is just the reason" (§39)). Then no wonder "The philosopher's treatment of a question is like the treatment of an illness" (§255), which Wittgenstein articulates as a sickness of the understanding (*RFM*, orig. edn., p. 157) as well as a sickness of the will ("Why does it occur to us to want to make this word . . . ?"; "[Philosophical problems] are solved . . . through an insight into the workings of language [which takes place precisely] *despite* a drive to misunderstand them" (§109)). Yet philosophy itself—the human creature in its grip—remains tormented, and must learn to give itself peace, which means to break itself off (§133), critically to break itself of the craving for completeness, perhaps to reconstitute the craving. Add to these features the *Investigations'* beginning with (apart from an unnoticed child, and a curiously mechanical shopping errand) a succession of primitive builders, and we recognize that the strangeness of the human to itself is always before us—epitomized in its philosophizing and in the uncertainty of its grip on itself, or on the concept of itself (is it a *language* the builders have? is it *words* they use? If I do not know such things about them, how can I know them about myself?).

My remarks about the pathos of the modern subject—finding its portrait in the *Investigations'* predicates (stated or implied) of torment, perverseness, disappointment, suffocation, illness, strangeness, etc.—is itself apt to seem perverse, anyway strange, or just remote, as a way of commending the Wittgensteinian text to the attention of contemporary thinkers inclined to the American-English side of the philosophical mind. Which would suggest that the dispensation of philosophy which indispensably protects Wittgenstein's teaching (that American-English side) at the same time resists or refuses it.

How shall I place—I who grew up in that dispensation—the remoter shore, let's call it, of perspicuousness, or call it the literariness of the *Investigations*? Let us figure it as, alluding to Kant, a standpoint from which to see the work of the *Investigations*, its leading words home, undoing the charms of metaphysics; a perspective apart from which there is no pressing issue of spiritual fervor, whether felt as religious, moral, or aesthetic. Standpoint implies an alternative, a competing standpoint, a near shore. For professional philosophers on the Western side of the North Atlantic, this shore is largely that of philosophical "problems"—say ones such as those Wittgenstein lists in the Preface to *Philosophical Investigations*, "[subjects such as] the concepts of meaning, of understanding, of a proposition, of logic, the foundations of mathematics, states of consciousness, and other things." Without *this* shore, the *Investigations* would not press upon, and not belong in, an academic philosophical curriculum. Because of the farther shore, its belonging is, and should be, uneasy.

I wish I could make the two shores equally palpable, and sufficiently so to make questions as to which shore is the more important seem as foolish to us as it must seem to the river of philosophy that runs between. One without the other loses the pivot of the ordinary, the pressure of everyday life; one without the other thus loses, to my way of thinking, the signature of the *Investigations*.

There remains a question of priority. From each shore the other is almost ignorable, and each imagines itself to own the *seriousness* of the *Investigations*' work. When the farther ignores the rigors of the near, it consigns philosophy to the perennial, the perhaps customary eternal. When the near ignores the yearning for the farther, it merely conforms to the customary institutional demands of the university, hence risks consigning philosophy to present intellectual fashion. Each position has its advanced and its debased versions.

To count, as I do here, on a willingness to maintain a continuity between near and far, is to count on a certain way of following the continuities implied between the pleasures I claimed for certain literary gestures in the *Investigations* and the portrait of human pathos I sketched from it. The way of following requires a willingness to recognize in oneself the moments of strangeness, sickness, disappointment, self-destructiveness, perversity, suffocation, torment, lostness that are articulated in the language of the *Investigations*; and to recognize in its philosophizing that its pleasures (they will have to reach to instances of the ecstatic) will lie in the specific forms and moments of self-recovery it proposes—of soundness, of finitude, of the usefulness of friction, of acknowledgement, of peace, of familiarity (hence of uncanniness, since the words of recovery were already familiar, too familiar).

But what kind of pleasure could be essential to philosophy, and worthy of it? I think it will help us find an answer if we pick up more concretely Wittgenstein's reiterated observation in *RFM* that "proof must be perspicuous," and look at a proof. Coming from me it had better be simple. I take an example remembered from Euclidean geometry, one of the two earliest discourses in which I remember experiencing something like ecstasy in arriving at a conclusion—the other discourse was music. I assume it is to be proved that the sum of the inner angles of a triangle equals 180 degrees, the measure of a straight line. I draw a triangle and construct through its apex a line parallel to its base (Fig. 5).

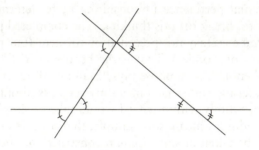

FIGURE 5

Proof: Assuming that we have proven that opposite interior angles of a transverse between parallel lines are equal, we know that the lower left angle is equal to the upper left angle beneath the parallel, and that the lower right angle is equal to the upper right angle beneath the parallel. Now since the remaining angle at the vertex of the triangle is identical with the remaining angularity of the line, namely that between those upper left and right angles, the line's angularity is equal to the sum of the three angles of the triangle; which is to say, the sum is 180 degrees. Q.E.D. Look at it. The three angles precisely exhaust the line. This is perspicuous. It is a glimpse at the ground of everything empirical.

The obvious predicates of this experience remain, I find, pleasure of some kind, and a kind of liberation or relief, and, we might now specify, a sense of arrival, or completeness, as of relationship perfected, not finished but permanent. As well, therefore, as manifesting "the understanding which consists in 'seeing connections'," as in the section naming perspicuous representation (§122), the proof also manifests, it seems, what Wittgenstein calls, a few sections later, "the clarity that we aspire to," about which he says, "[it] is indeed *complete* clarity." Then he goes on to characterize this completeness in ways that no longer seem pertinent to such a proof as I have remembered from Euclidean geometry, as follows: "But this simply means that the philosophical problems"—that is, a certain sense of being at a loss—"should *completely* disappear . . . The real discovery is the one that makes me capable of breaking off philosophizing when I want to. The one that brings philosophy peace." We don't seem to require a background of philosophical torment to ask for such proofs and to receive their pleasure. This difference between the philosophical and the geometrical mode (Spinoza's title for the *Ethics* emphasizes *Ordine Geometrico*) evidently goes with the fact that a proof is a structure that tells me something is over, a bottom reached; I do not have to consult my will, there would be no intellectual pertinence in consulting it, to determine whether I may, or want to, break off this thinking. The completed proof breaks it off. It affords me ecstasy not preceded by torment (but perhaps by the ups and downs of wonder). That is the beauty of it. (Were anyone to think me fool enough to suppose myself talking about the aesthetics of mathematics, let me state that I mean my remarks about the geometrical proof to be wholly within what I would take as simple and sensible aesthetic procedure. I mean, for example, that it begins by finding that pleasure is to be taken in some human construction, and communicated, and then determining the properties of the construction that seem to account for it. The little that I have encountered in what presents itself as the aesthetics of mathematics apparently begins the other way around, with mathematical properties that are somehow known to be aesthetic (symmetry, elegance, economy, etc.) which seems to beg the aesthetic question.)

We seem to have rearrived at the question whether the concept of perspicuousness invited by the experience of certain formal proofs is further invited by a certain unity or reordering of ordinary words—supposing this to be something Wittgenstein means by his discovery of (non-formal) moments of complete clarity; ordinary words, that is, which are not meant to line up as premises to a conclusion. Ones meant, perhaps, in a sense not to be taken as assertions at all—as what Wittgenstein calls theses—as claims for which we, let's say, have to go outside ourselves for confirmation. There is the force of a claim in question, but it is not one we are asked to place upon the world; it is a claim the words of the *Investigations* are placing upon its reader, as if he or she is to do something (evidently, do something about themselves—Thoreau words this as getting his reader to "look another way"). Is there, perhaps, an ordering of words that is its own bottom line, sees to its own ground—an ordering whose unity, we may say autonomy, strikes us as a kind of beauty? Would we, I mean, be prepared to describe any such philosophical ordering of words in this way?

In answering affirmatively, I need a name for forms of ordinary words that I will claim partake of (satisfy the criteria of) completeness, pleasure, and the sense of breaking something off (chief marks of perspicuous representation)—words that epitomize, separate a thought, with finish and permanence (one might say it is with beauty), from the general range of experience. To such a (non-formal) form of words I give the unsurprising, working name of the aphoristic. I am claiming that Wittgenstein's reconception of philosophy, or say of the form of a philosophical problem, requires an extension of the discovery of formal perspicuousness to a discovery of nonformal perspicuousness. I think of it as an extension from the work of what Wittgenstein calls grammatical methods or treatments of language to the primitive fact of everyday language itself—I might say, to the fact that there is such a thing as language—that it expresses desire, the point of language named by Augustine at the close of the citation with which Wittgenstein opens the *Investigations*. After Lacan's presentation of Freud, one could say the primitive fact is of language as the creation of (human) desire.

So here's the surprising premise in my argument for taking Wittgenstein's writing as essential to his philosophizing, the manner essential to the method: the concept of the perspicuous, governed by the criteria of completeness, pleasure, and breaking off—summarize these as defining a unity recognized through an impression of beauty—is as surely invited by contexts of aphorism as it is by those of proof and of grammatical investigation.

The aphoristic in Wittgenstein's writing is a mode of reflecting the clarity brought by grammatical methods, one that in itself, as itself, exhibits this clarity, together with a satisfaction or acknowledgment of the obscurity (the farther shore) from which clarity comes. To say that this exhibition is essential to the work of the *Investigations* is to say that appeals to the ordinary which fail this mode of reflection are not Wittgensteinian appeals, they do not take their bearing from the power to make philosophical problems completely disappear—hence appear. They do not, accordingly, express our interest in these problems, and so leave us subjected to them without understanding what kind of creatures we are, what our life form as talkers is, that we are thus fascinatable, that philosophy is seductive. (The philosophical sensibility here is radically different from Austin's.)

Since this claim for the aphoristic, say for its mode of expressiveness, rests upon experience, the claim's own perspicuousness depends upon attracting to itself sufficient pertinent experience. (The role of experience is critical. I am not supplying evidence for a hypothesis, but examples which, when successful, call for a particular concept.) I will in the time left undertake to provide objects of this experience, noting that in the *Investigations* the aphoristic does not always, or even usually take the form of free-standing aphorisms (as in the memorable cases of showing the fly the way out of the fly-bottle or the body as the best picture of the soul), but is mostly directed, as I have indicated, to reflecting details of its methodicalness, its searching out criteria, articulating grammar, spelling out fantasies, calling attention to a fixated picture, presenting intermediate cases, all in all mapping emptiness and insistence in philosophical assertion. To isolate and test the experience in independent aphorisms to show that it is reliably housed in specific, recognizable linguistic structures, I will go far outside *Philosophical Investigations* to Wittgenstein's aphorisms that find their way into Professor Von Wright's miscellany translated by Peter Winch under the title *Culture and Value* (pieces of prose palpably continuous with that of the *Investigations*) and select ten of them to pair with ten aphorisms composed between the last years of the eighteenth century and the end of the first half of the nineteenth. This is the period in which Wittgenstein, early in the entries of *Culture and Value*, locates his aspiration:

I often wonder whether my cultural ideal is new, i.e. contemporary, or whether it comes from the time of Schumann. At least it strikes me as being a continuation of that idea, though of course not the continuation that actually happened. Thereby the second half of the nineteenth century is excluded. (*CV*, p. 2)

(The excluded half-century includes Frege, *Tristan* and the future of music, Nietzsche, and, for example, Helmholtz.)

I present the ten pairs without beforehand identifying which member is Wittgenstein's.

I.   (a) One age misunderstands another; and a petty age misunderstands all the others in its own nasty way.
      (b) The age isn't ready for it, they always say. Is that a reason why it shouldn't happen?

II.   (a) A mediocre writer must beware of too quickly replacing a crude, incorrect expression with a correct one. By doing so he kills his original idea, which was at least still a living seedling.
      (b) How many authors are there among writers? Author means creator.

III. (a) Each of the sentences I write is trying to say the whole thing.
      (b) In poetry too every whole can be a part and every part really a whole.

IV.   (a) There is a pathos peculiar to the man who is happily in love as well as to the one who is unhappily in love.
      (b) A so-called happy marriage is to love as a correct poem is to an improvised song.

V.   (a) The idea is worn out by now and no longer usable . . . Like silver paper, which can never quite be smoothed out again once it has been crumpled.

(b) Isn't everything that is capable of becoming shopworn already twisted or trite to begin with?

VI.   (a) If in life we are surrounded by death, so too in the health of our intellect we are surrounded by madness.

(b) Like animals, the spirit can only breathe in an atmosphere made up of life-giving oxygen mixed with nitrogen. To be unable to tolerate and understand this fact is the essence of foolishness; to simply not want to do so is madness.

VII. (a) Is this the sense of belief in the Devil: that not everything that comes to us as an inspiration comes from what is good?

(b) On my saying, "What have I to do with the sacredness of traditions, if I live wholly from within?" my friend suggested,—"But these impulses may be from below, not from above." I replied, "They do not seem to me to be such; but if I am the Devil's child, I will live then from the Devil."

VIII. (a) My account will be hard to follow: because it says something new but still has egg-shells from the old view sticking to it.

(b) You're always demanding new ideas? Do something new, then something new might be said about it.

IX.   (a) One might say: Genius is talent *exercised with courage.*

(b) But one can never really have genius, only be one . . . Genius is actually a system of talents.

X.   (a) It may be that the essential thing with Shakespeare is his ease and authority and that you just have to accept him as he is if you are going to be able to admire him properly, in the way you accept nature.

(b) The simplest and most immediate questions, like, Should we criticize Shakespeare's works as art or as nature?

In each case the first member of the pair is from Wittgenstein; the second is, with one exception, either from Friedrich or from A. W. Schlegel (from either the *Critical* or the *Athenaeum Fragments*). (I am indebted, not I alone, to Jean-Luc Nancy and Philippe Lacoue-Labarthe for, among other matters, placing these writers on the contemporary philosophical table.) That the Schlegel brothers take the preoccupations of Wittgenstein's sensibility deep into, or into the origin of, German romanticism fits my sense of his continuing the romantic's response to the psychic threat of skepticism. (The exception to the Schlegels, among the writers of the aphorisms I paired with Wittgenstein's, is Emerson's declaration of readiness to be, if need be, the Devil's child.)

Naturally I will not attempt to argue for the resemblance between the members of the pairs; nor even argue here that the pairs present aphorisms, as opposed to adages, or maxims of practical wisdom—beyond noting that they do not present standing, sociable responses to life's recurrences, but rather new, eccentric, personal responses, to some present crossroads of culture, characteristically marked by the recurrences of a word, as if the thought were turning on itself ("One age misunderstands another; and a petty age misunderstands all the others in its own nasty way.") Nor shall I argue, on the basis of a score of examples, that aphorisms with this particular sense of breaking off complete fragments, so to speak, are apt to take on just these subjects—that of genius and talent, of life and death, of originality and banality, of human and animal, of madness, music, misunderstanding, religion. *Philosophical Investigations* touches on, and so continues, in its way, all of these topics—as, in its way, it continues to live on the sound of the fragment, the denial of system (while by no means the denial of the systematic).

But there is a coincidence of insight between a moment from the ones collected in *Culture and Value* and a moment from the *Investigations* which I find remarkable and to bear so precisely on recent work of mine on Emersonian Perfectionism, that I would like to end by citing it along with a thought or two about it. It dates from 1949, four years after the Foreword to *Philosophical Investigations* was written, two years before Wittgenstein's death.

"*Le style c'est l'homme*," "*Le style c'est l'homme meme*." The first expression has cheap epigrammatic brevity. The second, correct version, opens up quite a different perspective. It says that a man's style is a *picture* of him. (*CV*, p. 78e.)

The coincidence with the *Investigations* is—is it too obvious to mention, or too obscure to discuss?—with "The human body is the best picture of the human soul."

First let us venture a suggestion about what Wittgenstein finds cheap in the brief version—"Style is the man." Perhaps it is some resemblance to the saying "Clothes make the man," some unearned and cynical insight about the relation of social judgment to psychic reality, where the former is taken as open to view and the latter is taken to be of no interest even to the one in question. Or some resemblance to some such saying as "Life is the real work of art," which may at a stroke deny the seriousness and difficulty and beauty, such as they are, both of life and of art. How is the longer version different?—"Style is the man himself (the very man)." Well, immediately it has the air of discovery in it, the winning through to an insight, both about what the man, in his way, has made out of something (a talent, a circumstance) and hence something about the character of the maker. This speaks to the image of the human body as a picture of the human soul. I do not think we need more out of the concept of the soul in this passage than as a term for a subject's subjectivity, a thing possessed of mentality or mindedness or moodedness, one whose actions, as Heidegger roughly put it (making something of the German *Handlung* in his way), are ways of handling things. (This is something Charlie Chaplin knew as well as Heidegger is out of order on an assembly line.) We do not need more, I mean, in order to note Wittgenstein's implied refusal of a metaphysical insistence that the body is the mind or the man. This insistence is ruled, in Wittgenstein's aphorism about the body as a picture, to be a kind of literary error, a case of poor reading, a fixated (literalized?) way of taking something.

The importance of the aphorism is accordingly its undertaking to instruct us in reading, or to instruct us that we need such instruction, or really, to instruct us that to receive in writing instruction in reading we already must know how to read. The insight of the aphorism is— along with an implied claim that an insight is necessary here—that any handling by the man (of an impulse or of a circumstance) may be (none is assured to be) a signature, or a sketch that needs no signature for its attribution, a sally of identity, as if a mark of freedom; it may be forged. Perhaps the idea can be expressed as follows: It is assumed, explicitly since, say, Kant, that to originate one's actions, to be free, is to cause them in a certain way (to make the will practical). Kant claimed to be unable to explain this freedom. Wittgenstein's implied proposal assumes, rather, that freedom is to be found not in the will's effectiveness (the will already saturates the world), but in the will's distinctiveness. To originate an action is to act originally, to have the right to sign what you do as yours. In Nietzsche's *Beyond Good and Evil* the inability—or unwillingness—to find what you do to be yours presents itself as an inability to reach the future, the day after tomorrow, a new day (Nietzsche says *Übermorgen*, over-day, super-day. Emerson says: a new dawn at noon. Wittgenstein calls it the everyday.)

Allow me one further step. Prompted by Wittgenstein's reading of style as picturing the very man, I take his idea of the body's picturing to declare that his writing is (of) his body, that it is on the line, that his hand is in the manner of his text, in its melancholy accidents of

reception (cf. *Walden* I.15) as well as in its successes with happy intentions. It measures philosophical value not by the truth or falsity of its
theses (it knows nothing—it possesses no theses—everyone does not
possess) but by a distinction between impatience and perspective in
every word it utters. It is what you must expect of a perfectionist
author, whose authority, such as it is, lies only in his or her example.
Naturally, some find this attractive, others repellent; as some have
found it to be essential philosophy, others have by no means.

BIBLIOGRAPHY

ARMSTRONG, D. M., and MALCOLM, NORMAN. *Consciousness and Causality*. Oxford: Blackwell, 1984.

AUSTIN, J. L. *How To Do Things with Words*. Cambridge, Mass.: Harvard University Press, 1994.

—— "Other Minds," in *Philosophical Papers*, 2nd edn. Oxford: Oxford University Press, 1970.

AZZOUNI, JODY. *Metaphysical Myths, Mathematical Practice*. Cambridge: Cambridge University Press, 1994.

BAKER, G., and HACKER, P. M. S. *Scepticism, Rules and Language*. Oxford: Blackwell, 1984.

———— *Wittgenstein: Rules, Grammar and Necessity: An Analytical Commentary on the Philosophical Investigations*. Oxford: Blackwell, vol. 1, 1985; vol. 2, 1986.

BEN MENAHEM, YEMIMA. "Explanation and Description: Wittgenstein on Convention," *Synthese* 115 (1998): 99–130.

BENACERRAF, PAUL. "Mathematical Truth," in P. Benacerraf and H. Putnam, eds., *Philosophy of Mathematics: Selected Readings*, 2nd edn. Cambridge: Cambridge University Press, 1983.

BIGGS, MICHAEL, and PICHLER, ALOIS. *Wittgenstein: Two Source Catalogues and a Bibliography*. Working Papers from the Wittgenstein Archives at the University of Bergen, No. 7. Bergen, 1993.

BLACK, MAX. *A Companion to Wittgenstein's Tractatus*. Ithaca, N.Y.: Cornell University Press, 1982.

BLACKBURN, SIMON. *Spreading the Word*. Oxford: Oxford University Press, 1984.

CARNAP, RUDOLF. "The Elimination of Metaphysics through the Logical Analysis of Language," trans. Arthur Pap, in A. J. Ayer, ed., *Logical Positivism*. New York: Macmillan, 1959.

—— "Empiricism, Semantics and Ontology," in Leonard Linsky, ed., *Semantics and the Philosophy of Language*. Urbana: University of Illinois Press, 1952.

—— "Intellectual Autobiography," in P. A. Schilpp, ed., *The Philosophy of Rudolf Carnap*. Carbondale, Ill.: Open Court, 1963.

—— *The Logical Structure of the World*. Berkeley: University of California Press, 1967.

—— *The Logical Syntax of Language*. New York: Harcourt, Brace, 1937.

—— *Meaning and Necessity*. Chicago: University of Chicago Press, 1947.

—— *Philosophy and Logical Syntax*. First published 1935; repr. Bristol: Thoemmes, 1997.

CARNAP, RUDOLF (cont.). *Pseudo-Problems in Philosophy*. Berkeley: University of California Press, 1967.

—— "Überwindung der Metaphysik durch logische Analyse der Sprache," *Erkenntnis* 2 (1932): 219–41.

CAVELL, STANLEY. "The Argument of the Ordinary," in *Conditions Handsome and Unhandsome*. Chicago: University of Chicago Press, 1990.

—— *The Cavell Reader*, ed. Stephen Mulhall. Oxford: Blackwell, 1996.

—— *The Claim of Reason: Wittgenstein, Skepticism, Morality, and Tragedy*. New York: Oxford University Press, 1979.

—— *Must We Mean What We Say?* Cambridge: Cambridge University Press, 1969.

—— *A Pitch of Philosophy: Autobiographical Exercises*. Jerusalem–Harvard Lectures. Cambridge, Mass.: Harvard University Press, 1996.

—— *The Senses of Walden*. Chicago: University of Chicago Press, 1981.

—— *This New Yet Unapproachable America: Essays After Emerson After Wittgenstein*. Albequerque, N.Mex.: Living Batch Press, 1989.

CHURCHLAND, PATRICIA. *Neurophilosophy*. Cambridge, Mass.: MIT Press, 1986.

CHURCHLAND, PAUL. *Matter and Consciousness*. Cambridge, Mass.: MIT Press, 1988.

CONANT, JAMES. "The Method of the *Tractatus*," in Erich H. Reck, ed., *From Frege to Wittgenstein: Perspectives on Early Analytic Philosophy*. Oxford: Oxford University Press, 2000.

—— "On Wittgenstein's Philosophy of Mathematics II," *Proceedings of the Aristotelian Society* 97. 2 (1997): 195–222.

CRARY, ALICE, and READ, RUPERT, eds. *The New Wittgenstein*. London: Routledge, 2000.

DAVIDSON, DONALD, and HARMAN, GILBERT, eds. *Semantics of Natural Language*. Dordrecht: Reidel, 1972.

DERRIDA, JACQUES. "Signature Event Context," in *Margins of Philosophy*, trans. Alan Bass. Chicago: University of Chicago Press, 1982.

DIAMOND, CORA. *The Realistic Spirit: Wittgenstein, Philosophy, and the Mind*. Cambridge, Mass.: MIT Press, 1991.

—— "Rules: Looking in the Right Place," in D. Z. Phillips and Peter Winch, eds., *Wittgenstein: Attention to Particulars*. Houndmills: Macmillan, 1989.

DREBEN, BURTON, and FLOYD, JULIET. "Tautology: How Not to Use a Word," *Synthese* 87 (1991): 23–50.

DRURY, M. O'C. "Some Notes on Conversations with Wittgenstein," in Rush Rhees, ed., *Ludwig Wittgenstein: Personal Recollections*. Oxford: Oxford University Press, 1984.

DUMMETT, MICHAEL. *Frege: Philosophy of Language*. London: Duckworth, 1973.

—— "Wittgenstein on Necessity: Some Reflections," in Peter Clark and Bob Hale, eds., *Reading Putnam*. Oxford: Blackwell, 1994.

EMERSON, RALPH WALDO. *Selected Writings of Ralph Waldo Emerson*, ed. William H. Gilman. New York: New American Library, 1965.

EUCLID. *The Thirteen Books of the Elements*, vol. 2, trans. Thomas L. Heath. New York: Dover, 1956.

FIELD, HARTRY. *Science without Numbers*. Princeton: Princeton University Press, 1980.

FINE, ARTHUR. *The Shaky Game*. Chicago: University of Chicago Press, 1996.

FINKELSTEIN, DAVID. "Wittgenstein on Rules and Platonism," in A. Crary and R. Reed, eds., *The New Wittgenstein*. London: Routledge, 2000.

FLOYD, JULIET. "On Saying What You Really Want to Say: Wittgenstein, Gödel, and the Trisection of the Angle," in J. Hintikka, ed., *From Dedekind to Gödel: The Foundations of Mathematics in the Early Twentieth Century*. Dordrecht: Kluwer, 1995.

—— "Wittgenstein, Mathematics and Philosophy," in A. Crary and R. Reed, eds., *The New Wittgenstein*. London: Routledge, 2000.

FODOR, JERRY. *The Language of Thought*. New York: Thomas Y. Crowell, 1975.

—— *A Theory of Content and Other Essays*. Cambridge, Mass.: MIT Press, 1992.

FOGELIN, R. J. *Wittgenstein*. London: Routledge, 1987.

FOUCAULT, MICHEL. *The Archaeology of Knowledge*. New York: Pantheon, 1972.

FREGE, GOTTLOB. *The Basic Laws of Arithmetic*, trans. and ed. Montgomery Furth. Berkeley: University of California Press, 1967.

—— *Collected Papers on Mathematics, Logic, and Philosophy*, ed. Brian McGuinness. Oxford: Blackwell, 1984.

—— *The Foundations of Arithmetic*. Evanston, Ill.: Northwestern University Press, 1953.

—— *Translations from the Philosophical Writings of Gottlob Frege*. Totowa, N.J.: Rowman & Littlefield, 1952.

FRIEDMAN, MICHAEL. "Carnap and Wittgenstein's *Tractatus*," in W. W. Tait, ed., *Early Analytic Philosophy*. New York: Open Court, 1996.

GERT, HEATHER. "The Standard Meter by Any Name Is Still a Meter Long," *Philosophy and Phenomenological Research* (forthcoming).

GÖDEL, KURT. "On Intuitionistic Arithmetic and Number Theory," in Martin Davis, ed., *The Undecidable*. New York: Raven Press, 1965. Also in *Kurt Gödel: Collected Works*, vol. 1, ed. S. Feferman, J. W. Dawson, Jr., W. Goldfarb, C. Parsons, and R. Solovay. Oxford: Oxford University Press, 1986.

GOLDFARB, WARREN. "Kripke on Wittgenstein on Rules," *Journal of Philosophy* 82 (1985).

GRICE, PAUL. "Prolegomena," in *Studies in the Way of Words*. Cambridge, Mass.: Harvard University Press, 1989.

HACKER, P. M. S. *Insight and Illusion*. Oxford: Oxford University Press, 1986.

HARDY, GODFREY. "Mathematical Proof," *Mind* 38 (1929): 1–25.

HEIDEGGER, MARTIN. *Basic Writings*, ed. David Farrell Krell. New York: Harper & Row, 1977.

HERTZBERG, LARS. *The Limits of Experience*. Helsinki: Acta Philosophica Fennica, 1994.

HINTIKKA, JAAKKO, ed. *From Dedekind to Gödel: The Foundations of Mathematics in the Early Twentieth Century*. Dordrecht: Kluwer, 1995.

HINTIKKA, MERRILL B., and HINTIKKA, JAAKKO. *Investigating Wittgenstein*. Oxford: Blackwell, 1986.

HOBBES, THOMAS. *Human Nature and the De Corpore Politico: Elements of Law*. World's Classics. Oxford: Oxford University Press, 1994.

—— *Leviathan*. Penguin Classics. New York: Viking, 1986.

—— *Man and Citizen: De Homine and De Cive*. Indianapolis: Hackett, 1991.

HORWICH, PAUL. *Truth*. Oxford: Blackwell, 1990.

—— "Wittgenstein and Kripke on the Nature of Meaning," *Mind and Language* 2 (1990): 105–21.

HUMPHREY, NICHOLAS. *The Inner Eye*. London: Faber & Faber, 1986.

KEIL, F. C. *Concepts, Word Meanings, and Cognitive Development*. Cambridge, Mass.: MIT Press, 1989.

KOETHE, JOHN. *The Continuity of Wittgenstein's Thought*. Ithaca, N.Y.: Cornell University Press, 1996.

KRIPKE, SAUL. "Identity and Necessity", in Stephen Schwartz, ed., *Naming, Necessity, and Natural Kinds*. Ithaca, N.Y.: Cornell University Press, 1977.

—— "Naming and Necessity," in D. Davidson and G. Harman, eds., *Semantics of Natural Language*. Dordrecht: Reidel, 1972.

—— *Naming and Necessity*. Cambridge, Mass.: Harvard University Press, 1980.

—— "Time and Necessity." Cornell Lectures, unpublished.

—— *Wittgenstein on Rules and Private Language*. Cambridge, Mass.: Harvard University Press, 1982.

LEWIS, DAVID. *Parts of Classes*. Oxford: Blackwell, 1991.

MCCARTHY, TIMOTHY. *Radical Interpretation and Indeterminacy*. Oxford: Oxford University Press, 2001.

MCGINN, MARIE. *Sense and Certainty: A Dissolution of Scepticism*. Oxford: Blackwell, 1989.

MCGUINNESS, BRIAN. "On the So-Called Realism of the *Tractatus*," in Irving Block, ed., *Perspectives on the Philosophy of Wittgenstein*. Cambridge, Mass.: MIT Press, 1981.

MALCOLM, NORMAN. "Kripke and the Standard Meter," in G. H. Von Wright, ed., *Wittgensteinian Themes: Essays 1978–1989*. Ithaca, N.Y.: Cornell University Press, 1995.

—— *Nothing is Hidden: Wittgenstein's Criticism of His Early Thought*. Oxford: Blackwell, 1986.

MILL, JOHN STUART. *A System of Logic*. London: Longman, 1873.

MUNITZ, MILTON K., ed. *Identity and Individuation*. New York: New York University Press, 1971.

NAGEL, ERNEST. "Logic Without Ontology," in *Logic Without Metaphysics*. Glencoe, Ill.: Free Press, 1959.

NIETZSCHE, FRIEDRICH. *Beyond Good and Evil*, trans. Walter Kaufmann. New York: Vintage, 1966.

PEARS, DAVID. *The False Prison*. Oxford: Clarendon Press, 1988.

—— "Wittgenstein," in Jonathan Dancy and Ernest Sosa, eds., *A Companion to Epistemology*. Oxford: Blackwell, 1992.

PINKER, STEVEN. *The Language Instinct*. New York: William Morrow, 1994.

POUR-EL, MARIAN BOYKAN, and RICHARDS, IAN. "The Wave Equation with Computable Initial Data such that Its Unique Solution Is Not Computable," *Advances in Mathematics* 39 (1981): 215–39.

PUTNAM, HILARY. "Brains and Behavior," in *Philosophical Papers*, vol. 2: *Mind, Language and Reality*. Cambridge: Cambridge University Press, 1975.

—— "Convention: A Theme in Philosophy," in *Philosophical Papers*, vol. 3: *Realism and Reason*. Cambridge: Cambridge University Press, 1992.

—— "Is Water Necessarily H$_2$O?" in *Realism with a Human Face*. Cambridge, Mass.: Harvard University Press, 1990.

—— "Mathematical Necessity Reconsidered," in *Words and Life*. Cambridge, Mass.: Harvard University Press, 1994.

—— "On Wittgenstein's Philosophy of Mathematics I," *Proceedings of the Aristotelian Society*, Suppl. Vol. 70 (1996): 243–64.

—— "Philosophy of Logic," in *Philosophical Papers*, vol. 1: *Mathematics, Matter and Method*. Cambridge: Cambridge University Press, 1975.

—— "Philosophy of Mathematics: Why Nothing Works," in *Words and Life*. Cambridge, Mass.: Harvard University Press, 1994.

—— *Pragmatism*. Oxford: Blackwell, 1995.

—— "Pragmatism and Verificationism," *Proceedings of the Aristotelian Society* 95.3 (1995): 291–306.

—— *Reason, Truth, and History*. Cambridge: Cambridge University Press, 1981.

—— *Renewing Philosophy*. Cambridge, Mass.: Harvard University Press, 1991.

—— "Sense, Nonsense, and the Senses: An Inquiry into the Powers of the Human Mind" (the 1994 Dewey Lectures), *Journal of Philosophy* 91.9 (1994).

—— *The Threefold Cord: Mind, Body, and World*. New York: Columbia University Press, 2000.

—— *Words and Life*. Cambridge, Mass.: Harvard University Press, 1994.

—— and FLOYD, JULIET. "A Note on Wittgenstein's 'Notorious Paragraph' about the Gödel Theorem," *Journal of Philosophy* 97.11 (Nov. 2000): 624–32.

QUINE, W. V. O. "Facts of the Matter," in R. W. Shahan and K. R. Merrill, eds., *American Philosophy from Edwards to Quine*. Norman: University of Oklahoma Press, 1977.

—— *From a Logical Point of View*. Cambridge, Mass.: Harvard University Press, 1955.

—— "Natural Kinds," in Stephen P. Schwartz, ed., *Naming, Necessity, and Natural Kinds* (Ithaca, N.Y.: Cornell University Press, 1977).

QUINE, W. V. O. (cont.). *Ontological Relativity and Other Essays*. New York: Columbia University Press, 1969.

—— "Ontology and Ideology Revisited," *Journal of Philosophy* 80 (1983): 499.

—— *Pursuit of Truth*. Cambridge, Mass.: Harvard University Press, 1990.

—— "Success and the Limits of Mathematization," in *Theories and Things*. Cambridge, Mass.: Harvard University Press, 1981.

—— *Theories and Things*. Cambridge, Mass.: Harvard University Press, 1981.

RHEES, RUSH. *Discussions of Wittgenstein*. London: Routledge & Kegan Paul, 1970.

RORTY, RICHARD. *Contingency, Irony, Solidarity*. Cambridge: Cambridge University Press, 1989.

—— *Philosophy and the Mirror of Nature*. Princeton: Princeton University Press, 1979.

ROSENTHAL, DAVID. "Thinking that One Thinks," in M. Davies and G. W. Humphreys, eds., *Consciousness*. Oxford: Blackwell, 1993.

RUSSELL, BERTRAND. *The Analysis of Mind*. New York: Humanities Press, 1921.

—— *The Problems of Philosophy*. Oxford: Oxford University Press, 1912.

SALMON, NATHAN. "How To Measure the Standard Metre." *Proceedings of the Aristotelian Society* 88 (1987–8): 193–217.

SCHLEGEL, FRIEDRICH, and SCHLEGEL, A. W. *Philosophical Fragments*, trans. Peter Firchow. Minneapolis: University of Minnesota Press, 1991.

SCHWARTZ, STEPHEN P., ed. *Naming, Necessity, and Natural Kinds*. Ithaca, N.Y.: Cornell University Press, 1977.

SEGERDAHL, PÄR. *Language Use: A Philosophical Investigation into the Basic Notions of Pragmatics*. Houndmills: Macmillan, 1996.

SHANKER, S. G. *Wittgenstein and the Turning Point in the Philosophy of Mathematics*. Albany, N.Y.: SUNY Press, 1987.

SHER, GILA, and TIESZEN, CHARLES, eds. *Between Logic and Intuition: Essays in Honor of Charles Parsons*. Cambridge: Cambridge University Press, 2000.

TILGHMAN, BEN. *Wittgenstein, Ethics, and Aesthetics: The View from Eternity*. Albany, N.Y.: SUNY Press, 1991.

WELLMAN, HENRY M. *The Child's Theory of Mind*. Cambridge, Mass.: MIT Press, 1990.

WHITE, ROGER. "Wittgenstein on Identity," *Proceedings of the Aristotelian Society* 78 (1977–8): 157–74.

WHITEHEAD, ALFRED NORTH, and RUSSELL, BERTRAND. *Principia Mathematica*. London: Cambridge University Press, 1913.

WILLIAMS, MEREDITH. "The Philosophical Significance of Learning in the Later Wittgenstein," *Canadian Journal of Philosophy* 24 (March 1994): 173–204.

—— "Rules, Community and the Individual," in Klaus Puhl, ed., *Meaning-Scepticism*. New York: De Gruyter, 1991.

—— *Wittgenstein, Mind, and Meaning: Towards a Social Conception of Mind*. London: Routledge, 1999.

WINCH, PETER. *Ethics and Action*. London: Routledge & Kegan Paul, 1972.

—— *The Idea of a Social Science and its Relation to Philosophy*. London: Routledge & Kegan Paul, 1958.

—— "Persuasion," in Peter E. French, Theodore E. Uehling, Jr., and Howard K. Wettstein, eds., *Midwest Studies in Philosophy*, vol. 17: *The Wittgenstein Legacy*. Notre Dame, Ind.: University of Notre Dame Press, 1992.

—— *Simone Weil: The Just Balance*. Cambridge: Cambridge University Press, 1989.

—— *Trying to Make Sense*. Oxford: Blackwell, 1987.

WITTGENSTEIN, LUDWIG. "The Big Typescript," in *Philosophical Occasions, 1912–1951* (q.v.).

—— *The Blue and Brown Books*. New York: Harper & Row, 1965.

—— *Culture and Value*, ed. G. H. Von Wright and Heikki Nyman, trans. Peter Winch. Chicago: University of Chicago Press, 1994.

—— *Last Writings on the Philosophy of Psychology*, ed. G. H. Von Wright and H. Nyman, trans. C. G. Luckhardt and M. A. E. Aue. Vol. 1, Chicago: University of Chicago Press, 1982; vol. 2, Oxford: Blackwell, 1992.

—— *Lectures on the Foundations of Mathematics, Cambridge, 1939*, ed. Cora Diamond. Ithaca, N.Y.: Cornell University Press, 1976.

—— "Lectures on Personal Experience, Michaelmas Term, 1935," recorded by Margaret MacDonald, ed. Cora Diamond. Unpublished.

—— Letter to Moritz Schlick, 8 August 1932, in *Ludwig Wittgenstein: Sein Leben in Bildern und Texten*, ed. M. Nedo and M. Ranchetti. Frankfurt am Main: Suhrkamp, 1983.

—— *Letters to C. K. Ogden with Comments on the English Translation of the Tractatus Logico-Philosophicus*, ed. G. H. Von Wright. Oxford and London: Blackwell and Routledge, 1973.

—— *Ludwig Wittgenstein and the Vienna Circle: Conversations Recorded by Friedrich Waismann*, ed. Brian McGuinness. Oxford: Blackwell, 1979.

—— *Notebooks, 1914–1916*, ed. G. H. Von Wright and G. E. M. Anscombe, trans. G. E. M. Anscombe. New York: Harper & Row, 1969.

—— "Notes for Lectures on 'Private Experience' and 'Sense Data'," ed. Rush Rhees and David G. Stern, in *Philosophical Occasions, 1912–1951* (q.v.).

—— *On Certainty*, ed. G. E. M. Anscombe and G. H. Von Wright, trans. Denis Paul and G. E. M. Anscombe. Oxford: Blackwell, 1969.

—— *Philosophical Grammar*, ed. Rush Rhees, trans. Anthony Kenny. Oxford: Blackwell, 1974.

—— *Philosophical Investigations*, ed. G. E. M. Anscombe and Rush Rhees, trans. G. E. M. Anscombe. New York: Macmillan, 1953.

—— *Philosophical Occasions, 1912–1951*, ed. James Klagge and Alfred Nordmann. Indianapolis: Hackett, 1993.

—— *Philosophical Remarks*, ed. Rush Rhees, trans. Raymond Hargreaves and Roger White. Chicago: University of Chicago Press, 1975.

—— *Eine Philosophische Betrachtung*, ed. Rush Rhees, in *Schriften*, vol. 5. Frankfurt am Main: Suhrkamp, 1970.

WITTGENSTEIN, LUDWIG (cont.). *Remarks on Colour*, ed. G. E. M. Anscombe, trans. Linda L. McAlister and Margarete Schättle. Berkeley: University of California Press, 1984.

—— *Remarks on the Foundations of Mathematics*, ed. G. H. Von Wright, Rush Rhees, and G. E. M. Anscombe, trans. G. E. M. Anscombe. Original edn., Oxford: Blackwell, 1956; revised edn., Cambridge, Mass.: MIT Press, 1994.

—— *Remarks on the Philosophy of Psychology*, vol. 1, ed. G. E. M. Anscombe and G. H. Von Wright, trans. G. E. M. Anscombe. Chicago: University of Chicago Press, 1988; vol. 2, ed. G. H. Von Wright and Heikki Nyman, trans. C. G. Luckhardt and M. A. E. Aue. Chicago: University of Chicago Press, 1975.

—— *Tractatus Logico-Philosophicus*, trans. C. K. Ogden. London: Routledge, 1922. Also trans. David Pears and Brian McGuinness. London: Routledge, 1961. French edn. trans. Gilles-Gaston Granger. Paris: Gallimard, 1993.

—— *Zettel*, ed. G. E. M. Anscombe and G. H. Von Wright, trans. G. E. M. Anscombe. Berkeley: University of California Press, 1981.

WRIGHT, CRISPIN. Critical Notice of Colin McGinn, *Wittgenstein on Meaning. Mind* 98 (1989): 289–305.

—— "On Making Up One's Mind: Wittgenstein on Intention," in Weingartner and Schurz, eds., *Logic, Philosophy of Science and Epistemology* (Kirchberg: Hölder-Pichler-Tempsky, 1987).

—— "Self-knowledge: The Wittgensteinian Legacy," in C. Wright, B. C. Smith, and C. Macdonald, eds., *Knowing Our Own Minds*. Oxford: Oxford University Press, 1998.

—— *Wittgenstein on the Foundations of Mathematics*. Cambridge, Mass.: Harvard University Press, 1980.

—— "Wittgenstein's Rule-following Considerations and the Central Project of Theoretical Linguistics," in A. George, ed., *Reflections on Chomsky*. Oxford: Blackwell, 1989.

INDEX